CULTIVATING INNER RADIANCE AND THE BODY OF IMMORTALITY

In den reinen Strahlen des Lichtes
Erglänzt die Gottheit der Welt.
In der reinen Liebe zu allen Wesen
Erstrahlt die Göttlichkeit meiner Seele.
Ich ruhe in der Gottheit der Welt.
Ich werde mich selbst finden
In der Gottheit der Welt.

In purest outpoured light
Shimmers the Godhead of the world.
In purest love toward all that lives
Radiates the Godhood of my soul.
I rest within the Godhead of the world.
I shall find myself
Within the Godhead of the world.

—**Rudolf Steiner**

We are in a time of extremely serious trials; we must be ever-more conscious of this. Now everything good and everything evil is coming to the light of day, often in a most devastating way. Whoever is able to meditate can powerfully affect what is happening. Only very few have the possibility of understanding what is going on, let alone the strength to fulfill the task given to us. It is all the more important that the few who do have a true understanding now apply all their strength—in utmost conscientiousness and with the highest possible concentration…yes, with all the magic that they are able to call forth from the depths of their souls—to sacrifice themselves and work toward this: that humanity does not completely lose the Holy Spirit, which should lead the future evolution of humankind. Never before have we had to face the abyss so directly as in the present.

—**Rudolf Steiner**, from a letter of June 1924 to Moritz Bartsch (1869–1944)

These words are thought to have been written during the "Agricultural Course" in Koberwitz (June 7–16, 1924); quoted from Bastiaan Baan, *Christliche Meditation: Eine Einführung* ("Christian Meditation: An Introduction"; Stuttgart: Urachhaus Verlag, 2008).

CULTIVATING INNER RADIANCE and the BODY OF IMMORTALITY

Awakening the Soul through Modern Etheric Movement

ROBERT POWELL

Lindisfarne Books | 2012

2012
LINDISFARNE BOOKS
An imprint of SteinerBooks / Anthroposophic Press, Inc.
610 Main Street, Great Barrington, MA 01230
www.steinerbooks.org

Copyright © 2012 Robert Powell. All rights reserved. No part of this book may be reproduced, stored in a retrieval system, or transmitted in any form or by any means, electronic, mechanical, photocopying, recording, or otherwise, without written permission from Lindisfarne Books.

Original cover art by Malcolm Glover:
Cycle January, watercolor on paper, 20 x 30 cm.

Book layout concept by a friend who wishes to remain anonymous

LIBRARY OF CONGRESS CATALOGING-IN-PUBLICATION DATA

Powell, Robert, 1947–
 Cultivating inner radiance and the body of immortality : awakening the soul through modern etheric movement / Robert Powell.
   p. cm.
Includes index.
ISBN 978-1-58420-117-5
1. Eurythmy. 2. Eurythmics. 3. Spiritual life. I. Title.
BP596.R5P69 2012
299'.935—dc23

2011051302

Print edition: ISBN: 978-1-58420-117-5
eBook: ISBN: 978-1-58420-118-2

CONTENTS

	A Note from the Author	6
	Foreword	9
	Introduction	18
1	Foundational to the Practice of Cultivating Inner Radiance	24
	Index of Gestures	31
2	The Core of the Practice: Putting on the Resurrection Body	41
3	Inner Radiance: Introductory and Concluding Prayers	62
4	Deepening the Connection with the Etheric Christ	69
5	The Macrocosmic Background to the Core Practice	105
6	The Cosmic Nature of Christ in Light of the Hermetic Tradition	177
7	From the Eucharist to the Second Coming of Christ	195
	Index of Practices	196
8	Astrosophy and Scientific Research	225
	Afterword	230
	Acknowledgments	236
	About the Author	237
	Dedication	241

A NOTE FROM THE AUTHOR

Dear Reader,

In this much publicized year 2012, as we contemplate the world situation, we are faced with wave after wave of distressing news: wars and rumors of wars, a global financial crisis of unprecedented proportion, revolutions, travesties of social justice, the militarization of society (with accompanying brutality toward the people), death through famine, violence or natural catastrophes, and many other disturbing phenomena—for example, the ever-increasing "technological encroachment" described in my book *Prophecy-Phenomena-Hope: The Real Meaning of 2012*. One can have the impression that everything—all social, political, financial, cultural, and educational structures and institutions—are breaking down, gradually sinking into chaos. *Yet out of chaos something new can be born,* especially if we take to heart the words of Christ, "Lo, I am with you always, until the end of time," as a source of guidance and inspiration for our actions.

This book describes a series of practices—together comprising the Inner Radiance sequence—for coming into an experience of the truth and reality of these words of Christ. This experience is what is needed in our time as a strengthening elixir or "breath of life"—an elixir that one can partake of every day, that helps in the creation of an inner radiance, offering the possibility of finding support in encountering life's challenges—with the help of Christ.

At the heart of the Inner Radiance sequence is the Core Practice of *putting on the body of immortality*. This body, as discussed in chapter 5, is the highest member of the hu-

Hermes Trismegistus,
(mosaic panel on the floor of Siena Cathedral)

man being. It will arise/is arising by way of transformation of the physical body, the human being's lowest member. In other words, the highest member of the human being is mirrored in the lowest. It is a matter of bringing to realization the words "as above, so below," attributed to the ancient Egyptian sage Hermes Trismegistus, who is discussed at length in chapter 6. As outlined there, the physical body, here below on Earth, is to become a *body of immortality*—enjoying everlasting life. But how?

This book describes practices that can be taken up by almost everyone in some form or other, either by taking up the movement practices described in the follow-

A Note from the Author

ing pages or by engaging in the meditations and prayers purely meditatively.

Contemplating the adjacent image of Hermes Trismegistus, the Latin wording on the tablet on the right side (Hermes' left hand), when translated into English, reads: "God, the creator of all, brought forth a visible God from himself and made him his One and Only, in whom he rejoiced and whom he loved as his only Son, called the Holy Word." On the pages of the book on the left side (Hermes' right hand) we read, "Take up letters and laws O Egyptians."

Hermes greets you at the threshold

In the thirteenth century the basic structure of Siena Cathedral in Italy was completed. During the fourteenth and fifteenth centuries work on the interior continued. The inlaid marble mosaic floor is one of the most ornate of its kind in Italy, covering the whole floor of the cathedral, and is full of mysterious images comprising ancient wisdom teachings: the Sibyls, the symbols of the Tarot, Biblical figures, the four Platonic virtues, etc., all represented as mosaics on the floor of the cathedral, mirroring the wisdom of the heavens above. The artistic shaping of the mosaic floor went on from the fourteenth to the sixteenth centuries, with about forty artists making their contributions to it. The floor consists of fifty-six panels in different sizes. One of the most striking panels is that of Hermes Trismegistus (see image) from around 1488 attributed to Renaissance artist Giovanni di Maestro Stefano. It is this figure of Hermes, as a mosaic in the great panel located in the central position at the original main entrance, who would have greeted those entering as they stepped into the cathedral through this entrance. Beneath the feet of the figure of Hermes is inscribed "Hermes Mercurius Trismegistus, contemporary of Moses," since at that time it was believed that Hermes had lived at the same time as Moses. However, as discussed in chapter 6, Hermes lived more than one thousand years prior to the time of Moses, who during his time in Egypt imbibed something of the wisdom teachings transmitted from the days of Hermes.

For the Greeks, Hermes was identified with the planet Mercury, and the practice of the "Staff of Mercury," originally described by the great twentieth-century spiritual teacher, Rudolf Steiner, and further expanded upon in this book, is the *opening practice* of the Inner Radiance sequence. This is just one example of the persistent influence down through the ages of Hermes Trismegistus—an influence that implicitly and explicitly permeates this book, particularly with regard to the key significance of the teaching of Hermes summarized by "as above, so below" that is a primary focus throughout the following pages.

Having made the acquaintance of Hermes, dear Reader, you are invited to enter into the mystery of the creation of the body of immortality as a transformation of the physical body, in line with the Hermetic axiom "as above, so below" underlying the foundation of all true spiritual endeavor.

Robert Powell

Learn to dance,
  Or else the angels in Heaven
  will not know what to do with you.
  —Saint Augustine

He bade us therefore make as it were a ring…
And himself standing in the midst, he said:
  Answer "Amen" unto me.
He began, then, to sing a hymn and to say:
  "Glory be to thee, Father."
And we, going about in a ring, answered him:
  "Amen…"
Behold thyself in me…
  I would keep tune with holy souls."
  —Acts of John, 94–97

The sacred word and the holy prayer
  and the priestly sacrifice—
  Hold the Earth in its course.
  —Atharva-Veda

FOREWORD

By way of an introduction to *Cultivating Inner Radiance and the Body of Immortality*, it is important from the outset to bear in mind that this book is for everyone who has an interest in following a spiritual path based on movement.[1] The most widely known spiritual paths of this kind are yoga—more specifically, hatha yoga[2]—and qigong (also tai chi, which was originally part of qigong).[3] The path offered in this book is a western path arising from eurythmy—meaning "beautiful, harmonious movement." Eurythmy, as a new form of movement based on spiritual foundations, was born in the year 1912, and this book is written in honor of the one-hundred-year celebration of the birth of eurythmy. Eurythmy is known as a performing art comparable with ballet and as a pedagogical practice in the Waldorf Schools, and is also applied therapeutically as a healing practice. This book outlines another dimension to eurythmy, one that is universal, in that the exercises described in this book are simple enough for everyone to participate.

Like yoga, qigong, and tai chi, eurythmy is to be distinguished from gymnastics and other forms of physical activity in that it is focused upon the level of life energy (*prana* in India, *chi* in China, and the *etheric* in the west). The physical body is permeated by the life body (or etheric body), and the goal of the practice described in this book is the cultivation of currents of life energy through the gestures of eurythmy. These exercises are healing and invigorating, when practiced on a regular basis.

The healing aspect is one level. There is another level having to do with following a spiritual path. In this book a spiritual path emerges in relation to the practice of the sequence of exercises described here, the core of which is the sequence *Putting on the Resurrection Body*. First, in order to understand what is meant by this expression, let us consider these words of St. Paul:

> The Resurrection:...there is a natural body, and there is a spiritual body...and this mortal [body] must put on immortality...[then] death is swallowed up in victory: O death, where is thy sting? (I Corinthians 15:42–55)

St. Paul draws attention here to the body of immortality—also known as the Resurrection body. He admonishes us to "put on immortality" in order to overcome death. In other words, we are exhorted to put on the body of immortality, the Resurrection body. But how can we do this?

This book offers an answer. The central core of this book—the sequence *Putting on the Resurrection Body*—comes in celebration of the birth of eurythmy one hundred years ago and represents a metamorphosis of the content of my earlier book *The Morning Meditation in Eurythmy*. The inspiration for this discovery of a path of "putting on the body of immor-

---

1 Though initially some terms may seem unfamiliar, it is worthwhile to persist; the meaning will become clear.
2 *Yoga* = "union." It developed thousands of years ago in ancient India and has five main branches (raja, jnana, hatha, bhakti, and karma yoga), of which hatha yoga, focusing upon posture, breathing, and physical movement exercises activating the flow of life (*prana*) energy, is the most well known in the west. Like the other forms of yoga, hatha yoga has a profound dimension as a spiritual path.
3 Qigong is a practice of moving life energy. *Qi* (or *chi*) is life energy; and *gong* (or *kung*) is practice (or breath work). It is a very ancient movement practice originating in China thousands of years ago as a healing form of movement and also as a spiritual practice. *Tai chi* (or *tai chi chuan*) was originally that part of qigong that was used as preparation for self-defense. In the course of time tai chi developed independently of qigong, when Chinese martial arts practitioners adapted and modified qigong with the goal of improving their fighting abilities. Like qigong, tai chi is held to be Taoist in origin.

tality"—which is also a path of cultivating inner radiance—began for me with the practice described in *The Morning Meditation in Eurythmy*, and in the course of time the sequence described in this new book blossomed forth. Some practitioners will no doubt feel attached to the sequence as it is described in *The Morning Meditation in Eurythmy*, and this is understandable, as practice tends to inscribe its content into one's life (etheric) body. The new practice described in this book does not so much replace the earlier practice but rather deepens it, leading it through a metamorphosis and further expansion of the practice described in *The Morning Meditation in Eurythmy*. While acknowledging that with such practices it is always a matter of grace as to whether a particular practice really does signify the "opening of the gates of Heaven" or not, it is possible to say, based on direct experience, that a metamorphosis truly exists which leads to "putting on the Resurrection body"—initially experienced as a streaming out of inner radiance. A clairvoyant beholding of this reality is described by Estelle Isaacson on pages 13 and 14 of this foreword.

Why is such grace—as to be able to "put on the Resurrection body"—flowing at the present time? It is the grace of Christ in the etheric realm of life forces surrounding and permeating the Earth, the onset of which was prophesied by Rudolf Steiner to commence from around 1933 onward.[4] Since that time there exists the possibility that through etheric movement and gesture such as in the practice of eurythmy, when practiced in the right spirit—the spirit living in the words of Christ—we are led into connection with him. The discovery is then made that the movements and gestures of eurythmy are the language of the Angels, which is also the language of the Etheric Christ, who is now revealing himself in angelic form in the etheric realm. In this way it becomes a living experience that on an archetypal level eurythmy was originally born from Christ—the Divine Word—and that in a deeper sense he is the real teacher. We experience that through him our eurythmy practice becomes a portal to the world of spirit. It is a matter of *living* the words of the Beatitudes spoken by Christ at the Sermon on the Mount—for example, the sixth Beatitude: "Blessed are the pure in heart, for they shall see God." For beholding Christ *is* to behold God. And through the portal of purity of heart it is possible to behold him. He is with us now at this time of trial for the Earth and humanity. He is in the radiant blue light of the Earth's etheric aura, bestowing his eternal blessing upon all who truly seek him with purity of heart.[5]

It is important in the eurythmy practice of the central sequence—*Putting on the Resurrection Body*—that each gesture is done in consciousness of the significance of the words, expressed in conjunction with the gesture, in relation to the particular chakra to which the words correspond. In carrying out the eurythmy practice described in this book, it is best *not to hurry*, but rather always to practice with a sense of entering into the timelessness of spiritual realms—into the *great peace* that prevails there—where we unite with Christ through his words and gestures, the gestures of eurythmy, giving expression to the new universal language that Christ is now imparting, in the company of angelic beings, to all who seek him in purity of heart.

An example of the Risen Christ making eurythmy gestures is given by Judith von Halle in her description of the Ascension.[6]

---

4   This "greatest mystery of our time"—to use one of Rudolf Steiner's expressions for the return of Christ in the etheric realm—is central to the theme of my books *The Most Holy Trinosophia and the New Revelation of the Divine Feminine*, *The Sophia Teachings*, *Chronicle of the Living Christ*, *Christian Hermetic Astrology: The Star of the Magi and the Life of Christ*, *The Christ Mystery*, *The Sign of the Son of Man in the Heavens*, *Prophecy-Phenomena-Hope: The Real Meaning of 2012*, and *Christ & the Maya Calendar* (the latter written with Kevin Dann).

5   The qualities of the other Beatitudes—"seeking the spirit" (first Beatitude), "bearing suffering" (second Beatitude), "meekness" (third Beatitude), and so on—are also important. Yet the "purity of heart" of the sixth Beatitude is particularly significant, as it is this quality that especially underlies the beholding of Christ in the etheric realm.

6 Judith von Halle received the stigmata, the wounds of Christ, on Good Friday in 2004. In this connection Peter

> Then he [the Risen Christ on the Mount of Olives immediately prior to his Ascension] became brighter than the Sun itself... He was himself the Sun. Before it became impossible to make him out in this extremely bright Sun-like radiance, he bestowed his blessing upon the Earth by raising his left arm, as though allowing the power of the cosmos to flow into him, and then with his right arm pointing down to the ground allowed this [power] to flow through his right arm into the Earth.

[This is a description of the eurythmy gesture I—pronounced "ee" as in "see"—with the left arm raised and the right arm lowered.]

> Then he directed this stream by placing his left hand upon his breast to his heart, sending the stream through his right hand, that was making a gesture of blessing, to human beings.

[This is a description of the eurythmy gesture for the sound EU, pronounced "oy" as in "joy"]

> It was an indescribable cosmic stream of love, which sent the whole superhuman love of Christ out from its home in the stars to the Earth by flowing out of the cosmos through the left hand into the heart, and streaming out of the heart through the right hand to the Earth.
>
> So it appeared as though the resurrected Son of God was binding—by raising his left hand toward the heavens and holding his right hand down toward the Earth—the macrocosm and the microcosm together through an eternal divine bond of unbounded devotion and selfless love. (The statue of Christ by Rudolf Steiner bears witness to this.)

[The gesture of Christ in this statue, depicted by Rudolf Steiner (see page 4) is also a form of "I" in eurythmy.][7]

Judith von Halle here describes in a most inspiring way these examples of the Christ making eurythmy gestures. Her description of the I gesture made by Christ at the Ascension is something that can be held in consciousness and invoked every time that one forms the I gesture with the left arm raised—as in the "Christ in me" meditation, for example. There are many more examples of eurythmy gestures made by Christ that could be described, perhaps the most striking one being his gesture on the Cross, which is in essence the eurythmy gesture of Universal Love—as referred to in this book in the description of the correct pronunciation of the word AMEN as AUMEYN. The out-pouring of Divine Love from the Cross at the Crucifixion can be invoked each time one makes the gesture of Universal Love. Further research is being done into this "Christ dimension" of eurythmy that is very much part of the content of the Choreocosmos School.[8]

In writing this book, the author is aware that there may be readers who, for whatever reason, do not intend to take up the practice of eurythmy. It is important to remember that one can work solely with the words of Christ belonging to the various prayers and meditations described in this book, and in this way

---

Tradowsky describes: "Today we want to report on a specific event which has occurred right in our midst. It is a cosmic event manifesting in Judith von Halle. In Passiontide 2004, the stigmata, the wounds of Jesus Christ, appeared on Judith von Halle.... The stigmatization was accompanied by a radical change.... The altered body of Judith von Halle, who previously loved cooking and eating, now vehemently refuses any physical food... The Christ being provides humans with the power to develop their individual self, and also at the same time the possibility to transform, to spiritualize and individualize the sheaths of their being... [including] the individual form of the Resurrection body newly created by Christ... Humans will be reconnected by means of the Resurrection body with the karmic stream of nutrition which builds the substances in the human being.... The astonishing fact of someone living without eating or drinking... [is] an expression of a new form of health... a gradual stage-by-stage process of fusion with the Resurrection body" (report by Peter Tradowsky, in: Judith von Halle, *And if He Had Not Been Raised...: The Stations of Christ's Path to Spirit Man* (London: Temple Lodge, 2007), pp.10–20.

---

7 Ibid., p.155. Comments in brackets [ ] inserted by RP. Note that here RP has slightly modified the published English translation after comparison with the original German text.
8 See p.224.

come to the experience of uniting with him. For his grace is immeasurable and his mercy unfathomable. We are able through his words to enter into his Presence (Greek: *parousia*)—into the light, love, life, and peace that, streaming from the Etheric Christ, is now gracing humanity and the Earth at the present time.

A central purpose of my books *Christ & the Maya Calendar* (coauthored with Kevin Dann), *The Christ Mystery*, and *Prophecy Phenomena Hope: The Real Meaning of* 2012 has been to awaken in the reader the awareness that humanity and the Earth are passing through a great trial at the present time. As described in these books, it is Christ who is our guide through this trial. The purpose of this book is to offer a practice which, if followed in the right spirit, can open a path to union with Christ in the etheric realm.

The new art form of eurythmy, that came into the world through Rudolf Steiner, can thereby be experienced as having originated from Rudolf Steiner in relation to his beholding of Christ, who at that time was descending from cosmic realms to then commence in the twentieth century to manifest his Presence (*parousia*) to the Earth and humanity—the event referred to as the "Second Coming." On his path of descent, during the final stages some years before entering into the Earth's etheric aura in 1932–1933, Christ imparted to Rudolf Steiner something of the principles of and something of the actual content of the new universal language of eurythmy—one of the ways through which Christ can now be experienced.[9]

The discovery of eurythmy as a portal to the world of spirit came for me personally at a new level of experience in 2011, as a gift of grace, after working with eurythmy for thirty-three years—and coinciding with the celebration of the first beginnings of eurythmy one hundred years ago. I stress the gift of grace here, as I do not claim to be the discoverer of eurythmy as a path to the Etheric Christ. But rather it is for me now a matter of certainty of experience that eurythmy is—or holds the possibility of being—such a path. For me, also, knowing this to be true—that eurythmy is a path to Christ—I am certain that this is destined to become increasingly evident to more and more people in the course of time... *because it is true*.

Since its birth one hundred years ago (1912), eurythmy has signified a "breath of life" for very many people. All the great eurythmy endeavors in the artistic, pedagogical, social, and therapeutic realms are gratefully acknowledged and honored as extraordinary contributions to humanity's cultural life. The experience—over and beyond all the beauty, majesty, and healing power of artistic, pedagogical, social, and therapeutic eurythmy—that eurythmy is also a path to Christ in the etheric, does not in any way diminish the existing practice of eurythmy; rather, it heightens and elevates all eurythmy.

There is much more that could be described concerning the worldwide practice of eurythmy. In the realm of eurythmy, my particular focus is upon the cosmic aspects of eurythmy, for which I have chosen the name choreocosmos (from the Greek, meaning "cosmic dance"). Moreover, as described in this book, I have also worked upon the development of eurythmy in conjunction with prayer and meditation. This aspect I refer to as "sacred dance" or the "sacred dance of eurythmy"—see the afterword for further information about the cosmic aspects of eurythmy.

Concerning the intention held in the "moving meditation" of sacred dance, wherein prayer and meditation are expressed through movement and eurythmic gesture, we experience the "vertical axis of connection" through us, between Heaven and Earth, with Sophia, the divine matrix of creation, streaming down from above, and Christ, the power of Divine Love, radiating up from the Earth. The streaming of Sophia from above and the radiation of Christ from below unite in us, centered in the region of the heart. From the heart there can then take place a streaming out "horizontally" to all beings of good will—in the first instance to those closest to us. If we are engaged as a group in

---

9   Eurythmy, of course, is not the only way to experience Christ in the etheric realm.

eurythmic prayer and meditation, this comprises the community of those together with us in the circle of sacred dance. This horizontal stream from the region of the heart allows a peace-bestowing influence arising from the sacred union of Earth and Heaven, Christ and Sophia, the Lamb and his Bride, to flow out.

Community, true community, united in the spirit can serve as an antidote to all war and strife. In this way, sacred dance may also be a service to humanity, through which our love can spread out from our sacred dance community to eventually embrace all beings of good will, and our compassion may be able to extend ultimately to the entire circle of humankind and the Earth. This is a mystery of the heart—the threefold physical, etheric, and astral heart.

An example of the heightened effect of meditation and prayer in conjunction with the words of Christ together with eurythmy gestures is well described in the following words of Estelle Isaacson.[10]

> This vision happened in May 2011, during a class when Robert Powell was teaching the *Morning Meditation* in eurythmy, focusing on *Putting on the Resurrection Body*.
>
> We began with the Lord's Prayer as a chakra prayer and then moved into working with the Inner Radiance sequence, beginning with the prayer "Christ in me." While we were doing this, I became aware of the person who was to my left, and saw her heart unfold like a rose—being bathed in a lavender color. Her heart was very beautiful! I watched as it continued to grow. We then moved into the prayer "Sophia in me," and I saw shimmering crystal-clear lights touch each petal of the rose in her heart. The shimmering lights were the light that I see as part of Sophia's garment. I then felt all of this in my own heart—the light of Christ (lavender light) and the light of Sophia (the silvery prisms) coming together, and I felt great joy.
>
> By the time we moved into the central part of the Morning Meditation in eurythmy, I was seeing the building up of the Resurrection body approaching me as if from behind. I saw a sphere of rainbow light move into me through my back, and could feel the very point at which it entered, through my posterior heart chakra, coming into my core and then filling my entire being. It was a feeling of peace and love penetrating my whole soul. I felt lightness and joy—and it was as if all of my cells were so filled with light, that the matter of my physical body felt almost insubstantial. My limbs seemed to be absolutely weightless. I then became aware of everyone's hearts in the circle—they were each resonating with the lavender light, taking in the light, and also attuning to each other, so that the hearts were becoming more and more "one."
>
> I watched also the Resurrection body building up in Robert. Since he had been doing this eurythmy practice for so much longer than the rest of us, and was already very familiar with it, the light was much stronger and his aura was showing very beautiful sacred geometric forms that I have rarely seen in anyone's aura. It is my understanding that it takes a very special sort of consistent spiritual practice, coupled with a strong moral character in order to have such forms appear. This is a subject of spiritual research for me. Throughout the eurythmy, Robert's aura was moving through certain sacred geometrical forms—I saw such forms as the lemniscate, the seed of life, and the cross, all of which were multidimensional. At the end of the eurythmy, his aura was transformed into a "flower of life" form, which was a golden, pulsing light all around the periphery of the aura, and filled with a soft, healing green light.

---

10 Estelle Isaacson is a young woman who contributes to the *Journal for Star Wisdom*. In March 2008, she received the stigmata. Although they do not manifest outwardly, they are present more or less continuously on an inner level. She is an example of a contemporary mystic, who has had several experiences of Christ in the etheric realm. See also the article by Estelle Isaacson and the article about her, published in the Easter 2011 issue of *Starlight*, the newsletter of the Sophia Foundation; free download: http://sophiafoundation.org/newsletter/.

This flower of life contained within it all the other sacred forms I had seen in various layers of the aura, with all the colors of the rainbow. It was breathtakingly beautiful! It had the quality of creating humility for the beholder. For Divine Love was present in the forms, and one could only feel humbled to be in the presence of such love.

In my own soul, as the Resurrection body entered in through my heart chakra, I experienced my soul then becoming like a lens. Rainbow-colored light poured in through my crown and then refracted out to the hearts all around us—all colors searching out the hearts of others. I felt tremendous love for everyone in the room. I saw spiritual beings—angels raying out various colors—gathering around us. They were weaving a beehive-shaped vessel of light all around. This was in place as we closed our session at the end with the AUM meditation. The angelic realm was nourished by the gestures and sacred words we had just shared and in return had gifted us with the rainbow light of peace, love, and protection.

From Estelle Isaacson's description it emerges that the eurythmy practice of *Putting on the Resurrection Body* is spiritually effective. I am grateful to Estelle for her sharing this vision, and also for sharing another vision which inspired me to write the following words (below I have quoted directly from her vision). As indicated in this book, "putting on the Resurrection body" is a co-creative activity, together with Christ. There is an historical archetype for this: Christ's raising of Lazarus from the dead, described in chapter 11 of the Gospel of John. In connection with this greatest of Christ's miracles, he spoke the words: "I AM the Resurrection and the life" (John 11:25). These words convey something of a mystery: that when Christ raised Lazarus to new life, he bestowed his own life upon him. These words can be taken in a literal way. When we put on the Resurrection body, Christ literally becomes the life within us. He becomes our lifeblood. He dwells within us. In putting on the Resurrection body, we take on his body of life, which becomes our Resurrection body. This is the great mystery connected with the raising of Lazarus, serving as an historical archetype for putting on the Resurrection body.

A vision from the journals of Estelle Isaacson:

> After Lazarus' return to life, his body was not simply a revivified physical body, although it appeared to be. He had a Resurrection body, although it was not at the same level of glory that Christ's own Resurrection body would be at the Resurrection.
>
> As Lazarus lived in his Resurrection body, he found that he had the ability to traverse the boundary between the physical and spiritual realm. His body became a "vehicle" and enabled him to travel at will into the spiritual world, while also being able to be physically present in the physical realm, appearing like any normal human being. This ability did not present itself immediately, or all at once. It took some time for him to become used to the body, to learn how to work with it so that he could use the body in ever higher ways. His Resurrection body was a "star" in him—the star of his Resurrection body was his "vehicle" of travel. Moreover, his heart was in perfect entrainment with the heart of Jesus Christ. He had the heartbeat of the Lord.
>
> Lazarus had been spiritually reborn through the love of Christ—it was the Lord's love that had brought Lazarus back from the grave. It was by Christ's love for him that he was able to see that he still had work to do in the physical realm. It was the will of Christ that Lazarus should return, but this alone would not have brought Lazarus back. Through Christ's love for him, Lazarus' will was awakened such that he then desired to return to the physical world as well. Christ would never resurrect a person against their will. Resurrection could only happen through the merging of divine will with human will. The two together become sacred magic. Each of us may receive our Resurrection bodies

when we are ready to receive them—when our will is aligned with divine will.

Jesus Christ loved Lazarus, and Lazarus loved Jesus Christ. Their reunion in the physical realm after Lazarus' raising was so profound that Jesus Christ wept tears of joy. For Lazarus had chosen him over death. Lazarus recognized that Christ is the life and light of humanity, and he chose life. Lazarus' initiation fulfilled the purpose of the ancient death mysteries. Enacting the old mysteries is no longer relevant, for Christ is the great Initiator who takes us through the death of our old selves and then resurrects us to new life—a life in him. For he is the Resurrection and the life. Then we may truly say, "Not I, but Christ in me." Every time a part of us dies, such as an old belief, or a part of our ego, we have the opportunity to be restored to new life. When finally we are able to fully die in Christ, then we may be resurrected. This is what happened in Lazarus' soul—he died in Christ. His only desire was to be like Christ, to completely unite himself with him, and to dwell in the spirit. When he was raised to new life, Christ was then in him, in constant union with the soul of Lazarus. Lazarus was then able to live also in communion with the disciples on a spiritual level, most often with John, the son of Zebedee, and also with his sister Mary Magdalene.

Drawing upon Estelle Isaacson's vision, the above words indicate that alongside the archetype of the Risen One himself, the raising of Lazarus serves as an historical archetype for putting on the Resurrection body. This is not to say that Lazarus attained Resurrection to the same degree as Jesus Christ. In the case of Christ's Resurrection the final goal—the "Omega," the end—of human evolution was attained.[11]

With his raising from the dead, Lazarus attained the penultimate goal of evolution, signifying the putting on of the Resurrection body to a certain degree—a degree that still entails further evolution in order to attain the final goal. In terms of the cosmic stages of evolution the penultimate goal of evolution is the Venus stage of evolution (see chapter 5), that of the transformation of the etheric body into life spirit (*buddhi*). At this stage the etheric body becomes transformed—love-permeated, streaming out healing forces—as evinced by Jesus Christ in his healing miracles. As referred to in chapter 5, where the future Venus and Vulcan stages of evolution are discussed, the goal of eurythmy is the transformation of the etheric body into life spirit (*buddhi*). At the raising of Lazarus, because Lazarus had been out of his body for ten days, his etheric body had already dissolved back into the cosmic ether. In raising Lazarus from the dead, Jesus Christ not only called the soul and spirit of Lazarus back, but also bestowed upon him something of the Christ life body, which was completely love-permeated life spirit (*buddhi*). Even in the beating of his heart, Lazarus' life body was at one with the life body of Jesus Christ. Lazarus was thus endowed with a very special etheric body, bestowed by Jesus Christ, one which had been completely transformed into life spirit (*buddhi*), signifying that Lazarus had attained the goal of the Venus stage of evolution, which is the penultimate goal prior to that of the Vulcan stage. Thus Lazarus had reached the beginning of the Vulcan stage of evolution, that of the transformation of the physical body into the Resurrection body, whereas Jesus Christ at the event of his own Resurrection stood at a level signifying the attainment of the end of the Vulcan stage of evolution.

From this, it is evident that putting on the Resurrection body is a long process—one, however, that can be started at any time. The Risen One shows us the end stage of this process, and Lazarus raised from the dead indicates a significant stage toward the end of this process. Both are shining beacons for the activity of putting on the Resurrection body. The practice outlined in this book offers a path through eurythmy of beginning the putting on the Resurrection body. At the same time this is a path to beholding Christ in the etheric realm. In the words of Judith von Halle:

> This gaze into the etheric world—into that sphere in which the Christ being is [now] revealing himself in his

---

11 Christ in his Resurrection body indicates the level to which human beings will attain in the far-distant future, at the end of the Vulcan stage of evolution (see chapter 5).

etheric appearance—is essentially possible to human beings at the present time. And if one comes to the experience of the reality of Christ through gazing upon his etheric form, one beholds surrounding him a vast, seemingly infinite number of etheric seedlings, which through the Mystery of Golgotha the Representative of Humanity [Christ] has prepared for every human soul, for every one of us. They are preserved there until the moment when one—out of the freedom bestowed upon us—develops the impulse, taking the well deliberated decision in recognition of one's true spiritual being, to develop it further and thus also to shape and form one's own seedling of the new body from the etheric seedling preserved for one there. This shaping and forming of the seedling through a consciously cultivated moral–ethical self-education and spiritual consciousness training leads one step by step, from incarnation to incarnation, to be able to put on one's own phantom, the immortal body, just as the "first Adam"—the mortal body—was put on... It is a matter of the immortal body, which is not "given over to the elements at death" and which also does not, as with the etheric body, dissolve into the etheric realm after earthly death, but which—in so far as one has already begun shaping and forming it—is completely preserved during the spiritual life between death and a new birth, and which can then, when one reincarnates anew, be again re-membered into one as one's preciously and earnestly attained belonging. It is only in this way that one can—on the level of one's I—work from incarnation to incarnation on one's phantom, without losing what one had previously accomplished.[12]

Putting on the Resurrection Body is a very real work, one which extends from incarnation to incarnation. It is a work that is to be taken up consciously, as a co-creation together with Christ, whom one can now experience as the Cosmic Christ in his glorious Resurrection body in the etheric realm. The development of inner radiance, which accompanies the putting on the Resurrection body, is a protection against the various negative forms of radiation that are now increasingly encroaching upon human beings. This subject, addressed briefly in chapter 5, is treated at length in my book *Prophecy–Phenomena–Hope: The Real Meaning of 2012*.[13]

These negative forms of radiation cover a wide range from negative thought influences, electrical effects, electromagnetic and radioactive radiation, to new influences of a subtle nature—among which are the disorienting effects resulting from coming into high-energy fields (generated by laser beams, etc.) and also very powerful gravitational effects brought about directly through forces adversarial toward Christ. Since eurythmy works with the forces of levity, which are the forces of the etheric realm, eurythmy has the power to overcome effects such as the aforementioned gravitational ones—and other effects as well, particularly when done in conjunction with the words of Christ and in connection with *Putting on the Resurrection Body*. The cultivation of inner radiance can serve as an antidote to the encroachment of the various kinds of external radiation. It is a matter of aligning oneself with Christ in the etheric realm, as expressed in the meditation "Christ is already here." This is the intended purpose of the sequence of prayers and meditations described in this book.

As described in chapter 5, the cultivation of inner radiance can be of assistance in answering the challenges presented by the increasing encroachment upon human beings of "outer radiation" in various forms such as electromagnetism—for example, by way of mobile phones, cell phone towers, etc.—and can also help in a more general sense in relation to technological influences working upon us—for example, by way of television and computers—to name just two widespread forms of potentially detrimental influences to which human beings are now increasingly exposed. Upon nearing completion of the manuscript of this book, I was happy to see an article written by eurythmist

---

12 Judith von Halle, *Joseph von Arimathia und der Weg des Heiligen Gral* (*Joseph of Arimathea and the Path of the Holy Grail*) (Dornach, Switzerland: Verlag für Anthroposophie, 2011), pp. 34–36.

13 Robert Powell, *Prophecy–Phenomena–Hope: The Real Meaning of 2012* (Great Barrington, MA: SteinerBooks, 2011).

Elisabeth Göbel in which she refers to the value of eurythmy in connection with protecting school children from such influences. She writes: "There is the question what eurythmists can do so that the deeply effective strength of eurythmy—for example, also as a preventive and contrast to television and the computer world—can come more into the consciousness of teachers."[14] There are many other interesting points raised in her article, such as her brief discussion of eurythmy as a spiritual path. Her words quoted here reveal that it is now time for eurythmy to play a more widespread role in countering the potentially detrimental effect upon human beings through technological influences. Although in her article she is referring specifically to school children and is talking about the pedagogical application of eurythmy, her remarks could be considered to apply (by way of extension) also to adults and to other forms of eurythmy.

The Inner Radiance sequence of exercises presented in this book are not described perfectly—this would be impossible. Ideally one would learn these exercises from a eurythmist or graduate of the Choreocosmos School, but as this is not possible for everyone, this book is a substitute for the transmission by a "live teacher." Eurythmy is meant to be transmitted from person to person. However, in lieu of the possibility of receiving instruction in these exercises from someone in the living tradition of the etheric movement impulse of eurythmy, an appropriate attitude in working with the content of this book would be to turn directly to Christ as THE teacher.

The Etheric Christ is the focus and goal of many of the exercises in the Inner Radiance sequence. Ultimately, he is the teacher of eurythmy. For it was through the relationship between Rudolf Steiner and the Etheric Christ that eurythmy came into existence some one hundred years ago. He is the one to turn to inwardly with regard to all questions arising as a consequence of working with the exercises in this book.

To receive the content of the exercises belonging to the Inner Radiance sequence in the stream of the living tradition of eurythmy makes a deepening possible that otherwise would generally take much longer when working with the content by oneself. A teacher can usually impart direct guidance and give further explanations concerning the exercises. Notwithstanding this, it is possible to turn to Christ as THE teacher and—by way of schooling one's inner listening capacity—learn directly from the ultimate source of guidance in the new, universal language of the etheric movement of eurythmy, which is the language of the Angels and the language of the Etheric Christ.

Lastly, one question that often arises in doing the exercises of the Inner Radiance sequence is: Should I speak the words of the prayers and meditations out loud, or meditate upon them silently while shaping the gestures? In eurythmy it is the tradition not to speak out loud but to focus upon the content meditatively while forming the gestures—in order to really enter into the etheric flow of the movement. However, if one feels moved to speak the words out loud, this is fine, too, and can also be a powerful experience.

---

14 Elisabeth Göbel, "Von einigen Wirkungen des Eurythmie-Unterrichts und deren Voraussetzungen, ('Concerning Some Effects of Teaching Eurythmy and What This Presupposes"), *Rundbrief der Sektion für redende und musizierende Künste* (Newsletter of the Section for the Performing Arts) (Dornach, Switzerland: Rudolf Steiner Nachlassverwaltung, Michaelmas 2011), p. 41.

INTRODUCTION

It is necessary in the present age that an entirely new vista of life takes hold of human hearts. In the twentieth century there began for humanity the vision of Christ in the etheric realm. Just as it truly happened that at the time of the Mystery of Golgotha Christ walked among human beings in a physical form, in one known part of the Earth, so now the Etheric Christ walks among human beings the whole world over. This event must not pass by unnoticed by humanity. Humankind must awaken to Christ, so that a sufficient number of people may behold him in the etheric realm.

He is already present in the form in which more and more people will begin to see him. It is possible today, if we do but seek him, to be very near to Christ, to find him in a quite different way than has been possible hitherto.

Christ spoke some words, which should be deeply engraved in the human soul: "I am with you always, until the end of time." This is a truth, a reality. He is here. He is now making his presence felt in a new way.

Christ is not a ruler of human beings, but our brother. He wishes to be consulted on all the details of life. In everything we undertake we ought to ask of Christ: "Should we do this or not?" Then human souls may have the experience of Christ standing by them as the beloved companion, and they will then not only obtain consolation and strength from Christ, but will also receive instruction from him as to what is to be done. The figure of Jesus Christ is now able to draw near to us and give us the strength and force in which we can live more fully here on Earth. If we seek him, Christ is able to guide us, to stand beside us as a brother, so that our hearts and souls may be strong enough to grow in our further development.

O Light Divine,

O Sun of Christ,

Warm thou our hearts,

Enlighten thou our heads,

That Good may become

What from our hearts we found,

And from our heads direct

With single purpose.[15]

The above words by Rudolf Steiner set the stage for the content of this book by drawing attention to the Presence of Christ in the etheric realm. The Greek word that is used in the New Testament to signify this Presence is *parousia*, often translated as "Second Coming." To Rudolf Steiner's words I would like to add these from Valentin Tomberg:

> There, where the life body holding together the mineral substances penetrates the physical body, arises a new body: the body of love. [This is the Resurrection body.] Love is that cosmic essence which inwardly unites consciousness and life into a unity. This love body is still small and weak — it is as yet hardly perceptible behind the processes of death-giving consciousness and of unconscious life. But it will grow and gradually conquer ever more territory within the ordinary organism, the "old Adam." On through the millennia, human beings will gradually array themselves in the "new Adam," the love body, the Resurrection body. It is happening, but not by itself. It requires the working together of faith and grace in as much as human beings freely open themselves up to the Christ power which then streams into them,

---

15 This introductory text is based on Rudolf Steiner's lecture held in Berlin on February 6, 1917, the first lecture in *Cosmic and Human Metamorphoses* (Blauvelt NY: Garber, 1989) — with some editing by RP, and adding the closing words of the "Foundation Stone Meditation."

so reorganizing them that in the future a body will be theirs which has been won from death.[16]

These words are very important in relation to cultivating the body of immortality, also known as the Resurrection body. Valentin Tomberg draws attention to the fact that the manifestation of the Resurrection body for individual human beings does not happen by itself. It presupposes that human beings "open themselves up to the Christ power which then streams into them, so reorganizing them that in the future a body will be theirs which has been won from death." This love body arises as a co-creation between Christ and human beings who open themselves to him. The practice described in this book offers a path of embarking upon this co-creation, together with Christ, of the Resurrection body. It is an act of faith on the human side to embark upon this co-creation, and it a matter of experience that grace—the in-streaming Divine Love of Christ—responds. This is absolutely real and is of vital significance for the whole of future evolution, for each individual, for nature, and for the whole Earth. For the Resurrection body is essentially the physical body that has been spiritualized through the power of Divine Love, where this power is so strong that it can actually transform matter. In this way, death is overcome. The physical body (the "old Adam") is subject to death, whereas the Resurrection body (the "new Adam") has been "won from death." The practice of putting on the Resurrection body is one of entering more and more into Divine Love, thereby developing one's body of love, the Resurrection body. We are called to be gardeners of the integration of body, soul, and spirit.

Judith von Halle describes Christ's Resurrection body as a physical body:

> This physical body, however, does not decay, because it is *not material*. The level at which this appears is that of the etheric world. It is thus a matter of a *physical*—not a mineral—body, but on a higher, spiritual level, actually on the *etheric* level...a *physical* body which is not at the material level of appearances but at the etheric level.[17]

This helps to give us an understanding of the fact that Christ's Second Coming is in the etheric realm, not on the physical level. It is in the etheric realm that we behold him now, if our spiritual eyes are open, and feel his Presence—*parousia*—if we are attuned to him.

Since eurythmy is a form of etheric movement, whereby the physical body is moved according to the laws of the etheric body,[18] eurythmy leads us into connection with the etheric realm, where Christ is now to be found. In this sense eurythmy is well suited to open a path to Christ in the etheric realm. The degree of success in following this path depends upon various factors. The primary one is that of grace—the response of Christ by way of his Divine Love to our endeavor. This response is not automatically guaranteed. It is to a certain extent influenced by our inner attitude toward Christ and, also, whether we are committed to evolving spiritually and morally under his guidance. "For every one step that you take in the pursuit of higher knowledge, take three steps in the perfection of your own character" is the golden rule formulated by Rudolf Steiner in his book *Knowledge of the Higher Worlds*.[19] Very much depends upon our level of moral development. One is admitted to the mysteries of the higher worlds if one is found to be worthy. Of course, no one is perfect. It is a matter of the *intention* to strive toward perfection—"Be ye perfect as your Father in Heaven is perfect" (Matthew 5:48). To embark upon a path of self-perfection is to set about improving oneself morally and spiritually. This intention sets the tone for one's spiritual endeavor, and it is this tone to which Christ responds. In this

---

16 Valentin Tomberg, *Russian Spirituality and Other Essays* (San Rafael, CA: LogoSophia, 2010), p.56. Comment in brackets [ ] inserted by RP.

17 Judith von Halle, *Joseph von Arimathia und der Weg des Heiligen Gral* ("Joseph of Arimathea and the Path of the Holy Grail"; Dornach, Switzerland: Verlag für Anthroposophie, 2011), pp.41–42.

18 Rudolf Steiner, *Eurythmy: Its Birth and Development* (Weobley, England: Anastasi, 2002), p.113.

19 Rudolf Steiner, *Knowledge of the Higher Worlds: How Is It Achieved?* (London: Rudolf Steiner Press, 2009), chapter: The Stages of Initiation.

connection Judith von Halle—quoted at length in the following text concerning the Resurrection body—refers to a "consciously cultivated moral-ethical self-education and spiritual consciousness training."

> The figure in which the Risen One appeared to Mary Magdalene was not that of a normal physical-material body subject to death. This body of the Risen One is not at all of flesh and blood, skin and bones, as was the body of Jesus of Nazareth, who from the Cross on Golgotha breathed out his life and was then laid in the grave. The body of the Risen One is a completely physical one, yet it is a spiritualized physical body.... As Rudolf Steiner expressed it, it is a matter, with regard to this spiritualized body, of the true primal form of the physical body in which that original pure condition of the human being's "Adamic organization" as it was prior to the Fall, free of all the forces of temptation and decay, was restored. Rudolf Steiner spoke of the phantom in connection with Christ's Resurrection body—the phantom as the true primal form of the physical body—and he described that this spiritual body enjoys all the qualities of the physical body. This indication by Rudolf Steiner is of great significance if one wishes to come to an understanding of the Resurrection body, the phantom.... In truth, our mortal physical body is nothing more than a gross, shadowy copy of this living, spiritual true primal form.
>
> The similarity in appearance between the mortal body and this true primal form of the physical body is evident from Mary Magdalene's encounter with the Risen One, as she was initially convinced that it was a normal human being facing her, who was a caretaker of the garden of the holy sepulcher. Yet in reality, from the moment of the Mystery of Golgotha—which changed everything, including herself—she was in a special, heightened condition of spiritual perception, which made it possible for her to recognize the pure spirit body of Christ, the phantom of the physical body.... And since in this heightened condition of spiritual perception she was able to behold both the Angel and the Redeemer, an outer indication is thus given of the "level" at which the Redeemer revealed himself in his Resurrection body.
>
> An Angel appears in a realm transcending the mineral kingdom—thus transcending the physical-material—yet this realm is the next closest one to the mineral kingdom, namely the etheric realm. The etheric is closest to our physical-material world. Although the etheric realm is invisible for our normal organs of sense perception, this realm is the most "condensed" spiritual realm. And in this etheric realm, after [she beheld] the Angels in the recess of the grave, the Risen Christ himself appeared to Mary Magdalene. This means that the true primal form of the physical body in which he appeared on Easter Sunday morning revealed itself on the level of the etheric world.... This gaze into the etheric world—into that sphere in which the Christ being is [now] revealing himself in his etheric appearance—is essentially possible to human beings at the present time.... Through a consciously cultivated moral-ethical self-education and spiritual consciousness training the human being is led step by step, from incarnation to incarnation, to be able to put on their own phantom, the immortal body, just as the "first Adam"—the mortal body—was put on.[20]

These words of Judith von Halle indicate something which—in terms of this book—provides us with a deeper understanding as to what the intention is of the practice of putting on the Resurrection body as outlined in this book. Just as during the period of embryonic development between conception and birth we "put on" the physical body (the "old Adam"), so through a conscious practice of "putting on the Resurrection body" we have the possibility—though the grace of Christ in the etheric realm, and with the help of the new etheric form of movement known as eurythmy—to "put on" the phantom (the "new Adam"), which according to Valentin Tomberg is a body of love. Here the question arises: Is there any connection between the birth of eurythmy one hundred years ago and the coming of Christ in the etheric realm?

---

20 Judith von Halle, *Joseph von Arimathia und der Weg des Heiligen Gral* ("*Joseph of Arimathea and the Path of the Holy Grail*"; Dornach, Switzerland: Verlag für Anthroposophie, 2011), pp. 31–34.

Introduction

Rudolf Steiner's proclamation of the return of Christ in the etheric realm began at Easter 1909.[21] In his lecture of January 12, 1910, held in Stockholm,[22] he mentioned for the first time that the advent of the Etheric Christ for humanity would begin in 1933—a date which he confirmed again in a lecture he held on September 20, 1924.[23] What does this signify?

An answer is revealed when we consider Christ's Second Coming as a path of descent through the angelic hierarchies. On this path of descent, at the time (1909) when Rudolf Steiner began his proclamation, Christ was in the realm of the Archangels, having just entered that realm in 1908.[24] Rudolf Steiner was able to behold Christ in the realm of the Archangels, recognizing him on his path of descent, and cognizing that he would descend into the realm of the Angels around 1920 and, subsequently, into the earthly realm around 1932 to '33. He knew that by 1933 Christ would be in the etheric aura of the Earth. In one lecture he refers to the onset of Christ's Second Coming between 1930 and 1933.

The important point for our consideration is that with the beginning of Rudolf Steiner's proclamation of Christ's Second Coming at Easter 1909, the focus of Rudolf Steiner's activity—from his awareness of Christ's descent toward the earthly realm—turned to active preparation for Christ's coming. This active preparation assumed a variety of forms, the most striking being the focus upon the creation of a building which would serve as a temple for the Etheric Christ. The foundation stone of this temple—the First Goetheanum—was laid on September 20, 1913, approximately 4½ years after the proclamation began at Easter 1909. This time of Rudolf Steiner's teaching activity from Easter 1909 to the founding of the First Goetheanum in September 1913 marked a pronounced transition in his way of teaching, which grew more and more in intensity.

This was also the time of the birth of eurythmy. The first conversation that Rudolf Steiner had with Clara Smits, the mother of the first eurythmist, the young Lory Maier-Smits, who at that time was 18 years old, was in Berlin in mid-December 1911. It was during this conversation that Rudolf Steiner explained that he was willing to show Lory a new form of movement based on the spoken word rather than upon music. Clara then took Lory to meet with Rudolf Steiner in Kassel on January 29, 1912, for Lory's first lesson.[25] These lessons then continued during the following years; and thus eurythmy was born. This birth took place parallel to the building of the First Goetheanum which, with its performance stage, was intended to house eurythmy.[26]

The centerpiece—the holy of holies—of the First Goetheanum was to have been Rudolf Steiner's great statue of Christ known as the *representative of humanity*. The eurythmy performances would have taken place against the background of this great statue representing the Etheric Christ who, if one looks closely, is making the eurythmy gesture I, with the left arm

---

21 See my article "Kashyapa and the Proclamation of Christ in the Etheric" in the Easter 2011 issue of *Starlight*, the newsletter of the Sophia Foundation, available as a free download: http://sophiafoundation.org/newsletter. Steiner called this the "greatest mystery of our time," ushering in a New Age for humankind.
22 There was not a stenographer present at this lecture. However, Marie Steiner took notes—translated into English and published in the *Journal for Star Wisdom* 2012 (Great Barrington, MA: SteinerBooks, 2011), pp. 22–23.
23 Rudolf Steiner, *The Book of Revelation and the Work of the Priest* (London: Rudolf Steiner Press, 1998), p. 231.
24 Robert Powell, "Subnature and the Second Coming," in *The Inner Life of the Earth: Exploring the Mysteries of Nature, Subnature & Supranature* (ed. Paul V. O'Leary; Great Barrington, MA: SteinerBooks, 2008), p. 70. See also, Robert Powell, *The Christ Mystery: Reflections on the Second Coming* (Fair Oaks, CA: Rudolf Steiner College Press, 1999), p. 21.

25 Magdalene Siegloch, *How the New Art of Eurythmy Began: Lory Maier-Smits, the First Eurythmist* (London: Temple Lodge, 1997), pp. 11–17.
26 Among other activities, such as the performance of the Mystery Plays written by Rudolf Steiner precisely during this 4½-year period from Easter 1909 to the laying of the foundation stone of the first Goetheanum in September 1913.

raised and the right arm lowered (see page 2). All of this is to say that eurythmy was born out of Rudolf Steiner's preparation for Christ's Second Coming. Now, one hundred years later, a new and conscious understanding of eurythmy's relationship to the Etheric Christ is taking place.

The practice of *Putting on the Resurrection Body*, as described in this book, serves as one aspect of this celebration of the birth of eurythmy. In the spirit of the words of Rudolf Steiner quoted above, this book of meditations and prayers is presented with the intention of helping the spiritual seeker to progress along the path toward the Etheric Christ through the uniting of the power of the words of Christ with the etheric form of movement known as eurythmy. The kernel of this book is the sequence of prayers and meditations which gives this book its title—*Cultivating Inner Radiance and the Body of Immortality*. This sequence has been taken up by many people as a daily morning practice and has been found to be a source of strength and comfort as a way of drawing close to Christ.

The central meditation of *Putting on the Resurrection Body* resonates within the seven lotus flowers (chakras) on four different levels, relating to Christ's Transfiguration, Crucifixion, Resurrection, and Ascension. This is a most powerful meditation provided it is done conscientiously, each time consciously associating each chakra with the relevant words for the deeds, miracles, and gifts of Christ. Also important is a brief time of repose upon completing each of the four levels of the meditation, during the repose focusing upon the relationship of the seven lotus flowers to the stages of Christ's Transfiguration, Crucifixion, Resurrection, and Ascension. These four stages lead us into the future, to the transformation of our entire being, culminating with the level of the Resurrection body in the far-distant future. Putting on the Resurrection body aligns us with this ultimate goal of human and earthly evolution. This activity, focusing upon the seven lotus flowers at each of the four stages of the meditation, begins to take effect upon the etheric body. This interaction between the seven lotus flowers and the streaming of the etheric body is described in a beautiful way by Rudolf Steiner.

> When esoteric development has progressed so far that the lotus flowers begin to stir, much has already been achieved by the student which can result in the formation of certain quite definite currents and movements in his etheric body.
>
> The object of this development is the formation of a kind of center in the region of the physical heart, from which radiate currents and movements in the greatest possible variety of colors and forms. The center is in reality not a mere point, but a most complicated structure, a most wonderful organ. It glows and shimmers with every shade of color and displays forms of great symmetry, capable of rapid transformation.
>
> Other forms and streams of color radiate from this organ to the other parts of the body, and beyond it to the astral body, completely penetrating and illuminating it. The most important of these currents flow to the lotus flowers. They permeate each petal and regulate its revolutions; then streaming out at the points of the petals, they lose themselves in outer space. The higher the development of a person, the greater the circumference to which these rays extend.
>
> The twelve-petaled lotus flower [heart chakra] has a particularly close connection with this central organ. The currents flow directly into it and through it, proceeding on the one side to the sixteen- and the two-petaled lotus flowers, and on the other, the lower side, to the flowers of eight [ten], six and four petals. It is for this reason that the very greatest care must be devoted to the development of the twelve-petaled lotus, for an imperfection in the latter would result in irregular formation of the whole structure.[27]

---

27 Rudolf Steiner, *Knowledge of the Higher Worlds: How Is It Achieved?* (London: Rudolf Steiner Press, 2009), chapter: Some Results of Initiation. Comment in brackets [ ] inserted by RP.

Introduction

These words indicate how delicate and sensitive the subtle organs within the human being are, and what care must be taken with regard to their development. The student of Christian esotericism therefore places himself or herself under the guidance of Christ and, as indicated in the first quotation of Rudolf Steiner cited above, seeks the help and guidance of Christ with respect to all of life's questions, especially those connected with spiritual and moral development.

Initially, should the entire sequence of meditations seem too much, one can begin by focusing solely upon the central practice, that of the four levels connected with Christ's Transfiguration, Crucifixion, Resurrection, and Ascension.

As an introduction to the central sequence of *Cultivating Inner Radiance and the Body of Immortality*, the following discussion of the word AMEN, followed by the meditation on the AMEN as an esoteric name of the Etheric Christ, offers a direct attunement to Christ in the etheric realm, as well as indicating the significance of the correct pronunciation of the word AMEN. This is important in consideration of AMEN as the closing word of many prayers.

Later in this book are the meditations "Christ is already here" and the AUM meditation. The "Christ is already here" meditation addresses the apocalyptic dimension of the struggle of Christ with the embodiment of evil known as the Antichrist. This, too, is a very powerful meditation, but is more complex than the other prayers and meditations included in this book, and is thus included as an "optional extra," just as the AMEN meditation can be viewed as an "optional introduction" to the central sequence *Inner Radiance: Putting on the Resurrection Body*.

And finally, I would like to address something concerning the style in which this book is written. In this book it is a matter of describing a path with spiritual exercises. Trying to describe these exercises in a book is not easy. Normally they are communicated "live" in a group situation in three-dimensional space, where there is a direct perception—and therewith the possibility of immediate cognition—of what is being done. And in this situation oral instructions of a subtle nature can be given which are not possible to communicate otherwise. In the written description sometimes, in order to be able to indicate the subtlety and depth of a particular exercise, it is necessary to approach it from different perspectives.

To the reader, this might seem like a repetition of what has already been described, but this is not the case. It is, in such instances, a matter of "subtle overlays" in order to convey the profundity of a spiritual exercise. Just as a photographer might take photos of something from different angles in order to convey a true image through an array of various photos arranged in a sequence, so what might seem like a repetition of a description presented elsewhere in this book is not simply a repetition, it is a depiction bringing forth a different nuance—one that is important for that particular exercise. This should be borne in mind by the reader when he or she thinks something is being repeated. The style of this book is not intended to be repetitive; rather, it is an endeavor to portray something living and profoundly real in a comprehensive and understandable way. Thus, in connection with a particular exercise, a tapestry comes into vision, if one reads—scattered in different parts of the book—what is said about that exercise. The purpose of the index in chapter 7 is to enable the reader to easily find the "subtle overlays" making up the tapestry, as well as giving an overview and helpful comments—and also providing an over-arching panorama of the spiritual significance of the *Core Practice Putting on the Resurrection Body* and the entire Inner Radiance sequence.

Chapter 1

FOUNDATIONAL TO THE PRACTICE OF CULTIVATING INNER RADIANCE

The Relationship of Christ to the Sun

In connection with the *Salutation to the Sun*—the meditation which starts "I see the Sun"—the spiritual inspiration to this meditation is Mary Magdalene's encounter with the Risen Christ in the garden of the holy sepulcher on Easter Sunday morning. After not finding him (his body) in the recess of the cave of the tomb—although she did behold two Angels there—she went out from the cave and turned toward the East. Just at that moment the Sun was rising. Against the background of the rising Sun she beholds a figure, whom she takes to be the gardener. It is in this context that we can understand the words of a meditation given by Rudolf Steiner: "It is dawn. The Sun rises a little: *the face of Christ*."[28] And in another meditation: "The Sun slowly rises. Christ speaks from the Sun."[29] And in yet another meditation: "The rising Sun. I speak to Christ: May your Word dwell in my heart."[30]

In connection with the *Morning Meditation* "In purest out-poured light..." which is foundational for the content of this book, Rudolf Steiner indicated: "Here in this meditation we find Christ as our highest Leader, our highest Guru, who guides us in a direct and immediate sense, if we turn to him."[31]

Finally, there is the following version of the *Morning Meditation* given by Rudolf Steiner, the *Morning Meditation* being central to the eurythmy practice described in this book:

> Imagine the image of the Sun setting in white light as if the power of Christ radiates out from the light with these words:
>
> *In purest out-poured light*
>
> *shimmers the Godhead of the world.*
>
> Then in one's imagination let the image of the Sun become yellowish-red as if in the redness the love of Christ radiates in the words:
>
> *In purest love toward all that lives*
>
> *radiates the Godhood of my soul.*
>
> Then in one's imagination let the image of the Sun become transformed into green and at the same time let the four lower red roses [of the Rose Cross] appear upon the [green] image of the Sun with the words:
>
> *I rest within the Godhead*
>
> *of the world.*
>
> then [let] the three upper red roses [of the Rose Cross appear] with the words:
>
> *I shall find myself*
>
> then [imagine] a black cross on the green background with the words:
>
> *within the Godhead of the world.*

---

28 Rudolf Steiner, *Seelenübungen mit Wort- und Sinnbild-Meditationen* ("Soul Exercises with Meditations of Words and Images"), Complete Works vol. 267 (Dornach, Switzerland: Rudolf Steiner Verlag, 1997), p.400.
29 Ibid., p.405.
30 Ibid., p.257.
31 Rudolf Steiner, *Aus den Inhalten der esoterischen Stunden II, 1910–1912* ("Esoteric Lessons II, 1910–1912"), Complete Works vol. 266/II (Dornach, Switzerland: Rudolf Steiner Verlag, 1996), p.90.

Then [later] one can fall asleep in the mood which carries over from [meditating upon] these formulae.³²

The connection of this meditation with Christ in relation to the Sun is very clear—also, that it is a matter of the Etheric Christ, since the Rose Cross is a symbol for Christ in the etheric realm:

> What is new and what will now gradually be communicated (revealed) to human beings is a recollection or repetition of what St. Paul experienced at Damascus. He saw the etheric body of Christ. The reason why this will now become visible to us derives from the fact that a new Mystery of Golgotha has...taken place in the etheric world... Let us visualize once more how, at the Mystery of Golgotha, a cross of dead wood was erected on which the body of Christ hung. And then let us visualize the wood of that cross in the etheric world as green, sprouting, and living wood, which has been turned to charcoal by the flames of hatred and on which seven blossoming roses appear, representing Christ's sevenfold nature. There we have the picture of the second Mystery of Golgotha, which has now taken place in the etheric world. And through this dying, this second death of Christ, we have gained the possibility of seeing the etheric body of Christ.³³

Just as the crucifix is a symbol of Christ's death two thousand years ago, a death that took place on the physical plane of existence, so the Rose Cross is a symbol for Christ's sacrifice and "second death" now in the etheric realm. In particular, it is the addition of the circle of seven roses to the cross that lifts us from the physical (the cross) to the etheric level. The etheric permeates the whole of nature, and the rose is considered as the most beautiful representative of nature. Also, the rose, when it blossoms, is fivefold in the shape of its blossoms, and the pentagram (five-pointed star) represents the five primary streams of the etheric body.

> Streams of ether are always circulating out of the cosmos through the human body. One such stream enters through the head, passes from there into the right foot, then into the left hand, then into the right hand, then into the left foot, and from there back to the head. If we think of a human being standing in the position just described, with outstretched arms, then the streaming has the form of a pentagram... These fine streams circulate all the time in the human being and bring him [her] into connection with the entire cosmos.³⁴

Almost everyone is familiar with the cross as the symbol of Christ. This is the symbol of Christ on the physical level, relating to the Earth stage of evolution, which is the fourth stage of cosmic evolution (see chapter 5). This fits appropriately with the four arms of the cross. Christ's sacrifice on the Cross two thousand years ago was essential for humanity. Through the outpouring of Divine Love from the Cross, the birth of the true "I" of the human being is made possible, as expressed in the words of St. Paul, "Not I, but Christ in me"—see the meditation "Christ in me" presented in this book, which offers a daily practice for the birth of the true I, this being the goal of earthly evolution since the coming of Christ. It is a matter of the union of the human I with the I of Christ. Mystical union with Christ is the inner core of Christian esotericism, and the "way of the Cross" is the path to this union. Following upon this, the path then opens to the inner

---

32 Ibid., pp. 176–177. Words in brackets [ ] added by RP. The seven roses are imagined in a circle around the cross, with the four arms of the cross extending beyond the circle of seven roses. The Rose Cross meditation is described in detail in chapter 5 ('Knowledge of Higher Worlds') in Rudolf Steiner's *An Outline of Esoteric Science* (former title, *Occult Science: An Outline*) (Great Barrington: SteinerBooks, 1997).
33 Rudolf Steiner, *Concerning the History and Content of the Higher Degrees of the Esoteric School, 1904–1914*, Complete works vol. 265 (Isle of Mull, Scotland: Etheric Dimensions Press, 2005), pp. 369–370.

34 Rudolf Steiner, *Guidance in Esoteric Training* (London: Rudolf Steiner Press, 1972), p. 83.

transformation—through union with Christ—of the different members of the human being, a path that can be described as "putting on the Resurrection body."

Just as the cross is the symbol of Earth evolution and of Christ's coming upon the Earth, so the Rose Cross is the symbol of Christ's Second Coming, his return in an etheric body, which entails a new sacrifice—this time opening the path to Shambhala, to the heart of Mother Earth.

> Let us now picture the vision of Christ as it will appear...during the next 2,500 years and as it appeared to Paul on the way to Damascus. Human beings will ascend to a cognition of the spiritual world and will see the physical world permeated by a new sphere. The physical environment will present a totally different aspect in the course of the next 2,500 years through the addition of an etheric realm, which indeed is already here and which human beings will learn to perceive. This etheric sphere is even now spread out before the eyes of those who have carried their esoteric training as far as illumination...A part of the land from which initiates drew their forces...will be thrown open to a great part of humanity during the next 2,500 years...This land will return to Earth, and human beings will be guided to it by him whom they will see when, through a vision like that of the event in Damascus, they reach the land of Shambhala. Shambhala, for thus is the land called, has withdrawn from the sight of human beings...The Christ event, however, which will be granted to human beings in this century through their newly awakened faculties, will bring back the fairy land of Shambhala...Humanity is called upon to...find the way to the land of Shambhala that has disappeared...but that Christ will once more reveal.[35]

Concerning the "location" (spiritually understood) of the lost realm of Shambhala, it is interesting to consider Rudolf Steiner's words to Countess Johanna von Keyserlingk at the end of his *Agricultural Course* (Pentecost 1924), at which he laid the foundations for a new and conscious relationship to the Earth Mother, Demeter, through the spiritually based form of agriculture known as the biodynamic method:

> Rudolf Steiner had the kindness to come up to my room, where he spoke to me about the kingdom in the interior of the Earth. We know that, at the moment when Christ's blood flowed down onto the Earth at Golgotha, a new Sun globe was born in the Earth's interior. My search had always been directed toward studying the Earth's depths, because I had seen within the Earth a golden kernel light up, named by Ptolemy the primeval Sun. I could connect those golden depths only with the land that Steiner said was hidden from human sight, and that Christ would open the gates to lead those who seek it to the submerged fairy-tale land of Shambhala, of which the Indians dream... I asked Rudolf Steiner, "Is the interior of the Earth made of the gold that comes from the hollow cavity in the Sun and is destined to return there?" He replied, "Yes, the interior of the Earth is of gold."... I continued to question him for my assurance: "Doctor, when I am standing here on Earth...the golden land is beneath me, deep within the interior of the Earth; if I now attain sinlessness and remain in the depths, will the demons be able to harm me, and will I be able to penetrate beyond them and reach the golden land?" He replied, "If you pass through them accompanied by Christ, the demons will be unable to harm you—but otherwise they would indeed be able to destroy you." He added emphatically, "They can, nevertheless, become our helpers. Yes, this is true; the path is a true one, but very difficult."[36]

Against this background, it can be understood that the new sacrifice of Christ at this time of his Second Coming has to do with the Earth Mother and with restoring access for humanity to the "lost paradise" known in the East as Shambhala. This, in turn, is an

---

35 Rudolf Steiner, *The Christ Impulse and the Development of "I" Consciousness* (New York: Anthroposophic Press, 1976), pp. 111–113.

36 Johanna and Adalbert von Keyserlingk, *The Birth of a New Agriculture* (London: Temple Lodge Press, 1999), pp. 84–86.

aspect of the creation of the "new Earth" through the spiritualization of the present Earth. There is much more that could be said about this, in particular, that in the future eurythmy will increasingly—through connecting with Christ in the etheric—be able to draw upon the forces of Shambhala in the heart of the Earth. This is one of the goals of the practice of *Putting on the Resurrection Body* described in this book.

The foregoing will also help to illumine the significance of taking Rudolf Steiner's *Morning Meditation* as the point of departure for the sequence *Inner Radiance: Putting on the Resurrection Body*. This is evident by way of understanding both the inner connection of the Rose Cross meditation to the *Morning Meditation* and also the meaning of the Rose Cross as a symbol relating to Christ in the etheric realm.

Now let us return to the main theme: the Sun nature of Christ, which is brought out by a number of meditations given by Rudolf Steiner, some of which are quoted earlier in the text. Considering again the *Salutation to the Sun,* this meditation starts with the words "I see the Sun," which relate to Mary Magdalene's experience on Easter Sunday morning, beholding in the etheric realm the Risen One in his Resurrection body. The meditation continues with the words, "The Sun beholds me," which express that Mary Magdalene became aware of the gaze of the Risen One resting upon her, although still not recognizing him as her beloved Master. The next words, "I revere the Sun," bring to expression the mood of reverence that overcame Mary Magdalene, which deepened immensely when the Risen One greeted her by saying "Mary" and she recognized him as the Master: "The Sun greets me." She was profoundly moved to the depths of her being and the longing arose within her to mystically unite with him: "I unite myself with the Sun."

At that point in time the Risen One was "newly born" in his Resurrection body, which was still in the process of formation. When Mary Magdalene, overcome with longing, fell on her knees and stretched out her arms

to touch his feet, He gestured to her, saying: "Do not touch me." (This can be contrasted with the experience of the disciple Thomas on the following Saturday evening when the Risen One allowed Thomas to touch him—his Resurrection body during the intervening week having been more fully "born.")

What then transpired for Mary Magdalene is of extraordinary significance for grasping the "putting on of the Resurrection body" as a co-creation together with Christ. For her encounter with the Risen One can be understood as another archetype of this co-creation—different from that of the exchange between the Risen One and Lazarus at his raising. The experience of Mary Magdalene was that of a streaming of substance from the Risen One toward her, a streaming that can be differentiated into Light, Love, and Life—as expressed in the *Salutation to the Sun*: "The Sun blesses me with Light, Love, and Life." The Risen One was streaming toward her the light of *manas* (Spirit Self), the love of *buddhi* (Life Spirit), and the life of *atma* (Spirit Human). All three together she experienced as *spiritual power*: "The power of the Sun is immeasurably strengthening. Through the Sun's power one can pass through all trials peacefully. Through the power of the Sun one can endure to an extraordinary degree. The Sun bestows great power." It is this power, streaming from Christ in the etheric, which human beings are in need of at the present time in order to pass through the great trials described in my book *Prophecy–Phenomena–Hope: The Real Meaning of 2012* and which are alluded to briefly in chapter 5.

This transmission of spiritual power (Light, Love, and Life) from the Risen One to Mary Magdalene did not stop when he disappeared from her beholding of him in the etheric realm. It continued for the rest of her life. From that time onward Mary Magdalene was receiving the in-streaming substance of the Risen One into the region of her heart, which streamed out from her in three directions:

> *vertically, ascending upward*—through her crown chakra toward Heaven, to the Angels and the spiritual hierarchies as a constant hymn of praise and thanksgiving;
>
> *horizontally*—from her heart chakra outward, across the land (and ultimately around the world), in praise of creation and blessing human souls;
>
> *and vertically, descending downward*—streaming from the region of the heart what she received from Christ down through the root chakra and through her legs and feet toward Shambhala, for the transformation of the Earth—thus participating with Christ in the work of creating the "new Earth."

This is one of the goals, also, of the activity of the Choreocosmos School: to participate in the creation of the "new Earth" along the lines of this archetype described here in relation to Mary Magdalene and her life path. It was this activity that she was engaged in for some thirty years in the South of France, when she lived in the cave of Sainte-Baume in Provence. In this sense she was a forerunner for humanity, preparing for the present time of humankind's encounter with Christ in the etheric realm.

A further deepening into the *Salutation to the Sun*—and into the entire sequence *Inner Radiance: Putting on the Resurrection Body*—is helped by holding in consciousness, while engaged in the eurythmy practice of the sequence, the archetypal meeting of Mary Magdalene with the Risen One on Easter Sunday morning.

Also, the following words of Rudolf Steiner from an esoteric lesson held on September 24, 1907, can be a great source of inspiration with regard to connecting with Christ in the etheric:

> Christ is a Sun Spirit, a Fire Spirit. His Spirit is what reveals itself to us in the light of the Sun. His Breath of Life is what envelops the Earth in the air and penetrates into us with every breath [we take]. His Body is the Earth upon which we live.
>
> He really does nourish us with his Flesh and Blood. For what we also take into ourselves as nourishment is from the Earth, taken from his Body.
>
> We breathe his Breath of Life, which he streams to us through the plant covering of the Earth.
>
> We behold in his Light, for the light of the Sun is his Spirit Radiance.
>
> We live in his Love, also physically; for what we receive as warmth from the Sun is his Spiritual Power of Love, which we feel as warmth.
>
> And our spirit is attracted by his Spirit, as our body is bound to his Body.
>
> Therefore our body must become hallowed, since we walk upon his Body. The Earth is his Holy Body, which we touch with our feet. And the Sun announces his Holy Spirit, to which we are allowed to look up. And the air is the proclamation of his Holy Life, which we are allowed to take into ourselves.

So that we could become conscious of our self, our spirit, so that we ourselves would become spirit beings, this lofty Sun Spirit sacrificed himself, leaving his Royal Dwelling Place, descending from the Sun and taking up physical raiment on the Earth. Thus he is crucified physically in the Earth.

However, he spiritually embraces the Earth with his Light and his Power of Love—and everything that lives upon [the Earth] belongs to him. He waits only for us to want to be his. If we offer ourselves up to him wholly as his own, he gives to us not only his physical Life—no, also his higher spiritual Sun Life. Then he irradiates us with his Divine Light Spirit, with his Warming Rays of Love, and with his Creative Will of God. [As described above, this is what was experienced by Mary Magdalene through her encounter with the Risen One—the streaming of his Divine Light Spirit, his Warming Rays of Love, and his Creative Will of God—experienced as the transmission of spiritual power from the Risen One into her being.]

We can only be what he bestows upon us—that into which he makes us. Everything to do with us that corresponds to the Divine Plan is his Work. What can we do toward this? Nothing—other than to allow him to work within us. However, if we resist his Love, he is unable to work within us.

How could we possibly resist this Love?—from him, he who speaks: "I have always loved you and I have drawn you toward Me through the power of Goodness."

He has loved us from the beginning of the Earth. We have to allow his Love to become Being in us.

Only this signifies True Life; only there is True Spirit, True Blessedness possible, where this life becomes for us a Life of Being, the Christ Life in us.

It is not from ourselves that we are able to become pure and holy, but only from this Christ Life. All our struggle and endeavor is for naught as long as we are not filled with this Higher Life. This alone, as a cleansing, purifying stream, can wash away everything from our being that is still unclean.

This is the soul foundation from which this purifying Light-life can arise.

There we have to seek our dwelling place: at his feet, and in devotion to him [as was the case with Mary Magdalene].

Then he will transform us and irradiate us with his Divine Life-love until we become light and pure like him, similar to him—until he can share his Divine Consciousness with us.

Through his Light the soul becomes pure—that is, [she becomes] wise. Thus she can unite herself with his Life. This is then the union of Christ and Sophia, the union of the Christ Life with the human soul purified through his Light.[37] (Rudolf Steiner)

Keys to the Gestures

The prayers and meditations offered here in connection with eurythmy can also be worked with as prayers and meditations in their own right—and, as such, are extremely potent. The entire sequence of prayers and meditations is called *Inner Radiance*. The core sequence within the whole sequence is called *Putting on the Resurrection Body*.

The call to prayer and meditation bids us to participate in the great celebration of cosmic sounding—as in "In the beginning was the Word." Prayer, whether personal or communal, when coming from the depths of the wellspring of the human heart exudes a substance and movement into the aura of the Earth's mantle. The responding silence, if only a quiver, indicates that our

---

37 Rudolf Steiner, *Aus den Inhalten der esoterischen Stunden III, 1913–1923* ("*Esoteric Lessons III, 1913–1923*"), Complete Works vol. 266/III (Dornach, Switzerland: Rudolf Steiner Verlag, 1998), pp. 346–347. This esoteric lesson was held in Hanover, Germany, on September 24, 1907.

prayer and heartfelt thoughts—whether filled with joy and tender gratitude or despair—have been received by a hierarchy of spiritual beings who participate together with us in the life and love-filled wisdom that weaves between all beings, between Heaven and Earth.

The vowel sounds give expression to the interiority of the Word. Like the functioning organs of the physical body, the vowels give sound to the soul qualities of life and resonate within the chakras as active agents of movement and transformation. Prayerful movement tones the will forces in the limbs and strengthens the activation of the life currents that are imbued with the shaping forces of life.

Obviously, with our intention focused upon co-participating with Christ in the shaping of the Resurrection body, we are celebrating the "Word made flesh." Included in this section are some simple diagrams describing the vowel sounds with accompanying gestures and indications for the prayers and meditations which comprise the practice of "Cultivating Inner Radiance and the Body of Immortality."

The eurythmy gestures for the sounds accompanying the prayers and meditations are given with the prayers, with some descriptive indications and additional sketches. Herewith some examples of notation used in describing the gestures:

> "Above"— a gesture that is formed above the head
> "Upward"—the gesture is one of moving from below upward
> "Below"—a gesture that is formed below the solar plexus
> "Downward"—the gesture is one of moving from above downward
> AU: heart: formed at the heart chakra
> I: left: the left arm is raised and the right arm is diagonally down from the raised left arm
> I: right: the right arm is raised and the left arm is diagonally down from the raised right arm

The Sacred Movement of Eurythmy

It is Rudolf Steiner's great gift to humanity to have brought into existence a new form of sacred movement, which strengthens the life body and prepares us for union with Christ as the bearer of Divine Love—with him whose essential nature is unfathomable mercy and infinite compassion. This new form of sacred movement is by no means the only way, yet it is one of the ways offering a path leading to what is needed by way of preparation for the future World Pentecost—the approaching heavenly out-pouring of a great wave of Divine Love—and as a remedy in face of the attempt by adversarial forces to harden human beings through materialism and the more destructive aspects of modern technology.

These hardening forces tend to cut us off from the heavens, from Divine Love. With the help of this new form of sacred movement, we are able to strengthen and open ourselves to the meeting with Christ, whose being is Divine Love, and who is now extending his unfathomable mercy and infinite compassion to all human beings. It is important, though, that we turn to him in complete freedom, exercising our freedom of choice to open ourselves to him in order to receive his mercy and compassion.

The schooling offered in this book is one of cultivating inner radiance through connecting with Christ by way of the etheric form of movement known as eurythmy. The expression of Christ's words in conjunction with this etheric form of movement opens up a path to Christ, attuning oneself with Christ's presence, now living in the etheric aura of the Earth. The Core Practice of the Inner Radiance sequence described in the book is that of *Putting on the Resurrection Body*. Working with the words of Christ also offers protection against the adversarial forces, bearing in mind Christ's words that "Heaven and Earth will pass away, but my words will never pass away" (Matthew 24:35).

Chapter 1: Foundational to the Practice of Cultivating Inner Radiance

Resources

Among the books listed at the end of this book, the works *Cosmic Dances of the Planets, Cosmic Dances of the Zodiac,* and *The Foundation Stone Meditation in the Sacred Dance of Eurythmy,* coauthored by Lacquanna Paul and Robert Powell, are valuable for describing the gestures (usually accompanied by figures). The book *The Prayer Sequence in Sacred Dance* by Lacquanna Paul and Robert Powell contains a sequence of prayers and meditations that are complementary to the Inner Radiance sequence described in this book—complementary in the sense that the Inner Radiance sequence is best practiced in the morning and the Prayer sequence in the evening (although some people might appreciate the Prayer sequence in the morning and the Inner Radiance sequence in the evening or at some other time of day). The prayers and meditations belonging to the Inner Radiance sequence are not meant to replace—but rather to supplement—those belonging to the Prayer sequence. The "Lord's Prayer as chakra prayer" belonging to the Inner Radiance sequence in no way replaces the "Lord's Prayer" of the Prayer sequence. In practicing both, it is possible to experience that each works in its own unique and particular way—the former taking effect more in relation to enlivening the chakras, while the latter has an enlivening influence upon the whole etheric body and also elevates the soul to a new level of experience of the cosmos.

Index of Gestures

This index gives the page numbers where the most extensive description of the gesture is to be found.

A gesture 32
Artemis gesture 73
AU gesture (with arms extended) 54
AU-heart 32, 35
AUM/AUMEYN 38
Blessing Hands gesture 39
Cosmic Reverence gesture 38
D gesture 76
E gesture 32
E gesture (above head) 63
EI gesture 32
"Eye of God" gesture 35
Fulfillment gesture 37, 38
"Grail Cup" gesture 36
Holding Fast gesture 73
I gesture 32
L gesture 42, 46

M gesture (horizontal) 64
M gesture (lemniscates—figure 8) 57
Moon gesture 38
N gesture 64
O gesture 32
Octave gesture (musical interval) 62
Pentagram-IAO gesture 39, 62
Prayer gesture 35, 36
R gesture 48
Reverence gesture 40
Saturn gesture (start)—see "Grail Cup" gesture 36
Sixth gesture (musical interval) 62
Sun gesture 38, 66
U gesture 32
Universal Love gesture 38
Veneration gesture 64
Warmth of Heart gesture 64

Planets and Corresponding Vowel Sounds

The correspondence of the vowel sounds to the planets was given in eurythmy by Rudolf Steiner in the German language, as listed below. However, in the English language the vowel sounds are not spoken in a pure way, so the pure pronunciation of the vowel sounds in eurythmy is listed in parentheses.

In addition to the five pure vowel sounds for the five planets, there are two diphthong vowels (AU and EI) corresponding to the Sun and the Moon.

Saturn U ("oo" as in "soon")
Raise arms straight up above head (arms parallel and palms facing each other).
Feel the etheric connection of the feet with the earth and also flowing between the hands.

Sun AU ("ow" as in "now")
—also called AU-heart

Draw hands into the region of the heart, right hand cupped loosely over the left, which is closed softly over the heart chakra (*drawing the earth, creation, and life experience into the human and cosmic heart*).

Moon EI ("eye"—or "I")
As the right arm extends gracefully out to the right (palm down blessing the earth); the left palm simultaneously strokes along the aura of the extending arm, from hand to shoulder. This gesture can be done by reversing the right and left arms. *Allow warmth of heart to stream lovingly from the heart through the arms and hands toward the earth, all the way to the heart of the earth.*

Mars E ("eh"—or "a" as in "say")
Bring the arms to the cross "X" position between the larynx and heart—lower arms touching and hands opened out, fingers extended, wrists in alignment with crossed arms. The completion of this gesture is "crisp" and clearly defined. Mars-E gives rise to the experience of *setting boundaries for oneself* and is complementary to the openness of Venus-A. Can also be formed above head, *reaching up to the higher self.*

Mercury I ("ee" as in "feet")
Arms form a diagonal line, opening from the heart, left arm up (diagonally forward) and right arm down diagonally back). (This gesture can also be formed with the right arm up and the left arm down.) Hands are open (fingers together) in alignment with extended arms.
Experience oneself, in freedom, connecting heaven and earth.

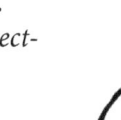

Jupiter O ("oh" as in the exclamation "oh")
Arms open to form an open O.
Embrace the whole world with the light and warmth and strength of the heart.

Venus A ("ah" as in the exclamation "ah")
Palms open in a gesture of praise and gratitude.

AMEN in the Teaching of Jesus Christ from Anne Catherine Emmerich

Near the city of Salamis on the island of Cyprus, on Monday, April 30 in the year AD 31, Jesus taught about the creation. He said that from one seed-corn a whole harvest was gathered, that all things came forth from one, Almighty God, the Creator of Heaven and Earth, the Father and Supporter of all human beings....

Four weeks later, on Monday, May 28, at Mallep, where there was a Jewish colony on the island of Cyprus, Jesus "delivered a grand discourse on the word AMEN which, he said, was the whole summary of prayer. Whoever pronounces it carelessly, makes void his prayer. Prayer cries to God; binds us to God; opens us to his mercy, and with the word AMEN uttered rightly, we take the asked-for gift out of his hands. Jesus spoke most forcibly of the power of the word AMEN. He called it the beginning and the end of everything. He spoke almost as if God had by it created the whole world. He uttered an AMEN over all that he had taught them, over his own departure from them, over the accomplishment of his own mission, and ended his discourse by a solemn AMEN. Then he blessed his audience, who wept and cried after him." [38]

From the foregoing text it is apparent that it is important not to pronounce the word AMEN carelessly. On this account it is helpful to know the deeper meaning of AMEN and its correct pronunciation. Knowing both the deeper meaning of the word AMEN and its correct pronunciation helps us not to pronounce it carelessly, i.e., without caring. Obviously this does not mean that all the millions of people down through the ages who have spoken the word AMEN have spoken it carelessly. That they spoke it with care is what counts in the first place. Over and above speaking it with care, however, it is helpful to know the deeper meaning of AMEN and its correct pronunciation, which allows us to speak AMEN not only with care but also to pronounce it in the right way—simultaneously being conscious of its deeper meaning.

From the visions of Anne Catherine Emmerich quoted above, it emerges that the word AMEN is an expression of the primal Word of creation. "In the beginning was the word..." as it is stated in the Gospel of St. John.

In the Hindu tradition the primal word of creation is AUM. AMEN is AUM to which the letters "E" and "N" have been added by Jesus Christ. A–Father / U–Son / M–Holy Spirit refer to the Holy Trinity.

Christ incarnated on the earth into Jesus of Nazareth as a fourth power of the Good—the divine-human being, Jesus Christ—in addition to the three primal powers of the Good known as the Father/Creator—A; the Son/Maintainer—U; and the Holy Spirit/Transformer—M.

The "E" and the "N" were added by the fourth power of the Good, Jesus Christ, to the AUM of the Holy Trinity. The "E" expresses the gift of selfhood that came into the world with Jesus Christ as a result of his sacrifice on Golgotha, bringing down from the Central Sun the true I AM for human beings and pouring it out from his sacred heart with his blood. Christ on the Cross holds the "E" gesture in its cosmic form. The "N" is the power to resist evil —initially stemming from the overcoming of the three temptations in the wilderness and then from the triumph over the fourth temptation that presented itself during the night of Gethsemane, but above all owing to Christ's vanquishing of evil on his path of descent through the subearthly spheres toward the heart of Mother Earth, followed by his triumphant Resurrection as the conqueror over evil and death. The "N" gesture expresses the descent—entering into connection with the depths—followed by the triumphant ascent.

---

[38] Anne Catherine Emmerich, *The Life of Jesus Christ* (Charlotte NC: TAN Books, 2004), vol. 3, pp. 351, 424. See also, *Anne Catherine Emmerich, Visions of the Life of Jesus Christ* (San Rafael, CA: LogoSophia Press, 2012)—this work includes the chronology of Christ's ministry as determined by Robert Powell.

The correct pronunciation of AMEN is "A-U-MEYN" (which is an abbreviated form of A-OO-MEYN).

AMEN is the esoteric name of Christ in our age, at this time of his Second Coming in the ethereal realm enveloping the Earth:

> Thus speaks the AMEN, the faithful and true witness, the beginning of God's creation.
>
> (Revelation 3:14)

Contemplating these words brings us into contact with the mystery of the Resurrection body. *Putting on the Resurrection Body*, which is the focus of this entire sequence of prayers/meditations, is the goal of all humanity.

> The head of the AMEN is the kingdom of stars in the heavens;
>
> The heart and outstretched arms (cosmic "E") of the AMEN comprise the power of the radiant cross of the Sun's light;
>
> The limbs of the AMEN comprise the rainbow of glory when matter is permeated by spirit.
>
> The kingdom, the power, and the glory of the AMEN stand over and against the false kingdom, the false power, and the false glory of the adversarial forces confronting Christ and humanity today. In essence, the AMEN is Christ in his cosmic garment.

As quoted in the previous paragraph, in Revelation we read these words concerning the AMEN:

> Thus speaks the AMEN, the faithful and true witness, the beginning of God's creation.
>
> (Revelation 3:14)

Here the AMEN is related to the primal beginning ("in the beginning was the Word"). There is another reference in Revelation, where the AMEN is signified in relation to the Coming One:

> Behold the AMEN who makes all things new.
>
> (see Revelation 21:5–6)

In this connection we think of Christ in his Second Coming:

> Behold, he is coming in the clouds...
>
> (Revelation 1:7)

Now follows the AMEN/AUMEYN meditation with indications for the gestures accompanying the speaking of this meditation, which, like all the prayers and meditations in this work, can be spoken silently, purely inwardly.

Since the AMEN/AUMEYN meditation is a deepening into the closing words of the Lord's Prayer,[39] first of all the Lord's Prayer is prayed.

---

[39] The closing words of the Lord's Prayer—"Deliver us from evil" (spoken by Jesus Christ at the Sermon on the Mount, as recorded in the Gospel of St. Matthew)—ultimately signify "Deliver us from the evil one" (the translation offered by the New International Version of the Bible in the 2011 edition). In the early Christian centuries the words "For thine is the kingdom and the power and the glory, for ever and ever, AMEN" became added to "Deliver us from evil" as closing words to the Lord's prayer. These closing words are not found in the earliest versions of the Matthew Gospel. The first reference—albeit abbreviated to: "For thine is the power and the glory for ever"—is in the Teaching of the Twelve Apostles (8:1), written shortly after AD 100. In a complete form, these words are subsequently found in the second (or third) century Syriac Peshitta Bible—James Murdock, *The Syriac New Testament* (Boston: H. L. Hastings, 1896), p.9. How did these words come to be added to the Lord's Prayer? It is not generally known that they were inspired by the Risen One himself. Deeper study and contemplation reveals that these closing words were communicated by the Risen One as a prophetic announcement of his Second Coming and are a powerful means of connecting with the *parousia*, the Divine Presence of Christ in his Second Coming. It is significant that these words follow directly after "Deliver us from the evil one" relating to the encounter with the evil one as the personification of evil. The words "For thine is the kingdom and the power and the glory, for ever and ever. AMEN" were given by the Risen Christ to guide and strengthen humanity through the trial of the encounter with the evil one expressed in the words "Deliver us from the evil one." This is the deeper significance of working with the AMEN/AUMEYN meditation at the present time.

Chapter 1: Foundational to the Practice of Cultivating Inner Radiance

The Lord's Prayer as Chakra Prayer

If one knows the words of the Lord's Prayer in the Aramaic language, this can be spoken in Aramaic. [40]

Heart gesture AU-heart

The heart gesture is formed by gently closing the palm of the left hand at the level of the heart chakra and cupping the right palm over the spiral formed by the closed left hand.

Form the Heart gesture over the Heart chakra.

Prayer gesture

Forming the Prayer gesture, move the hands upward above the head.

With the Prayer gesture the tips of the thumbs and fingers and also the base of the palms are gently touching, while leaving an open space between the palms.

Our Father, who art in heaven

"Eye of God" gesture

Form the "Eye of God" gesture at the level of the Crown chakra.

The "Eye of God" gesture is formed by making an upward-pointing triangle, where the tips of the thumbs (base of triangle) are touching and the tips of the forefingers are also touching one another (pointing upward).

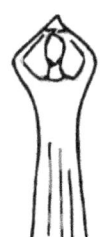

Hallowed be thy name

"Eye of God" gesture

Maintaining the "Eye of God" gesture, move the hands downward and hold the gesture over the chakra of the "Third Eye."

Thy kingdom come

"Eye of God" gesture

Maintaining the "Eye of God" gesture, move the hands downward and hold the gesture over the Throat chakra.

Thy will be done, on earth as it is in heaven

---

40   For a commentary on the Lord's Prayer in Aramaic, see Neil Douglas-Klotz, *Prayers of the Cosmos* (New York: HarperCollins, 1990).

(Lord's Prayer continued)

Heart gesture AU-heart
Move the hands downward, forming the Heart gesture over the Heart chakra.

Give us this day, our daily bread

Saturn gesture ("Grail Cup")
Moving the hands downward, form the Saturn gesture (Grail Cup) over the chakra at the solar plexus. The hands (palms facing upward) are cupped one above the other with the tips of the thumbs touching each other.

And forgive us our trespasses, as we forgive those who trespass against us

Saturn gesture ("Grail Cup")
Maintaining the Saturn gesture (Grail Cup), move the hands downward over the Sacral (Life Center) chakra.

And lead us not into temptation

Saturn gesture ("Grail Cup")
Maintaining the Saturn gesture (Grail Cup), move the hands further down to align with the Root chakra.

But deliver us from evil

Prayer gesture
Move the arms and hands upward, forming the Prayer gesture over the chakra of the "Third Eye," and with the tips of the forefingers lightly touch the brow in the region of the "Third Eye."

For thine…

Heart gesture
Move the hands down to form the Heart gesture AU-heart over the Heart chakra.

is…

Prayer gesture (hands downward)
Move the hands downward, forming the Prayer gesture with the fingers pointing toward the earth.

the kingdom

36

Chapter 1: Foundational to the Practice of Cultivating Inner Radiance

(Closing to the Lord's Prayer)

Prayer gesture (crossing from left to right shoulder)
With the hands still forming a downward facing Prayer gesture, leave the left hand pointing toward the Earth (in the Prayer gesture) and move the right hand up toward the left shoulder. While speaking the words "and the power," the tips of the fingers of the right hand first touch the left shoulder and then move across horizontally to touch the right shoulder. After saying the words, move the right hand back to join the left hand in the downward facing Prayer gesture.

 *and the power*

Prayer gesture (crossing from right to left shoulder)
Move the left hand up toward the right shoulder (leaving the right hand pointing toward the Earth in the Prayer gesture). While speaking the words "and the glory," the tips of the fingers of the left hand first touch the right shoulder and then move across horizontally to touch the left shoulder.

 *and the glory*

Fulfillment gesture (curved chalice above head)
Move the arms upward from the downward facing Prayer gesture to form the Fulfillment gesture above the head. The palms are facing each other and the uplifted arms form a chalice to receive the grace that streams down after praying the Lord's Prayer. In releasing the Fulfillment gesture, return to the gesture for "Universal Love" with arms extended horizontally at the sides and palms facing forward in preparation for speaking AMEN/AUMEYN.

 *for ever and ever*

A: arms form a horizontal V-shaped A

U: arms parallel and extended forward horizontally in the U gesture

M: hands return in the M gesture toward heart, palms facing heart

AU: heart gesture (hands cupped over heart chakra).

 AMEN/AUMEYN

It can be helpful in attuning to Christ in the etheric realm to face toward the south while practicing the Lord's Prayer and the following prayers and meditations (see pages 71 and 199).

AMEN/AUMEYN *Meditation*

"For thine is the kingdom,	**Sun gesture** Extend right arm up (diagonally forward) and left arm down (diagonally back); simultaneously rotate arms: right arm clockwise, left arm counterclockwise (*radiating love from the heart, connecting Heaven and Earth*) With the Sun gesture, circle forward, counterclockwise to the right, coming to the front of the form—a small circle. (*Focus on the Father*)	
and the power,	**Moon gesture** Slowly close palms, hands lightly clenched, as arms move to cross over the life center (*concentrating the currents of Heaven and Earth, and aligning human will with divine will; becoming firmly rooted and deeply connected to the Earth*) With the Moon gesture, continue circling back counterclockwise to complete the circle—back to the starting point. (*Focus on the Son*)	
and the glory,	**Cosmic Reverence gesture** (*receiving the imprint of divine order in awe and wonder*) Raise arms above head, palms facing up; gaze directed up toward Heaven, leaning back slightly. (*Focus on the Holy Spirit*)	
For ever and ever	**Fulfillment (Grail) gesture** Arms open to form a rounded chalice above head; palms facing in toward each other, creating a connecting current (*opening to receive the fullness of divine grace*)	
AMEN/AUMEYN"	**Universal Love gesture** Slowly open arms and extend them horizontally, palms facing forward (*radiating divine energy into the world*)	

A: arms form a horizontal V-shaped A
U: arms parallel and extended forward horizontally in the U gesture
M: hands return in the M gesture toward heart, palms facing heart
AU: heart gesture (hands cupped over heart chakra).

Thus speaks the AMEN, the faithful and true witness, the beginning of God's creation.	AU – heart gesture
The AMEN bears the World Word within as the kingdom,	Blessing Hands gesture As indicated by Rudolf Steiner—connecting with the world of divine energy which is streaming down upon us, and letting it ray out through our arms and hands. The Blessing Hands gesture is formed with the palms facing outward, separating: thumb—forefinger / middle finger—ring finger / little finger, (similar to the gesture of the Risen Christ from the Isenheim altar—see page 55)
And in the miracles and stages of the Passion wields the power,	Universal Love gesture
And as the Risen One is the glory.	IAO standing in the form of a pentagram (five-pointed star) • Body upright (upright body represents I) • Arms and hands downward (A), palms facing down • Feet apart and knees pressed outward, with weight lightly pressed upon the outer edge of the soles of feet (O)

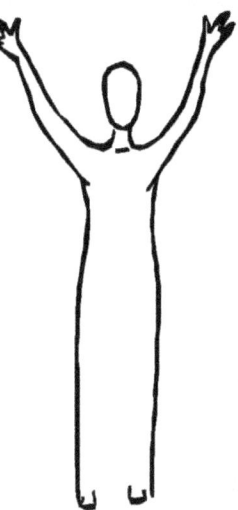

This pentagram–IAO gesture is that of Christ as depicted on the first seal of Revelation (see page 60). This is the Cosmic Christ. His uprightness represents I, his arms (palms facing down toward the Earth) are extended in a downward A, and his legs form a slight O. Together, this gesture of the Cosmic Christ represents IAO, which can be read as "I AM the Alpha and the Omega" —the words spoken by Christ in Revelation (verses 1:8, 21:6, and 22:13). As the I AM, he is I. As the Alpha, the beginning of creation, he is A. And as the final goal of evolution, as the Risen One, he is the Omega—that is, O. This gesture is both in the form of a pentagram—the overall form and figure of the Cosmic Christ—and it is the IAO, the esoteric name of Christ, signifying "I AM the Alpha and the Omega." With the I he is inwardly extending his head to the realm of stars, embracing the entirety of the starry heavens. With the A he is pouring Divine Love from his sacred heart through his arms and hands as a blessing to Mother Earth. And with the O he is inwardly extending his legs down to the heart of the Earth, to Shambhala, the golden realm of the Mother.

In connecting with Shambhala through the O, the O is experienced as very long and elongated, the top of the O being the region of the legs and the bottom of the O coinciding with Shambhala. We experience O in the practice of Right Standing (page 41), which is key to all the standing prayers and meditations in eurythmy.

Cultivating Inner Radiance and the Body of Immortality

The kingdom, the power, and the glory are united	Bringing feet together, U-upward
in Jesus Christ,	I-left
and their fulfillment	U-upward
is the AMEN.	Releasing the U, form the Blessing Hands gesture
His head is the kingdom, embracing all the stars in the heavens.	Blessing Hands gesture
His breath is the power to continue the work of creation: a breathing, radiant cross of light against the background of the starry heavens.	Universal Love gesture
And his limbs are the glory of spirit-permeated substance like a rainbow in the foreground.	Pentagram: IAO gesture
And the unity of the rainbow,	Pentagram: IAO
The radiant cross of light,	Universal Love gesture
And the starry heavens	Blessing Hands gesture
Is the all-encircling circle of the AMEN.	Lower arms form the Reverence gesture
"*For thine is the kingdom,*	Sun gesture (circling forward counterclockwise)
and the power,	Moon gesture (circling back counterclockwise)
and the glory,	Cosmic Reverence gesture (palms facing upward)
For ever and ever...	Fulfillment gesture

Releasing the Fulfillment gesture, the arms extend out into the Universal Love gesture.

- A arms form a horizontal V-shaped A
- U arms parallel and extended forward horizontally in the U gesture
- M hands return in the M gesture toward heart, palms facing heart
- AU heart gesture (hands cupped over heart chakra).

AMEN/AUMEYN"

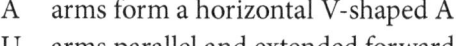

Chapter 2

THE CORE OF THE PRACTICE:
PUTTING ON THE RESURRECTION BODY

Introduction—Right Standing

In ancient times there was the practice of *Right Standing*, and the goddess of Right Standing was Vesta. In their underground temple the Vestal virgins practiced Right Standing, connecting with the heart of the Earth in the depths and with the starry heavens in the heights.

To practice Right Standing, stand with the feet a little apart, positioned approximately beneath the shoulders, with the knees relaxed. Feel the vertical, sensing one's connection with the stars; especially with one's own star, which one pictures to be vertically above—one's Eternal Star that supports one all the time—and through one's Eternal Star one feels one's connection with the Central Sun in the heart of the galaxy, the kingdom of the Father.

Feeling this vertical connection, one sends one's love and gratitude up from the heart toward the Heavenly Father, opening oneself like a flower in the region of the Crown to receive the flow of Divine Light pouring down from above.

Holding in consciousness the kingdom of the Heavenly Father above, one turns one's attention to the realm of the Mother below. One feels love and gratitude in one's heart toward the Divine Mother for her selfless, loving, nourishing support of all living beings. To find one's root connection with the Mother, one allows the love-filled warmth in the heart to stream downward, pouring through the legs and feet into the Earth, streaming all the way to the golden realm of Shambhala in the heart of the Earth, the kingdom of the Mother, and one feels the Mother's response as a breath of warmth streaming from Shambhala through the feet and up the insides of the legs into the region of the heart chakra.

This is Right Standing: to feel oneself as a vertical pillar, experiencing the Heavenly Father above in the heights and at the same time connecting with the Divine Mother below in the depths.

Through Right Standing one realizes one's true humanity, to the extent that one feels one's connection with the Father in the heights and with the Mother in the depths, finding the balance point between above and below in the region of the heart—sensing heavenly peace in one's heart chakra and sending this out:

> *Glory to the Father in the heights,*
> *and to the Mother in the depths,*
> *and peace on Earth to all beings of good will.*

This is essentially a living experience of the St. John's Imagination, bringing it to expression through inner identification with the Son by way of the words "Not I, but Christ in me."

St. John's Imagination

The silver-sparkling blue below, arising from the depths of the Earth and bound up with human weakness and error, is gathered into a picture of the Earth Mother. Whether she is called Demeter or Mary, the picture is of the Earth Mother. So it is that in directing our gaze downward, we cannot do otherwise than bring together in Imagination all those secrets of the depths which go to make up the material Mother of all existence. While in all that which is concentrated in the flowing from above, we feel and experience the Spirit Father of everything around us. And now we behold the outcome of the working together of the Spirit Father with the Earth Mother, bearing so beautifully within itself the harmony of the earthly silver and the gold of the heights. Between the Father and the Mother we behold the Son. (Rudolf Steiner)

In the spirit of inner identification with the Son in the St. John's Imagination, from the heart one sends out peace in the horizontal toward one's fellow human beings.

And one sends one's heartfelt love and gratitude above to the Heavenly Father through the crown chakra—picturing this chakra opening like a sunflower—sending one's love and gratitude above to starry heights all the way to the Central Sun at the heart of the galaxy, the throne of God.

At the same time one sends one's love and gratitude below through the root chakra—down through the legs and feet—to Shambhala, the realm of the Divine Mother, thanking Her for continually supporting and sustaining all living beings.

The knees should not be taut and rigid; rather, they should be slightly bent and relaxed. Then, pressing the knees gently outward, one senses the contact of the outer edges of one's feet with the Earth and becomes conscious of two currents, one from above and one from below.

This is the macrocosmic orbit, which comprises two currents. There is the stream of light from above, coming from the Central Sun, the kingdom of the Heavenly Father:

*In purest out-poured light shimmers
the Godhead of the world.*

And there is the stream of life from below, coming from Shambhala, the realm of the Divine Mother:

Thou art the Mother of everything living.

Right Standing entails becoming aware of the two currents comprising the macrocosmic orbit: Radiant spiritual light cascading down from the Heavenly Father pouring all around one as a shower of light, and the fountain of life gushing up from the Divine Mother as an inner stream ascending from the feet to the heart and from there to the crown of the head, where it joins the cascade of light from above.

The cascade of spiritual light from above streams down to the crown and envelops one in a shower of light. Sensing the enveloping shower, one concentrates upon the light streaming down, particularly upon the light streaming down the sides of the body.

The ability to sense the stream of light from above—passing via the crown down the body (focusing here upon the light passing down the sides of the body)—is enhanced by feeling the contact of the outer edges of one's feet with the Earth.

At the same time this position—in which the knees are relaxed and pressed outward slightly so as to establish the contact between the outer edges of the feet and the Earth—enhances one's awareness of the fountain of life gushing up from Shambhala and surging through the soles of the feet upward to the region of the heart, and from there streaming up to the crown of the head and radiating out as a fountain of life to merge with the cascade of light streaming down from above.

The fountain of life is felt most intensely streaming up the insides of the legs through the root chakra and bubbling up to the heart region. The cultivation of an awareness of the flow of the fountain of life on its further course from the heart chakra up to the crown chakra and beyond is enhanced especially through accompanying this flow by movement of the hands and arms as in the eurythmy gesture for the sound L, since normally the flow of vital force streams out from the heart center through the arms and hands, flowing out through the fingers.

Chapter 2: The Core of the Practice: Putting on the Resurrection Body

To form the L gesture, with palms open, facing up, raise arms up along the mid-line of the body. When the hands reach above the crown, turn the palms over and bring the arms out and down in a flowing movement. With the L gesture the flow of the fountain of life up to the heart is stimulated to flow up further, continuing from the heart up to the crown of the head and issuing forth from the crown as a gushing fountain, which then merges with the light cascading down from above.

One image for the flow of life force set in motion by the L gesture is that of a tree in the human being—a tree mirroring the Tree of Life.

With the help of the L gesture—formed slowly and purposefully—one can begin to experience the macrocosmic orbit: the radiant spiritual light flowing down from the Heavenly Father above and the fountain of life gushing up from the Divine Mother below, experiencing how one is placed between these two macrocosmic currents. This is the experience of Right Standing.

One can practice the following meditation anywhere—indoors or outdoors—at any time of day or night. Clearly it is easier to experience love and gratitude for the Mother—sending one's appreciation down toward the Mother's realm (Shambhala) through the legs and feet—when one does this meditation outside in Nature rather than inside. But often it is only possible inside, and one can nevertheless still feel one's profound connection with Mother Nature through one's power of recollection. If one has the opportunity to do the meditation outside in a beautiful natural setting, it is wonderful to take the opportunity to do the meditation outside, and the optimum time of day is around sunrise, since at this time the Earth is most receptive to the instreaming cosmic influences that are harvested through the eurythmy gestures. In the sense of St. Paul's words "Not I, but Christ in me," one can imagine that one is doing the eurythmy together with Christ, who imbues one's gestures with love, strength and beauty.

Moreover, if one is doing the meditation in a natural setting, one can imagine that Christ is doing the eurythmy with one and through one for the healing of Mother Nature, sensing moral warmth streaming out through the eurythmy gestures into Nature as a healing force for the redemption of the Earth and all the beings and kingdoms of Nature.

Then it is possible for eurythmy to be applied in service of landscaping in the ethereal realm and for the creation of ethereal "landscape temples" in service of Christ's work of redemption of Mother Earth and all the beings and kingdoms of Nature.

In the following sequence, the prayers and meditations are described one after the other. It is helpful to pause between each prayer or meditation in order to allow the realm of spirit to pour in blessing as a silent response to the prayer or meditation. The AU-heart gesture or the Reverence gesture or holding the hands in the Prayer gesture (*Namasté*) are all suitable and appropriate for remaining in silent repose between the various prayers and meditations, as these gestures were commonly used by the holy women in Christ's presence.

Christ himself often had his hands in the AU-heart gesture—for example, when in the company of the Blessed Virgin Mary. This gesture elevates one into the cosmic condition of consciousness that is experienced in the womb, prior to birth, and activates the streaming of the "inner sun" of one's heart chakra, whereby light and warmth begin to stream from the heart chakra, which is the organ in the astral body corresponding to the Sun.

Right Standing, holding the AU-heart gesture, can be done as a conscious practice to connect with the life force of Shambhala, in the heart of the Earth. Right Standing is the basic way of standing throughout the entire sequence of prayers and meditations described in this book. As alluded to above, at the end of each exercise one can consciously take up the posture of Right Standing, together with the AU-heart gesture of the hands cupped over the heart chakra or, if one prefers, with the hands in the Prayer gesture or the Reverence gesture. Holding this posture and gesture at the end of each exercise allows an opportunity not only for the grace of the spiritual world but also the grace of the Earth Mother to flow in as an "echo" or response after each prayer or meditation consciously opening to receive the in-streaming life force of Shambhala needed for the formation of the Resurrection body. There are other eurythmy exercises—for example, the eurythmy exercise of threefold walking—which offer an opportunity of opening the path to Shambhala, when practiced in the right way and with the right consciousness, together with the Etheric Christ.

Correspondences to the Seven Chakras and the Octave[41]

	SATURN	JUPITER	MARS	SUN	MERCURY	VENUS	MOON
SYMBOL	♄	♃	♂	☉	☿	♀	☽
CHAKRA	Crown	Third eye	Larynx	Heart	Solar plexus	Sacral	Root
LOTUS	8-petal	2-petal	16-petal	12-petal	10-petal	6-petal	4-petal
SOUND	U "oo"	O "oh"	E "eh"	AU "ow"	I "ee"	A "ah"	EI "eye"
DAY OF WEEK	Saturday	Thursday	Tuesday	Sunday	Wednesday	Friday	Monday

In the four stages of the Core Sequence—Transfiguration, Crucifixion, Resurrection, and Ascension—discussed below, there is a sevenfoldness inherent in each stage relating to the seven chakras, to which, however, an eighth is added. Eight is the symbol of infinity, and it is also the number associated with Jesus Christ, who rose from the dead on Easter Sunday, the "eighth day" (as the octave of Palm Sunday). Christ transcended time, expressed by the seven days of the week. The eighth day is the one on which he—the Risen One, the "first born of the dead" (Revelation 1:5)—is born. Christ in his Resurrection body is the octave of the human being in the physical body. This relationship of the Risen One to the "eighth" can be borne in mind whenever an "eighth" is added to the sevenfoldness in the following sequence.

For example, in the first part of *Putting on the Resurrection Body*, in forming the seven L's with the seven "I AM sayings" in relation to the seven chakras ascending from the root chakra to the crown chakra, an eighth L can be shaped in connection with the "star above the head" referred to in the meditation "A star is above my head, Christ speaks from the star…" described on page 62.[42] This "star above the head" is an expression of *manas* (spirit self), when the astral body is purified and transfigured.

For each of the four stages of the meditation an eighth gesture can be formed: with an eighth L commemorating the Transfiguration, an eighth R commemorating the Crucifixion, an eighth AU commemorating the Resurrection, and an eighth M commemorating the Ascension.

The Core Sequence is key to the practice of *Putting on the Resurrection Body,* whereas the prayers and meditations preceding and following the Core Sequence comprise the entirety of the Inner Radiance practice and can be built up over time as a series of invocations for the protection of the Earth and all life on Earth.

---

41 Lacquanna Paul & Robert Powell, *Cosmic Dances of the Planets.*

42 The eighth I AM saying—"I AM the Alpha and the Omega"—is the I AM saying for the "star above the head."

Chapter 2: The Core of the Practice: Putting on the Resurrection Body

---

> *In purest out-poured light shimmers the Godhead of the world"*
>
> *The Transfiguration*
>
> *The Seven I AM Sayings*
>
> *The Seven Healing Miracles*
>
> *"L"*

In purest out-poured light shimmers the Godhead of the world.

The archetype for this experience is to be found by contemplating the Transfiguration in the life of Christ.

Christ is the divine I AM. At the Transfiguration the Divine Light of the Godhead was streaming through his seven chakras. This experience is evoked through the seven I AM sayings spoken by Christ.

Each I AM saying corresponds to one of the seven chakras:

Root	I AM the true vine
Sacral	I AM the way, the truth, and the life
Solar plexus	I AM the door: the entrance and the exit
Heart	I AM the bread of life
Larynx	I AM the good shepherd
Third eye	I AM the light of the world
Crown	I AM the Resurrection and the life

Just as light passing through a prism refracts into the seven colors of the visible color scale, the light of the Divine refracts in the human astral body as the seven I AM sayings corresponding to the seven chakras, which are the primary organs of the astral body.

The seven I AM sayings spoken by Christ are for the healing of the seven chakras, which became disfigured as a consequence of the Fall, and correspond to the seven healing miracles of Christ described in the Gospel of St. John:

The changing of water into wine at the wedding at Cana	I AM the true vine
The healing of the nobleman's son	I AM the way, the truth, and the life
The healing of the paralyzed man at the pool of Bethesda	I AM the door: the entrance and the exit
The feeding of the five thousand	I AM the bread of life
The walking on the water	I AM the good shepherd
The healing of the man born blind	I AM the light of the world
The raising of Lazarus from the dead	I AM the Resurrection and the life

The seven healing miracles took place in this order for the healing of the seven chakras from below ascending above, from the root chakra to the crown chakra.

For this reason the I AM sayings are listed above alongside the seven chakras in the sequence ascending from the root chakra below to the crown chakra above, and this is the order of working with the I AM sayings in the context of this first stage of the Core Practice.

Preceding the working with the L gesture, one practices Right Standing and contemplates the words:

> *Glory to the Father in the heights,*
>
> *and to the Mother in the depths,*
>
> *and peace on Earth to all beings of good will.*

Then one crosses one's arms across one's breast in the eurythmy gesture for reverence.

Holding the Reverence gesture, one can meditate on the words "Christ in me" or on the mantra:

> *In Christo morimur*

(literally: "In Christ we die"—through here focusing on the words "Christ in me" one merges [dies] into the being of Christ and experiences "In Christ death becomes life"; see page 217).

Then one steps forward with the right foot (right foot forward, left foot behind) and begins the L gesture, inclining gently back when the hands are moving upward with the L and inclining gently forward when the hands are moving downward with the L gesture, synchronizing the rocking motion forward and backward with the L such that one is always at the low point of the L when most inclined forward and at the high point of the L gesture when one is most inclined back. With this rocking motion—and this applies also to the rocking motion during the subsequent stages with the R and M gestures—one takes care that when one is inclined back one maintains contact with the ground (with the foot that is forward) through the toes, i.e., that the toes remain touching the ground (rather than the heel).

With the first three L's one contemplates the words:

> L: *In purest out-poured light shimmers the Godhead of the world*
>
> L: *Putting on the Resurrection Body*
>
> L: *The first stage: the Transfiguration*

With the following seven L's one contemplates an I AM saying in relation to the corresponding chakra (in ascending sequence)

    I AM *the true vine*

    I AM *the way, the truth, and the life*

    I AM *the door: the entrance and the exit*

    I AM *the bread of life*

    I AM *the good shepherd*

    I AM *the light of the world*

    I AM *the Resurrection and the life*

In forming the eighth L one focuses upon the I AM Presence in all seven chakras, bringing the Light of Christ into all seven chakras simultaneously, as at the Transfiguration. Then one reverses the feet so that the left foot is forward and the right foot is behind and repeats seven L's, this time contemplating the healing miracle associated with each chakra (again in ascending sequence).

The changing of water into wine at the wedding at Cana

The healing of the nobleman's son

The healing of the paralyzed man at the pool of Bethesda

The feeding of the five thousand

The walking on the water

The healing of the man born blind

The raising of Lazarus from the dead

With the eighth L one speaks (or contemplates) again the words "In purest out-poured light shimmers the Godhead of the world."

Throughout the entire first stage of the morning exercise, and also during the resting contemplation holding the AU-heart gesture after completing the exercise, one focuses one's inner gaze upon the scene of the Transfiguration, inwardly invoking the Divine Light of the Transfiguration that was streaming through all seven of Christ's chakras.

The Transfiguration *by Fra Angelico*

> *"In purest love toward all that lives radiates the Godhood of my soul"*
>
> *The Crucifixion*
>
> *The Seven Words (Sayings) from the Cross*
>
> *The Seven Stages of the Passion*
>
> *"R"*

At this second stage of the Core Practice it is a matter of entering into an experience of the microcosmic orbit activated through the eurythmy gesture for the sound R.

The microcosmic orbit is the flow of vital energy that circulates in the embryo up through the region where the spine forms and down the front of the embryo as a circulating current of life energy, the place of influx being the navel. Through the umbilical cord the embryo receives nourishment and vital energy, which circulates around this orbit. The circulating life energy of the microcosmic orbit continues in a subtle form after birth and throughout life.

Just as the L gesture helps to bring the macrocosmic orbit to consciousness, so the eurythmy gesture for the sound R enables us to come to an experience of the circulating flow of energy in the microcosmic orbit.

The L gesture follows the downward flow and the upward stream that comprise the macrocosmic orbit. Likewise, the R gesture follows the circulating flow of energy around the microcosmic orbit. Arms rotate back/up, then out/forward, down and around, palms open facing Earth (*receiving and blessing the Earth*).

Following the movement of the R up the back, one focuses upon the flow of life force upward along the spinal column, and with the downward movement of the R in the front, one follows the flow from above to below through the seven chakras, from the crown chakra down to the root chakra, accompanied by the words "In purest love toward all that lives radiates the Godhood of my soul."

One endeavors to enter into the flow of movement of the R gesture, at the same time sensing the circulation of the microcosmic orbit as a river of life within.

The cultivation of an awareness of the flow of the river of life on its course up the spinal column to the crown chakra and then down the front from the crown to the root chakra is enhanced especially through accompanying this flow by movement of the arms and hands as in the eurythmy gesture for the sound R, and also by touching the tip of the tongue to the roof of the mouth to complete the circuit. Placing the tip of the tongue against the roof of the mouth ensures that the current continues on its downward flow, rather than collecting in the region of the crown and possibly causing pressure there. This is particularly important with respect to the subtle flow of life currents activated by the eurythmy gestures for the R and for the M (to be described in the fourth stage) but holds also to a certain extent for the currents activated by the eurythmy gestures for the L (first stage) and the AU (third stage). With the R gesture the inner streaming of the river of life around the microcosmic orbit is stimulated and brought to consciousness, especially when warmth of heart is allowed to stream from the heart through the arms and hands in pure love toward all that lives.

One image for the flow of life force set in motion by the R gesture is that of the great circle of the Milky Way in the heavens—a circle extending from the heights of Heaven to the depths below—mirrored in the orbit between the crown chakra above to the root chakra below and then back up again up the spine. It is interesting to note that in various cultures of antiquity the Milky Way is referred to as a celestial river—the heavenly Nile in Egypt, the heavenly Ganges in India, and so on. In forming the R gesture—slowly and purposefully—one can begin to experience the microcosmic orbit: the radiant, love-filled flow of vital energy circulating around the inner Milky Way.

Moses was the teacher of the people of Israel, and Hermes was the great teacher of the Egyptians, whose teaching is summarized in the words "As above, so below." In light of this correspondence between above and below, the microcosmic orbit is the inner Milky Way, mirroring within the human being the Milky Way in the heavens.

With the R gesture the ideal is to infuse the circulation of the inner Milky Way with love and warmth streaming from one's heart, in contemplating the words "In purest love toward all that lives radiates the Godhood of my soul."

The historical archetype for this experience is to be found by contemplating the Crucifixion in the life of Christ, who is Divine Love. At the Crucifixion the pure love of the Godhead was streaming through all seven chakras of Jesus Christ. This experience is evoked through the seven words (sayings) from the Cross spoken by Christ. Each word (saying) from the Cross corresponds to one of the seven chakras:

Crown	"Father, into thy hands I commend my spirit"
Third eye	"My God, my God, why hast thou forsaken me?" (*Eli, Eli, lama sabachthani*)
	(Alternate translation: "My God, my God, how thou hast glorified me!")
Larynx	"I thirst"
Heart chakra	"Today you shall be with me in paradise"
Solar plexus	"Father, forgive them, for they know not what they do"
Sacral	"Behold thy son; behold thy mother"
Root	"It is fulfilled"

The pure love of Christ, who is Divine Love, permeates the human being on seven levels as the seven words (sayings) from the Cross corresponding to the seven chakras are held in consciousness. The seven words (sayings) from the Cross spoken by Christ signify the infusion of Divine Love into the seven chakras on these seven different levels.

Crown	"Father, into thy hands I commend my spirit"

– brings to expression love of the Heavenly Father, to whom the crown chakra opens.

Third eye	"My God, my God, why hast thou forsaken me?"

– has to do with the I AM consciousness associated with the third eye chakra. The experience of utter loneliness ("being forsaken") is a great challenge on the one hand, and on the other hand it offers the possibility of an extraordinary enhancement of spiritual self-consciousness, that of the true I AM centered in the third eye chakra.

Larynx	"I thirst"

– expresses the great thirst for the redemption of all beings through the Word.

Heart	"Today you shall be with me in paradise"

– has to do with the expression of pure compassion from this central chakra.

Solar plexus	"Father, forgive them, for they know not what they do"

—gives expression to the capacity to forgive, associated with this chakra.

Sacral	"Behold thy son; behold thy mother"

– is concerned with the ability to unite polarities—the impulse of this chakra.

Root	"It is fulfilled"

– brings to expression love for the Divine Mother, who is addressed primarily through deeds.

In the context of this eurythmy meditation, the seven words from the Cross are spoken in this order for the infusion of love into the seven chakras, descending from the crown chakra (love of the Heavenly Father) to the root chakra (love of the Divine Mother).

For this reason the words from the Cross—listed above—are indicated alongside the seven chakras in the sequence descending from the crown chakra above to the root chakra below, and this is the order of working with the words from the Cross in the context of the second stage of the Core Practice.

One steps forward with the right foot (right foot forward, left foot behind) and begins the R gesture, inclining gently back when the hands are moving upward with the R and inclining gently forward when the hands are moving downward with the R gesture.

With the first three R's one contemplates the words:

> R—*In purest love toward all that lives radiates the Godhood of my soul.*
>
> R—*Putting on the Resurrection body*
>
> R—*The second stage: the Crucifixion*

Then with seven R's with the right foot forward, focus with each R upon a chakra:

Crown	*Father, into thy hands I commend my spirit*
Third Eye	*My God, my God, why hast thou forsaken me?/how thou hast glorified me!*
Larynx	*I thirst*
Heart	*Today you shall be with me in paradise*
Solar plexus	*Father, forgive them, for they know not what they do*
Sacral	*Behold thy son; behold thy mother*
Root	*It is fulfilled*

In forming an eighth R one focuses upon Divine Love in all seven chakras, bringing the Love of Christ into all seven chakras simultaneously, as at the Crucifixion. Then one reverses the feet so that the left foot is forward and the right foot is behind and repeats seven R's, each time contemplating one of the seven stages of the Passion:

Crown	*The washing of the feet*
Third Eye	*The scourging*
Larynx	*The crowning with thorns*
Heart	*The carrying of the cross*
Solar plexus	*The Crucifixion*
Sacral	*The Entombment*
Root	*The Resurrection*

With the eighth R one speaks (or contemplates) again the words "In purest love toward all that lives radiates the Godhood of my soul."

Throughout the entire second stage of the morning exercise, and also during the resting contemplation holding the AU-heart gesture after completing the exercise, one focuses one's inner gaze upon the scene of the Crucifixion, inwardly invoking the Divine Love poured out at the Crucifixion while contemplating the seven words from the Cross and the Seven Stages of the Passion in connection with the eurythmy gesture R.

The San Damiano Cross of St. Francis

> *"I rest within the Godhead of the world"*
>
> *The Resurrection*
>
> *The Seven Sayings of the Risen One*
>
> *The Seven Gifts of the Risen One*
>
> *"AU"*

At this third stage of the Core Practice it is a matter of entering into the spiral circulation through the chakras with the help of the eurythmy gesture for the sound AU.

The L gesture follows the downward flow and the upward stream of the macrocosmic orbit; the R gesture follows the circulating flow of energy around the microcosmic orbit; and the eurythmy gesture for the sound AU enhances the flow of the spiral circulation through the seven chakras.

This radiant life energy of the spiral circulation through the seven chakras is activated through contemplation of the Resurrection and the Divine Breath transmitted by the Risen One—just as the Crucifixion has to do with the out-pouring of Divine Love and the Transfiguration has to do with the radiation of Divine Light.

The building up of the Resurrection body was the goal of Jesus Christ that was attained at the Resurrection, thereby attaining the highest level—*atma*. The Sanskrit word *atma* and the German word *atmen* ("to breathe") come from the same root.

One begins by attuning to the Peace of Resurrection in the heart chakra and sensing how this spirals out in a clockwise direction—mirroring the clockwise movement of the Sun in 227 million years around the Central Sun located at the center of the galaxy.

Similarly, the current of peace is pictured emanating from the heart in a clockwise direction, which in eurythmy is the "Sun direction." This current ascends on the left to the region of the larynx (Mars chakra) and then descends on the right to the region of the solar plexus (Mercury chakra). From the solar plexus it ascends on the left to the region of the third eye (Jupiter chakra) and then descends on the right to the sacral region of the abdomen (Venus chakra). From the sacral chakra it ascends on the left to the region of the crown (Saturn chakra) and then descends on the right.

As it descends on the right, the heart chakra (Sun) is engaged in this spiral circulation more at the periphery, whereas at the starting point the focus is more upon the center of the heart chakra as the point of departure for the emanation of the Peace of Resurrection. And the descending stream, flowing down on the right, then streams down further from the periphery of the heart chakra to the region of the root chakra (Moon), and then flows out—upward and beyond the human form—in a continually expanding spiral.

Chapter 2: The Core of the Practice: Putting on the Resurrection Body

---

In forming the AU gesture the ideal is to infuse the spiral circulation through the chakras with peace streaming from one's heart, in contemplating the words "I rest within the Godhead of the world." The historical archetype for this experience is to be found by contemplating the Resurrection in the life of Christ, who is now the Risen One, breathing out Divine Peace through all seven chakras. This experience is evoked through the seven sayings spoken by the Risen Christ, each saying of the Risen One corresponding to one of the seven chakras as indicated above.

The Divine Breath of the Risen One transmits something unique through each chakra:

Crown	Transmission of spiritual power	
	"All power in Heaven and on Earth has been given unto me"	
Third eye	Transmission of spiritual presence	
	"Lo, I AM with you always, until the end of time"	
Larynx	Transmission of active spiritual force	
	"Go forth and baptize all peoples, in the name of the Father, and of the Son and of the Holy Spirit"	
Heart	Transmission of spiritual union, the union of the heights and depths in the heart	
	"Behold a new Heaven and a new Earth"	
Solar plexus	Transmission of healing	
	"You shall cast out demons, speak in new tongues, and heal through the laying on of hands"	
Sacral	Transmission of peace	
	"Peace be with you"	
Root	Transmission of the Holy Spirit	
	"Receive the Holy Spirit"	

The Breath of the Risen Christ, who is Divine Peace, permeates the human being on seven levels as the seven sayings of the Risen One corresponding to the seven chakras. The seven sayings spoken by the Risen One are for the infusion of Divine Breath into the seven chakras on these seven different levels.

In the context of this eurythmy meditation the seven sayings of the Risen One are spoken in the order related to the planets during the course of the week, considering the chakras as the inner planets (the heart chakra being the inner Sun, the crown chakra the inner Saturn, etc.). For this reason the sayings of the Risen One—listed above—are indicated alongside the seven chakras in the sequence beginning with the larynx chakra (Mars) and ending with the root chakra (Moon), and this is the order of working with the sayings of the Risen One in the context of the third stage of the Core Practice.

One begins in "Right Standing" with the "inward" AU gesture (AU-heart), of one hand cupped over the other lightly clenched hand held to the region of the heart chakra, inwardly contemplating the words:

> AU: *I rest within the Godhead of the world*
>
> AU: *Putting on the Resurrection Body*
>
> AU: *The third stage: the Resurrection*

Concentrating upon the heart chakra, one contemplates the Peace emanating from the Risen One—who said "Peace be with you." The Peace of the Risen One expresses the attainment of union of the highest and the deepest—of pure spirit with the depths of matter—resulting in *atma*, the Resurrection body. The seed of *atma* is implanted in the heart of everyone. The Resurrection is the seed for a new creation, that of spirit-permeated matter—the new Earth.

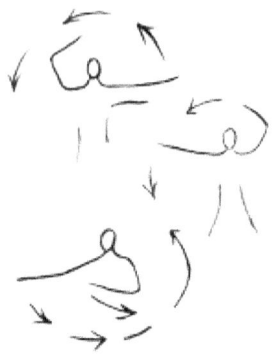

Continue by stepping to the left so that the left foot and the right foot are parted by about the same distance as the shoulders are apart. The outward-raying AU gesture starts with the arms extended out to the left, palms facing forward—an expression of the rising of the Sun at sunrise. Rotate arms clockwise, moving up on the left and down on the right, while maintaining the forward facing position of the palms of the hands (except for a brief moment when the arms are directed vertically downward and palms face toward the body). In this circular clockwise movement, following the cycle of the Sun (as seen in the Northern Hemisphere) during the course of the day, the solar forces stream from the heart and ray out through the extended arms and hands.

To maintain the outstreaming of life energy through the arms and hands, it is important with the AU gesture that the hands and fingers are extended in a straight line from the arms without bending the wrist, since any bending at the wrist can impede the smooth flow of energy streaming out through the arms and hands and fingers.

Following the movement of the AU around, one focuses upon the flow of radiant life force spiraling out through the chakras accompanied by the words of the Risen One in the following sequence:

Larynx	Go forth and make disciples of all peoples, baptizing them in the name of the Father and of the Son and of the Holy Spirit
Solar plexus	You shall cast out demons, speak in new tongues, and heal through the laying on of hands
Third eye	Lo, I am with you always, until the end of time
Sacral	Peace be with you
Crown	All power in Heaven and Earth is given unto me
Heart	Behold a new Heaven and a new Earth
Root	Receive the Holy Spirit

With the eighth AU one focuses upon Divine Life in all seven chakras, bringing the Life of the Risen Christ into all seven chakras simultaneously, as at the Resurrection. One endeavors to enter into the flow of movement of the AU gesture, at the same time sensing the spiral circulation of the radiance of the inner Sun expanding out from the heart chakra. The cultivation of an awareness of the flow of this spiral circulation on its course of expansion from the heart chakra through the other chakras to the root chakra and its further spiraling out is enhanced especially through accompanying this flow by movement of the arms and hands as in the eurythmy gesture for the sound AU. With this gesture the inner Sun radiance spiraling out through the chakras is stimulated and brought to consciousness, especially when peace of heart is allowed to stream from the heart through the arms and hands as a blessing toward all that lives.

In forming the AU gesture—done slowly and purposefully—one can begin to experience the spiral circulation through the chakras: the radiant, peace-filled flow of vital energy spiraling out from the heart chakra.

Still keeping the feet at shoulder width apart, one then reverses the direction of rotation of the arms, repeating seven AU's with extended arms, each time contemplating one of the seven gifts of the Risen One.

The rotating circular movement of the arms and the positioning of the palms of the hands are exactly the same as for the clockwise AU, except that the direction of rotation is counterclockwise, moving up the right and down the left. With this circular counterclockwise movement of the arms, in which the cycle of the Sun as seen in the Southern Hemisphere is followed during the course of the day, the hands, facing forward, are raying out the solar forces streaming from the heart through the extended arms and hands.[43]

Larynx	The power of the Word in me
Solar plexus	The gift of healing in me
Third eye	The divine I AM in me
Sacral	Eternal peace in me
Crown	Heavenly power and earthly power in me
Heart	The heavenly Jerusalem in me
Root	The Holy Spirit in me

When the arms are moving from the midnight (down) to midday (up) positions, one inclines gently to the right when the hands are moving around with the AU, and one inclines gently to the left when the hands are moving with the AU gesture from the midday (up) to the midnight (down) positions.

With the eighth AU one speaks (or contemplates) again the words "I rest within the Godhead of the world."

Throughout the entire third stage of the meditation, and also during the resting contemplation holding the AU-heart gesture after completing the exercise, one focuses one's inner gaze upon the scene of the Resurrection, inwardly invoking the Divine Breath transmitted by the Risen One.

The Resurrection *by Grünewald*

---

43   This movement describes the new direction of rotation of the chakras, as indicated by Rudolf Steiner, *An Esoteric Cosmology*, CW 94 (Great Barrington, MA: SteinerBooks, 2008), lecture of June 6, 1906 (translation amended by RP after comparison with the German original): "The lotus-flower with sixteen petals lies in the region of the larynx. [Previously] this lotus-flower turned counterclockwise.* Now this lotus-flower has ceased to turn....With the new conscious clairvoyance the lotus flowers rotate clockwise.* (*The clairvoyant sees his/her own aura reversed: thus the outer as the inner and the inner as the outer, because he/she sees from outside.)"

> *"I shall find myself within the Godhead of the world"*
>
> *The Ascension / The Appearance of the Cosmic Christ to John on Patmos*
>
> *The Seven* THOU ART *Sayings*
>
> *The Seven Seals (corresponding to the Seven Chakras)*
>
> "M"

At this fourth stage of the Core Practice it is a matter of entering into the cosmic circulation through the seven chakras with the eurythmy gesture for the sound M. The circulation of cosmic life through the chakras is an expression of the human being's relationship with the solar system, and since the Ascension it also has to do with the Divine Peace streaming from the Cosmic Christ.

After the building up of the Resurrection body that was attained at the Resurrection, Jesus Christ began his ascent to the realm of the Father at the Ascension, that began forty days after the Resurrection.

This transition to cosmic realms of existence signified a stepping into the cosmic circulation of spiritual energy flowing through the solar system, the cosmic circulation which is mirrored in every human being during the hours of sleep, when the human being (indwelling the astral body) is outside of the physical body. The cosmic circulation flows in the form of a lemniscate ("figure 8") with the heart—corresponding to the Sun at the center of the solar system—at the center.

Mirrored in the human being, the upper part of the lemniscate includes the head and the entire human being from the heart upward. Similarly, the lower part of the lemniscate embraces the lower human being from the heart downward.

The transition undergone by the Risen One in stepping into the cosmic circulation of the solar system is readily apparent if we contemplate the difference in appearance of the Risen One at his appearance to Mary Magdalene in the garden of the Holy Sepulcher on Easter Sunday morning, to that of the appearance of the Cosmic Christ some sixty years later to John on the island of Patmos.

Mary Magdalene thought at first that he was the gardener—he appeared more like a human being than a cosmic being. However, at the appearance of the Cosmic Christ to John on Patmos, his face shone like the Sun, his eyes were like flames of fire, in his right hand he held seven stars, and his whole appearance was unmistakably cosmic in nature. Jesus Christ had found himself within the Godhead of the world as a cosmic being.

In forming the M gesture the ideal is to infuse the chakras with the cosmic life streaming from the Cosmic Christ according to the words "I shall find myself within the Godhead of the world."

Chapter 2: The Core of the Practice: Putting on the Resurrection Body

---

Jesus Christ as the Cosmic Christ manifested himself to John on Patmos as a being of Divine Power, whereas at the Resurrection it was a matter of the transmission of Divine Breath, just as the Crucifixion has to do with the radiation of Divine Love, and the Transfiguration has to do with the out-pouring of Divine Light.

The heavenly energy of the cosmic circulation through the seven chakras is activated especially through contemplation of the Ascension and the Divine Power of Eternal Peace transmitted by the Cosmic Christ.

Just as the L gesture helps to bring the macrocosmic orbit to consciousness, and the eurythmy gesture for the sound R enables one to come to an experience of the circulating flow of energy in the microcosmic orbit, and just as the eurythmy gesture for the sound AU enhances the flow of the spiral circulation through the seven chakras—clockwise and counterclockwise—so the M gesture helps to activate the lemniscatory movement of cosmic circulation through the chakras.

The might of the whole universe comes to expression in the radiant appearance of the Cosmic Christ, who wields the Divine Power of Eternal Peace. The Ascension is the archetypal event signifying the re-integration of Heaven and Earth. The sound M—the final sound in the sacred word AUM—leads us into the future, toward the far-distant event of the re-integration of Heaven and Earth.

At the center of the lemniscate is the heart chakra, and the cosmic circulation streams around the figure 8 embracing all the chakras. First the upper chakras—the crown chakra (Saturn), the third eye chakra (Jupiter), and the larynx chakra (Mars)—are activated by the lemniscatory movement of the M on the downward path of the upper half of the lemniscate. Then the lower chakras—the root chakra (Moon), the sacral chakra (Venus), and the solar plexus chakra (Mercury)—are activated through the lemniscatory movement of the M on the upward path of the lower half of the lemniscate. The culmination of this lemniscatory movement is at the place of the heart chakra (Sun), and this is also the point of departure for the beginning of the next figure 8 of the M moving up the back of the head to the crown and then descending again at the front—by way of the three upper chakras—to return to the heart.

To form the M gesture following the stream of the figure 8, one steps forward with the right foot (right foot forward, left foot behind).

1. Begin with palms facing the heart.
2. Circle arms back and up over the head, tracing the lemniscatory path from the heart up the back to the crown, at the same time inclining back gently. Here it is important to place the tongue against the roof of the mouth in order to complete the circuit of the flow of energy up the back with the flow of energy down the front.
3. Continue circling down toward the heart, leaning gently forward.
4. Then back and down, inclining gently back as the arms and hands move back down to the region of the root chakra, feeling the continuation of this movement streaming down the back of the legs.
5. Complete the lemniscate by bringing palms up and in toward the heart. One feels a streaming up the front of the legs accompanying this movement.

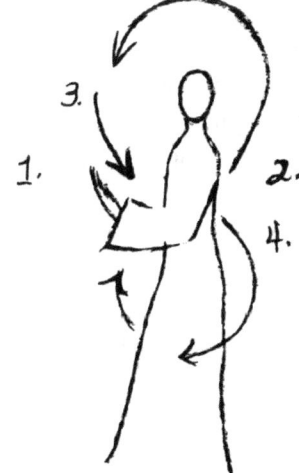

With the first three M's, in tracing out the lemniscate, one contemplates the words

> M—*I shall find myself within the Godhead of the world*
>
> M—*Putting on the Resurrection Body*
>
> M—*The fourth stage: the Ascension*

With the subsequent seven M's, in tracing out the lemniscate, one meditates upon the words

Crown	Ancient Saturn	THOU ART the Alpha and the Omega
Third eye	Ancient Sun	THOU ART the Lamb of God
Larynx	Ancient Moon	THOU ART the Word
Root [+ legs and feet]	Moon + Earth	THOU ART the Tree of Knowledge and the Tree of Life (where the right leg represents the Tree of Knowledge and the left leg the Tree of Life)
Sacral	Future Jupiter	Sophia is the Bride; THOU ART the Bridegroom
Solar plexus	Future Venus	Michael is the Guardian; THOU ART the Greater Guardian of the Threshold
Heart	Future Vulcan	THOU ART the Holy Grail

In forming an eighth M one focuses upon Divine Peace in all seven chakras, bringing the Peace of the Cosmic Christ into all seven chakras simultaneously, as at the appearance of the Cosmic Christ to John on Patmos.

The only one of the seven sayings listed above that was actually spoken by the Cosmic Christ is the first one—"I AM the Alpha and the Omega" (chapter 1 of Revelation)—in connection with the appearance of the Cosmic Christ to John on the island of Patmos.

The other six "sayings" of the Cosmic Christ were not actually spoken, yet they are implicit in the images of the seven seals, and are thus the unspoken words that characterize the essence of the various manifestations of Christ through the stages of cosmic evolution presented by the images of the seven seals. This sequence corresponds to the order of the planets connected with the stages of cosmic evolution, as described in chapter 5.

Ancient Saturn	took place within the heliocentric orbit of the planet Saturn
Ancient Sun	took place within the heliocentric orbit of the planet Jupiter
Ancient Moon	took place within the heliocentric orbit of the planet Mars
Moon + Earth	taking place now in the heliocentric orbit of the Earth together with the Moon
Future Jupiter	will take place within the heliocentric orbit of the planet Venus
Future Venus	will take place within the heliocentric orbit of the planet Mercury
Future Vulcan	will take place in the sphere of the Sun

Chapter 2: The Core of the Practice: Putting on the Resurrection Body

One endeavors to enter into the flow of movement of the M gesture, at the same time sensing the lemniscatory circulation of cosmic life streaming through the chakras, mirroring the course of cosmic evolution.

The sayings of the Cosmic Christ reflect the course of cosmic evolution through these seven stages, summarized pictorially by the seven seals, described in detail in chapter 5:

Ancient Saturn	Crown	1st Seal	*Christ as the Alpha and the Omega* (pages 60, 109)
Ancient Sun	Third eye	2nd Seal	*Christ as the Lamb of God* (page 110)
Ancient Moon	Larynx	3rd Seal	*Christ as the Word* (page 112)
Present Earth	Root	4th Seal	*Christ as the Tree of Knowledge and the Tree of Life* (page 129)
Future Jupiter	Sacral	5th Seal	*Sophia as the Bride* (implicitly Christ as the Bridegroom; page 112)
Future Venus	Solar plexus	6th Seal	*Michael as the Guardian of the Threshold* (implicitly Christ as the Greater Guardian of the Threshold; page 110)
Future Vulcan	Heart	7th Seal	*Christ as the Holy Grail* (page 153)

The italicized words relate to the images presented by the seven seals, some of the images—for example, the image of the second seal showing the Lamb of God surrounded by the four holy living creatures (Bull, Lion, Eagle, Angel or the holy living creature with a human face) described in chapter 4 of Revelation—being more readily identifiable than others—see page 110.

The cultivation of an awareness of the lemniscatory flow of cosmic life on its descent from the crown chakra through the upper chakras to the root chakra and then back up from the root chakra to the heart chakra is enhanced especially through accompanying this flow by movement of the arms and hands as in the eurythmy gesture for the sound M, in conjunction with the seven THOU ART sayings associated with the Cosmic Christ listed above, at the same time holding in consciousness the images of the seven seals corresponding to each chakra.

With the M gesture the streaming of cosmic life through the chakras is stimulated to flow in the lemniscatory form, especially when holding the images of the seven seals in consciousness, accompanied by the seven THOU ART sayings corresponding to the seven chakras.

In forming the M gesture—done slowly and purposefully—one can begin to experience the streaming of cosmic life through the chakras: the powerful flow of vital energy circulating from the crown to the feet in a "figure 8" centered in the heart. Just as the arms and hands are an extension of the heart chakra (its "wings," so to say), so the legs and feet are an extension of the root chakra and are included in the lemniscatory flow.

The historical archetype for this experience is to be found on the one hand by contemplating the Ascension in the life of Christ, who thereafter became the Cosmic Christ, transmitting the Divine Power of Eternal Peace through all seven chakras, and on the other hand by meditating upon the appearance of the Cosmic Christ to John on Patmos.

Continue the meditation by reversing the feet so that the left foot is forward and the right foot is behind and repeat seven M's in tracing out the lemniscate, each time contemplating one of the seven seals, starting with

Crown	Image from the 1st Seal	*The Cosmic Christ in me*
Third eye	Image from the 2nd Seal	*The Lamb of God in me*
Larynx	Image from the 3rd Seal	*The Divine Word in me*
Root	Image from the 4th Seal	*The Tree of Knowledge and the Tree of Life in me*
Sacral	Image from the 5th Seal	*Divine Sophia in me*
Solar plexus	Image from the 6th Seal	*The Archangel Michael in me*
Heart	Image from the 7th Seal	*The Holy Grail in me*

With the eighth M one speaks (or contemplates) again the words "I shall find myself within the Godhead of the world."

Throughout the entire fourth stage of the morning exercise, and also during the resting contemplation holding the AU-heart gesture after completing the exercise, one focuses one's inner gaze upon the Ascension and upon the scene of the appearance of the Cosmic Christ to John on Patmos, inwardly invoking the Divine Peace transmitted by the Cosmic Christ while contemplating the seven sayings in connection with the eurythmy gesture for the sound M.

Close the meditation—at the end of these four stages—by folding the arms across the breast in the gesture of reverence and contemplate the words

"Not I, but Christ in me" (or simply, "Christ in me")

inwardly recalling the four stages in connection with the Transfiguration, Crucifixion, Resurrection, and Ascension (including the appearance of the Cosmic Christ to John on Patmos).

Above we see the first of the seven seals designed by Rudolf Steiner and painted by Clara Rettich. This first seal depicts the Cosmic Christ in the form of a pentagram. His gesture is IAO—
- I (ee): the head and the upright posture extending upward
- A (ah): the arms extended downward, palms facing down
- O (oh): the legs form part of an O that continues down into the Earth below

The Cosmic Christ speaks "I AM the Alpha and the Omega"—this is IAO—
I—I AM / A—the Alpha / O—and the Omega
His right hand holds the seven stars: Saturn—Sun—Moon—Mars—Mercury—Jupiter—Venus representing the stages of cosmic evolution as described in chapter 5.

Chapter 2: The Core of the Practice: Putting on the Resurrection Body

Conclusion

The four stages of this Core Practice through the eurythmy gestures for the sounds L, R, AU, M is an elaboration of the *Morning Meditation* given by Rudolf Steiner and activates four different currents or streaming of life forces within the human being.

The macrocosmic current activated by the L gesture

Streaming of Divine Light from above, from the Father, and streaming of Divine Warmth from below, from the Mother, together creating a fountain ascending through the chakras.
Archetype: the Transfiguration
    The seven I AM sayings (ascending)
    The seven healing miracles (ascending)

The microcosmic current activated by the R gesture

Inner circulation (microcosmic orbit) of the flow of life initiated during the embryonic phase, permeated with one's heart forces so that this becomes an inner circulation of Love ascending the spinal column and descending through the chakras.
Archetype: the Crucifixion
    The seven words from the Cross (descending)
    The seven stages of the Passion (descending)

The spiral current activated by the AU gesture

Spiraling out from the heart chakra, circulating through all the chakras in the order corresponding to the days of the week: the spiral circulation of Divine Life.
Archetype: the Resurrection
    The seven sayings of the Risen One (clockwise)
    The seven gifts of the Risen One (counterclockwise)

The lemniscatory current activated by the M gesture

Circulation of Divine Peace in a figure 8, the upper circle of the flow of Divine Peace circulating up the back from the heart and down through the three upper chakras, and the lower circle of the flow of Divine Peace circulating down the back from the heart and back up again (including the flow down the legs to the feet and then up the legs) through the three lower chakras, returning to the heart chakra.
Archetype: the Ascension and the Appearance of the Cosmic Christ to John on Patmos
    The seven THOU ART sayings associated with the Cosmic Christ
    The seven sayings relating to the seven seals of Revelation

With regard to each of the four stages discussed above it may be that for any given saying one might wish to do the corresponding gesture twice or more. One may wish to slow down the external movement so much that to an observer it would appear as if one is standing motionless in a posture. In fact, it is possible to do the entire exercise meditatively without any outward movement at all, following the gestures purely inwardly, or meditating upon the words, deeds, gifts, and powers of Christ without any accompanying gestures at all.

CHAPTER 3

INNER RADIANCE

INTRODUCTORY PRAYERS AND CONCLUDING PRAYERS

A Star is above my Head

A star is above my head—	Starting gesture AU-heart
Christ speaks from the star:	"Sixth" followed by "octave"*
"Let your soul be borne	I: left
through my strong force—	A: downward (palms facing down)

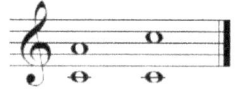

I am with you;
I am in you;
I am for you;

Universal love gesture
Reverence gesture
standing in the form of pentagram–IAO
- body upright (upright body represents I)
- Arms and hands downward (A), palms facing down
- Feet apart and knees pressed outward, weight on outer soles of feet (O)

I am your I."

The arms and hands are raised slightly, at the same time bringing the feet back together, coming into the gesture of Universal Love and then closing with the horizontal AUM as at the close of the AMEN/AUMEYN meditation (see page 79; also foot of page 63).

Return to starting gesture AU-heart

---

*For those who know the eurythmy for the "Our Mother" prayer, the "sixth" followed by the "octave" are the two gestures made at the end of the "Our Mother" prayer in connection with the words "boundless wisdom" (Sixth) and "all-merciful grace" (Octave).

Sixth gesture (musical interval #6): Starting with the "AU-heart" gesture, the arms open outward and upward, radiating in a streaming gesture from the heart up toward heaven, streaming though the arms, hands, fingertips toward the infinite, reaching out from the soul/heart level toward the universal wisdom.

Octave gesture (musical interval #8): From the finishing point of the "sixth" gesture, bring the raised hands up further toward one another so that the hands are back to back to one another, then continue the movement further so that the hands trace a movement from the front to the back of the head—during this movement the backs of the hands can lightly touch one another—then lead the hands from the back of the head, opening out, around in a circular movement above and to the sides of the head, so that the palms of the hands sculpt the sphere of the higher self above the head, however without completing the sphere (it is about ⅔ completed and about ⅓ left open at the front).

Chapter 3: Inner Radiance: Introductory Prayers and Concluding Prayers

Christ In Me ["Not I, but Christ in me"]

Starting gesture AU-heart

Christ in me:	I:	left
His radiant, light-filled Spirit in my spirit.	I:	right
His pure, loving Thoughts in my soul.	A:	downward (palms facing down)
His grace-filled Sacred Heart in my heart.	O:	horizontal
Christ, I receive Thee:	I:	left
For the healing of my body.		Standing in the form of the Pentagram-IAO
For the healing of my soul.	O:	horizontal
For the healing of my spirit.	I:	right
		Return to starting gesture AU-heart

Sophia In Me ["Not I, but Sophia in me"]

Sophia in me:	O:	opens to A– above head
Her radiant, light-filled Spirit in my spirit.	I:	right
Her pure, loving Thoughts in my soul.	A:	downward (palms facing down)
Her grace-filled Immaculate Heart in my heart.	O:	horizontal
Sophia, I receive Thee:	O:	opens to A—above head
For the healing of my body.		Standing in the form of the pentagram-IAO
For the healing of my soul.	O:	horizontal
For the healing of my spirit.	I:	right
		Return to starting gesture AU-heart

Michael–Sophia in Nomine Christi ["Michael and Sophia in the name of Christ"]

—the gestures form a pentagram (five-pointed star)

Michael	[right upper point]	I:	right
Sophia	[two lower points]	A:	downward, palms facing forward
			and the feet apart to form a pentagram
			[then drawing the feet together again
			for the following gestures]
in Nomine	[top point]	E:	gesture above head
Christi	[left upper point]	I:	left

AMEN/AUMEYN   [form the Universal Love gesture]
  A: arms form a horizontal V-shaped A
  U: arms parallel and extended forward horizontally in the U gesture
  M: hands return in the M gesture toward heart, palms facing heart
  AU: heart gesture (hands cupped over heart chakra).

Prayer for the Protection of Mother Earth and Her Creatures

	Starting gesture AU-heart
Heavenly Father	A: above head
Hear our prayer	Prayer gesture—Bring palms together at heart level; keeping palms together, slowly raise palms above head
May destructive modern technology be stopped	U: downward
May the assault on Mother Earth and her creatures be halted	M: horizontal: palms vertical, hands flow forward and back

In the name of Jesus Christ   I: left

For the sake of his sorrowful Passion
In atonement for our transgressions   Universal Love gesture: Open arms out to the side horizontally, palms open, facing forward

Have mercy on us   Universal Love gesture—alternatively, Warmth of Heart gesture: Standing on the ball of the foot, with the heel slightly (only very slightly) raised from the ground, both arms extended forward, curving up, with palms facing up and tips of thumbs touching the tips of the forefingers

And on the whole world   Veneration gesture toward the Earth: Raise arms and bow forward, slowly sweeping arms down toward the Earth, palms down (*as though gently touching into the Earth's aura*)

Now   Quickly return upright with the N gesture: hands withdraw upward, returning to head and heart

And forever   Fulfillment gesture: arms open and rounded above head; palms facing each other, forming a chalice

AMEN/AUMEYN   Return to Universal Love gesture: followed by the AUM gestures, and the closing AU-gesture with hands cupped over heart chakra (as described at the foot of the previous page).

Chapter 3: Inner Radiance: Introductory Prayers and Concluding Prayers

These words bear a strength intended to align our thoughts with the "Deliver us from evil" petition in the Lord's Prayer, and may seem harsh upon hearing them for the first time. However, just as one becomes accustomed in the course of time to speaking the words "Deliver us from evil," so also one can become used to praying, "May destructive modern technology be stopped." These words—and also the words of the next line "May the assault on Mother Earth and her creatures be halted"—are prayed out of love and care for the Earth and for all living beings, including human beings, whose lives are bound up with Mother Earth. The fact is that there are aspects of modern technology, which are harmful to the Earth. It is these destructive aspects, which are addressed in this prayer—not modern technology as such—rather that which is used (or intended to be used) in a harmful way, without consideration for the welfare of the planet or the beings (creatures) whose lives are dependent upon the wellbeing of Mother Earth.

The spiritual world hears our prayers, particularly those prayed in the name of Jesus Christ. When a prayer such as that for the "Protection of Mother Earth and her Creatures" is prayed, it gives the angels and higher beings who are in service of the Heavenly Father permission to intervene on behalf of humanity in relation to that which may be threatening to the very life of Mother Earth. Without our prayers, the various ranks of angelic beings are not allowed to intervene. It is heavenly law that human beings are left free, and, generally speaking, this law is adhered to, except by demonic beings, who do not respect human freedom. Hence the need in relation to certain destructive forms of modern technology in our time—such as nuclear weapons, for example—of praying this kind of prayer, which calls upon the help of the Divine for problems that go beyond the capacity of most individuals to heal and/or transform them.

The second half of the "Prayer for the Protection of Mother Earth and her Creatures" is the Mercy Prayer of Sister Faustina, slightly adapted. Sister Faustina (1905–1938) was a Polish nun who, from 1931 until the end of her life, experienced numerous visions and prayers relating to Christ. In the year 2000 she was declared a saint and is now known as St. Faustina. In 1933, God gave Sister Faustina a striking vision of his Mercy:

> I saw a great light, with the heavenly Father in the midst of it. Between this light and the Earth I saw Jesus nailed to the cross in such a way that God, wanting to look upon the Earth, looked through Our Lord's wounds. I understood that in this way the heavenly Father blessed the Earth for the sake of Jesus.

On September 14, 1935, her inner voice taught her to say this prayer, known as the Mercy Prayer:

> For the sake of his sorrowful Passion,
>
> In atonement for our transgressions,
>
> Have mercy on us and on the whole world.

The words of the Mercy Prayer, spoken in the name of Jesus Christ and in contemplation of the Crucifixion as a portal to the heart of the Heavenly Father, are a potent means of offering up this "Prayer for the Protection of Mother Earth and her Creatures." The same formulation is found in the "Prayer for Putting on the Resurrection Body" (see page 67).

Salutation to the Sun

The Sun Spirit is the Risen One, whose face "shines like the Sun" (Revelation 1:16).
In this meditation the Sun is an image for the Christ–Sun ("O Sun of Christ," addressing the Etheric Christ; see pages 18, 24, 27–29, 215). Each time in speaking the word "Sun" one can either think "Christ–Sun" or one could explicitly say "Christ–Sun" if, in the context of the words of the *Salutation to the Sun,* one is able to sense Christ in the etheric realm as the Christ–Sun.

	Starting gesture AU-heart
I *see the* (Christ) *Sun,*	I: right
The (Christ) *Sun beholds me.*	Sun gesture
	Extend right arm up (diagonally forward) and left arm down (diagonally back); simultaneously rotate arms, clockwise right side, counterclockwise left side (*radiating love from the heart, and connecting Heaven and Earth*)
I *revere the* (Christ) *Sun,*	Reverence gesture
The (Christ) *Sun greets me.*	Sun gesture
I *unite myself with the* (Christ) *Sun,*	U: upward
The (Christ) *Sun blesses me with Light, Love and Life.*	Sun gesture L, L, L
The power of the (Christ) *Sun is immeasurably strengthening.*	AU: clockwise
Through the (Christ) *Sun's power, one can pass through all trials and remain peaceful.*	AU: clockwise
Through the power of the (Christ) *Sun, one can endure to an extraordinary degree.*	AU: clockwise
The (Christ) *Sun bestows great power.*	AU: clockwise
	Repeat this section with the four AU's in a counterclockwise direction

AUM

[form the Universal Love gesture]
A: arms form a horizontal V-shaped A
U: arms parallel and extended forward horizontally in the U gesture
M: hands return in the M gesture toward heart, palms facing heart
AU: heart gesture (hands cupped over heart chakra).

Chapter 3: Inner Radiance: Introductory Prayers and Concluding Prayers

Prayer for Putting on the Resurrection Body

The Gestures are the same as for the "Prayer for the Protection of Mother Earth and her Creatures" (page 64) and for the AUM meditation (page 78).

	Starting gesture AU-heart
Heavenly Father	A: above
Hear our prayer	Prayer gesture Bring palms together at heart level; keeping palms together, slowly raise palms above head
May we be clothed in the power of the Sun[44] *With the Resurrection body*	U: downward
May we receive the breath of eternal life	M: horizontal: palms vertical, hands flow forward and back
In the name of Jesus Christ	I: left
For the sake of his sorrowful Passion *In atonement for our transgressions*	Universal Love gesture: Open arms out to the side horizontally, palms open, facing forward
Have mercy on us	Universal Love gesture—alternatively, Warmth of Heart gesture: Standing on the ball of the foot, with the heel slightly (only very slightly) raised from the ground, both arms extended forward, curving up, with palms facing up and tips of thumbs touching the tips of the forefingers
And on the whole world	Veneration gesture toward the Earth: Raise arms and bow forward, slowly sweeping arms down toward the Earth, palms down (*as though gently touching into the Earth's aura*)
Now	Quickly return upright with the N gesture: hands withdraw upward, returning to head and heart
and forever	Fulfillment gesture: arms open and rounded above head; palms facing each other, forming a chalice
AMEN/AUMEYN	Return to Universal Love gesture, followed by the AUM gestures, and the closing AU-gesture with hands cupped over heart chakra.

---

44 In this meditation the Sun is an image for the Christ-Sun ("O Sun of Christ," addressing the Etheric Christ; see pages 18, 24, 27–29, 215). Thus, one could pray, "May we be clothed in the power of the Christ-Sun."

INNER RADIANCE: CONCLUDING PRAYERS

Christ In Me   ["Not I, but Christ in me"]   Starting gesture AU-heart

Christ in me:	I: left
His radiant, light-filled Spirit in my spirit.	I: right
His pure, loving Thoughts in my soul.	A: downward (palms facing down)
His grace-filled Sacred Heart in my heart.	O: horizontal
Christ, I receive Thee:	I: left
For the healing of my body.	Standing in the form of the Pentagram-IAO
For the healing of my soul.	O: horizontal
For the healing of my spirit.	I: right
	Return to starting gesture AU-heart

Sophia In Me   ["Not I, but Sophia in me"]

Sophia in me:	O opens to A, above head
Her radiant, light-filled Spirit in my spirit.	I: right
Her pure, loving Thoughts in my soul.	A: downward (palms facing down)
Her grace-filled Immaculate Heart in my heart.	O: horizontal
Sophia, I receive Thee:	O opens to A, above head
For the healing of my body.	Standing in the form of the Pentagram-IAO
For the healing of my soul.	O: horizontal
For the healing of my spirit.	I: right
	Return to starting gesture AU-heart

Michael–Sophia in Nomine Christi ["Michael and Sophia in the name of Christ"]

—the gestures form a pentagram (five-pointed star)

Michael	[right upper point]	I: right
Sophia	[two lower points]	A: downward, palms facing forward
		and the feet apart to form a pentagram
		[then drawing the feet together
		again for the following gestures]
in Nomine	[top point]	E gesture above head
Christi	[left upper point]	I: left
		[Form Universal Love gesture]
AMEN/AUMEYN		A: arms form a horizontal V-shaped A
		U: arms parallel and extended forward horizontally in the U gesture
		M: hands return in the M gesture toward heart, palms facing heart
		AU: heart gesture (hands cupped over heart chakra).

Chapter 4

DEEPENING THE CONNECTION WITH THE ETHERIC CHRIST

The Star of the Lamb

Rudolf Steiner spoke about the Star of the Lamb in his lecture held in Munich on April 22, 1907,[45] and drew a figure, commenting on the words, "I saw a Lamb standing, as though it had been slain, with seven horns and with seven eyes" (Revelation 5:6).

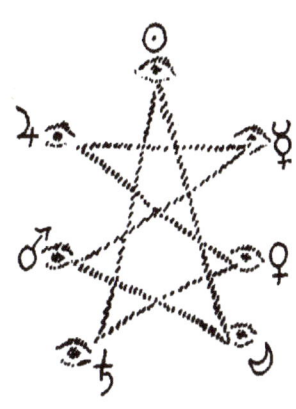

> The seven corners of the sign [of the Star of the Lamb] are called horns. However, what do the [seven] eyes signify? In esoteric schools the symbols for the seven planets are written here [at the seven corners] as the seven eyes. The seven eyes [of the Lamb] are nothing other than the seven planets, and the names of the planets designate the Spirits who are incarnated in them as Intelligences. Saturn is the name of the Saturn Soul. The names of the planets are the seven planetary Spirits who surround the Earth and influence human life. The Lamb, Christ, contains all seven. Christ is the Alpha and the Omega, and the seven planets relate to him as limbs belonging to the entire body. The interweaving of the lines of the sign [of the Star of the Lamb] represents in a wonderful way the working together of the seven planets. From Saturn one rises up to the Sun; from there back down to the Moon, then to Mars, to Mercury, and so on. The same is expressed by the names of the days of the week—Saturn, Saturday; Sun, Sunday; Moon, Monday; Mars, Mardi, Tuesday; Mercury, Mercredi, Wednesday; Jupiter, Jeudi, Thursday; Venus, Vendredi, Friday. Christ is the regent of all these heavenly spheres; they are only parts of him; he connects them all. (ibid., p. 121, German edition).

As stated in the first chapter of Revelation, Christ is the "Alpha and Omega"; he comprises all stages (globes) of world evolution from Saturn (Alpha) to Vulcan (Omega). Rudolf Steiner says, "One must conceive of the planets more as principles, which are really always active in all the globes, but in a special way in certain ones" (CW 264, p 181, English edition).

At the seven corner points he wrote the names of the seven planets in the sequence of the days of the week. For the eurythmy exercise of the Star of the Lamb, the sequence is: Saturn, Saturday (left foot); Sun, Sunday (head); Moon, Monday (right foot); Mars, Tuesday, Mardi (left hip); Mercury, Wednesday, Mercredi (right shoulder); Jupiter, Thursday, Jeudi (left shoulder); Venus, Friday, Vendredi (right hip). In this sense, when moving along the seven "ways" of the Star of the Lamb in the eurythmy meditation on the Etheric Christ, the first "way" is from Saturn to Sun; the second "way" is from Sun to Moon; the third "way" is from Moon to Mars, the fourth "way" is from Mars to Mercury; the fifth "way" is from Mercury to Jupiter; the sixth "way" is from Jupiter to Venus; and the seventh "way" is from Venus back to the starting point, Saturn (Vulcan). Note that here, at the conclusion, instead of "Saturn," one could say "Vulcan," since Vulcan is the octave of the Saturn stage of world evolution.

---

45 *Aus der Bilderschrift der Apokalypse des Johannes*, cw 104a ("From the Picture-script of John's Apocalypse").

	FIVE-POINTED STAR PENTAGRAM	SIX-POINTED STAR HEXAGRAM	SEVEN-POINTED STAR HEPTAGRAM
Saturn	Sense-creating (lower "I")	Sense-creating	Physical foundation
Sun		Eternally flowing and evolving life	Eternal progress: *Eternally growing, eternally flowing*
Moon	Form-creating (rigidifying)	Form-creating (rigidifying)	Holding fast: *Creating form*
Mars		Fiery, courageous (infusing with fire)	Leading into sensory existence
Mercury	Soul-freeing, dissolving	Soul-freeing	Leading out of sensory existence
Jupiter	"I"-liberating (higher "I")	"I"-liberating	Liberation of the "I" (freeing of the "I")
Venus	Love of deeds		Ascending in love (consummation of love/in pure love)
Vulcan			Fulfillment

The expressions listed in the above table are from Rudolf Steiner's complete works.[46] In the heptagram column the expression "eternal progress" for the Sun is the one used by Rudolf Steiner, but the expression "eternally flowing"—carried over from the hexagram column—is preferable for the eurythmy exercise of the seven-pointed star. Similarly, for the eurythmy the term "creating form" for the Moon, carried over from the hexagram column, is preferable to the expression "holding fast" used by Rudolf Steiner (he gives for the Moon "holding fast/retarding/rigidifying").

The expressions in the pentagram column were given by Rudolf Steiner in relation to the pentagram exercise for the etheric body, and the expressions in the hexagram column were given by him in relation to the hexagram exercise for the astral body.[47] If one deepens into these two exercises in relation to the expressions listed in the above table,

one can experience their inner connection with the expressions listed in the heptagram column, which relate to the stages of world evolution, whereby Vulcan is the octave of the Saturn stage.[48] The seven-pointed star relates, in turn, to the level of the I. There is clearly a continuity between the different levels of the heptagram for the I, the hexagram for the astral body, and the pentagram for the etheric body. This is evident from the expressions listed in the above table—especially in the Jupiter row. Even though Rudolf Steiner did not give a seven-pointed star meditation for the level of the I, on account of the inner continuity between the three levels indicated in the columns of the above table, the correspondence of the heptagram expressions to the seven points on the Star of the Lamb, in turn related to the seven stages of world evolution, emerges clearly from the tabulation above.

---

46 Vol. 264, pp. 188–193 (trans. RP). In the English edition of vol. 264, *From the History & Contents of the First Section of the Esoteric School 1904–1914*, the expressions (or similar ones) in the pentagram column are on page 182, those in the hexagram column are on page 183, and those in the heptagram column are on page 184 (and in a slightly different form on page 185).
47   Cw 264 (English ed.), pp. 181–189.

48 *Vulcan*, "fulfillment," is not an expression used by Rudolf Steiner. He does not mention Vulcan at all in relation to the pentagram and hexagram exercises. However, the expression "fulfillment" for Vulcan is obvious. The Vulcan stage is the octave of the Saturn stage and is the last and highest level of world evolution, thus the Vulcan globe is the fulfillment of the stages of world evolution.

Chapter 4: Deepening the Connection with the Etheric Christ

Meditation on the Etheric Christ

How is it possible to come to an experience of Christ's Second Coming? This is an event that is impacting the whole Earth. In order to find a connection to the *parousia*—the Greek word used to describe Christ's Second Coming—the Presence of Christ—one way is to come to a true Imagination of the Earth and of Christ's relationship to the Earth at the present time.

A true image of the Earth is that of a tetrahedron with its apex at the South Pole and its other three points located in Japan, Caucasus, and Mexico.[49] The interesting thing about this is that it is the reverse of how we normally think of the Earth—being "upright" with the apex at the North Pole. Thus, there is a reversal from the physical to the etheric level, since on the etheric level the apex is at the South Pole.

With Christ's coming in the etheric realm it is, in the first place, the South Pole which is the place where his initial activity is focused. As a help to enter into an experience of Christ's activity at this time of his Second Coming,

we can hold in consciousness his magnificent and radiant being streaming in now in the region of the South Pole, and also the waves that are proceeding from here—the Earth's etheric apex—around the world as an enlivening strength for the whole Earth and all the kingdoms of nature.

One can intensify this Imagination of Christ's Second Coming by simultaneously focusing inwardly on Raphael's great (and last) painting, that of the Transfiguration on Mt. Tabor—with the Earth's etheric apex (South Pole) in place of Mt. Tabor—in the sense that Raphael's painting of the Transfiguration was, while depicting a historical event, at the same time in some way a prophetic vision of Christ's Second Coming.

Then one can further intensify the whole experience with the help of the "Meditation on the Etheric Christ" by Valentin Tomberg, while moving to the figure below. The figure describes working with a seven-pointed star in the Meditation on the Etheric Christ. This seven-pointed star fits very well with this meditation, as Rudolf Steiner spoke of it as the Star of the Lamb—and so it has a direct relationship with Christ. (It should be noted that this seven-pointed Star of the Lamb is different from the usual eurythmic seven-pointed star).

From the starting-point at the "left foot" of the star, move on straight lines for seven "star ways" (it is helpful to picture the seven-pointed star horizontally on the ground):

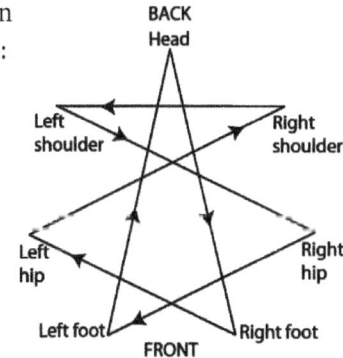

1. Left foot back to head
2. Head forward to right foot
3. Right foot back to left hip
4. Left hip back to right shoulder
5. Right across to left shoulder
6. Left shoulder forward to right hip
7. Right hip forward to left foot

---

49 Rudolf Steiner, *The Evolution of the Earth and Man and The Influence of the Stars,* lecture of September 18, 1924, CW 354 (Hudson, NY: Anthroposophic Press, 1987), p. 194. Steiner drew a map showing a tetrahedron with one vertex at the South Pole, another vertex in Japan, a third vertex in the Caucasus, near Mt. Ararat, and the fourth at the Colima Volcano in west Mexico.

Introduction to the Meditation

The following description assumes that one is facing south. In this imagination, one is facing toward Christ, who is streaming radiant blue etheric light toward one from the south. It is also possible to face north, having one's back to the south, and to imagine that Christ is behind one streaming radiant blue etheric light through one from behind. (It is possible to imagine this even if one is not physically facing north.)

Start the meditation facing the south. Whether one is moving around the circle surrounding the seven points of the star, or whether one is moving on a straight line (as indicated in the diagram of the seven-pointed star), one is always facing toward the south.

One walks the Star of the Lamb while forming the corresponding planetary gestures silently, or one can accompany the planetary gestures in connection with the following words for the planets related to the indications given by Rudolf Steiner, where the "ways" of the seven-pointed star are indicated in the figure on page 71.[50]

Saturn	*Physical foundation*	Saturn gesture (standing)
Sun	*Eternally growing, eternally flowing*	Sun gesture (1st way)
Moon	*Creating form*	Moon gesture (2nd way)
Mars	*Leading into sensory existence*	Mars gesture (3rd way)
Mercury	*Leading out of sensory existence*	Mercury gesture (4th way)
Jupiter	*Liberation of the "I"*	Jupiter gesture (5th way)
Venus	*Ascending in love*	Venus gesture (6th way)
Vulcan	*Fulfillment*	Vulcan gesture (7th way)

In terms of moving the "ways" of the Star of the Lamb as described above, Saturn coincides with the left foot; the Sun with the head; the Moon with the right foot; Mars with the left hip; Mercury with the right shoulder; Jupiter with the left shoulder; Venus with the right hip; and Vulcan with the left foot (at the same place as Saturn, but as the octave of Saturn).[51]

The following three-part meditation is given in three versions.

1. A simplified version which does not include all the gestures, and does not include movement on the seven-pointed star.
2. Straight-line movement on the seven-pointed star is added to the middle section, and additional gestures to the last section.
3. Circular movements around the star are added in the first and last sections.

---

50 CW 264, pp. 183–185 (trans. RP). English edition pp.184–185.

51 Added by RP: "Fulfillment" also as part of the eurythmy gesture for Vulcan. The Vulcan gesture begins as the Octave gesture, which then concludes with the Fulfillment gesture.

Meditation on the Etheric Christ

Version One

Christ is already here.	I: Left
From the south of the Earth	Standing in the form of the Pentagram-IAO
Waves are proceeding from him across the world.	V sound, moving forward
Every human being is now able to create a connection with him.	Universal Love gesture, stepping back to starting point
The human being has to do this out of free will.	L gesture, circling back in a clockwise direction, completing the circle with the I gesture, right arm raised
Christ is opening	I gesture, left arm raised, finishing with O above head (while stepping back with the right foot)
the path	A gesture above head, bringing feet together
to Shambhala,	A gesture slowly lower arms to the horizontal, palms facing down blessing the Earth

And human beings are able to approach him,	Step forward with Artemis gesture: small U, lower arms forward horizontally, upper arms remain close to body, bring feet together
to create a connection with him.	Universal Love gesture
For this, two things are necessary:	E gesture

Knowledge of Christ	I - left
and Antichrist	Gesture of Holding Fast, formed with hands lightly clenched and held down, while stepping back with right foot, and looking straight ahead

And aligning oneself with Christ.	A gesture, from below to above I: left
If one chooses one of the two streams now streaming through the world:	U gesture, from below to above
Christ	I: left
or Antichrist	Gesture of Holding Fast
a radiant blue stream,	U gesture, from below to above
and an ahrimanic stream –	Gesture of Holding Fast
when one chooses, one is already taken into one of the two streams.	U gesture upward, leading to I: left

The Power of Christ 　*is immeasurably strengthening.*	AU gesture, starting with the arms raised and circling clockwise down on the right and then up on the left, while moving back to the right and then forward to the left around a small circle clockwise
With him one can pass through all trials 　*and remain peaceful.*	[same again]
Through his Power one can endure to an *extraordinary degree.*	[same again]
He bestows great Power.	[same again]
AUM	A　arms form a horizontal V-shaped A U　arms parallel and extended forward horizontally 　　in the U gesture M　hands return in the M gesture toward heart, 　　palms facing heart AU　heart gesture (hands cupped over heart chakra).

Meditation on the Etheric Christ: Version Two

Version two includes version one through to the words "to create a connection with him," accompanied with the gesture for Universal Love. Then with the same gestures as described above, one follows the seven "star ways" added as a middle section; and ending with a final section accompanied with further petitions and gestures (indicated on the next page). For an overview of the planetary symbols, see page 44.

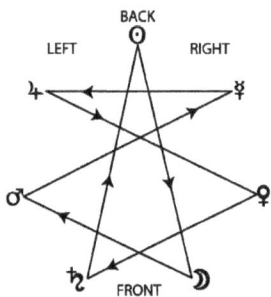

For this, two things are necessary:	1st way: back to right, from Saturn to Sun
Knowledge of Christ and Antichrist	2nd way: forward to right, from Sun to Moon
And aligning oneself with Christ.	3rd way: back to left, from Moon to Mars
If one chooses one of the two streams *now streaming through the world:*	4th way: back to right, from Mars to Mercury
Christ or Antichrist –	5th way: straight left, from Mercury to Jupiter
a radiant blue stream, and an ahrimanic stream –	6th way: forward to right, from Jupiter to Venus
when one chooses, one is already taken *into one of the two streams.*	7th way: forward to left, from Venus to Vulcan 　　　("octave" of Saturn)

Chapter 4: Deepening the Connection with the Etheric Christ

Meditation on the Etheric Christ: Version Two (last section)

The Power of Christ	AU gesture, with the arms circling clockwise up on the left and down on the right, initially moving forward to the left, then continuing back all the way around a small circle clockwise to return to the starting point
is immeasurably strengthening.	E gesture
With him one can pass through all trials	AU gesture, as described above, while initially moving forward to the left, then continuing back clockwise in a small circle, to return to the starting point
and remain peaceful.	Universal Love gesture
Through his Power one can	AU gesture, starting with the arms raised and circling clockwise down on the right and then up on the left, while moving back to the right and then forward to the left around a small circle clockwise
endure to an extraordinary degree.	D gesture with hands extended up as in the A gesture, with forefinger and middle finger (together) pointing heavenward or with the thumb and all the fingers together (flattened hand)
He bestows great Power.	AU gesture, as described above, starting with the arms raised and circling clockwise down on the right and then up on the left, while moving back to the right and then forward to the left around a small circle clockwise

AUM
[Form Universal Love gesture]
A: arms form a horizontal V-shaped A
U: arms parallel and extended forward horizontally in the U gesture
M: hands return in the M gesture toward heart, palms facing heart
AU: heart gesture (hands cupped over heart chakra).

Meditation on the Etheric Christ: Version Three

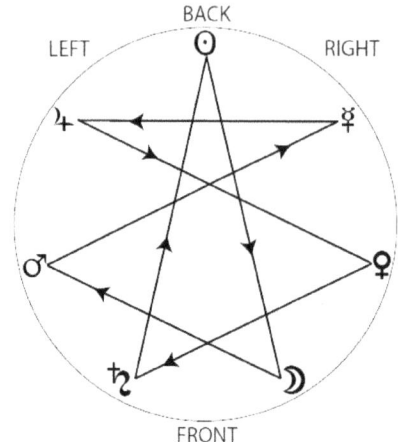

Facing south, and starting at the "left foot" (Saturn) of the Star of the Lamb. Keep facing south in the movements around the circle

Christ is already here.	I: left
From the south of the Earth	Standing in the form of the Pentagram-IAO
Waves are proceeding from him across the world.	V gesture, moving around the circle clockwise from Saturn to the Sun (V is the sound corresponding to the zodiacal sign of Aries)
Every human being is now able to create a connection with him	Universal Love gesture, moving around the circle clockwise from the Sun back to Saturn
The human being has to do this out of free will.	L gesture, moving around the circle clockwise from Saturn to the Sun, and finishing with the I gesture, right arm raised, from the Sun back to Saturn
Christ	I gesture, left arm raised, as in the Christ statue (see page 2)
is opening	O gesture above head, moving around the circle clockwise from Saturn to the Sun
the path	A gesture above head, continuing the clockwise movement toward the place of the Sun
to Shambhala,	At the place of the Sun: bring A gesture down slowly to horizontal, palms facing down blessing the Earth
And human beings are able	Continue clockwise from the Sun to Mars with Artemis gesture: small U, lower arms forward horizontally
to approach him,	Complete the Artemis gesture, close feet together
to create a connection with him.	Universal Love gesture, moving forward around the circle clockwise from Mars to Saturn
For this, two things are necessary:	E gesture (see Mars—E, page 32), formed while moving diagonally back on a straight line from Saturn to the Sun
Knowledge of Christ	I: left, moving diagonally forward on a straight line from the Sun to the Moon
and Antichrist	At the place of the Moon: Gesture of Holding Fast
And aligning oneself	A gesture from below to above, while moving on a straight line from the Moon to Mars
with Christ.	At the place of Mars: I—left gesture

Chapter 4: Deepening the Connection with the Etheric Christ

If one chooses one of the two streams now streaming through the world—	U gesture from below to above, while moving diagonally back to the right on a straight line from Mars to Mercury
Christ	I: left, while moving on a straight line from Mercury to Jupiter
or Antichrist;	At the place of Jupiter: gesture of Holding Fast
A radiant blue stream,	U gesture from below to above, while moving diagonally forward to the right on a straight line from Jupiter to Venus
and an ahrimanic stream—	At the place of Venus: gesture of Holding Fast
when one chooses one is already taken into one of the two streams.	U gesture upward, leading to I left, while moving on a straight line diagonally forward from Venus to Saturn–Vulcan
The Power of Christ	AU gesture, with the arms circling clockwise up on the left and down on the right, while moving around the circle clockwise from Saturn to the Sun
is immeasurably strengthening.	E gesture, finishing at the place of the Sun
With him one can pass through all trials	AU gesture, with the arms circling clockwise up on the left and down on the right, while moving all the way around the circle clockwise from the Sun back to the Sun
and remain peaceful.	Universal Love gesture at the place of the Sun
Through his Power one can endure	AU gesture, with the arms circling clockwise up on the left and down on the right, while moving all the way around the circle clockwise from the Sun back to the Sun
to an extraordinary degree.	Concluding at the place of the Sun with the D gesture with hands extended up as in the A gesture, with forefinger and middle finger (together) pointing heavenward, or with the thumb and all the fingers together (flattened hand)
He bestows great Power.	AU gesture, with the arms circling clockwise up on the left and down on the right, while moving all the way around the circle clockwise from the Sun back to the Sun, concluding with the Universal Love gesture.
	Repeat the AU gesture (together, as indicated above, with the other gestures: E, Universal Love, D) four times circling in a counterclockwise direction, each time moving all the way around the circle counterclockwise from the Sun back to the Sun.
AUM	Form the Universal Love gesture; close with the AUM gestures: A: arms form a horizontal V-shaped A U: arms parallel and extended forward horizontally in the U gesture M: hands return in the M gesture toward heart, palms facing heart AU: heart gesture (hands cupped over heart chakra).

AUM *Meditation*

AUM is a sound that drives out evil influences. Spoken properly, AUM connects the human being with the Creative Godhead, the three Logoi, and no evil being—seeking to draw the human being away from the Godhead—can stand up to it. AUM must be spoken in consciousness of:

O Self from whom all originates,

O Self dwelling in me,

O Self to whom all returns—

Toward Thee I strive.

Peace, peace, peace.

AUM

Manas is spiritual consciousness as such, and becomes divine consciousness when the human being unites it with *buddhi*. This is possible only for the human being who has given birth to the higher self, which lies hidden in AUM:

A = *atma*

U = *buddhi*

M = *manas*—the wisdom that leads the higher self to AUM.

A: past—descent from the Spirit

U: present—life in the material realm

M: future—return to the Spirit[52]

Past, present, and future are united harmoniously, as set by the great masters into language in the holy sound AUM. This is one of the interpretations that can be given to this sound.

When we speak this sound the great masters are with us and the air resounds with the spiritual power of the sound AUM.[53]

Another comment from Rudolf Steiner:[54]

A: I dedicate myself to myself

U: I dedicate myself to humanity

M: I dedicate myself to life

AUM ("AU-OO-M") connects the human being with the Central Sun, the Heart of the Creative Godhead in the galaxy.

A = *atma*   oneness with the Father
eurythmy gesture A → Father

U = *buddhi*   oneness with the Son
eurythmy gesture U → Son/Sun

M = *manas*   oneness with the Holy Spirit
eurythmy gesture M

*The Spirit of God **moves***

over the face of the waters.

(Genesis 1:2)

---

52 Lectures of November 6 and 14, 1906, and January 29, 1907, in Rudolf Steiner, *Esoteric Lessons 1904–1909*, CW 266/1 (Great Barrington, MA: SteinerBooks, 2007), pp. 137, 142, 168 (trans. amended by RP after comparing with the German original).

53 Ibid., p 166, lecture of January 29, 1907 (trans. amended by RP after comparing with the German original).

54 Notebook entry no. 3147.

Chapter 4: Deepening the Connection with the Etheric Christ

O Self, from whom all originates	Stepping back, A: above
O Self, dwelling in me	Stepping forward, U: downward, drawing feet together
O Self, to whom all returns	Stepping forward then back, with M forward then back–hands parallel
Toward Thee I strive	I: left
Peace, Peace, Peace	Peace gesture: the cross of Universal Love with arms extended horizontally at the sides and palms facing forward, as in Fra Angelico's depiction of the Transfiguration on page 47
AUM	A: arms form a horizontal V-shaped A U: arms parallel and extended forward horizontally in the U gesture M: hands return in the M gesture toward heart, palms facing heart AU: heart gesture (hands cupped over heart chakra).

One way to work with the meditation is to do it three times—the third time in Sanskrit, using the transliteration of the original Sanskrit verse from Shankara's Commentary to the *Taittiriya Upanishad*: [55]

yasmājjātam jagatsarvam (*jj* pronounced "tch")

yenedam dhāryate chaiva

yasminneva pralīyate

tasmai jñānātmane namah

shāntih, shāntih, shāntih[56]

AUM

In the Hindu tradition, it is customary to sing the closing words *"Shantih Shantih Shantih."* Two of the traditional ways of singing these words are indicated below. The first, taught by Sreedevi Bringi of the Buddhist-inspired

---

55 In the original Sanskrit verse, the second and third lines are reversed, which does not really make sense, as can be seen by considering Rudolf Steiner's explanation when he presented this verse in 1906 to students of the Esoteric School: A—descent from the Spirit / U—life in the material realm / M—return to the Spirit (see previous page). See also the quote by Ludwig Kleeburg on page 80, which is also in *Esoteric Lessons 1904–1909*, p. 489 (trans. amended by RP after comparing with the German original).

56 *Shanti shanti shanti, AUM* does not belong to Shankara's original verse, but was added by Rudolf Steiner. This line is in the *Taittiriya Upanishad* 2.9.5.

Naropa University in Boulder, Colorado, concludes with *AUM*; the second, taught by Joy of the Sri Aurobindo-inspired "universal town" of Auroville in Southern India, sets *AUM* before *Shantih Shantih Shantih*. In the Hindu tradition *AUM* is written (and spoken) "OM."

Joy from Auroville[57]

According to Ludwig Kleeburg:

In the esoteric lesson held in Munich [November 6, 1906] Rudolf Steiner spoke about the syllable AUM *(in Sanskrit an elongated diphthong: the past is designated by* A, *the present by* U, *the future evolution by* M). *When he concluded by singing these three sounds, it effected a sacred consecration. After the sounding of the* M *faded, there was a presence in the room as though invisible spirits were blessing us; and only slowly did the devotional silence ebb away.*

It is not known how Rudolf Steiner sang AUM. The following way of singing AUM comes from the Bulgarian spiritual teacher Peter Deunov (1864–1944), also known as Beinsa Douno.[58] It is wonderful, as well as closing with this sung version of AUM after the AUM meditation, to also begin the entire Inner Radiance sequence with this because of the special evocative power of AUM.

---

57 http://www.aurovilleradio.org/spirituality/the-path/915-learning-about-mantras.
58 With grateful acknowledgments to Ardella Nathanael, who wrote the book *Dance of the Soul: Peter Deunov's Pan-Eu-Rhythmy* (Carlsbad, CA: Esoteric Publishing, 1998). The music and original Bulgarian vocalization, as well as the English vocalization for "Aoum," are on page 115 of Ardella's book.

Chapter 4: Deepening the Connection with the Etheric Christ

If the AUM is sung at the beginning of the entire Inner Radiance sequence, it can be followed by singing the concordances in relation to the chakras, which prepares the way for the Lord's Prayer as a chakra prayer.

Concordances

Rudolf Steiner gave concordances between the tones and certain vowel sounds in language. The following table gives the concordances for the C Major scale and also the intervals have been added to the tabulation. For the English language these concordances have been slightly adjusted in the case of the intervals of the fourth (AU instead of Ö) and the sixth (EI instead of Ü), since the sounds Ö and Ü hardly occur in English (except perhaps for some special dialects). The correspondence with the chakras, as worked with in the Choreocosmos School, has also been added to the table.

TONE	INTERVAL	CONCORDANCE	CHAKRA
C	prime	U (oo)	root
D	second	O (oh)	sacral
E	third	A (ah)	solar plexus
F	fourth	AU (ow)	heart
G	fifth	E (eh)	throat
A	sixth	EI (eye)	third eye
B	seventh	I (ee)	crown
C	octave	U (oo)	star of the higher self, above the crown chakra

(see the meditation "A Star is above my Head," page 62)

As a toning for the chakras, the scale can be sung with the concordances (vowel sounds) and with the same gestures in relation to the chakras as in the Lord's Prayer as a chakra prayer—first ascending from the root (C) to the star of the higher self (C-octave), and then descending from the star of the higher self (C-octave) back to the root (C), as indicated in the following notes.

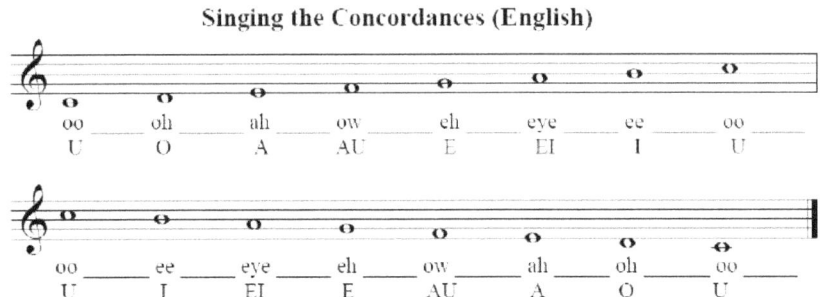

Singing the Concordances (English)

oo	oh	ah	ow	eh	eye	ee	oo
U	O	A	AU	E	EI	I	U

oo	ee	eye	eh	ow	ah	oh	oo
U	I	EI	E	AU	A	O	U

From the description of the Lord's Prayer as a chakra prayer, the gestures can be seen to be the "Grail Cup" gesture for the three lower chakras, the "AU-heart" gesture for the heart chakra, the "Eye of God" gesture for the three upper chakras, and the Prayer gesture (as for "Our Father, who art in Heaven") when it comes to C-octave in relation to the star of the higher self above the head.

For German-speaking readers, the concordances in the German language, as mentioned already, are different from those indicated above for the English language:

The concordance for F in German is Ö—approximately English "ir" (as in "birth").

The concordance for A in German is Ü—approximately English "eu" (as in "feud").

Since "ir" and "eu" are only approximate equivalents of the German ö and ü, the sounds "ow"(AU) and "eye"(EI) are substituted as appropriate concordances in the English language for Ö and Ü. It thus transpires that the English language concordances are the seven vowel sounds corresponding to the seven planets, and as experience shows, the AU ("ow") sound really does resonate in the heart chakra and the EI ("eye") sound in the Third Eye chakra.

When he presented the concordances in eurythmy, Rudolf Steiner—speaking of the German language concordances—indicated that "This is the approximate correspondence between the scale and the main vowels, purely according to their sound."[59]

Singing the Concordances (German)

oo	oh	ah	ir	eh	eu	ee	oo
U	O	A	Ö	E	Ü	I	U

oo	ee	eu	eh	ir	ah	oh	oo
U	I	Ü	E	Ö	A	O	U

---

59 Rudolf Steiner, *Eurythmy as Visible Singing* (CW 278, Stourbridge, UK: Anderida Music Trust, 1998), p. 34.

It should be remembered that the concordances are vowel sounds that resonate with the chakras *as sounds*, which must be distinguished from the correspondence between the planets and the eurythmy *gestures* of these vowel sounds. The sound and the gesture are two different levels. Great confusion would be possible if these two levels are not clearly distinguished. The concordances—the singing of the seven planetary vowel sounds in relation to the chakras, ascending and descending through the musical scale—apply on the sound level in their own right. The gestures have to do with setting in motion etheric currents relating to the chakras, in turn corresponding to the planets, and these also apply in their own right.

For example, the eurythmy gesture for EI ("eye") activates an etheric streaming in relation to the root chakra, corresponding to the Moon, and thus in eurythmy EI ("eye") is the Moon sound. However, intoning EI ("eye") activates a vibration in the third-eye chakra, which corresponds to Jupiter. This sound vibration is experienced on a different level to the etheric streaming of the eurythmy gesture. From this example, it can be seen how important it is to distinguish between these two levels of sound (sound vibration) and gesture (etheric streaming).

Interestingly, in the case of the sound E ("eh"), which vibrates in the region of the larynx, there is an agreement between the sound vibration and the etheric streaming in so far as the throat chakra corresponds to Mars and also the eurythmy gesture E ("eh") is the Mars sound in eurythmy. And in the case of the sound AU ("ow"), which vibrates in the region of the heart chakra, there is likewise an agreement between the sound vibration and the etheric streaming since the heart chakra corresponds to the Sun and also the eurythmy gesture AU ("ow") is the Sun sound in eurythmy.

Regarding the sound level, Rudolf Steiner indicated:

> One can feel the vowels also [by] sounding the vowels in the organism: I ("ee") above in the head; E ("eh") more in the larynx; A ("ah") in the breast [region]; O ("oh") in the lower body; U ("oo") deep down.[60]

Having made this indication, Rudolf Steiner went to some length to point out that this correspondence—and this, he said, applies also to other such esoteric correspondences—needs to be viewed in the context of a spiritual-scientific understanding of the human being. It is precisely because of the remarkable potency of singing the concordances in relation to the chakras that it needs to be borne in mind that the chakras are the seven primary organs of the human astral body and that these are the "seven seals" in the human being which only the Lamb can open (as it is expressed in Revelation, chapter 5; this is discussed in chapter 5). The singing of the concordances in relation to the seven chakras and the subsequent praying of the Lord's Prayer as a chakra prayer thus (as presented in this book) need to be experienced together—connected with one another, the one preparing for the other—so that the singing of the concordances is placed into relationship with the work of the Lamb (Christ) in transforming the astral body.

It is also interesting that the concordances given by Rudolf Steiner in 1924 are to be found in a book written by the Austrian composer and music theorist Josef Matthias Hauer (1883–1959). Hauer claimed to have been the first to compose music in full consciousness of the twelve-tone law, and he is among the most important early writers in twelve-tone music theory and aesthetics. In his book *Deutung des Melos* ("*Interpretation of Melos*") published in 1923, he wrote:

> "Pure *Melos* presents the spiritual connection between all these things including the connection between the individual notes of the melody. The meaning of a

---

60 Rudolf Steiner, *Das Wesen des Musikalischen und das Tonerlebnis im Menschen* ("*The Inner Nature of Music and the Experience of Tone in the Human Being*"; CW 283, Dornach, Switzerland: Rudolf Steiner Verlag, 1989), p. 64. The existing English translation of these lectures, published by Anthroposophic Press in 1983, does not contain the lecture of September 30, 1920, from which the above quotation is taken.

word, a melody with vowels and consonants, lies in its *Melos*. The vowels are fixed notes with clear tone-colors which move within the compass of an octave (U, O, A, Ö, E, Ü, I—[phonetically: oo, oh, ah, ir, eh, eu, ee]), and their absolute pitch depends on the speech organ."[61]

As Alan Stott, who translated these words of Hauer from German into English (and added in brackets the English phonetic equivalents), points out:

Singers, too, speak of *whispered vowels*; it is unclear whence the tradition originates.[62]

In other words, evidently there is a tradition concerning the concordances which was written down by Hauer and was taken up by Rudolf Steiner for eurythmy. Although it could be that Rudolf Steiner came to the concordances entirely through his own spiritual research, independently of the existing tradition recorded by Hauer, and that in this way Rudolf Steiner confirmed the correctness of this tradition. As is evident from Rudolf Steiner's indications—E (eh) more in the larynx, etc.—the relationship of the concordances to the chakras is implicitly stated. However, it is only now, with the publication of this book, that the correspondence between the concordances and the chakras is made explicit.

---

[61] These words from page 16 of Josef Matthias Hauer's book *Deutung des Melos* ("*Interpretation of Melos*") published in Vienna in 1923 were translated into English by Alan Stott and are quoted from his book *A Companion to Rudolf Steiner's "Eurythmy as Visible Singing"* (Stourbridge, England: Anderida Music Trust, 1995), p.41.

[62] Ibid., p.41.

Chapter 4: Deepening the Connection with the Etheric Christ

The IAO Meditation

Breathing with the Consciousness of Christ

> One has to learn to breathe in such a way that one breathes in the Christ stream, holding it within, and then breathing it out—that through this one's being expands with the Christ stream.[63]
> —Valentin Tomberg

These words of Valentin Tomberg relate on an inner level to the following IAO meditation given by Rudolf Steiner in three parts:

[Part one]   Concentrate on your breathing in the following way:
  Concentrate on inhalation and experience the in-flowing air as   I (ee)
  Concentrate on the inhaled air filling your body and experience it as   A (ah)
  Concentrate upon exhalation and experience the out-flowing air as   O (oh)

In closing part 1 of the IAO meditation, concentrate upon the region of the Third Eye between the eyebrows, feeling "therein as though the word IAO were resounding; holding this tone for one or two minutes; then *nothing but empty consciousness*, awaiting what comes":

[Part two]   While focusing on IAO as the name of the Cosmic Christ, imagine:
  A stream of light from [the region of the Third Eye] between the eyebrows to the neck   I (ee)
  The stream of light [pours down] along the spinal column   A (ah)
  The stream of light returns [streaming up] within the spinal column back to
  [the region of the Third Eye] between the eyebrows   O (oh)

[Part three] Contemplate the following three statements (as often as possible)

   IAO penetrates into me—through me—from me
   IAO creates forces in me—through me—from me
   IAO lives in me, weaving in me—through me—from me

Mood [for all three parts of this IAO meditation]

IAO as the name of Christ—
this has to do with the mystery
of how Christ works within human beings.[64]

(The first seal shows Christ in the Pentagram-IAO gesture.)

---

63 Valentin Tomberg, "Mitteilungen über das Geheimnis des ätherischen Christus" ("Communications Concerning the Mystery of the Etheric Christ") (diary entry for June 3, 1933) previously unpublished.
64 Rudolf Steiner, *From the History & Contents of the First Section of the Esoteric School 1904–1914* (Great Barrington, MA: SteinerBooks, 1998), pp. 167–168. Words in brackets [ ] added by RP; and some alterations to the English translation have been made after comparing with the original German text.

This IAO meditation is related to the Pentagram–IAO gesture from the first seal image of the Cosmic Christ from Revelation chapter 1,[65] where the Cosmic Christ speaks the words: "I AM the Alpha and the Omega" (Revelation 1:8).

I AM	I (ee)
the Alpha	A (ah)
and the Omega	O (oh)

In this sense Rudolf Steiner's indication that IAO is the name of Christ can be understood, since the Cosmic Christ announces himself as the IAO with the words:

"I AM the Alpha and the Omega"

By standing in the pentagram–IAO eurythmy gesture from the first seal image of the Cosmic Christ from Revelation chapter 1, one can enter into inner union/communion with Christ in the etheric realm, whose name is IAO.

This Pentagram–IAO gesture relates to the Cosmic Christ, as depicted on the first seal of the seven seals of the Apocalypse, and is practiced as follows:

IAO—body upright
(I is experienced in the head and also in the upright, vertical posture of the head and body, reaching up toward Heaven)

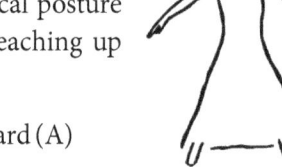

Arms and hands downward (A) palms facing down

Feet apart and knees pressed slightly outward with weight lightly on outer soles of feet (O)[66]

---

65 Revelation 1:13–16—these words underlie the image of the Cosmic Christ sketched by Rudolf Steiner and painted (on the basis of this sketch) by Clara Rettich. The description of the eurythmy gesture of the pentagram–IAO from the first seal image of the Cosmic Christ is first described on page 39 in connection with the AMEN/AUMEYN meditation. See also page 60.

66 This is the description of the Pentagram–IAO gesture from the AMEN/AUMEYN meditation on page 39.

In particular, holding in consciousness the opening of the path to Shambhala, the golden heart of Mother Earth, by Christ, as central to his Second Coming, one can imagine the O of the legs—although formed only slightly—as elongated, stretching down to Shambhala. In a strict geometrical sense it is then no longer a circular O, but an extremely long, elongated ellipse. Nevertheless, on a feeling level it can be sensed eurythmically as an O, with the legs open and connecting to the golden heart of the Earth. Through this eurythmy gesture one can come into an inner identification with the Cosmic Christ, now opening the path to Shambhala, and through Christ one can begin to draw from the life force of Shambhala—the life force that Christ took into himself when he descended down to Shambhala after the Crucifixion, taking in the life force of Shambhala for the final stage of formation of his Resurrection body. Through the O done in this way and with this consciousness, it is possible to allow the life force of Shambhala to flow up through the soles of the feet, through the legs, into the heart chakra, where it is experienced as a warm breath of the sacred life energy of the Divine Mother. With the I one allows the light of one's Eternal Star in heavens, the source of which streams from the Central Sun at the heart of our galaxy, also known as the *throne of God*, to flow down into the heart chakra, there to commingle with the warmth streaming up from the Mother. The commingling of light from the Father with warmth from the Mother is experienced as a sense of peace and blessedness, which is allowed to stream out from the heart chakra through the arms and hands, extended in the A gesture downward (palms facing down), as a blessing toward Mother Earth.

In coming into an inner identification with Christ in his Resurrection body, instead of facing south,[67] it is

---

67 From the time of Christ's Resurrection, in light of Mary Magdalene's experience of facing east and beholding the Risen One against the background of the rising Sun, it was natural for human beings—following Mary Magdalene—to turn to the east in search of the Risen Christ, to receive the forces of Light, Love, and Life streaming from him, as Mary Magdalene did, who on Easter Sunday

Chapter 4: Deepening the Connection with the Etheric Christ

appropriate to face north, as may be understood from the meditation given by Valentin Tomberg: "Christ is already here, from the south of the Earth waves are proceeding from him across the world." Facing north in this Pentagram–IAO gesture as that of the Cosmic Christ on the first seal, one can then do parts one and two of the IAO meditation given by Rudolf Steiner, holding in consciousness the "Christ is already here" meditation and the waves of radiant blue ether emanating from the Etheric Christ streaming from behind (from the south) around the world. Rudolf Steiner's recommendation is to do both parts one and two of the IAO meditation seven times. Later, though, as he did not subsequently recommend specific breathing exercises to members of the esoteric school, the question remains as to whether this indication of inhaling, holding, and exhaling the breath seven times in the IAO meditation is still to be considered as an essential part of the meditation. This is a matter for each person to decide for themselves individually.

Perhaps the most important thing in connection with breathing is to hold in consciousness these words from Rudolf Steiner's esoteric lesson of September 24, 1907:

> His Breath of Life is what envelops the Earth in the air and penetrates into us with every breath [we take]. We breathe his Breath of Life, which he streams to us through the plant covering of the Earth. And the air is the proclamation of his Holy Life, which we are allowed to take into ourselves.

The following words from the description of a participant in the Choreocosmos School express the sense of the Etheric Christ that can arise in connection with "breathing with the consciousness of Christ":

morning (and continuing for the rest of her life) received the *spiritual power* (Light, Love, and Life) of the Risen One into the region of her heart chakra. Since the Second Coming of Christ, starting in the twentieth century, it is appropriate to face south to receive the Light, Love, and Life streaming from Christ in the etheric. However, to express an inner union/identification with the Etheric Christ, it is appropriate to face north—like Christ—toward the Father, who is associated (esoterically) with the north.

The trees in the distance were shrouded by a vibrational force, like a breathing atmosphere. I understood and felt the presence of Christ in the etheric realm. The air that surrounds all life is his Breath. Air is the Breath of Love. Inwardly I heard, "I AM here. Breathe in my Love." I understood that we can co-create our Temples by breathing with the consciousness of Christ.[68]

These words express something of the magical "Shambhala quality" that is possible to experience in nature now that the *parousia*, the Presence of Christ in his Second Coming, is pervading the life and atmosphere of Mother Earth. To take up the life force of Shambhala is an important mission for eurythmy in the future, and the following exercise, which can be practiced as an "optional extra" after the closing AUM exercise, is a conscious step in this direction. Many of the exercises described in this book represent steps in the direction of taking up the life force of Shambhala. The description given at the start of the following exercise assumes that throughout the entire sequence one has been facing south—facing toward Christ in the etheric in order to receive the Light, Love, and Life streaming from him. However, when expressing an inner identification with the Etheric Christ—it is then appropriate to face north, holding in consciousness that the "Etheric Christ is standing in the south and waves are preceding from him across the Earth."[69]

---

68 In the ancient mysteries it was expressed that, "The body is the temple of the spirit." As described in this book, in a deeper sense it is the Resurrection body, co-created with Christ, which is the temple of the spirit. This is the deeper meaning of the exercises presented in this book.

69 It is also possible, following the experience of Mary Magdalene (see page 24), to do the entire sequence facing east, connecting onto the archetypal experience of Mary Magdalene, and this is most powerful at the time of sunrise. This also honors the second hierarchy (Exusiai, Dynamis, Kyriotetes), whose abode is in the Sun.

IAO *Gestures Express the Cosmic Christ on the First Seal*

From facing south toward the Etheric Christ, turn to face north, toward the Father.

Take up the Pentagram–IAO gesture (see pages 39 and 85) as that of the Cosmic Christ on the first seal, and then begin part 1 of the IAO meditation given by Rudolf Steiner, holding in consciousness the "Christ is already here" meditation and the waves of radiant blue ether emanating from the Etheric Christ streaming from behind (from the south) around the world.

[1] Be aware of your breathing in the following way:

Concentrate on inhalation and experience the in-flowing air as	I (ee)
Concentrate on the inhaled air filling your body and experience it as	A (ah)
Concentrate upon exhalation and experience the out-flowing air as	O (oh)

Repeat seven times.

Through the O done in this way eurythmically with the legs, holding in consciousness that the Etheric Christ is opening the path to Shambhala, it is possible to allow the life force of Shambhala to flow up through the soles of the feet, through the legs, into the heart chakra, where it is experienced as a warm breath of the sacred life energy of the Divine Mother. With the "I inhalation" one allows the light of one's Eternal Star in heaven, the source of which streams from the Central Sun at the heart of our galaxy, also known as the throne of God, to flow down into the heart chakra, there to commingle with the warmth streaming up from the Mother. The commingling of light from the Father with warmth from the Mother (holding the breath) is experienced as a sense of peace and blessedness, which is allowed to stream out from the heart chakra through the arms and hands, extended in the A gesture downward (palms facing down), as a blessing toward the Earth Mother. With the O (exhalation) one can allow the Christ stream of blessing to flow down through the legs and feet to Shambhala.

After having repeated this part of the IAO meditation seven times, one adopts the Right Standing posture described earlier in this book and folds the arms across the region of the heart chakra in the Reverence gesture. Holding this position, one can be conscious that with the legs one is making an U (oo) gesture extending down to the heart of the Earth—keeping the connection for the flow of life force from Shambhala open—and that with the Reverence gesture one is doing a form of the E (eh) gesture (see page 32). One closes part 1 of the IAO meditation with the UE (U with the legs, E with the arms). At this point Rudolf Steiner indicates to concentrate upon the region of the Third Eye between the eyebrows, feeling "therein as though the word IAO were resounding; holding this tone for one or two minutes; then nothing but empty consciousness, awaiting what comes."

When one is ready, one can then begin part 2 of the IAO meditation. One again takes up the Pentagram–IAO gesture as that of the Cosmic Christ on the first seal:

[2] While focusing upon IAO as the name of the Cosmic Christ, imagine:

A stream of light from [the region of the Third Eye] between the eyebrows to the neck: I (ee)

The stream of light [pours down] along the spinal column: A (ah)

The stream of light returns [streaming up] within the spinal column back to [the region of the Third Eye] between the eyebrows: O (oh)

Repeat seven times.

After having repeated part 2 of the IAO meditation seven times, one adopts the Right Standing posture and folds the arms across the region of the heart chakra in the Reverence gesture. Holding this position, one can be conscious that with the legs one is making an U (oo) gesture extending down to the heart of the Earth—keeping the connection for the flow of life force from Shambhala open—and that with the Reverence gesture one is doing a form of the E (eh) gesture. With this UE, one continues with part 3 of the IAO meditation:

[3] Contemplate the following three statements]

IAO penetrates into me—through me—from me

IAO creates forces in me—through me—from me

IAO lives in me, weaving in me—through me—from me

For the closing part of part 1 and again during part 3 (as the closing of part 2), one can take up the posture of Right Standing, consciously holding the U (oo) in one's standing, together with the E (eh) of the Reverence gesture of the arms folded across the region of the heart chakra. Holding this posture and gesture allows an opportunity not only for the grace of the spiritual world but also the grace of the Earth Mother expressed by UE, flowing in as an "echo" or response after doing the various parts of the IAO meditation—done consciously as an opening to receive the in-streaming life force of Shambhala needed for the formation of the Resurrection body. The IAO together with the UE forms the divine name IAOUE, so that holding the IAO in consciousness together with the U and the E in one's posture and gesture allows the divine name to resound within one's whole being.

One then closes the IAO meditation by releasing the hands to the sides and coming into a normal standing position. As Rudolf Steiner indicates, the three statements in part 3 of the IAO meditation can be contemplated "as often as possible." One interpretation—actually a metamorphosis—of his remark "as often as possible" would be to contemplate the three statements as often as possible during the course of the day. Since he gave this IAO meditation as part of a longer exercise to be done each evening, it is likely that he intended the recipient of the exercise to go through the three statements as many times as possible at one sitting (remembering that it was understood that the meditation would be done in a seated position). Now, in this book, the IAO meditation is put forward as a meditation for any time of day, and hence the remark, "as often as possible" can be considered in the sense of "as often as possible during the course of the day."

Regarding part 2 of the IAO meditation, Rudolf Steiner indicated that one could spend two minutes each time one visualizes the circuit of light in connection with IAO, so that—doing each circuit seven times—the whole meditation would last for fourteen minutes. Obviously, then, he did not have in mind that one would visualize the circuit of light in connection with the breathing as described in part 1, because for anyone but an advanced practitioner of breathing exercises, it would be impossible to take two minutes for inhalation, holding the breath, and exhalation.

This way of doing the IAO meditation in connection with the Pentagram–IAO gesture offers an opening through eurythmy to begin to take up the life force of Shambhala, which is essential for the formation of the Resurrection body, as is evident from contemplating Christ's descent down to Shambhala after his Crucifixion and prior to his Resurrection. Just as the creation of a physical body requires a father (male) and a mother (female), so the creation of the Resurrection body requires the forces of both the Father and the Mother—that of the Heavenly Father streaming as Light from the Central Sun at the heart of the galaxy, also known as the throne of God, and that of the Earth Mother radiating as Life from below from the golden heart of the Earth (Shambhala). It is the confluence of these two in the human being which creates the Resurrection body. This confluence or commingling is experienced first in the region of the heart chakra as heavenly peace and blessing—this being a sign, albeit in seed form, of the Resurrection body.

The foregoing description of the IAO meditation in connection with the Pentagram–IAO gesture is given in consciousness that the first exercise involving speech sounds that Rudolf Steiner gave, near the beginning of his communication of instructions for the new art form of eurythmy, was for the exercise IAO. This was one hundred years ago in Munich, at the beginning of September 1912. Here follows an account of this early eurythmy exercise. Rudolf Steiner's description of the exercise was recorded by Lory Maier-Smits and the text is interspersed with her comments:

IAO

"Stand upright, and try to feel that you are a column whose base is the balls of your feet and whose capital is your own head, your forehead. And this upright column, learn to perceive it as I [ee]." As I was making the effort, he called out once more, emphatically, "The weight rests on the balls of the feet, not on the entire foot!" Then it worked better, and led to a very strong experience, especially in contrast to the first unsuccessful attempts.

"Now shift the head of the column so that it is behind the base, and that you will learn to perceive as A [ah]." And thirdly, "Tilt the head of the column so that it is in front of the base, and learn to perceive that as O [oh]." Rudolf Steiner gave only these three sounds and only in this form that evening in Munich. That is, there was still no movement of the arms. [The addition to this exercise of the eurythmy gestures for A (ah) and O (oh) made with the arms came later. Initially this IAO exercise was simply a matter of experiencing the quality of I (ee) in the upright posture, A (ah) in the leaning back posture, and O (oh) in the leaning forward posture.][70]

Now, one hundred years later, to celebrate the one-hundredth anniversary of the birth of eurythmy, the IAO meditation is described in a new way, in connection with the Pentagram–IAO gesture as that of the Cosmic Christ on the first seal, thus making this exercise explicitly an expression of the Etheric Christ, whereas the connection was implicit when Rudolf Steiner taught the IAO exercise one hundred years ago. May this exercise (IAO) as it is presented in this new way in this book serve as a stimulus now, one hundred years later, for the taking up of the life force of Shambhala—through the Etheric Christ—in the practice of eurythmy.

Rudolf Steiner knew, of course, about IAO as the

---

70 Rudolf Steiner, *Eurythmy: Its Birth and Development*, Complete Works vol. 277a (Weobley, England: Anastasi, 2002), p.23. Comments in brackets [ ] added by RP.

Chapter 4: Deepening the Connection with the Etheric Christ

esoteric name of Christ, having already given the IAO meditation, where he had written, "IAO as the name of Christ," prior to having taught this first eurythmy exercise (IAO) involving speech sounds in September 1912. In giving this eurythmy exercise he was implicitly founding eurythmy upon the name of the Etheric Christ. And it is the purpose of this book—now explicitly—to give an impulse for the future of eurythmy: not only for eurythmy to serve as a path to Christ in the etheric but also for eurythmy to be in service of the work of the Etheric Christ in the creation of the "new Earth" by opening the path to Shambhala.

This work can be considered as a metamorphosis of the central mystery cultivated at the temple of Artemis of Ephesus in antiquity. There the neophytes and initiates contemplated the birth mystery, the incarnation of the human being into a physical body. They focused upon the sounds IOA, relating them to the three members of the human being beyond the physical body: the "I," the astral body, and the etheric body:

"I"	the sound I (ee)
astral body	the sound O (oh)
etheric body	the sound A (ah)[71]

The sequence IOA metamorphoses into IAO, which also clearly has to do with the three members of the human being beyond the physical body—and, over and above this, is "the name of Christ."

The IAO Meditation in Relation to the Sacred Name IAOUE

In connection with IAO, Rudolf Steiner alludes to something quite remarkable. Putting this in my own words: it was that the neophytes and initiates of the Artemis mysteries celebrated at Ephesus experienced the vowel sounds—E (eh) and U (oo)—resounding up from the Earth Mother (Artemis) below.[72] Here we come to the mystery of the holy name of God celebrated in the ancient Hebrew mysteries.

IAOUE

The holy name of God, written with the four Hebrew letters *Yod-Hé-Vav-Hé*, also written *Yod-Heh-Vav-Heh* (abbreviated YHVH)—and now usually written *Yod-Heh-Waw-Heh* (abbreviated YHWH)—is referred to as the *Tetragrammaton*. This name in the ancient Jewish religious tradition could only be pronounced once a year by the high priest in the temple on the holy day of Yom Kippur, the Day of Atonement; otherwise its name was not pronounced.[73] Subsequently when the Hebrew Bible was translated and the translators came across these four Hebrew letters *Yod-Hé-Vav-Hé*, they did not know where the vowel sounds were to be inserted and thus they were at a loss as to how this divine name of God should be translated from the Hebrew into English. It was incorrectly translated as Jehovah on account of a misplacing of the vowel sounds. Nowadays scholars have agreed upon YAHWEH,

---

71 Rudolf Steiner, *The Easter Festival in the Evolution of the Mysteries* (Great Barrington, MA: SteinerBooks, 1988), Compete Works vol. 233a, lecture of April 22, 1924.

72 Ibid.

73 Observant Jews write down but do not pronounce the Tetragrammaton, because it is considered too sacred to be used for common activities. The Tetragrammaton was pronounced by the high priest on Yom Kippur when the temple was standing in Jerusalem. Since the destruction of the Second Temple of Jerusalem in AD 70, the Tetragrammaton is no longer pronounced, and it is not generally known what this pronunciation is. Instead, common Jewish use has been to substitute the name "Adonai" ("My Lord") where the Tetragrammaton appears—http://en.wikipedia.org/wiki/Tetragrammaton

which gives a good sense as to how this sacred name of God was actually pronounced, although it is still not quite accurate, as will emerge in the following.

Beyond the scholarly level, there is an esoteric significance to this very profound name. In the English language the alphabet is comprised of vowels and consonants. There are twenty-one consonants and five vowels. Almost every word comprises both vowels and consonants. In the understanding of language based on eurythmy, the consonants correspond to the constellations of the zodiac and give the outer form of a word, whereas the vowels correspond to the planets and give the inner soul quality of that word. The vowels are thought of as issuing from within the soul of the human being. In our language the vowels are: A, E, I, O, U. If one runs the vowels together in a certain sequence—IAOUE—one arrives at YAHWEH, provided that the vowels are pronounced in a pure way.[74] The vowels are an expression of the human soul, since the vowel sounds issue from within and express different qualities of the human soul—for example, A (ah) expresses wonder, O (oh) expresses astonishment, and so on.

In the ancient Hebrew language the vowels were considered so sacred that they were not written down. One has to judge from the context how a word in ancient Hebrew is pronounced. This sequence of vowel sounds IAOUE is the most holy name one can think of because it expresses the inner life of the human being—the quintessence of what lives *within* the human soul: YAHWEH. YAHWEH expresses the inner life of the soul, in face of which the ancient Hebrews were filled with holy awe, experiencing this as something so sacred that it was not allowed to be spoken aloud (except in the one instance mentioned earlier; see footnote 73).

It can be seen that the sacred name IAOUE is comprised of IAO as the name of Christ resounding from cosmic heights together with UE as the answer from the Earth Mother from the depths below. It is interesting that the original name of Artemis of Ephesus was *Oupis* or *Upis*, where the U (oo) sound is prominent. Also, the E (eh) sound predominates in the word Ephesus. Thus, "Upis of Ephesus" could be expressed—in abbreviated form—UE. Moreover, the great temple of the Earth Mother at Eleusis, near Athens, was named in honor of Demeter, where the E (eh) sound predominates.

In the context of the IAO meditation, one can inwardly hold the mission of the Etheric Christ in consciousness, identifying with him through the Pentagram–IAO gesture as that of the Cosmic Christ on the first seal, whose mission is to open the path to Shambhala, the realm of the Earth Mother, who responds to the IAO of the name of Christ with her reply UE sounding up from below, from Shambhala, the golden heart of the Earth. The U (oo) expresses the life force streaming up from Shambhala, which one receives through the soles of the feet, streaming up through the legs, into the region of the heart chakra, and the E (eh) expresses the quality of inner warmth in the region of the heart chakra that is experienced when the life force of Shambhala is received there. (In eurythmy there is an inward, warm form of E used, for example, in the therapeutic exercise "heart-E" and this inward form of E is of the nature of the Reverence gesture—also a form of E—rather than the expanded E of the Universal Love gesture, which is that of Christ on the Cross.) In this way one's connection—through Christ—with the Earth Mother and with Shambhala is heightened, when doing the IAO meditation. Receiving the UE sounding up from Shambhala into oneself, while holding the IAO of the Cosmic Christ through one's gesture, allows the holy name of God IAOUE to come to expression in its fullness, uniting the heights and the depths within oneself.

---

74 Today scholars write YAHWEH as the sacred name of God, but without knowing exactly how it is pronounced. It is only when the sequence of vowels IAOUE is pronounced in a pure way—as is the case in eurythmy—that the word YAHWEH is yielded in its correct pronunciation. The vowels in eurythmy are spoken I (ee), A (ah), O (oh), U (oo), E (eh). The sequence IAOUE should be spoken with the eurythmy vowel sounds by running them together as if gliding from one vowel to the next. Then the correct pronunciation of YAHWEH is yielded.

Thus, eurythmy can be in service of the work of the Etheric Christ in the creation of the "new Earth" by opening the path to Shambhala.

In conclusion, for the sake of completeness and as a stimulus intended to connect onto the foregoing description as to how to allow the holy name IAOUE to come to expression in doing the IAO exercise, herewith some further indications from Rudolf Steiner. The significance of the holy name IAOUE is highlighted by the esoteric lesson held by Rudolf Steiner on May 27, 1923.[75] This was the final esoteric lesson of the first esoteric school. As part of this esoteric teaching, Rudolf Steiner returned to the mystery of the sequence of the vowels IAOUE:

Concerning the vowels—
the hierarchies are involved in them.

IAO Seraphim, Cherubim and in part the Thrones [first hierarchy]

U Kyriotetes, Dynamis, Exusiai [second hierarchy]

E Archai, Archangeloi, Angeloi [third hierarchy]

All of this together signifies the primordial sacred YAHWEH-Word[76] ...To create this YAHWEH-Word from the hierarchies signifies a deed.[77]

At this point in this final esoteric lesson Rudolf Steiner gave several meditations.[78] In his handwritten notes concerning the last three esoteric lessons that he held—the following translation is from these notes—he made these notes concerning the sacred IAOUE (YAHWEH-Word):

---

75 In discussing the holy name IAOUE, it is important to bear in mind that the name IAOUE (YAHWEH) is not the *actual* name of God referred to in the Lord's Prayer with the words, "Hallowed be thy name." Nevertheless, IAOUE can be considered as a *reflection* of the name of God in the following sense. YAHWEH is understood to be the name of God in the Old Testament. The earliest extra-Biblical mention of YAHWEH as Israel's God is in Moabite on King Mesha's stele from about 840 BC. However, Moses lived several centuries prior to this date, and these words are attributed to him: God said to Moses, "I AM THE I AM" And he said, "Say this to the people of Israel, 'I AM has sent me to you.'" God also said to Moses, "Say this to the people of Israel, 'YAHWEH, the God of your fathers, the God of Abraham, the God of Isaac, and the God of Jacob, has sent me to you.' This is my name forever, and thus I AM to be remembered throughout all generations" (Exodus 3:14-15). The God of Israel clearly identifies himself here as YAHWEH—I AM—I AM THE I AM (Hebrew: *Ehyeh asher ehyeh*). However, according to Rudolf Steiner, YAHWEH is a spiritual being of the rank of an Elohim (Greek: Exusiai), and is thus not identical with the One Whom Jesus spoke of as the Father (beyond the spiritual hierarchies). Nevertheless, since YAHWEH was clearly acting on behalf of the Father in preparing the way for the incarnation of the Son (Christ), YAHWEH was *representing* the Father. his name, therefore, reflects something of the essence of the Father, since the name of a spiritual being expresses its mission, and the mission of YAHWEH was to represent the Father.

76 The German way of writing YAHWEH is *Jahve*, which in English would be pronounced Yahveh. Regarding this difference between the English and the German: The letter known to modern Hebrew speakers as *vav* was in ancient Hebrew a semivowel "w" rather than a "v" (an English "w," not a German "v"). This letter is thus referred to as *waw* in the academic world, and—because of this difference between the ancient pronunciation and the modern pronunciation—academics have opted for YAHWEH rather than Yahveh, in order to remain true to the ancient Hebrew way of speaking the holy name. From the eurythmic way of pronouncing the sequence of vowel sounds IAOUE—this being the authentic pronunciation of the holy name of God—it is evident that YAHWEH is closer to the true pronunciation than Yahveh (German *Jahve*).

77 Rudolf Steiner, *Concerning the History and Content of the Higher Degrees of the Esoteric School*, 1904-1914, Complete works vol. 265 (Isle of Mull, Scotland: Etheric Dimensions Press, 2005), pp.499-500. Words in brackets [ ] added by RP. The words: "To create this YAHWEH-Word from the hierarchies signifies a deed" are followed by these words, "The putting into practice of this deed on Earth: the *Butterfly meditation*" (see next footnote).

78 Ibid., pp.500-505. The central meditation that Rudolf Steiner gave during this last esoteric lesson is the "Butterfly Meditation." In the middle of this meditation there are the words, "Where cosmic will works," alongside which (in the notes from this esoteric lesson) is written: IAOUE.

I: still within oneself

A: one opens oneself to the world, which says much

O: the Angels come, join hands [with them—the Angels representing the third hierarchy comprising Angels, Archangels, Archai]

U: the second hierarchy then comes, surrounding one with light

E: the first hierarchy comes, burning one in the fire[79]

The mysterious words about "burning in the fire" relate to the Seraphim, the Spirits of Love, the highest rank of the first hierarchy, whose name (from the Hebrew) means "the burning ones"—and in this context "burning in the fire" relates to the experience of the fire of Divine Love of the Seraphim, who are closest to the throne of God.

It is interesting that these handwritten notes concerning the sacred IAOUE *ascend* from the third to the second to the first hierarchy, whereas the preceding indication given in the esoteric lesson—

IAO: Seraphim, Cherubim and in part the Thrones

U: Kyriotetes, Dynamis, Exusiai

E: Archai, Archangeloi, Angeloi

—indicates a *descent* through the hierarchies in relation to the sacred YAHWEH-Word. This apparent contradiction contributes to the profound mystery surrounding the sacred name, which can be experienced on the one hand *macrocosmically* as streaming from the Father downward through all the hierarchies and on the other hand *microcosmically*, beginning within the human being, streaming upward through all the hierarchies toward the Father. On the reverse of the page on which he wrote the IAOUE words quoted here ("I—still within oneself," etc.), the following notes—which are obviously directions given by Rudolf Steiner for the carrying out of the meditation—appear in Edith Maryon's handwriting:[80]

"…the sounds connect one with the hierarchies. Then say: IAOUE" [81]

Speaking the sacred name IAOUE in the right way—as described here in connection with the eurythmic understanding of the vowel sounds—is a deed for our time. And connecting with the hierarchies through IAOUE is also something very profound—evidently relating on the one hand to Rudolf Steiner's indication regarding the *descending* passage through the hierarchies:

IAO: Seraphim, Cherubim and in part the Thrones

U: Kyriotetes, Dynamis, Exusiai

E: Archai, Archangeloi, Angeloi

and, on the other hand, to the *ascending* passage through the hierarchies:

I: still within oneself

A: one opens oneself to the world, which says much

O: the Angels come, join hands [with them—the Angels representing the third hierarchy]

U: the second hierarchy then comes, surrounding one with light

E: the first hierarchy comes, burning one in the fire

From this indication, the significance of the holy name IAOUE can be grasped as an expression of the

---

79 Ibid., pp.506–526—Rudolf Steiner's handwritten notes concerning the last three esoteric lessons that he gave, with the IAOUE words quoted here from p.523.

80 Edith Maryon (1872–1924) was one of Rudolf Steiner's closest co-workers. She worked closely together with Rudolf Steiner from 1914/1915 until the end of her life. Together they created the great statue of Christ as the *Representative of Humanity*, and she participated in a very active way in the building of the first Goetheanum.

81 Rudolf Steiner, *Concerning the History and Content of the Higher Degrees of the Esoteric School*, 1904–1914, Complete works vol. 265 (Isle of Mull, Scotland: Etheric Dimensions Press, 2005), p.525. Here, and also in the foregoing quotations from this book, the English translation has sometimes been slightly amended by RP after comparison with the original German text.

name of God, whose essence streams through all the ranks of the spiritual hierarchies—from above down (in the direction from the Father to the Mother) and from below up (in the direction from the Mother back to the Father).

As described above, one's connection—through Christ—with the Earth Mother and with Shambhala is heightened, when doing the IAO meditation while holding the IAO of the Cosmic Christ through one's gesture and at the same time receiving the UE of the Earth Mother, sounding up from Shambhala, into oneself. This allows the holy name IAOUE to come to expression in its fullness, uniting the heights and the depths within oneself. And now Rudolf Steiner's indication that the sounds IAOUE "connect one with the hierarchies"—macrocosmically streaming down through the hierarchies and microcosmically ascending through the ranks of the hierarchies—can be incorporated into the meditation, adding a whole new dimension to the sacred name IAOUE.

Finally, herewith some indications by Valentin Tomberg concerning the name YAHWEH (IAOUE):

> The name of God which was revealed to Moses corresponds completely with the Being of the God who transcends the self ("I"). The name I AM THE I AM (Hebrew: *Ehyeh asher ehyeh*) is not the name which Moses gave God, but on the contrary it was given and revealed by God himself. It is, then, of such a kind that it cannot be used in the sense of "He" or "It" but only in the sense of transsubjective Being. It contains no analogy, no likeness or image from the entire realm of existence, except for the analogy with the "I AM" experience of the human being. The most intimate, intuitive experience of the human being, that of "I AM," is the only "image and likeness" which it contains.
>
> In fact, two names were revealed to Moses—one name that is absolute: I AM THE I AM (or I AM); and a second, the name of the God of Abraham, Isaac, and Jacob, YAHWEH, which is to be his name for ever and which, "to his remembrance," is to be valid throughout all generations. Thus was revealed to Moses the timeless, absolute, and cosmic name I AM, and also the name valid for historical time, the name of the "God of the fathers," YAHWEH (YHWH).
>
> I AM is the name for the realm of eternal being, while the name YAHWEH is meant for the realm of temporal history, i.e., for the realm of existence. YAHWEH is the name for the "upper" partner of the covenant: ISRAEL—YAHWEH. It contains within it and also reveals the meaning and nature of the divinely willed mission of Israel, the "chosen people"—historically actually "the people of YAHWEH."
>
> The God of Being—HE WHO IS—revealed himself to Moses as I AM THE I AM (*Exodus* 3:14). This was followed by the I AM sayings in the Gospel of St. John, which reveal Christ as the I AM:
>
> I AM the True Vine
>
> I AM the Way, the Truth, and the Life
>
> I AM the Door
>
> I AM the Bread of Life
>
> I AM the Good Shepherd
>
> I AM the Light of the World
>
> I AM the Resurrection and the Life
>
> —and "I and the Father are One."
>
> The words I AM THE I AM (HE WHO IS) of the Mosaic revelation are like a seed or germ which by the time of Christ had ripened through stages of growth—to blossom and to fruit.[82]

In celebration of the sacred names of the Divine, a suggested practice would be to follow the AUM meditation with singing the AUM/AOUM, according to a composition by the Bulgarian spiritual teacher Peter Deunov (1864-1944), then to follow with the IAO meditation (described earlier), closing with

---

82 Valentin Tomberg, *Lazarus, Come Forth!* (former title: *Covenant of the Heart*) (Great Barrington, MA: SteinerBooks, 2006), pp. 148, 161.

singing the sounds for the IAOUE.

It is thanks to Rudolf Steiner that the true and authentic pronunciation of YAHWEH as IAOUE is now known—at least, among those who are acquainted with Rudolf Steiner's spiritual research. (This statement does not preclude the possibility that there are others in our time who, independently of Rudolf Steiner, know that YAHWEH is pronounced IAOUE). Given the profound significance of this divine name, it is a privilege to be able to speak or sing it with the correct pronunciation, which is otherwise unknown to millions of people in the world who revere the holy name in its written form. It can be spoken/sung in consciousness that it is the name of the sacred covenant between the Divine and Abraham—the father of the three traditions of Judaism, Islam, and Christianity—as well as of the covenant with the greatest of the prophets of Israel: Moses, who appeared at the right hand of Christ at the Transfiguration on Mt. Tabor, and that Jesus Christ—HE WHO EMBODIED THE DIVINE NAME—was the fulfillment of this sacred covenant.

The following composition for singing IAOUE is based on Peter Deunov's composition *"Izgryava Sluntseto"* (usually rendered as "Behold the Rising Sun" but a more exact translation from the Bulgarian is "Rising is the Sun").

In singing IAOUE it is good to hold in consciousness that this sequence of vowel sounds flows together as a word—the sacred name YAHWEH. Rudolf Steiner's indications about connecting with the hierarchies in both an ascending and a descending sequence in relation to IAOUE can also be held in consciousness when singing IAOUE ascending and descending.

YA = IA ("YA" as in YAHWEH)

Chapter 4: Deepening the Connection with the Etheric Christ

The Esoteric Dimension of Peter Deunov's (Beinsa Douno's) Compositions

Before we enter more specifically the esoteric dimension of Peter Deunov's compositions, it is helpful to consider the general background to this theme. The following analysis of two compositions by Peter Deunov—the two that have been adopted in this book—shows that his compositions (at least, this applies to these two) have a profound esoteric dimension. This esoteric dimension emerges by way of considering the chakras in relation to the tones of the scale. This subject is addressed briefly in appendix 2 of *Cosmic Dances of the Planets*.[83] The correspondence indicated there, proceeding from the heliocentric perspective of the planets, and following Rudolf Steiner's indication that "C = 128 Hz = Sun," is as follows:[84]

Tone	Chakra (Lotus flower)	Planets (heliocentric)
C = 128 Hz	Heart (12-petal lotus)	Sun
D = 144 Hz	Solar Plexus (10-petal lotus)	Mercury
E = 162 Hz	Sacral (6-petal lotus)	Venus
F = 170⅔ Hz	Larynx (16-petal lotus)	Mars
G = 192 Hz	Third eye (2-petal lotus)	Jupiter
A = 216 Hz	Crown (8-petal lotus)	Saturn
B = 243 Hz	Root (4-petal lotus)	Moon

---

83 Lacquanna Paul & Robert Powell, *Cosmic Dances of the Planets* (San Rafael, CA: Sophia Foundation Press, 2007), appendix 2: "Musical Tones and the Planets," especially p.174 & p.177.
84 In addition to indicating "C = 128 Hz = Sun," Rudolf Steiner also indicated that A = 432 Hz, which one octave lower signifies that A = 216 Hz, as given in the table. It is only possible to reconcile these two indications by adopting the Pythagorean intervals (rather than the natural intervals). The values 128 Hz, 144 Hz, 162 Hz, and so on, given in the first column are derived from the Pythagorean intervals. For an in-depth discussion of this theme, see Maria Renold, *Intervals, Scales, Tones and the Concert Pitch C = 128 Hz* (London: Temple Lodge, 2004).

The table gives Rudolf Steiner's indication concerning the correspondence between the tones and the parts of the body, which in turn correspond to the chakras.[85] Although he did not speak explicitly of the chakras, it is evident that the chakras underlie the indication he has given concerning the parts of the body. It should be noted that here the tones *descend* through the scale starting with A for the crown (head) and that in this indication Rudolf Steiner interchanges Mercury and Venus, as discussed on page 155. On this account the Mercury chakra located in the region of the solar plexus is designated with "Venus" and the Venus chakra located in the sacral region is designated "Mercury."

Tone	Chakra (Lotus flower)	Planets
A	Crown (8-petal lotus) Head	Saturn
G	Third eye (2-petal lotus) Forehead	Jupiter
F	Larynx (16-petal lotus) Larynx	Mars
E	Heart (12-petal lotus) Heart	Sun
D	Solar Plexus (10-petal lotus) (no indication)	"Venus"
C	Sacral (6-petal lotus) Stomach	"Mercury"
B	Root (4-petal lotus) (no indication)	Moon

For the sake of comparison the following table integrates the correspondence indicated by Rudolf Steiner from the above table with the correspondence from the preceding table (heliocentric sequence). The earlier table is reproduced again below, with the correspondence indicated by Rudolf Steiner given in the last column:

Tone	Chakra (Lotus flower)	Planets (heliocentric)	Rudolf Steiner's indications
C = 128 Hz	Heart (12)	Sun	E
D = 144 Hz	Solar Plexus (10)	Mercury	D
E = 162 Hz	Sacral (6)	Venus	C
F = 170⅔ Hz	Larynx (16)	Mars	F
G = 192 Hz	Third eye (2)	Jupiter	G
A = 216 Hz	Crown (8)	Saturn	A
B = 243 Hz	Root (4)	Moon	B

Comparing the first and the last columns, there is agreement except that (1) C-heart in the first column is given as E-heart in the last column, and (2) E-sacral in the first column is given as C-sacral in the last column, i.e., there is an interchange between the tones for the Sun and Venus.

---

85 *Eurythmische Korrespondenz Nr. 15, "Eurythmisten im Gespräch 1952–1958,"* herausgegeben von Hans Reipert (Berlin: Otanes Verlag, 2006), pp. 17–19: Olga Samyslowa reported that Mr. Lewerenz read the following indications from his notebook, which he had received from Rudolf Steiner in response to his questions: "The tones descending from above: A-Saturn-head / G-Jupiter-forehead / F-Mars-larynx / E-Sun-heart / D-Venus-not effective in any organ / C-Mercury-stomach / B-Moon-not effective in any organ."

Chapter 4: Deepening the Connection with the Etheric Christ

According to Peter Deunov, "The heart represents the tone C."[86] It could be that the interchange according to Rudolf Steiner's indication has to do with considering the sequence geocentrically rather than heliocentrically. At any rate, although the indications are not completely in accordance between the first and the last columns, there is nevertheless a basic agreement. The foregoing table (excluding Rudolf Steiner's indications in the last column) depicts the absolute correspondence between the tones and the chakras. This absolute correspondence emerges in relation to the heliocentric structure of the solar system and (for the Earth and humanity) has to do with the primacy of the tone C and the key of C major. "C=128 Hz is indeed the foundational prime tone for humanity and the Earth, having been carried over from the Sun to the Earth by Christ."[87]

Whereas Peter Deunov's correspondence C-heart agrees with the C=128 Hz indication in the Tone column of the foregoing table, the remaining correspondences indicated by Peter Deunov do not fit so clearly and unambiguously. In this connection it is important to bear in mind that Peter Deunov was referring to the *organs*, which in turn correspond to the planets, and that the correspondence between the *tones and the organs* is different from the correspondence between the *tones and the chakras*.[88] The latter correspondence derives archetypically from the cosmic (heliocentric) perspective—what is referred to earlier as the *absolute correspondence*—whereas the correspondence between the tones and the organs relates to the earthly (geocentric) perspective.

When it comes to exploring the esoteric dimension of Peter Deunov's compositions, it is not a matter of the absolute correspondence, but of the correspondence *within each key*. In the music of Peter Deunov the correspondence between the tones and the chakras changes according to the key in which the music is written. If a piece of music is written in C major, the tone for the heart chakra is C. If it is written in G major, the tone for the heart chakra is G; and so on. This can be seen in the following two pieces composed by Peter Deunov.

The first piece—composed for singing the sacred mantra AUM/AOUM—is in the key of C major, and thus the tone corresponding to the heart chakra is C. This yields the following table of correspondences between the tones and the chakras, whereby the eighth chakra—the "star above the head" (to use Rudolf Steiner's expression, see the exercise A Star Is above My Head, page 62)—is experienced above the crown chakra. "This...[is] a point of light approximately 20 to 30 centimeters [8–12 inches] outside our head...above.... With this...I must think of my higher I outside of me."[89] The eighth chakra—when it develops it is visible to clairvoyant perception as a point of light some 10 inches above the head—is that of the higher I associated with the "star above my head." This eighth chakra develops through the permeation by the divine I AM of the seven chakras, as outlined in the first part of *Putting on the Resurrection Body*.

Including the eighth chakra, and beginning with the correspondence C-heart, ascending and descending from the heart the complete correspondence is shown in the following table. As in Rudolf Steiner's indication (see table on page 98), where the tone E corresponds with the heart as central to the scale of tone/chakra correspondences, so in the AUM/AOUM composition of Peter Deunov, once the correspondence of the tone C with the heart chakra is established, the remaining correspondences between the tones of the

---

86 Beinsa Douno [Peter Deunov], *The Wellspring of the Good* (Sofia, Bulgaria: Kibea, 2002), p. 317.

87 Maria Renold, *Von Intervallen, Tonleitern, Tönen und dem Kammerton c=128 Hertz* (Dornach, Switzerland: Verlag am Goetheanum, 1998), p. 238. English translation: *Intervals, Scales, Tones and the Concert Pitch c=128 Hz.* (trans. Bevis Stevens; London: Temple Lodge Press, 2004).

88 Concerning this difference, see Lacquanna Paul & Robert Powell, *Cosmic Dances of the Planets* (San Rafael, CA: Sophia Foundation Press, 2007), appendix 2: "Musical Tones and the Planets," pp. 176–178.

89 Rudolf Steiner, *Esoteric Lessons 1904–1909*, Complete Works vol. 266/1 (Great Barrington, MA: SteinerBooks, 2007), pp. 424–425.

scale and the chakras follow in ascending/descending order. This is a geocentric approach in contrast to the absolute correspondence tabulated (see table on page 97) in relation to the heliocentric structure of the solar system. This geocentric approach is valid in so far as we are incarnated upon the Earth.

Tone/Interval (the interval from G)	Chakra (Lotus flower)	Planets/Star
G/8	Eighth chakra ("star above the head")	Sirius
F/7	Crown (8-petal lotus)	Saturn
E/6	Third eye (2-petal lotus)	Jupiter
D/5	Larynx (16-petal lotus)	Mars
C/4	Heart (12-petal lotus)	Sun
B/3	Solar Plexus (10-petal lotus)	Mercury
A/2	Sacral (6-petal lotus)	Venus
G/1	Root (4-petal lotus)	Moon

The "star above the head" is the microcosmic equivalent to the *individual's star*, which is different for each person.

> The human being, inasmuch as he [she] comes down from cosmic spiritual spaces into an earthly life, comes always from a certain star. We can trace the very direction of it, and it is not unreal—on the contrary, it is most exact to say "The human being has his [her] star." If we take what is experienced beyond all space and time between death and a new birth, and translate this into its spatial image, we can say: Every human being has his [her] star, which determines what he [she] has attained between death and a new birth...We can certainly not speak of "the midnight hour of existence" between death and a new birth without thinking of some star which the human being indwells between death and a new birth.[90]

Thus, each individual has a star, which holds the mystery of the higher I, just as the Sun holds the mystery of the I. On a cosmic level, the star Sirius serves as the "higher I" for the Sun, which is why Sirius is listed in the "Planet/Star" column of the table.

Making use of the aforementioned correspondences in relation to the AUM/AOUM composition of Peter Deunov, the following music indicates the relationship of the tones to the chakras while singing this composition.

---

90 Rudolf Steiner, *Karmic Relationships,* vol. 3 (CW 237; London: Rudolf Steiner Press, 2009), lecture of July 7, 1924.

Singing AUM

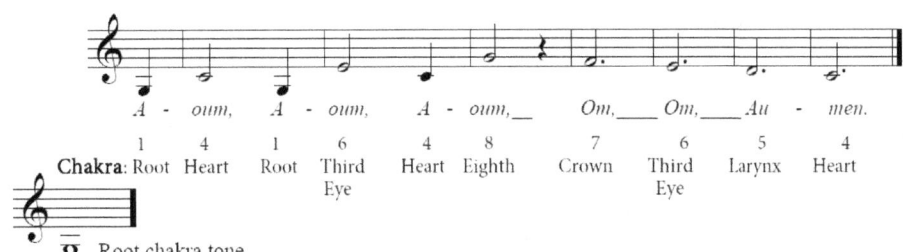

Singing the words with the music and holding in consciousness the chakras corresponding to each tone offers a remarkable deepening into the music, whereby the resonance between the tones and the chakras—not in an absolute sense, but within the context of the particular composition—opens up an esoteric dimension to music. Evidently Peter Deunov was aware of this. It is extraordinary how the music starts with the root chakra, ascends to the heart chakra, goes back to the root chakra, and then ascends to the third eye chakra; then, returning to the heart chakra, the music ascends to the Star of the Higher Self (eighth chakra), and from there descends down through each chakra from the crown to the third eye to the larynx back to the heart chakra—corresponding to the tone C, which serves as the "Sun-heart" of this composition in C major. The more one sings this, the more one experiences a quality of perfection in this composition. Over and above this, as Peter Deunov said

> If you are sorrowful, ill, or with an indisposed spirit, then pronounce AOUM a few times. Sacred words exist, one of which is AOUM, that you need to pronounce often, even if you do not understand their meaning. AOUM is a word of the Spirit. When you sing this word, the Spirit hears you and will assist you, because the Spirit comprehends and knows your needs. [91]

Keep this sacred exercise as a sacred part of yourself. When you sing a sacred song, your soul opens like a flower opening to the light; you put yourself in a pure and carefree state like that of a child, with no fear of what is around you. In this state you unite with beings of the World of Reason and will then understand what music is, what song is, and what science is...It produces magnificent forms in the soul, linking us to the cosmos, elevating us to the divine realms, and activates the 1,000-petal lotus flower [crown chakra]. This song calms and appeases the cells [of the body]. [92]

Regarding the esoteric dimension of Peter Deunov's compositions, he said:

> Our songs exist in the world above and are brought down to us from there. When we sing them, evolved beings come to help us. Through our songs we go to them, and they come to us. Each of our songs is brought down from above and corresponds to a song that exists in the divine world. Each of our songs is created according to the plan of the sublime scales which comes from above. And if we here, while singing or playing, are in accordance with the real essence of these heavenly songs which are brought from above, we will then receive the blessing of the divine world. When one sings with purity, love, and total harmony of mind, heart, and will—all three turned toward the divine—then at this very moment we will connect with the rhythm of these heavenly songs from which

---

91 Beinsa Douno [Peter Deunov], *Paneurythmy* (Sofia, Bulgaria: Bialo Bratstvo, 2004), p.68. See also, Beinsa Douno, *Paneurythmy* (Sofia, Bulgaria: Vsemr, year unknown), p.32.

92 The translation of this Peter Deunov text concerning AOUM was made in a private communication by Maria Mitovska, Sofia, Bulgaria.

ours are derived. As a result, we will receive the living divine stream and its blessing. These divine songs are sung above—unto eternity. They resonate there forever. It is through them that the universe is created and built.[93]

Having considered Peter Deunov's composition AUM/AOUM, let us now turn our attention to the music that we have adapted—from another of his compositions—for the singing of IAOUE. This music is composed in the key of G major, and so G is the "Sun-heart" of this composition. Before tabulating the correspondences between the tones and the chakras for this composition, with this one it emerges that we need to take account not only of the "star above the head" (eighth chakra) but also the "earth beneath the feet."

In the ancient Jewish esoteric teaching concerning the Tree of Life, there is a sphere of life connected with the feet—in particular with the soles of the feet—where the feet connect with the Earth, and this sphere in the Hebrew tradition of the Cabbala is called *Malkuth*, which means "kingdom" (see page 137). This "Earth sphere" in the region of the feet is of great significance as it is through Malkuth that we connect with the realm of Shambhala, the golden heart of the Earth. The tone in this composition corresponding to Malkuth is a low B, which occurs only once—at the very start of the music—as a kind of "springboard" from the Earth sphere (Malkuth) to the root chakra, the first chakra. This starting tone B in relation to Malkuth is taken into account in this composition as step 0—from here jumping immediately to the tone D corresponding to the root chakra as step 1 (see table).

---

93 Beinsa Douno [Peter Deunov], *The Wellspring of the Good* (Sofia, Bulgaria: Kibea, 2002), p.304.

Tone/interval (the interval from D)	Chakra (Lotus flower)	Planets/Star
D/8	Eighth chakra ("star above the head")	Sirius
C/7	Crown (8-petal lotus)	Saturn
B/6	Third eye (2-petal lotus)	Jupiter
A/5	Larynx (16-petal lotus)	Mars
G/4	Heart (12-petal lotus)	Sun
F#/3	Solar Plexus (10-petal lotus)	Mercury
E/2	Sacral (6-petal lotus)	Venus
D/1	Root (4-petal lotus)	Moon
B/0	Malkuth (Earth sphere)	Earth

Using this table in relation to the composition by Peter Deunov adapted for singing the IAOUE music, the following music indicates the relationship of the tones to the chakras while singing the composition.

As remarked upon earlier (see page 96), this music composed by Peter Deunov for the song "Izgryava Sluntseto" is usually rendered in English as "Behold the Rising Sun." Concerning this music and song, he said:

> Here, with perfect simplicity in music and lyrics, a magnificent picture of the rising Sun is created. The most beautiful—the most solemn—moment in Nature is the rising of the Sun. And within human consciousness a Sun is rising as well. It sends its life into the human being's life and gives the impulse to work... In order to sing this exercise, one needs to enter into a harmonious relationship with divine Nature. There is no being more intelligent, more tender, more responsive, and more sensitive than She. Therefore one needs to listen to Her call. [94]

Here, instead of singing the words relating to the rising Sun, the IAOUE invites us to sing one of the sacred names of the Divine, whereby the same inner quality of beauty and solemnity in addressing a higher source of life, divine intelligence, and spiritual grace is called for. For those readers already used to singing "Behold the Rising Sun" to this music composed by Peter Deunov, it may at first seem quite different to sing IAOUE to this music. However, as with singing the AUM/AOUM, the discovery can be made that the majesty of this sequence of tones—especially when sung in consciousness of the relationship to the chakras, as indicated below—can be also a blessed experience.

---

[94] Beinsa Douno [Peter Deunov], *Paneurythmy* (Sofia, Bulgaria: Bialo Bratstvo, 2004), p.71.

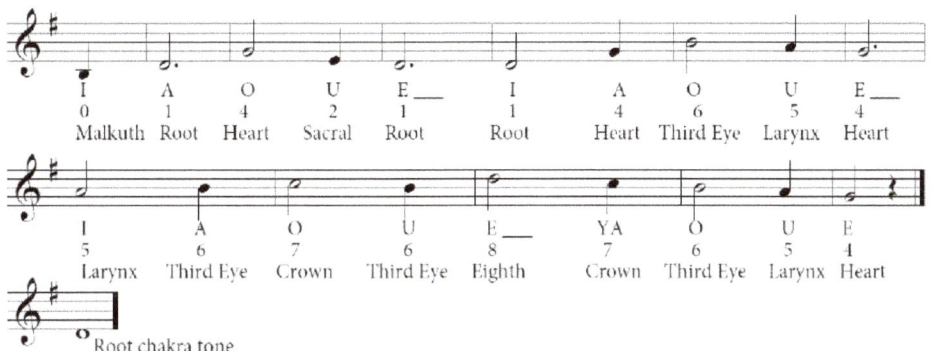

Thus we honor the sacred name IAOUE.

In singing IAOUE, holding in consciousness that this sequence of vowel sounds flows together as the sacred name YAHWEH, at the same time paying attention to the relationship of the tones to the chakras, can be an extraordinary experience. As with the AUM/AOUM composition, this other sublime composition by Peter Deunov ascends to the "star above the head" and then at the end descends from there through the crown chakra, the third eye chakra, the larynx chakra, back to the heart chakra—corresponding to the tone G, which serves as the "Sun-heart" in this composition in G major. Here it can be seen that the same compositional principle—of tones in relation to the chakras—is followed in both compositions.

Singing the AUM, the concordances, and the IAOUE in relation to the chakras is conducive to the opening of the lotus flowers—as, also, are the eurythmy practices described in this book. Ultimately, however, it is the grace of Christ in connection with the human being's moral/spiritual development that opens the chakras, as indicated in Rudolf Steiner's book *Knowledge of the Higher Worlds* and in Valentin Tomberg's "Lord's Prayer Course." And, as described in the book *Meditations on the Tarot*:

> It is a matter...of choosing between the method of vibrating particular sounds...and the method which has in view spiritual communion with the seven rays of the I AM or the seven aspects of the perfect SELF, who is Jesus Christ. The first method aims at awakening the centers [chakras] *such as they are*; the second aims at the *christianization* of all the centers [lotus flowers], i.e., their *transformation* in conformity with their divine-human prototypes. It is a matter here of the realization of the words of the apostle Paul: "Therefore, if anyone is in Christ, he is a new creation" (2 Corinthians 5:17).[95]

To conclude these considerations, herewith some further indications of Peter Deunov concerning music and singing:

> There exist sentient beings who sing as a chorus in the forest as they roam. There is a harmony within their music.
>
> This singing cannot be perceived with physical ears— it is an etheric singing. And yet, this singing is real: the wind, the storms are musical, but the human ear does not possess the musical sensibility for perceiving this music.
>
> Which is the most sublime of concerts?—the sunrise. In the storm, the thunder, the falling raindrops—I hear music. It is a great concert. We will make an experiment with the sunlight. Let it speak to you: music is hidden within. No harmony of tones more sublime exists than that which emanates from the vibrations of the rays of the Sun...Music and song exist in all things. Every living thing produces sound. Imagine that the whole of Nature is one great orchestra...
>
> The Angels need to open the music centers in the human being that one may hear the songs which are sung and the music which is from above. In the future, the human being will hear the music of the Angels. And an even greater music exists—the divine music. When you hear this music, you will forget everything...
>
> Every tone can be sublime when it is suffused with light, warmth, and power. The mind receives the light of tones; the heart receives the warmth; and the soul—the power. Some music carries predominantly light; other kinds of music—warmth; still others— power...These are the three fundamental qualities of music...Music awakens the Divine within people...
>
> The Gospel of Music is Love.[96]

---

95 *Meditations on the Tarot* (trans. R. Powell; New York: Tarcher-Putnam, 2002), p. 228.

96 Beinsa Douno [Peter Deunov], *The Wellspring of the Good* (Sofia, Bulgaria: Kibea, 2002), pp. 316–319, 375–376.

Chapter 5

THE MACROCOSMIC BACKGROUND TO THE CORE PRACTICE

The Seven Seals of the Apocalypse[97]

The Apocalypse is another name for Revelation, the Third Testament of the Holy Bible after the Old Testament and the New Testament. Apocalypse signifies "unveiling." What is the Third Testament unveiling? Herewith some background to cosmic evolution which will help to answer this question.

Rudolf Steiner describes the occurrence of seven cultural epochs (historical periods of time, each 2,160 years long) contained within each of seven great ages of the evolution of the Earth. These seven great ages are called: Polaris, Hyperborea, Lemuria, Atlantis, fifth great age, sixth great age, seventh great age. We are now in the fifth great age, which began with the Flood, or deluge, that destroyed Atlantis—the Flood that is referred to in connection with Noah and the Ark in the Book of Genesis, chapters 6 to 9. As with each of the preceding great ages, a sequence of seven cultural epochs unfolds within this fifth great age—these seven cultural epochs running parallel to the seven zodiacal ages indicated by the precession of the equinoxes: Cancer, Gemini, Taurus, Aries, Pisces, Aquarius, Capricorn. The Flood took place historically around the time of the transition from the Age of Leo (the last zodiacal age/cultural epoch of Atlantis) to the Age of Cancer (the first zodiacal age/cultural epoch of the fifth great age). It is prophesied that toward the end of the seventh cultural epoch, corresponding to Capricorn, there will be another catastrophe—one of the same order of magnitude as the flood that destroyed the continent of Atlantis that was located in the region of the Atlantic Ocean. At the present time we are living in the fifth cultural epoch, corresponding to Pisces—or, to be more exact, unfolding parallel to the age of Pisces. To summarize: within the fourth stage of evolution—known as *Earth evolution*—we are living in the time of the fifth cultural epoch (Pisces) within the fifth great age.

Three stages of cosmic evolution (known as Ancient Saturn, Ancient Sun, and Ancient Moon) preceded the current fourth stage (that of present Earth evolution) and three stages of cosmic evolution (Future Jupiter, Future Venus, and Future Vulcan) will follow the current stage (Earth evolution). This panoramic image of the evolution of humanity from out of the Godhead, to our present time and into the future, is referred to—albeit in words and images that are not easy to understand—in a veiled way in Revelation. In our time the mysteries of the Apocalypse, which have to do with the deeper truths of our existence, are being unveiled.

In the fourth cultural epoch that ran parallel to the Age of Aries (preceding our present Age of Pisces) something of the mystery of death was unveiled. This took place through the Mystery of Golgotha, which comprises the death, descent into hell, and Resurrection—the overcoming of death by Christ. As the Risen Christ said, "Do not be afraid; I am the first and the last; I am the Living One; I was dead, and behold I am alive for ever and ever! And I hold the keys of death and Hades" (Rev. 1:17–18). Implicit in this message is, "Do not be afraid of death."

---

[97] With grateful acknowledgment to Kelly Calegar, who organized the Chapel Hill 2011 workshops during which these two lectures serving as the basis for this chapter were held, and who transcribed and edited the recording of the lectures. These two lectures—held in Chapel Hill, NC, July 27, 2011, morning and afternoon—have been edited and expanded upon for inclusion in this book. To hear an audio recording of the first lecture: http://www.eastcoastschoolofchoreocosmos.com/Audio_Files.html.

At the present time in the fifth cultural epoch, which began in the year 1414 (1,199 years after the beginning of the zodiacal age of Pisces in AD 215),⁹⁸ it is the mystery of evil that is being unveiled for the divine purpose of the awakening of consciousness and conscience. Whereas the mystery of death was unveiled with the first coming of Christ—unveiled through the Resurrection as the overcoming of death—the mystery of evil is being unveiled now with the Second Coming of Christ, which began in 1899, but which did not become generally perceptible until around 1933.⁹⁹ With the Second Coming, Christ is manifesting not in a physical body, but in his Resurrection body within the etheric aura of the Earth. Thus he is called the Etheric Christ. He is able to manifest in multiple places at the same time. With this we can imagine that just as Christ came to the Earth two thousand years ago, sent by the Father to overcome death ("Do not be afraid"), now he has come to communicate a message along these lines: "I have been sent by the Father to overcome evil." But how is evil to be overcome?

The mystery of evil has to do with an age-old conflict which began when Ahriman (the Persian term for Satan) issued a challenge to Ahura Mazda who, as spiritual research shows, was for the Persians the same being whom we now call Christ. As Rudolf Steiner indicated, Ahura Mazda (also known as Ohrmazd) was Christ as he was beheld by the Persians at that time in his pre-incarnatory form, united with the Sun.¹⁰⁰ In Persian mythology Ahriman was known as the *evil twin*, and Ahura Mazda was spoken of as the *good twin*. According to this mythology, Ahriman was jealous of Ahura Mazda, to whom he issued a challenge, saying that he would win over all human beings to his side and substitute his own creation in the place of divine creation. This challenge was issued because Ahriman saw that all human beings were intrinsically united with the goodness of Ahura Mazda and with his work of divine creation as the Logos, the creative Word. This infuriated Ahriman, who decided to try and win over all human beings to his side and to undertake to substitute his own creation in the place of divine creation.

This ancient Persian mythology stems from the great prophet Zarathustra, the founder of the Zoroastrian religion, known as the *religion of the good*. Zarathustra, the high initiate of the Persian cultural epoch (running parallel with the Age of Gemini, the Twins), beheld Ahura Mazda in the Sun sphere. Ahura Mazda could be translated as "the aura of the Sun." Zarathustra also beheld the opponent of Ahura Mazda, whom he called Ahriman (also known as *Angra Mainyu*). The only way that Ahriman can progress toward his evil goal is through finding human beings who are willing to act in his service. He has had to prepare the ground for this goal over many centuries, and what he gradually foisted upon humanity during this time has given rise to materialism. During the preceding, i.e., the fourth, cultural epoch, which flourished during the 2,160-year period from the time of the founding of Rome in 747 BC until the beginning of the Renaissance (the present, i.e., the fifth, cultural epoch started in AD 414),¹⁰¹ there was

---

98 As described in Robert Powell & Kevin Dann, *The Astrological Revolution* (Great Barrington, MA: SteinerBooks, 2010), the present Age of Pisces lasts 2,160 years and extends from AD 215 to 2375. The corresponding cultural epoch, known as the age of the consciousness soul, began in 1414—after a time-lag of 1,199 years—a period of almost twelve hundred years after the start of the Age of Pisces. The rhythm of 1,199 years is an astronomical period associated with the planet Venus, comprising two 600-year cultural waves. According to Rudolf Steiner, a cultural wave lasts for six hundred years, whereas a cultural epoch—like a zodiacal age—lasts for 2,160 years. The cultural epochs run parallel to the cycle of zodiacal ages, always starting 1,199 years after the start of the corresponding zodiacal age.
99 Robert Powell, "Subnature and the Second Coming," in: *The Inner Life of the Earth* (ed. Paul V. O'Leary; Great Barrington, MA: SteinerBooks, 2008).

100 Rudolf Steiner, *The Deed of Christ and the Opposing Spiritual Powers: Lucifer, Ahriman, and the Asuras*, lecture of March 22, 1909 (CW 107): "Although Christ appeared only later, he was already present.... Zarathustra in ancient Persia spoke of Ahura Mazda.... [He] spoke of Christ" (Great Barrington MA: Steiner Books, 1976).
101 It is difficult to pinpoint the exact beginning of the Renaissance. The architect Brunelleschi is the pioneer who first consciously applied a Renaissance outlook to the arts

hardly anything along the lines of what we could call materialism. Almost everyone had a religious belief and believed that life is created by God. Since then, what has gradually happened in the age of the consciousness soul, with the unfolding of the fifth cultural epoch, has been a slow but steady emancipation from all traditional beliefs and ideas, including emancipation from the belief that we are created by God.

Darwin and the Rise of Materialism

Step by step this program for inculcating materialism as the basic world view of human beings has marched steadily forward in our time. A key figure in the history of this spread of materialism was Charles Darwin. With the introduction of Darwin's ideas in the nineteenth century, primarily through the publication of his book *Origin of the Species* in 1859, a complete reversal from what had existed in human consciousness prior to that time began. In his book Darwin traces his belief that the evolution of the human being took place through various processes of nature, culminating with the purported "final step" asserting that human beings developed from the apes. This idea has led to the view that the human being has evolved to attain the pinnacle of animal creation—a complete reversal from the previous widespread worldview of humanity occupying the lowest rank in the celestial hierarchies: Humanity, Angels, Archangels, Archai, Exusiai, Dynamis, Kyriotetes, Thrones, Cherubim, and Seraphim in service of the Creator.[102] Then, because of Darwin's assertion that human beings evolved from the apes, there began a great—to this day unsuccessful—search for the "missing link" between the human being and the ape. Nevertheless, Darwinistic thinking has taken hold increasingly in the Western world and has greatly contributed to the spread of materialism.

A primary consequence of the introduction of Darwinism has been that it has supplanted the teaching of Moses. This teaching from the Book of Genesis, outlining the activity of the Creator through the seven days of creation, was the backbone of Western civilization in the stream of the Judeo-Christian tradition. The biblical account of the seven days of creation was the most widespread belief, down through the centuries, concerning the origin of the Earth and the human being. On account of Darwinism, however, the biblical narrative was put into question, and more and more people began to doubt Moses' description of creation. The facts collected by Darwin, put together in such a convincing way, proved to be enticing to the human intellect, laying a foundation for the materialistic worldview—a perspective of evolution inspired by Ahriman in which the divine-spiritual element is eradicated altogether. This incursion of ahrimanic thinking into the modern world through Darwinism is just one example alongside many others in the realm of science. For ahrimanic thoughts took hold in many scientific disciplines, signaling the beginning of a triumphant march toward the capture of the minds of people in an ahrimanic worldview that excludes the divine. What was the answer to this situation from the divine-spiritual realms?

It was envisaged that Christ's coming in the etheric would be an answer to the ahrimanic threat facing humanity and the Earth—the threat of a complete take-over by Ahriman. However, the coming of Christ in the etheric realm had to be prepared. To this end, the divine plan was that a succession of three teachers would come to prepare the way. In my book *The Most Holy Trinosophia* I refer to three teachers—without

---

and is thus considered the seminal figure of the Renaissance. His most famous work is the dome of Santa Maria del Fiore cathedral in Florence. It was in 1419 that he received the commission to design the dome.

102 See, for example, Dante's *Divine Comedy* for a classic exposition of the world view of humanity as part of the "great chain of being" extending through the spiritual hierarchies to the Creator. Dante uses the Latin names, rather than the Greek names favored by Rudolf Steiner—for the ranks Archai (Principalities), Exusiai (Powers), Dynamis (Mights or Virtues), and Kyriotetes (Dominions). Note that "Thrones" is from the Greek "Thronoi" and that Seraphim and Cherubim are both Hebrew names.

explicitly naming them—who incarnated at successive intervals of time as ambassadors for the coming of Christ in the etheric, with Rudolf Steiner being the first of these three to incarnate. Rudolf Steiner's task was to build a bridge between science and spirituality, and thus to contribute to the overcoming of materialism, which had arisen on the foundation of scientific thinking—Darwinism being just one example of this. It is interesting that Steiner was born in 1861, just two years after the publication of Darwin's work *The Origin of the Species*. What Rudolf Steiner arrived at by applying his method of spiritual-scientific research is that the genesis of the human being together with the Earth involves a process of cosmic stages of evolution—specifically, the seven days of creation from ancient Saturn, through ancient Sun, ancient Moon, present Earth, future Jupiter, future Venus, and future Vulcan. He brought this panoramic vista of spiritual evolution to expression in 1909 with the publication of his book *An Outline of Esoteric Science* (originally published as *Occult Science: An Outline*). This book was—and is—the answer to Darwinism. Out of Rudolf Steiner's depth of spiritual experience, presented in such a clear and scientific—yet spiritual—way, one can come to understand that the genesis of humanity and the Earth is from divine-spiritual realms according to a divine plan. This depiction indicates the true *origin of the species*.

Rudolf Steiner's teaching concerning the divine plan of evolution provides a modern form of Moses' teaching of the seven days of creation—a teaching which, in contrast to the biblical account, speaks to the intellectual capacities of our times. In our time, neither pure science nor pure spirituality suffices for seekers of truth. The demand of our time is for perspectives that have a solid foundation in contemporary thinking and yet also open a path to the spirit. The majestic pictures of spiritual evolution unfolding in seven great stages, as described by Rudolf Steiner, bring profound meaning to those rooted in the scientific world view who at the same time are also open to spiritual perspectives—in short, who have a consciousness which seeks to bridge science and spirituality. This modern panorama of the genesis of humanity that came through Rudolf Steiner was the answer from the spiritual world to the materialistic assertion of Darwinism.

The First Seal

In 1907, two years prior to the publication of *An Outline of Esoteric Science*, Rudolf Steiner artistically portrayed the seven cosmic stages of evolution in seven images drawn from Revelation. He called these seven images the "seven seals." The first image, or seal, portrays the description from chapter 1 of Revelation of the Cosmic Christ who is holding seven stars (represented by planetary symbols) in his right hand, which are arranged in a certain sequence: Saturn, Sun, Moon, Mars, Mercury, Jupiter, and Venus—where Mars and Mercury are the two halves of Earth evolution.[103] Given that these planets are arranged in this order, which is the sequence of the cosmic stages of evolution, and given that the first seal, that of the Cosmic Christ, offers an archetypal image of the Etheric Christ, this image reveals that the new teaching of the seven days of creation that Rudolf Steiner brought into the world was in service to the Etheric Christ—to Christ in his Second Coming. This is very important to grasp, because—seen through the lens of the divine plan—Christ's Second Coming is to wrest humanity and the Earth from the clutches of Ahriman, and this means, eventually, the overcoming of materialistic thinking.[104] The emergence of

---

103   See pages 60 and 109 for a reproduction of the first seal, showing the Cosmic Christ. The stages of cosmic evolution depicted by the seven stars in the right hand of the Cosmic Christ are Saturn, Sun, Moon, Earth, Jupiter, and Venus—with Earth evolution divided into two halves: the first half leading up to Christ's coming being the descending (incarnatory) phase associated with Mars, and the ascending (spiritualizing) phase, inaugurated by the coming of Christ, encompassing the second half of Earth evolution that is associated with Mercury.

104   Rudolf Steiner describes how the task of the present—i.e., the fifth—cultural epoch (the "fifth post-Atlantean epoch" as he calls it), is to completely eradicate ("extirpate") materialism, indicating that this will be achieved

Rudolf Steiner and his new teaching of the seven days of creation—filling the gap left by the displacement from Western civilization of Moses' teaching of the seven days of creation—provided humanity with an antidote to Darwinism, preparing the way for this event of the Second Coming of Christ.

With regard to the image of the first seal, depicted above, we can come to understand its meaning in terms of the great imagination of the Cosmic Christ from Revelation, chapter 1, where the Cosmic Christ speaks, "I am the Alpha and the Omega" (Revelation 1:8). These words point to the fact that Christ is the overseer of all seven days of creation beginning with ancient Saturn (Alpha) and ending with future Vulcan (Omega). The first seal has an inner connection with ancient Saturn—Christ is the Alpha (the beginning)—and at the same time Christ is the Omega (the end), the goal, or the final stage of the seven cosmic stages of evolution, which is Vulcan. Although Vulcan is not represented on the first seal by a planetary symbol—as discussed above, the planetary symbols in the right hand of the Cosmic Christ are: Saturn, Sun, Moon, Mars, Mercury, Jupiter, Venus—Vulcan is the "octave" of the Saturn stage of evolution; it is the same "tone" but at a higher octave. Ancient Saturn was the stage of the laying of the foundation of the physical body, and future Vulcan is the stage of perfecting the development of the Resurrection body, which is the transformed, spiritualized physical body.

Each of the three future stages of cosmic evolution will be a metamorphosis of one of the three past stages of evolution. The example of Vulcan (the "octave") as the transformed Saturn (first) stage of cosmic evolution has already been given. During ancient Saturn the foundation for the physical body was laid. At a certain point in the ancient Saturn evolution, into the coldness and immobility of pure *being*, the spiritual hierarchy of the Thrones, known as the Spirits of Will, poured forth their forces of divine will, and the resulting warmth became the seed of the human being's physical body. A metamorphosis of this will occur during future Vulcan with the perfecting of the development of the Resurrection body, which is the transformed and spiritualized (Christ-permeated) physical body. Part three of the exercise Putting on the Resurrection Body relates to this level.

Summarizing part 3: The higher consciousness that is developed through the transformation and spiritualization of the physical body—eventually to become the Resurrection body—is called "*atma* consciousness." To bring this higher consciousness to realization, the seven sayings of the Risen Christ are allowed to stream through the I into the seven chakras of the astral body and from there they are mirrored in the etheric body, then, finally, are echoed within the physical body. By living the words spoken by St. Paul in his letter to the Galatians (2:20), "Not I, but Christ in me," the I aligns with Christ and can become a vessel for the in-streaming of the I AM (Christ). A path toward the aligning of the I with the I AM is indicated in the "Christ in me" meditation outlined in this book and—from another perspective—also in the I A O meditation described in chapter 4.

When Christ says, "I am the Alpha and the Omega," relating to the image of the Cosmic Christ holding seven stars in his right hand, he announces himself as the beginning and the end of the whole process of evolution. But Christ is also the overseer of everything

---

through a "more spiritual being" (i.e., the Etheric Christ) counteracting materialism. "Humanity will come to a true healing when one works so thoroughly in the life of spirit that one knows absolutely that the fifth post-Atlantean epoch is there for the purpose of extirpating materialism from the general evolution of humanity. A more spiritual being, however, must counteract materialism"—Rudolf Steiner, *The Reappearance of Christ in the Etheric*, (Great Barrington MA: SteinerBooks, 2003) chapter 10, lecture of November 18, 1917.

that happens in between the beginning and the end. With these stages of evolution, Christ is the one who, through his deeds, which are deeds of sacrifice, brings each phase of evolution to its next level of unfolding. Christ's deeds of sacrifice during the various stages of cosmic evolution are described in a remarkable way in a series of lectures which Valentin Tomberg held in 1939 in Rotterdam, seven lectures on "The Four Sacrifices of Christ and the Reappearance of Christ in the Etheric." These lectures are published as an appendix to his book *Christ and Sophia*.[105]

Having looked at the metamorphosis from ancient Saturn (first stage) to future Vulcan (final stage), both of which are related—as prime interval (Saturn, first seal) and octave (Vulcan, seventh seal)—let us now contemplate the correspondence between the second stage, that of ancient Sun, imaged in the second seal, and the sixth stage, that of future Venus, related to the sixth seal.

The Second Seal and the Sixth Seal

Looking at the correspondence between the second and sixth seals, this has to do with the correspondence between the ancient Sun (second) and the future Venus (sixth) stages of evolution. In the image of the second seal there is in the center *the Lamb as if slain*. This relates to the creation of the human etheric body. For the human etheric body was created

by an out-pouring of etheric substance, entailing sacrifice on the part of lofty spiritual beings dwelling upon the Sun who, in turn, were guided by the Lamb from a still higher level. The four holy living creatures around the Lamb represent the four different qualities of the etheric, which are in turn related to the four elements: the Lion (warmth ether, element of Fire), Eagle (light ether, element of Air), Waterbearer (tone ether, element of Water), and Bull (life ether, element of Earth). Generally speaking, according to the constitution of the human etheric body, one element usually predominates, and this gives rise to the four temperaments: choleric, if the element of Fire is predominant; sanguine, Air; phlegmatic, Water; and melancholic, Earth.

Although Revelation refers to the twenty-four elders in connection with the text of the second seal, the twenty-four elders are not depicted explicitly on the image of the second seal, but are there implicitly in the hours of the clock around the outside of the second seal—remembering the twenty-four hours in the cycle of the day. The etheric body is a time body, attuned to the unfolding of the various cosmic rhythms—that of the Earth being the cycle of the day. The second seal has an inner correspondence with ancient Sun, when the human etheric body was bestowed upon the human being. Looking from the vantage point of present Earth to the future, to the next-but-one stage of evolution represented by the sixth seal, the image of this seal is that of Michael holding the dragon underfoot, bound with a great chain, and holding in his raised left hand the key to the bottomless pit. In this image the dragon (the ahrimanic influence in the etheric body) has been cast out of the etheric body and has been bound through

the power of truth and justice (righteousness) represented by Michael, who also holds the key to Ahriman's realm known as *Sheol* (Hebrew), which is the bottomless pit. This seal relates to future Venus, which will be the future evolutionary condition that will be a metamorphosis of the ancient Sun evolution.

---

105 Valentin Tomberg, *Christ and Sophia* (Great Barrington, MA: SteinerBooks, 2006).

Since the incarnation of the divine I AM—Christ—the human etheric body is able to receive the transformative power of the I AM streaming through the I into the etheric. This is the endeavor of the second part of the exercise *Putting on the Resurrection Body*. The seven sayings (words) of Christ from the Cross are expressions of Divine Love, which can stream into the seven chakras of the astral body—and then from the astral body, with the help of eurythmy, into the etheric body.[106] Thereby the human being is able to ascend on a path of further development through transformation of the etheric body by way of the activity of the I AM through the I, toward the future Venus stage of evolution, where the etheric body will be transformed and spiritualized through becoming more and more permeated by the love of Christ—as made manifest in the historical archetype of the healing powers of Christ and in the stages of the Passion, especially at the stage of the Crucifixion (see part 2 of the exercise *Putting on the Resurrection Body*). The higher consciousness that is developed through the transformation of the etheric body is called *buddhi consciousness*. To bring this higher consciousness to realization, the I AM of Christ has to stream through the I into the human etheric body. (A path toward the aligning of the I with the I AM is indicated in the "Christ in me" meditation outlined in this book.)

Then, as described in this book in relation to the second stage of the exercise *Putting on the Resurrection Body*, the love of Christ streaming through the seven sayings of Christ from the Cross is allowed to radiate into the seven chakras as a transforming power, while holding the archetype of Christ's Crucifixion in consciousness. As indicated in connection with this exercise, there is a saying from the Cross relating to each of the seven chakras—for example, "Today you shall be with me in paradise" is the Christ mantra for the transformation of the heart chakra by bringing the love of Christ into this chakra when the mantra "Today you shall be with me in paradise" is allowed to resonate within the heart chakra. The etheric body is to be transformed on the human being's path of development in order to attain the level of Crucifixion—with accompanying *buddhi* consciousness—by the end of the cosmic stage of evolution known as *future Venus*. The transformation of the etheric body is a stage (to be fully attained on future Venus) on the path toward the Resurrection body. Thus, the permeation of the I by the I AM is the goal of the second half of Earth evolution, where we stand at present, and the transfiguration of the astral body through the I AM streaming through the I into the astral body is the goal of future Jupiter. Then the transformation of the etheric body through the I AM streaming through the I into the etheric body is the goal of future Venus—and this is the ideal, also, of eurythmy: to transform the etheric body into a Christ-permeated, love-filled, radiant healing body. A start toward this goal can be undertaken through working with the seven sayings (words) from the Cross at the second stage of the practice described in this book as *Putting on the Resurrection Body*. This process of transformation of the etheric body into *buddhi*, also known as *life spirit*, is the penultimate stage on the evolutionary path—it is the stage prior to the transformation of the physical body into the Resurrection body (*atma* or spirit human), which is the goal of the future Vulcan stage of evolution.

---

106 Eurythmy is one way of working upon the transformation of the etheric body. There are other ways/practices as well, which can help to facilitate the carrying over of the Christ impulse into the etheric body. Here, again, it is important to emphasize that it is in particular the working in eurythmy with the words of Christ that helps to carry over the Christ impulse into the etheric body, when undertaken in the right way—and this is dependent not only upon one's inner attitude toward Christ but it is always a matter, also, of the grace of Christ.

The Third Seal and the Fifth Seal

Let us now look at the correspondence between the third and fifth seals, which has to do with the correspondence between the ancient Moon (third) and the future Jupiter (fifth) stages of evolution. In the image of the third seal there is in the center the *book with seven seals*. This relates to the creation of the human astral body, for the book with seven seals represents the human astral body. The seven seals in this book are the chakras, which are the seven primary organs within the human astral body. The third seal has an inner correspondence with ancient Moon, when the human astral body began to flower. This was prior to the incarnation of the Divine I AM, the Christ, during the present Earth stage of evolution, to bring to birth the true I of the human being.[107] Looking to the future, to the next stage of evolution, the fifth seal is an image of Sophia, the woman clothed with the Sun, with the Moon under her feet, and a crown of twelve stars upon her head. This seal relates to future Jupiter, which will be the future evolutionary condition that will be a metamorphosis of the ancient Moon evolution.

To elaborate, since the incarnation of the Divine I AM—Christ—the human astral body is able to receive the transformative power of the I AM streaming through the I. Thereby the human being is able to ascend on a path of further development through purification of the astral body by way of the activity of the I AM through the I, toward the future Jupiter stage of evolution, where the astral body will be transformed and spiritualized through becoming more and more permeated by the light of Christ—as manifested in the historical archetype of the Transfiguration of Christ on Mt. Tabor (see part 1 of the exercise *Putting on the Resurrection Body*). The higher consciousness that is developed through the transfiguration of the astral body is called *manas consciousness*. To bring this higher consciousness to realization, the I AM of Christ has to stream through the I into the human astral body. By living the words spoken by St. Paul in his letter to the Galatians (2:20), "Not I, but Christ in me," the I aligns with Christ and can become a vessel for the in-streaming of the I AM. A path toward the aligning of the I with the I AM is indicated in the "Christ in me" meditation and in the meditation "A Star Is above My Head," outlined in chapter 3 and—from another perspective—in the I A O meditation described in chapter 4.

Then, as described in this book in relation to the first stage of the exercise *Putting on the Resurrection Body*, the light of Christ streaming through the seven I AM sayings is allowed to radiate into the seven chakras as a transforming power, while holding the archetype of Christ's Transfiguration in consciousness. As indicated in connection with this exercise, there is an I AM saying relating to each of the seven chakras—for example, "I AM the Resurrection and the life" is the Christ mantra for the transformation of the crown chakra by bringing the light of Christ into this chakra when the mantra "I AM the Resurrection and the life" is allowed to resonate within the crown chakra. All seven chakras of the human astral body are to be transfigured on the human being's path of development in order to attain the level of Transfiguration—with accompanying *manas* consciousness—by the end of the cosmic stage of evolution known as *future Jupiter*. The transfiguration of the astral body is a stage (to be

---

107 The I (self) is the innermost core of the human being and is an expression of the spirit, just as the astral body reflects the soul, and the etheric body sustains the physical body.

Chapter 5: The Macrocosmic Background to the Core Practice

fully attained on future Jupiter) on the path toward the Resurrection body (which in turn will be fully attained on future Vulcan). Thus, the permeation of the I by the I AM is the goal of the second half of Earth evolution, where we stand at present, and the transfiguration of the astral body through the I AM streaming through the I into the astral body is the goal of future Jupiter. A start toward this goal can be undertaken through working with the seven I AM sayings of Christ at the first stage of the practice described in this book as *Putting on the Resurrection Body*. What is to be found in the Bible in connection with this process of transformation of the astral body into *manas*, also known as *spirit self*?

There are some profound words in the fifth chapter of Revelation pertaining to the third seal, the image of which depicts the book with seven seals at its center:

> And I saw a mighty angel proclaiming with a loud voice, "Who is worthy to receive the book and open its seven seals?" And no one in Heaven or on Earth or beneath the earth was...found worthy to receive the book and open its seven seals. Then one of the elders said to me, "Weep not. Lo, the Lion of the tribe of Judah, the Root of David, has conquered...He can receive the book and open its seven seals." (Revelation 5:2–5)

An angel says, "Who is worthy to receive the book and open its seven seals?" For a time, John is completely downcast, to the point of weeping, because there is no one who is worthy. Then, however, one of the twenty-four elders says to him, "The Lion of Judah...can receive the book and open its seven seals." That is a very clear and important indication that the opening of the chakras, which are the seven seals in the human being, is a work that is undertaken together with the Lamb, or Christ, who is referred to here as the Lion of Judah. It has to be borne in mind that the third seal relates to the ancient Moon stage of evolution, during which the astral body was bestowed upon the human being, and that the book with the seven seals is an image for the astral body with its seven primary organs, which are the seven chakras. The seven lotus flowers (chakras) are the seven seals within the human being.

That the seven chakras or seals are to be opened by Christ is important in relation to the following considerations. Rudolf Steiner points out that there is a counter impulse to Christ's coming in the etheric. Through the Etheric Christ—as indicated in the exercises described in this book—there is an opportunity to develop spiritually with Christ's help and guidance. On the other hand, according to Rudolf Steiner, the counter impulse to that which is shepherded by Christ is an occult schooling offered by Ahriman, who also will open up spiritual faculties, but *not objectively*—people will be locked into their own clairvoyance, which will not relate to objective reality but will be a counterfeit or "virtual" reality. Many of the different spiritual paths offered in the world at the present time promise clairvoyance, the unfolding of psychic powers, developing the chakras, and so on and so forth. Rudolf Steiner warns about possible dangers associated with this, and Christ even said, "False Christs and false prophets will appear and perform great signs and miracles to deceive even the elect—if that were possible" (Matthew 24:24). Thus, with respect to all spiritual teachings we have to ask: Is it true? Is there moral depth to it? Is it relevant? Does it resonate with what I already know to be true? For it is always a matter of *truth*. And, as Christ said, "I AM the way, the *truth*, and the life." We see how important the words of Revelation are: *It is the Lamb, or Christ, the Lion of Judah, who is worthy to open the seven seals, the chakras*. The "opening of the seven seals" through Christ is a primary goal of the exercises outlined in this book, exercises which are described in relation to the words of Christ such as the seven I AM sayings, the seven sayings from the Cross, the seven sayings of the Risen One, and the seven THOU ART sayings in relation to the Cosmic Christ.

Through the unveiling of the mystery of the third and fifth seals one can begin to grasp the significance of the development of the chakras through the words of Christ. It was the Russian esotericist Valentin Tomberg who revealed that the seven I

AM sayings of Christ are mantric formulae for the seven chakras. This correspondence, as well as the other correspondences indicated by Valentin Tomberg—the correspondences to the chakras of the seven sayings from the Cross and the seven sayings of the Risen One—form the central content of the Core Practice of *Putting on the Resurrection Body* described in this book. Previously, in my booklet *Morning Meditation in Eurythmy*, I had already developed the rudiments of working with this profound esoteric teaching of Valentin Tomberg concerning the correspondences between the words (sayings) of Christ and the seven chakras.[108] Now, in this book, his teaching is developed and expanded upon as a contribution to eurythmy at this time of the celebration of one hundred years since the birth of eurythmy. What is outlined in this book is a way of deepening into the path of "opening the seven seals" (which are the seven chakras), and this practice is taken up here in partnership with Christ—calling upon Christ who is the shepherd for this path.

---

108 Robert Powell, *Morning Meditation in Eurythmy* (San Francisco: Sophia Foundation of North America, 2005)—www.sophiafoundation.org.

Four Levels of Putting on the Resurrection Body

What has been developed and brought to expression in the booklet *Morning Meditation in Eurythmy*, which is expanded upon and deepened into in this book, takes its point of departure from the *Morning Meditation* given by Rudolf Steiner and includes the teaching of Valentin Tomberg regarding the correspondences of the words of Christ to the chakras—and it also includes the gestures of eurythmy. Valentin Tomberg not only taught the correspondences of the "I AM sayings" of Christ with the seven chakras, but he also taught the correspondences of the "seven words (sayings) from the Cross" with the seven chakras. In addition, he taught the correspondences between the "seven sayings of the Risen Christ" and the seven chakras. These three sets of words (sayings) from Christ correspond respectively to the first three stages of the exercise of *Putting on the Resurrection Body*.

In the fourth stage of *Putting on the Resurrection Body*, with the words "I shall find myself within the Godhead of the world," we work with the correspondences between the seven seals and the seven chakras. These seven images or seals are macrocosmic seals reflecting the vast panorama of our path of emergence from the Godhead and our future evolution. These macrocosmic seals are mirrored in us microcosmically in the seven chakras, and serve as very powerful images in relation to opening the chakras.

One can complete all four of these stages of the sequence *Putting on the Resurrection Body* on a daily basis each morning—or at any other time of day—in a relatively short space of time, once one is familiar with them. One can go through all four of these levels of correspondence with the chakras, and if one does this on a daily basis one finds that day by day an increasing resonance is created and the chakras begin to respond more and more to the words and sayings of Christ. In other words, there is a direct relationship of Christ, the Lamb of God, to the seven chakras (the microcosmic seven seals), and when we work with the words of Christ, this takes effect upon the chakras—in different ways at each level. Of course, it is always a matter of grace and having the right attitude—see Rudolf Steiner's words on pages 28 to 29 from his esoteric lesson held on September 24, 1907, concerning the right inner attitude toward Christ.

To summarize the four levels of *Putting on the Resurrection Body*: at the first level (Transfiguration), the I AM sayings bring the *light* of Christ into the seven chakras; at the second level (Crucifixion) the words from the Cross bring the *love* of Christ into the chakras; at the third level (Resurrection) the seven sayings of the Risen One bring in the *life* of Christ—the *eternal life* of Christ—into the seven chakras. Then at the fourth level—working with the seven seals—through grace the *peace* of Christ may be received into the seven chakras. As indicated in the following, the peace of Christ stems from a realm beyond the foreseeable human stages of evolution, beyond Vulcan.

Receiving the light, love, and life of Christ contributes to the realization of purification on various levels of the human being. What comes to expression with the light of Christ takes effect in the astral body as the light of *manas*, or the spirit self. (*Manas* is the Hindu term for spirit self.) It refers to the realization of the spirit-permeated—or I AM (Christ)-permeated, transfigured astral body. When the light of Christ is received into the astral body, this light differentiates into seven colored rays on the astral level, each corresponding to a particular chakra, and these seven rays of light stream into and through the various chakras. Buddha at his enlightenment, and Christ at the Transfiguration, are examples of those whose astral bodies were radiantly pure, manifesting the light of *manas*—as also was the case with the Virgin Mary.

With regard to the *love* of Christ, what comes to expression is *buddhi*, or the life spirit. (*Buddhi* is the Hindu term for life spirit.) This refers to the realization of the spirit-permeated and transformed etheric body. When one—through grace—receives the love of Christ into the chakras, this love differentiates into seven moral tones, each corresponding to a particular chakra, and these seven moral tones stream into and through the chakras supersensibly, resonating from the astral into the etheric, so that in the course of time the etheric body is transformed into love-permeated, healing substance. The etheric body of Jesus Christ was completely transformed into *buddhi* and thus was a transmitter of healing, raying out love-permeated etheric substance. He is an example of one whose presence emanated the healing force of love-permeated, transformed life substance.

With respect to the *life* of the Risen Christ, this is an expression of *atma*, or the spirit human, which is also known as the Resurrection body. (*Atma* is the Hindu term for spirit human.) This refers to the realization of the Resurrection body as the spirit-permeated physical body, into which the power of Divine Love works so deeply that the substance of the physical body is turned into spirit: spirit-permeated matter. When one is graced with receiving the life of Christ into the chakras, they become increasingly "solarized" (Sun filled), which attunes them more and more to the Central Sun, the throne of the Father, who wields the power of *atma*, just as the Son is the regent of *buddhi*, and the Holy Spirit is the transmitter of *manas*.

Just as the Christianizing of the I (in the spirit of St. Paul's words, "Not I, but Christ in me") is the goal of the present Earth stage of evolution, so the development of *manas, buddhi,* and *atma* is the goal of the three future stages of evolution: Jupiter, Venus, and Vulcan. These three future stages of evolution of the human being are within the seven stages of cosmic evolution from ancient Saturn to future Vulcan. Beyond this, beyond Vulcan, the *peace* of Christ is transcendental to these stages of evolution. The peace of Christ is actually the *source* for the light, love, and life of Christ. When we come to the fourth stage of *Putting on the Resurrection Body*, the focus is upon the Cosmic Christ, seven aspects of whom are revealed in the seven seals of the Apocalypse—the essence of the Cosmic Christ being eternal peace. At the fourth stage of *Putting on the Resurrection Body* we strive to attune to this transcendental level of expression: eternal peace ("the peace that surpasses understanding"—Philippians 4:7). It is this transcendental level of eternal peace to which the Cosmic Christ ascended—beginning his ascent forty days after his Resurrection—and it is this transcendental level from which he has returned by way of his descent, his Second Coming (*parousia*), entering the Earth's etheric aura during the 1930s of the last century.

Rudolf Steiner was the prophet of Christ's Second Coming. As described in this book, the birth of eurythmy into the world one hundred years ago through Rudolf Steiner was a consequence of his relationship—as the "John the Baptist" of Christ's Second Coming—to the Cosmic Christ, to whom Rudolf Steiner referred as the Etheric Christ, emphasizing his return into the Earth's etheric aura. The arising of eurythmy as a new etheric form of movement unfolded in tandem with Rudolf Steiner's proclamation of the coming of the Etheric Christ. Eurythmy thus has a special relationship with Christ in the etheric, and it is the intention of this book to help an ever-greater circle of people enter into a living connection with the Etheric Christ through the eurythmy exercises described in this work.

Putting on the Resurrection Body: Protection against Ahrimanic Encroachment

In addition to this intention there is another purpose to this book. In my book *Prophecy-Phenomena-Hope: The Real Meaning of* 2012 two central prophecies of Rudolf Steiner are described.[109] The first prophecy, starting 1909, was that of the return of Christ in the etheric. The second prophecy, from November 1, 1919, concerns the incarnation of the being whom he referred to as Ahriman (more generally known as Satan). *Prophecy-Phenomena-Hope* starts by considering this second prophecy in relation to the present time and then looks at various phenomena which indicate that the ahrimanic/materialistic influences are becoming stronger and stronger. The last part of the book discusses the hope for humanity and the Earth for the future, which is the Etheric Christ.

This new book, outlining the practice of *Putting on the Resurrection Body*, offers a path not only for coming into a relationship with the Etheric Christ but also offers a degree of protection against the steady encroachment of ahrimanic influences such as those described in *Prophecy-Phenomena-Hope*. The combination of the words of Christ in correspondence with the chakras, together with eurythmy, comprises learning, initially at a rudimentary level, something of the language of the Etheric Christ. This practice can lead to a certain degree of protection against ahrimanic influences through aligning ourselves in body, soul, and spirit with Christ. When we consider the words of Christ, "Heaven and Earth will pass away, but my words will never pass away," we can grasp that when we are working with the words of Christ in the way described in this book we are working with something eternal, allowing it to penetrate into the depths of our being through our chakras. And when we begin to take these words into ourselves on a daily basis they begin to create a condition—the putting on of the Resurrection body—that endures beyond death.

This practice—using an earthly analogy—is like a deposit into our heavenly bank account. We each have a heavenly bank account and the deposits into this account are our good and noble thoughts, our pure and elevated feelings, and our selfless deeds—all of which connect us with Christ, Sophia, and Michael. That is our heavenly bank account. Many people nowadays think only of their earthly bank account. We also have a heavenly bank account and, as well, a bank account with Mother Earth. Everything we do toward nature and her creatures is recorded and remembered. Those human beings who work for the redemption of

---

109 Robert Powell, *Prophecy-Phenomena-Hope: The Real Meaning of* 2012 (Great Barrington, MA: SteinerBooks, 2011).

the Earth are depositing into their bank account with Mother Nature. Those human beings who never give nature a thought will have an empty bank account. It can even go into the negative. It is important to hold this in consciousness. Materialism has cut us off not only from the heavenly world, but also from Mother Nature—this great Being of Mother Earth, who is a living organism, but who has unfortunately come to be regarded simply as a thing that can be plundered and utilized at will. *It is not only for our sakes but also for the sake of Mother Nature that we need to become equipped to counteract what is coming through Ahriman and as a consequence of materialism.*

In the 2011 and 2012 issues of the *Journal for Star Wisdom* there is a translation of part of the visions of Daniel Andreev from his book *Rose of the World*.[110] *Rosa Mira*, as the Russian book whose English title is *Rose of the World* is known, is an enormously valuable work by this Russian mystic and poet, written in Russian, and read by hundreds of thousands of Russians. The last part of the book contains Daniel Andreev's visions of the coming of the Antichrist, which he goes into in great detail. No one has described this in such extraordinary detail as he has. Because of the significance of this hitherto (in English) unpublished material, I have translated part of it in the 2011 *Journal for Star Wisdom*[111] because it is very significant in terms of understanding where we are in world history at the present time.

Taken together with the works of Rudolf Steiner, in particular holding the larger picture he offers through the seven seals of the Apocalypse, it emerges that the visions of Daniel Andreev come to expression in the fifth and sixth seals. With the image of the fifth seal we see beneath Sophia the great red dragon, which has to do with Lucifer—but only a certain aspect of Lucifer, because there is one aspect of Lucifer that has been on an ascending path of redemption since Christ's sacrifice on Golgotha. However, there is still part of Lucifer that is unredeemed, and that is what is represented here by the red dragon. On the other hand, in the sixth seal we see Michael coming down from Heaven, holding in his hand the key to the bottomless pit, and a great chain with which he binds the dragon. That dragon is Ahriman and Michael is holding him underfoot. Let us recall that the fifth seal is about the development of the spirit self (*manas*). It is above all Sophia—working together with Christ—who helps us on the path of evolution of consciousness leading to the development of *manas*, the purified astral body. The sixth seal, on the other hand, is about the development of *buddhi* or life spirit, and here the Archangel Michael—together with Christ—helps us.

Manas, or spirit self, is the transformed astral body, and it was in the astral body that the intervention of Lucifer took place at the time of the Fall. When we are working on the astral body we are working on the transformation of the luciferic nature within us, which comes to expression as desire, passion, instincts, and so forth. And it is Sophia's purity that helps us to tame our desires and passions and to place ourselves in service of the divine plan. But we see in the fifth seal the red dragon that is trying to devour Sophia. She is a being of ineffable purity, who is helping us forward on the path toward *manas* consciousness. As described in my book *Christ & the Maya Calendar*, the red dragon emerged historically with the Bolshevik revolution and with everything that followed in the wake thereof, in the form of communism.[112]

To understand this historical manifestation of the red dragon, it is helpful to consider the plan of evolution.

---

110 *Journal for Star Wisdom* (ed. Robert Powell; Great Barrington, MA: SteinerBooks, 2010), pp. 12–15. The original title of Daniel Andreev's book (written in Russian) is *Rosa Mira*. The first half of *Rosa Mira* was translated into English and published as *The Rose of the World* (Great Barrington, MA: SteinerBooks, 1997). The translation and publication of some of Andreev's material in the *Journal for Star Wisdom* is from the second half of *Rosa Mira* (not yet translated into English).
111 Published also in Robert Powell, *Prophecy-Phenomena-Hope*, appendix 1.

112 Robert Powell & Kevin Dann, *Christ & the Maya Calendar* (Great Barrington, MA: SteinerBooks, 2009), chapter 8.

The divine plan is that a new culture—called by Daniel Andreev the *Rose of the World*—is to arise in Russia and the Slavic world in the age of Aquarius, whereby this new culture will have the task of preparing in seed form the development of *manas* consciousness under the guidance of Sophia working together with Christ. This new culture will arise initially in the Slavic world and will then spread around the globe to become a world culture. This new culture could also be called the "Sophia culture," seeing that Sophia is known as the "Rose of the World" on an archetypal level and that she is the inspirer of the new Sophia culture. Preparation for this new culture was underway in Russia through figures such as the great Russian philosopher Vladimir Solovyov (1853–1900), the founder of the spiritual movement known as "Russian Sophiology," and through others in Russia and the Slavic world.[113] This preparation was suddenly and devastatingly interrupted when the Bolshevik revolution broke out in 1917, which brought the "Reds" to power. Seen in the context of the unfolding of history, against the background of the meta-history presented in the fifth seal of the Apocalypse, this was the attack of the red dragon on Sophia.

What is the message of the sixth seal? The development of *buddhi* (life spirit), which on an archetypal level is the theme of the sixth seal, relating to the sixth stage of cosmic evolution (future Venus), entails the transformation of the etheric body. And eurythmy, as an etheric form of movement, works upon the transformation of the etheric body. Through Rudolf Steiner's collaboration with the Etheric Christ, the gift of eurythmy came into the world one hundred years ago. As indicated already, eurythmy can lead on the one hand to an ever-deeper relationship with the Etheric Christ, and on the other hand offers a degree of protection against the ahrimanic encroachment into the etheric body which, as described in *Prophecy–Phenomena–Hope*, is well underway and is accelerating in intensity at the present time. The image of the sixth seal shows Michael with the dragon underfoot, bound with a chain. Michael—as a mighty leader of the celestial hosts—is at the right hand of Christ in the struggle with the ahrimanic forces symbolized by the dragon. We receive help and support from Michael in the battle with Ahriman, which is also a battle for the human etheric body and for the entire etheric aura of the Earth. How does the encroachment of ahrimanic forces into the etheric body and into the Earth's etheric realm in which the etheric body is immersed take place?

It is, in the first place, materialism that gives Ahriman an opportunity to intervene into the human etheric body. By and large, materialistic thinking is of a mechanistic nature—a thinking that applies well to the physical level of existence but is ill suited to come into relationship with the etheric level. This materialistic, mechanistic thought has the effect of hardening the etheric body—ahrimanic influences harden and scleroticize—by way of removing the human being from the living flow of thought activity that belongs naturally to the etheric level of existence. In earlier times—for example, at the time of Plato and Aristotle—thinking was more fluid and organic, and was thus better suited to come into relationship with the etheric realm—a realm that is "watery" in comparison to the solid earth. Materialistic thinking, in general, represents a descent from the level of "living, organic thinking" to a level of "materialistic, mechanistic thinking." This can be thought of as a "fall"—in the following sense.

Compare a sage, who has attained self-mastery, with someone who is unable to control their instinctual urges. In the latter case, it can be observed that untamed desires and passions rule the astral body, whereas the sage has exercised his consciousness, his I, to establish mastery over his passions and desires. His I has tamed them. Going back into the far-distant past, there was

---

113 Also important as a great spiritual teacher who was a contemporary of Rudolf Steiner and who through his teaching was imparting the principles to the Bulgarian people (and the Slavic people in general) of the new coming culture based on love and wisdom is Peter Deunov (1864–1944), also known as Beinsa Douno, who is referred to in chapter 4; see also http://www.beinsa-douno.net and http://en.wikipedia.org/wiki/Peter_Deunov.

a time when the astral body was more connected with the heavens—hence the name "astral body," which indicates a relationship with the stars (Latin: *astra*). Due to Lucifer's intervention into the astral body, however, the astral body became permeated with desire, which led to the event known as the Fall that took place long ago. At that time, the I was generally not developed, and human beings "fell" out of their cosmic connection with the starry realms and became more and more bound up with the Earth. From an evolutionary perspective, this was a necessary step, in order for the I to develop. As part of the Divine Plan, the Fall was allowed to happen. Although the consequences—toil, suffering, and death—were devastating for human beings, the possibility was given of freedom and independence, through the development of the I. And Christ's incarnation was for the purpose of overcoming the consequences of the Fall, culminating with the overcoming of death through Resurrection.

The Second Fall

Just as in the far-distant past humankind went through the Fall as a result of Lucifer's penetration into the astral body, so in our time humanity is going through a second Fall through Ahriman's intervention into the etheric body. Through materialistic thinking the way was paved for the second Fall. Our thoughts are deposited in the etheric body, and materialistic thinking—by its very nature hardened and empty (devoid of life)—brings about a hardening and hollowing out of the etheric body. Then with the advent of technological media—during Rudolf Steiner's lifetime—it became increasingly possible for ahrimanic thoughts to insert themselves into the human being, into the etheric body, with the help of gramophone records, slide shows, radio, and cinema, which are the four technological media that he spoke about.[114] Then, after Rudolf Steiner's death, there came television, representing a much more powerful means for Ahriman to influence a large segment of the world population. And subsequently more direct intervention into the etheric body through technology began on a global scale through increasing exposure to invisible forces like electromagnetism and electricity (the harmful effects of exposure to high levels of electricity are now well-documented), which we are subject to all the time. These invisible forces—such as electricity, electromagnetism, and radioactivity—are encroaching upon human beings more and more in a penetrating way, and this comprises a substantial aspect of the ahrimanic invasion into the human etheric body. There are, however, other aspects, which I have gone into in *Prophecy–Phenomena–Hope*.

On October 20, 1923, the *Deutsche Rundfunk* (German Radio) commenced regular broadcasts. On the same day, Rudolf Steiner spoke about "the terrible law of the sounding in unison of vibrations."[115] He was then asked whether a radio station could be set up in Dornach, so that his lectures could be heard by many more people. Rudolf Steiner's response is revealing. He did not reject the idea outright, but the conditions that he specified would have meant, if they were to have been realized, the invention of a completely different kind of radio. He said that for him to use radio for transmitting his lectures: (1) there would have to be a microphone through which *only he* could speak; (2) this would have to function

---

114 Rudolf Steiner, *Das esoterische Christentum und die geistige Führung der Menschheit* ("Esoteric Christianity and the Spiritual Guidance of Humanity") (Dornach, Switzerland: Rudolf Steiner Verlag, 1995), lecture of January 29, 1911: "Many things in present-day cultural life are destructive—especially, for example, slide shows, which damage the etheric body." This is just one example of many of Rudolf Steiner's critical remarks concerning the aforementioned technological developments. He was not against technological progress as such, but in pointing out the harmful consequences of exposure to the influences of these technological innovations (such as the damaging effects of slide shows on the etheric body) indicated that there needed to be a counterbalance in terms of spiritual practice and development. For an overview of his comments, see Werner Schäfer, *Rudolf Steiner über die technischen Bild- und Tonmedien. Eine Dokumentation* ("Rudolf Steiner: A Documentation on the Technological Image and Sound Media"; Freiburg, Germany: Wege Verlag, 1999).
115 Rudolf Steiner, *Man as Symphony of the Creative Word*, lecture of October 20, 1923 (Blauvelt NY: Garber Communications, 1989).

through the power of a flame, not electromagnetically; and (3) it would have to transmit not only the physical vibration of sound but also the soul-spiritual qualities [of the voice] as well.[116] From this response it emerges implicitly that at that time when radio was starting to be used commercially,[117] Rudolf Steiner chose not to give his lectures over the radio, nor did he choose to appear on film. Having said that "there is no better school for materialism than the cinema, for what one sees there is not reality,"[118] how could he possibly have taken to using the radio or to appearing on film? Evidently—at least, this is the implication of what he said—Rudolf Steiner rejected the use of radio, even though it would have been for the purpose of promoting the truth. In other contexts he spoke of the transmission of spiritual truth as something to be communicated as a living experience—through the power of the spoken word; or, if by way of books, that it is up to readers to bring the text alive within themselves. Spirit manifests through living human beings. Whereas Rudolf Steiner implicitly rejected the radio, Adolf Hitler's minister of propaganda, Joseph Goebbels, immediately recognized the great significance of radio.[119] Under the National-Socialists there was a drive for every household to have a radio, the idea being that then everyone would be able to hear the Führer's voice. From this it is clear that radio was recognized to be ideal for promoting the LIE (Hitler's message) and for mesmerizing the masses.

Now it is not radio but television that is the primary tool for mesmerizing the masses. Almost every home has a television. Research shows that television has a mesmerizing, hypnotic effect.[120] This is intensified through modern high-density television—with which, moreover, there are also concerns about the potential health impacts of the increased radiation levels that accompany the digital television transmitters. And now there are further concerns regarding ultra high-density television, since the fast-moving images produced by this technology are not suitable for watching at close-quarters as they can induce disorientation and nausea in viewers.[121] We are living in an ahrimanic world and gradually are waking up to the realization concerning what is at work—that modern technology is *not harmless*. From Ahriman's standpoint, the goal is to harden the sensibilities and the constitution of human beings—literally so as to

---

116 Werner Schäfer, *Rudolf Steiner über die technischen Bild- und Tonmedien. Eine Dokumentation* ("*Rudolf Steiner: A Documentation Concerning the Technological Image and Sound Media*") (Freiburg, Germany: Wege Verlag, 1999), pp. 32–33. Words in brackets [ ] added by RP.
117 The first radio signal was sent and received by Marconi in 1895, the year in which the cinematograph was invented and demonstrated in Paris by Louis and August Lumière. Radio broadcasting experiments took place from 1906 to 1919, when the Radio Corporation of America (RCA) was formed. The period 1923 to 1926 saw the beginnings of broadcasting on a commercial basis, and from 1926 to 1930 commercial radio became solidly established. Parallel to this, from 1895 to 1906 the cinema moved from a novelty to an established large-scale entertainment industry. Throughout this time, and continuing until 1923, this was the era of silent film, since combining the image with synchronous sound was not possible until 1923. Thus, during the first three decades of their history, films were silent.
118 Rudolf Steiner, *Cosmic and Human Metamorphoses*, lecture of February 27, 1917 (Blauvelt, NY: Garber, 1989).
119 "I hold radio to be the most modern and important instrument for influencing the masses…to inwardly so immerse them in the content of our time that no one will be able to escape any more"—Joseph Goebbels (1933)—Werner Schäfer, *Rudolf Steiner über die technischen Bild- und Tonmedien. Eine Dokumentation* ("*Rudolf Steiner: A Documentation Concerning the Technological Image and Sound Media*") (Freiburg, Germany: Wege Verlag, 1999), p.1.
120 "Watching television, like playing video games, causes the viewer's brain waves to slip into a hypnotic, post-REM type—or delta—sleep. Brainwaves of television viewers are similar to those in deep sleep, though their eyes are still open. While in this state, any number of post-hypnotic suggestions can be implanted in the mind of the viewer"—Craig Elliott, "The Hypnotic Effects of Television"—http://craigelliottmusic.blogspot.com/2009/12/hypnotic-effects-of-television.html.
121 "The Japanese public broadcaster, NHK, has mentioned that Ultra HDTV may not be ideal for consumer use. At close range, the fast moving pictures of an Ultra HD signal on a minimum 60″ screen may cause nausea for viewers. Recall that Ultra HDTV requires 60 FPS to display images at high-speed. Humans may not be able to process movement at this speed, causing confusion and nausea"—http://www.ultrahdtv.net/ultra-hdtv-health-concerns/.

render the human being "stuck" on the Earth and unable to follow the ascending path of evolution under Christ's guidance. When we grasp this, we begin to understand the magnitude of what is happening now—what I call the "second Fall"—through the ahrimanic invasion of the etheric body.[122] We can begin to see the significance of eurythmy as an activity through which we engage in enlivening the etheric body. The intention of the eurythmy exercises described in this book, is to bring our etheric body into alignment with the Etheric Christ, serving as an antidote and protection to the ahrimanic snares of modern technology.

Not too long ago I was one of several presenters at a congress at which several speakers were giving Power Point presentations. They came up on the stage one after the other, and several of them at the outset of their presentation had to struggle with adjusting the computer for several minutes. Sometimes it just did not work and the presenter had to address the audience, "There is something wrong, can someone help?" All this time they could have been presenting their lecture, if they were not dependent upon the computer for their presentation. And the tragedy is that afterward one generally does not feel nourished from such a presentation—not to mention the negative impact upon the etheric body of this kind of thing.[123] One misses the experience of the human spirit, when someone has grasped something profound and is offering to share it through their presentation. Instead, the equipment and the influence of the technological presentation—which may be spectacular—becomes the central experience.

I mention this example just to illustrate how the ahrimanic presence in the world is all-pervasive. In relation to our gathering here at this workshop, it is becoming ever more a precious opportunity to come together in community, not via telephone or text message or email or Facebook or an internet "chat room," but in "real life" community. This is becoming precious in our time because there are forces at work to take the experience of true community away from us. On the one hand there are anti-community forces that utilize separation and polarization to divide and conquer—*divide et impera* being the age-old strategy—knowing that "A kingdom divided against itself cannot stand" (Mark 3:24). On the other hand, using technology, there is the drive to substitute "virtual community" for the real thing. Ahriman would like us to be doing everything via computers, by teleconference, for example, to eliminate the experience of, "*Where two or three are gathered in my name*," (Matthew 18:20), which can only happen in real, not virtual, community. Ahriman gains a victory over human souls, if they come to believe that in virtual community they are really experiencing community. The reality is that each person is sitting alone at their computer. It is this that Ahriman sees, which delights him all the more because of the illusion into which the participants have come.[124]

Having said all this, of course, we know that there are appropriate uses of such technology, but it cannot be a substitute for coming together in community. We cannot do eurythmy or Choreocosmos cosmic dances

---

122 Robert Powell & Kevin Dann, *Christ & the Maya Calendar* (Great Barrington, MA: SteinerBooks, 2009), chapter 10. See also Robert Powell, *Prophecy–Phenomena–Hope: The Real Meaning of 2012* (Great Barrington, MA: SteinerBooks, 2011).
123 If, as Rudolf Steiner indicated, slide shows have a detrimental effect upon the etheric body, this effect is boosted considerably when watching a highly sophisticated "slide show" such as a Power Point presentation.

124 However, a virtual gathering via an internet "chat room" or teleconference or conference call need not be a complete illusion. If the participants are conscious of the true nature of what they are participating in, they can consciously endeavor to overcome the illusion. On the basis of a spiritual understanding, the situation can be redeemed to a certain extent—with gratitude that technology makes something possible which could otherwise be extremely difficult. As with Rudolf Steiner's indication concerning a new kind of radio that would transmit not only the physical vibration but also the soul-spiritual level of the voice, that which is lacking (i.e., the soul and spiritual levels) from the technological forms of communication under discussion here has to be consciously activated by the participants in order to redeem the situation. There are other aspects to this question which, owing to lack of space in this book, have to be omitted from this brief discussion of a very important and significant topic.

via internet! When we come together in the spirit of Christ and Sophia, in service of the spiritual hierarchies, to do the cosmic dances together, our endeavor is to create an "Ahriman-free zone"—from which the ahrimanic element is altogether absent.

Rudolf Steiner summarized this development in the last words that he wrote in March 1925 (he died on March 30, 1925):

> In *this* [materialistic–mechanical aspect]...the purely ahrimanic dominates this sphere. In the science of the spirit another sphere is created, from which an ahrimanic element is altogether absent. It is precisely by consciously taking up that form of spirituality to which the ahrimanic powers have no access, that the human being gains the strength to meet Ahriman *in the world*. [Summarizing:]
>
> 1 In the age of science, beginning about the middle of the nineteenth century, there is in human civilization a gradual downslide...not only into the lowest regions of nature, but down *below* nature. Technological civilization becomes sub-nature.
>
> 2 This makes it necessary for one, in living inner experience, to come to spirit knowledge in which one rises as high above, into that which is beyond nature, as one goes down below nature through one's occupation with the technological belonging to sub-nature. One thereby creates within oneself the power *not to go under*.[125]

This is the purpose of this book, focusing upon eurythmy as a path to the Etheric Christ, offering a sequence of exercises as a daily eurythmy practice which can be taken up by anyone, to create the inner resources comprising the power *not to go under*—in the sense that putting on the Resurrection body, drawing upon the power of Christ's Transfiguration, Crucifixion, Resurrection, and Ascension (from which the spiritual practice outlined in this book draws), strengthens one, creating an inner radiance to counter the harmful external radiation coming toward one.

In daily life we are more or less constantly exposed to harmful electromagnetic fields and it is now increasingly recognized that electromagnetic fields pose a serious threat to our health—i.e., they affect the etheric body, which is the source of health and vitality in the human being. For example, radio waves and microwaves are forms of electromagnetic radiation, differing from one another in terms of their wavelength. Let us recall that the origin of the word "radio" comes from the word "radiation." Radio waves and microwaves together span a particular range which is referred to as *radio frequency*. One of the primary sources of harmful radiation—impacting the etheric body and causing damage to it—is the high level (microwave) radio frequency radiation to which the human being is exposed by way of cell phones and cell phone towers. Humanity is exposed to high levels of radio frequency radiation not only from cell phones and cell towers, but also from cordless phones, garage and other door openers, wireless devices known as PDAs (personal digital assistants such as wireless laptop computers, blue tooth devices, blackberries, iPads, etc.), microwave alarm system sensors and store security systems, wireless video cameras, TV extenders, walkie-talkie type radios, and satellites, etc. It should be noted that the frequencies of radio waves used in normal radio broadcasting pass through the human being with minimal damage to the etheric body, although FM (frequency modulation) broadcasting operates at frequencies approaching the microwave spectrum of radio frequency radiation, where the radiation starts to become harmful. In terms of health hazards, the real problems start with the devices operating at higher frequencies such as those used by cell phones and the other devices mentioned above. As the cell phone industry is a multi-billion-dollar industry, it has an interest in concealing the health hazards of cell phones (mobile phones) from the public, and official

---

[125] Rudolf Steiner, *Anthroposophical Leading Thoughts. Anthroposophy as a Path of Knowledge. The Michael Mystery* Complete Works, vol. 26 (London: Rudolf Steiner Press, 1998). Words in brackets [ ] added by RP, and the existing translation has been slightly modified after comparing with the original German.

websites tend to downplay the harmful effects of cell phones and other devices operating in the microwave spectrum of radio frequency radiation—microwave ovens being one of the most well-known example of such devices, where there is some degree of consciousness of the harmful effects associated with using them.

The first commercially available cell phone system in the United States came out about thirty years ago in the early 1980s. Now, with around seven billion people in the world, there are over five billion cell phone subscriptions, which—even taking into account that many individuals have multiple cell phones—still means that a high percentage of the world's seven billion people has a mobile phone. Cell phones need cell towers and/or satellites. The number of satellites orbiting around the Earth has skyrocketed, and cell towers, with their antennas, and micro-cell antennas have rapidly spread as a network across the globe. Cell tower antennas (on the cell towers) are directional antennas dividing a geographical area into cells of service, and each antenna is a powerful source of radiation—obviously much stronger in the direction in which it is radiating, depending upon proximity to the antenna. Covert micro-cell antennas (mini cell towers) come in many forms, often concealed in fake trees or fake cactus, gas station signs, and even in fake church steeples replacing the original church steeples. The electromagnetic radiation coming from cell phones is bad enough. What is coming from cell tower antennas is much stronger. Whereas the health hazards due to exposure to cell towers decrease significantly with distance—the cell phone is usually held directly to the head and is thus, generally speaking, more detrimental in terms of its impact upon the etheric body. All of this is only a small part of the story of the encroachment upon the etheric body through external radiation! Obviously, we cannot negate technology altogether, because there can be very positive uses for modern technology. However, it is important to bear in mind the consequences of using the ever advancing modes of technology, taking note that there is a steady and alarming encroachment of harmful energies into the human etheric body, not to mention the etheric body of Mother Earth. It is thus no exaggeration to say that a second Fall is underway through Ahriman's intervention into the human etheric body and the etheric aura of the Earth. Thus now, in the twenty-first century, Ahriman's plan is now emerging in its twin aspects: first, to win over human beings through materialism; and second, to take hold of them through technology. This plan has progressed so rapidly that it has become like a runaway train, and many people are on the train with little or no consciousness of where it is headed.

The "Staff of Mercury" Exercise

As mentioned throughout the foregoing discussion, the eurythmy practice described in this book offers a certain degree of protection from Ahriman's endeavor to penetrate into the etheric body. How is it possible, though, to protect oneself from Ahriman's invasion as an imprint on the level of consciousness as a further encroachment into the body of the Earth and humanity? The following answer is offered by Rudolf Steiner. As described in *Christ & the Maya Calendar*, Ahriman's intervention on the level of consciousness takes place via the mind soul (intellectual soul),[126] which is a domain belonging to the astral body that is affected by human consciousness through our thought life, and thus can be elevated by way of the thinking activity of the I. The antidote to ahrimanized thinking is given by Rudolf Steiner in the form of a meditative practice which hinders "ahrimanic beings from penetrating into our consciousness":

> There is a remedy that will hinder ahrimanic beings from penetrating into our consciousness, a symbol that one must enliven within oneself. This is the Staff of Mercury, the luminous staff with a black snake and a bright luminous shining snake. The snake is a symbol for the astral body. Every night the astral body sheds its skin; it throws off the used-up skin. The black snake is a symbol for this. Overnight it gets a new, shimmering skin, and this newly enlivened, beautiful, shining skin of the astral body is symbolized by

---

126 Robert Powell & Kevin Dann, *Christ & the Maya Calendar* (Great Barrington, MA: SteinerBooks, 2009), p. 114.

the shining snake... this symbol, the Staff of Mercury, who is the "messenger of the gods," [is what he] holds in his hand... [It] bans everything that wants to push into our consciousness and disturb.[127]

The vertical axis of the Staff of Mercury, also known as the caduceus, can be pictured inwardly as radiant yellow.[128] In addition to the powerful protective symbol of the Staff of Mercury, Rudolf Steiner recommends:

> ...imagining that we feel ourselves as if enclosed in a blue aura and thereby protected from all evil thoughts and feelings that want to attack us from outside. We inwardly feel how we are closed off from all evil influences by this aura. Only good powers can find entry into our soul. This can be effectively connected with the following meditation.

Meditation for Protection against Outer Influences

> May the outer sheath of my aura grow stronger.
>
> May it surround me with an impenetrable vessel against all impure, self-seeking thoughts and feelings.
>
> May it be open only to divine wisdom.[129]

This meditation is particularly significant in relation to the "radiant blue stream" of the Etheric Christ referred to in the meditation "Christ is already here" on page 73. Imagining a protective sheath of a radiant blue aura thus links us directly to the in-streaming of the Etheric Christ. In addition, the symbol of the Staff of Mercury—the deeper significance of which is elucidated on page 135—can also be effective when used before going to sleep, as sometimes ahrimanic thoughts penetrate into us at night, while asleep. As Rudolf Steiner indicated: "While the human being is asleep, ahrimanic beings approach and say: Good is evil, and evil is good.... Through this insinuation these ahrimanic beings believe they can attain their goal of nefarious evil [that human beings should become totally dependent upon their lower nature]."[130] Here it is a matter of consciously protecting the physical and etheric bodies when the astral body and the I separate from the physical/etheric bodies during the hours of sleep. What is also very effective is to imagine one's body as a cross of light before one goes to sleep—or, as the Staff of Mercury.

At the time of Rudolf Steiner during the first quarter of the twentieth century, it was a matter primarily of becoming conscious of the driving force of materialism and of how spiritual science can serve as a complementary perspective to what is offered by materialistic science. During his life, and especially toward the end of his life, Rudolf Steiner drew attention to the dimension of sub-nature as the source for the forces made use of by the advancing technology of his day,[131] in relation to which he emphasized the need to access the fountainhead of spiritual science in higher worlds, in order to create *within* a counterbalance and how *not to go under* (as Rudolf Steiner expressed it). Now, given that the ahrimanic encroachment is not just on the level of consciousness but is also laying hold of the human etheric body and the Earth's etheric body—this having already progressed to quite an extraordinary extent—it is a matter of defending oneself against this encroachment. Eurythmy, particularly in conjunction with the words of Christ, offers a powerful practice for developing the inner radiance needed in order to defend oneself against external radiation in its various forms. In our consideration of this path thus far, we

---

127 Rudolf Steiner, *Esoteric Lessons 1904–1909*, Complete Works vol. 266/I (Great Barrington, MA: SteinerBooks, 2007), p. 393.
128 Ibid., p. 379.
129 Ibid., p. 380.

130 Rudolf Steiner, *Geistige Zusammenhänge in der Gestaltung des menschlichen Organismus* ("Spiritual Relationships in the Shaping of the Human Organism"), Complete Works vol. 218 (Dornach, Switzerland: Rudolf Steiner Verlag, 1992), p. 150.
131 Robert Powell, "Subnature and the Second Coming," in: *The Inner Life of the Earth: Exploring the Mysteries of Nature, Subnature & Supranature* (ed. Paul V. O'Leary; Great Barrington, MA: SteinerBooks, 2008), pp. 69–141.

Chapter 5: The Macrocosmic Background to the Core Practice

have come to a more conscious understanding of the sixth seal of the Apocalypse, whose image shows Michael holding the dragon underfoot—an inspiring image and a source of inspiration in the struggle of our time with the ahrimanic encroachment.

In using the expression "defending oneself," something needs to be added. It is not just a matter of defending *oneself*, but also of defending Mother Earth and all her creatures—including humanity—as it is expressed in the prayer "Heavenly Father, hear our prayer, may destructive modern technology be stopped…" (see page 64). Defense of oneself is thus expanded to include the whole world. In this way we join together with Christ, who is the true Regent of the Earth. He—together with the Archangel Michael at his right hand, and Divine Sophia to his left—comprise the true defenders of the Earth and humanity. The fifth seal (the Sophia Mystery) expresses the transformation of the luciferic element in the astral body. In light of what is depicted in the image of the sixth seal (the Michael Mystery), the sixth seal expresses the archetype of *buddhi* (life spirit), which entails the casting out of the ahrimanic influence from the etheric body—the ahrimanic influence represented by the dragon. Since eurythmy is an art form that embodies the ideal of *buddhi*, it is an activity which, by its very nature, is able to cast out the ahrimanic influences from the etheric body, when practiced in the right consciousness.

In a broader sense the goal of this chapter is to attain an overview of the messages inherent in the Apocalypse as expressed through Rudolf Steiner's spiritual-scientific rendering of the images of the seven seals. What can we understand from the image of the sixth seal, which is that of Michael holding the dragon underfoot and bound with a great chain? To understand this message, to understand what this seal is communicating, there is in addition to the archetypal level referred to above also the earthly level, and here we have to have the courage to look at what is transpiring in the world at the present time. We have to understand exactly what it is that we need to overcome, how we are to do it, and who is helping and guiding us. We cannot completely eradicate Ahriman from the world, but we can put him in his right place if we become *masters of technology* rather than slaves to it. How are we to do this? Ultimately we have to activate certain forces within ourselves so that the external radiation that is coming toward us can be countered by our own inner radiance. The inner radiance of Christ is an answer to what is being directed toward us from outside and that is the goal of the *Putting on the Resurrection Body* sequence and also of the entire Inner Radiance sequence described in this book. It is a matter of the practice of developing inner radiance. It is a schooling of, or connecting onto, the stream of Christ, which is the stream of the Resurrection body. It is this for which Christ stands.

As physical human beings we are all descended from Adam and Eve, the progenitors of the physical human race. Jesus Christ is referred to as the *new Adam*. In Revelation he is described as the *first born of the dead*. The expression "first born" indicates there will be others who will overcome death, i.e., who will attain Resurrection, and this is the ultimate goal for humanity. The *Risen* Christ, the *new* Adam, is the progenitor of the *spiritual* human being who steps into the stream leading to Resurrection, which passes through the stages of spirit self (*manas*), life spirit (*buddhi*), and spirit human (*atma*).

Thus, through the practice of developing inner radiance, as described in this book, we focus upon the goal of evolution: the Resurrection, and we focus upon putting on the Resurrection body. We choose to school this inner radiance to overcome what is coming toward us from outside. *In this way we put Ahriman in his position.* Rudolf Steiner, as I said earlier, is an example of someone who was in this stream of the Resurrection body, and who was able, out of that, to "put Ahriman in his place," as indicated on the sixth seal. And that is what we see in the image in the sixth seal—that Ahriman is underfoot. If we observe this seal and behold the Archangel Michael holding the dragon underfoot, and simultaneously call Rudolf Steiner to mind, as a human being who—with the help of Michael, and through being permeated by Christ—

was able to hold Ahriman underfoot, we can begin to have a sense of Rudolf Steiner serving at the right hand of the Etheric Christ, fulfilling on Earth that which Michael fulfills in Heaven. As reported by those who knew him, Rudolf Steiner was permeated with the radiance of Christ, and this is what we can aspire to as well. It is what we have to come to in our future development, and we can begin already now through connecting onto the stream of the Resurrection body.

An important question to consider is: "How is Christ going to overcome evil in the world?" The answer is: *through* Ahriman. It is precisely through the incarnation of Ahriman, coming as the embodiment of evil, and through our overcoming this figure that evil will be overcome. Exactly how this is to happen is a mystery, *but it will happen*, and when it happens, it will be for our time the equivalent to what two thousand years ago the Resurrection was in relation to the mystery of death. The mystery of our time is that of the overcoming of evil, and it is to this that Daniel Andreev draws attention when he refers to the incarnated Ahriman as the Antichrist, the Prince of Darkness: "The Prince of Darkness will terrify human beings. Christ however, will take on as many forms as there are conscious beings on Earth to behold him. He will adapt himself to everyone and will converse with all. His forms will simultaneously yield an image in an unimaginable way—one who appears in Heaven surrounded by unspeakable glory. There will not be a single being on Earth who will not see the Son of God and hear his word."[132]

What is indicated in these words is an event we are approaching, a tremendous event enacted by the Etheric Christ for the overcoming of evil. However, this event will not signify the overcoming of evil once and for all. We can understand this by way of analogy with the momentous event of the Resurrection that took place two thousand years ago.

The Resurrection was a great triumph over death—the overcoming of death—but it did not mean that thereafter people no longer died. The Resurrection took place as a seed impulse for us to follow. In the same way that through the Resurrection the seed was planted for the overcoming of death, now a seed will be planted for the overcoming of evil. Looking toward the coming great event that will be enacted by the Etheric Christ, serving as a seed impulse for all human beings to overcome evil, we can begin to prepare ourselves through practicing the exercise of *Putting on the Resurrection Body*. We are approaching this tremendous event of the Antichrist, the incarnated Ahriman, being overcome by Christ—treading Ahriman underfoot—and then appearing to every human being in the world in his unspeakable glory. That is what is on the horizon, and this will be the overcoming of evil.

We can begin to understand why Rudolf Steiner said that everything he was communicating in his imparting of spiritual science could be considered as thoughts of Christ. We can begin to understand that his whole teaching is an expression of Christ's coming in the etheric, and that Rudolf Steiner's life activity as a spiritual teacher, which began in 1899 with his Christ experience, and should have extended until 1933, had he not died prematurely, was in the service of preparing for Christ's coming in the etheric in 1933. This is why he opened the mysteries of the Third Testament—Revelation—with its seven seals, as the testament of the overcoming of evil as part of the divine plan for the evolution of humanity through the ages, leading ultimately to the Resurrection in future Vulcan.

---

132 Daniel Andreev, *Rosa Mira*—quoted (translated by Robert Powell) in Robert Powell, *Prophecy-Phenomena-Hope: The Real Meaning of 2012* (Great Barrington, MA: SteinerBooks, 2011), p.89.

Chapter 5: The Macrocosmic Background to the Core Practice

The Seven Days of Creation in Relation to the Structure of the Solar System

We return now to review the relationship of the seven days of creation—as described for our time by Rudolf Steiner—to the spatial structure of our solar system.[133] In this way, we are going to continue to look at the relationship of the seven seals with the chakras but this time from a different perspective. As background, it is important to review the stages of evolution.

The descending path of evolution is the sequence from ancient Saturn, ancient Sun, ancient Moon, to the present Earth evolution. Through the coming of Christ in the middle of the Earth evolution a major shift began—a shift to an ascending phase of evolution. The first half of Earth evolution was the descending phase, followed by the ascending phase in the second half of Earth evolution. The first planetary embodiment, after the Earth, on the ascending phase of evolution will be future Jupiter, which will be followed by future Venus, then future Vulcan. Thus, Earth (second half), Jupiter, Venus, and Vulcan comprise the *ascending phase* of evolution.

The seed of the physical body was developed on ancient Saturn. The transformation of the physical body, which will occur at the Vulcan stage, will be the Resurrection body, or *atma*. At the stage of *atma* humanity will bring to realization the transformation of the physical body into the Resurrection body. At the ancient Sun stage it was the etheric body that was developed on a seed level. The metamorphosis of the etheric body will occur at the future Venus stage of evolution. The result of this metamorphosis will be the transformed etheric body, *buddhi*, which Rudolf Steiner called *life spirit*. On future Jupiter humanity will bring to realization the metamorphosis of the ancient Moon stage of evolution, where the astral body was developed. This metamorphosis in the future Jupiter stage of evolution will result in the transformation of the astral body into *manas*. To summarize: the gift of the physical body stems from ancient Saturn, that of the etheric body from ancient Sun, and that of the astral body from ancient Moon—these three comprise the descending phase of evolution. During the ascending phase of evolution, the transfiguration of the astral body into *manas* will take place on future Jupiter, the transformation of the etheric body into *buddhi* on future Venus, and the metamorphosis of the physical body into *atma* on future Vulcan.

The I is the gift of Earth evolution. How do we receive the I? The gift of the I began already during the Atlantean period of evolution, the fourth stage of the Earth evolution. The religion of ancient Atlantis centered on what was called the Great Spirit, comprising the community of the Sun Elohim (Greek *Exusiai*), who at that time were bestowing upon human beings the first seed of the I. In turn these Sun Elohim were working together with Christ. They were mediating from Christ the bestowal of the I upon human beings. Then, with the incarnation of Christ on the Earth, there arose, on the foundation of I consciousness which was prepared from the Atlantean period onward by the Great Spirit comprising the community of the Sun Elohim (also referred to as the *Pleroma*, meaning "fullness") the possibility of developing the higher level of I consciousness which came through Christ—through the Mystery of Golgotha (see page 131).

We see this transformation most strikingly with Saul who became Paul. Saul represents the rudiments of the I *before* receiving the gift of the incarnation of Christ, and Paul represents the transformation of the I through receiving Christ into the I. In the shift from

---

133 Robert Powell, *Hermetic Astrology*, vol. 2: *Astrological Biography* (San Rafael, CA: Sophia Foundation Press, 2007).

Saul to Paul we see the transition from the old level of I consciousness, which is not yet at the level of a direct Divine Presence within the I, to Paul who experienced an extraordinary transformation. This transformation from Saul to Paul mirrors the two halves of Earth evolution—with Saul representing the culmination of the first or descending phase, and Paul representing the beginning of the second or ascending phase.

What is depicted in this transformation from Saul to Paul is the divine plan of the "turning point of time." However, no one is obliged to receive Christ. It is only in freedom, completely out of free choice, that one can connect with Christ and receive the gift of the higher aspect of the I from him.[134] At the same time, we can also hold in consciousness the activity of Ahriman, who is challenging the divine plan. His plan is to strengthen the lower I—which could also be called the "egotistical I"—and his formula, which is the opposite of Christ's formula, is: *My will be done*. Self-will is expressed in this formula, and it is a key problem in the modern age, when we have certain human beings who have developed the principle of self-will to such an extent that they can seemingly accomplish whatever they wish to do by way of having acquired a great deal of money and power. *My will be done*, when brought to realization as a universal principle, would lead to the fulfillment of Ahriman's vision for the future of humankind. That is an ahrimanic vision of the future. However, this is not in accordance with the divine plan, which will be realized through the fulfillment of *Thy will be done on Earth as it is in Heaven* (*not my will, but Thy will*—i.e., the divine will, according to the divine plan—*be done*).

The vision of Christ is something quite different from that of Ahriman. Instead of intensifying the development of self-will, Christ's vision is that we step into our divine heritage as members of the spiritual hierarchies. We can only do this if we receive the Christ I into ourselves through living the formula of St. Paul: "Not I, but Christ in me" in our daily lives—for which the eurythmy practice described in this book on page 63 is intended. This is of primary significance in relation to the Second Coming of Christ in our time, when a new "turning point of time" has occurred. The unfolding of the divine plan at the present critical "turning point of time" (twentieth/twenty-first centuries) signifies receiving the Christ into one's I, thereby stepping into the living stream of the Spirit, a stream guided by Christ, leading into the future, leading one into connection with the Angels and even higher spiritual beings of the spiritual hierarchies. The fulfillment of the divine plan in its first stages would entail a sufficient number of human beings taking up this path leading humanity to become the tenth hierarchy: Seraphim (Saturn), Cherubim (Jupiter), Thrones (Mars), Kyriotetes, Dynamis, Exusiai (Sun), Archai (Venus), Archangels (Mercury), Angels (Moon), and Human Beings (Earth), where the names in parentheses indicate the relevant planetary spheres of activity of these beings of the celestial hierarchies.

Returning again to our main theme, in working with the significance of the Apocalypse and with the seven seals we are led to contemplate some very difficult aspects of the unfolding of evolution. One of these is the second Fall, already referred to, which is taking place at the present time. Part of the driving force taking effect upon the egotistical I leading humanity into the second Fall is self-will (selfish will), which is being promoted by Ahriman, who has his own agenda in opposition to the divine plan. *Self-will* (*selfish will*) is the motivating impulse, the underlying impetus, for the second Fall, just as *desire* implanted by Lucifer into the astral body was the primary impulse underlying the first Fall. From one perspective, Ahriman's agenda could be characterized

---

134 At first, it might seem as if Saul had not made a free choice to receive Christ into his I. In an earlier incarnation, however, Saul already had a connection with Christ in his pre-Christian manifestation in ancient India through Krishna, and when he reincarnated as Saul, it was a pre-birth decision to become a messenger of Christ. Thus, he had already made the decision to receive Christ into his I long before.

as promoting self-will in order to harden us into our egotistical I so that we will not take the ascending path of evolution. This hardening would result in the creation of an ahrimanic human race, which is Ahriman's goal. This is the antithesis of receiving the Christ impulse and taking the ascending path.

A prerequisite for this ascending path, developing *manas, buddhi,* and *atma,* is to receive Christ into one's I. Then, after receiving the Christ I, signifying the birth of Christ consciousness, to allow the light, love, and life of Christ into our astral, etheric, and physical sheaths. We can do this by entering into relationship with the events of the Transfiguration, Crucifixion, and Resurrection in Christ's life. The eurythmy sequence of *Putting on the Resurrection Body* described in this book is an exercise for orienting ourselves daily to the Christ mystery. We open to his light through the I AM sayings, to his love through the Seven Words from the Cross, and to his life through the Seven Sayings of the Risen One. Over and above that we have the possibility of coming into connection with the peace of Christ in the fourth level of this exercise, which is connected with the seven seals. This level of the peace of Christ goes beyond the seven stages of evolution. Christ's peace is the *source* from which the life, love, and light of Christ proceed. "My peace I give unto you" (John 14:27)—this is "the peace of God which surpasses understanding" (Philippians 4:7).

As an example, let us now consider the image of the fourth seal. The fourth seal is significant because it represents the present Earth evolution, which has no precedent. In this fourth seal we see two pillars, one red and one blue, with the red pillar representing the Tree of Knowledge and the blue pillar representing the Tree of Life. These pillars are the "bookends" of present Earth evolution—the Tree of Knowledge, being associated with the (first) Fall, representing the descending path, and the Tree of Life, brought to the Earth by Christ, representing the ascending path. An alignment with Christ consciousness brings the Tree of Knowledge into service with the ascending path. The descent into physical incarnation upon the Earth

was represented symbolically by eating from the Tree of Knowledge of good and evil—the red pillar, resting on the sea. Now, with the coming of Christ, we have the possibility of nourishment from the Tree of Life, represented by the blue pillar, resting on the land, which will lead us upon the ascending phase of Earth evolution—whereby as mentioned above, partaking of the Tree of Knowledge in the spirit of Christ comes into service on the ascending path of evolution. We can see how the imagery of the fourth seal is connected with the two phases of Earth evolution—the Mars or descending phase (red pillar), and the Mercury or ascending phase (blue pillar).

With the fifth seal (the Sophia Mystery) we come to the future Jupiter evolution, with the sixth seal (the Michael Mystery) to the future Venus evolution, and with the seventh seal to the Mystery of the Holy Grail, having to do with the future Vulcan evolution. These seals are macrocosmic realities. They exist in spiritual realms as part of what is known as the Eternal Apocalypse. It was out of the Eternal Apocalypse that Christ communicated Revelation, the Third Testament, to John, and these images represent macrocosmic realities into which one can enter meditatively and also experientially, because they are realities mirrored within us microcosmically within the seven chakras. How can we deepen into these realities?

To do this, let us shift the way we have been contemplating the stages of evolution. We have been contemplating them so far as a progression of time periods, such as the time period of ancient Saturn, the time period of ancient Sun, and so on. However, we can also look at the stages of evolution spatially. This perspective arises in connection with the evolution of our Sun, when we contemplate the spatial contractions of the Sun globe—

referred to in astronomy as the solar nebula—that have occurred periodically in the course of evolution. In astronomy the solar system is depicted heliocentrically, with the Sun in the center. The first planet from the Sun is Mercury, and then Venus is farther out from the Sun at the center. Then comes the Earth together with the Moon, then Mars, then the planet Jupiter, then Saturn. (The outer planets are left out of consideration here, as there is no correspondence of the chakras to Uranus, Neptune, and Pluto.)[135] Picturing the heliocentric structure of our solar system, one can begin to grasp how our Sun contracted from the orbit of Saturn to the present orbit of the Earth—contracting first to the orbit of Jupiter, then to the orbit of Mars, and then to the orbit of the Earth—and then how the solar nebula further contracted to where the Sun is presently located at the center of our solar system. This is the spatial extent of the Sun globe now at this stage within the present Earth evolution.

At one time our Sun was a gigantic cosmic body which extended spatially all the way to the current orbit of the planet Saturn. This was the spatial extent of the solar nebula during the ancient Saturn evolution. During this time our solar nebula was even larger than the red supergiant Betelgeuse (whose periphery, if Betelgeuse were to be placed within our solar system, would extend out somewhere between the orbits of Mars and Jupiter). The orbit of Saturn, indicating the spatial extent of our Sun globe during ancient Saturn, allows us to picture the spatial aspect of ancient Saturn. We can think of a correspondence: orbit of Saturn (space)—ancient Saturn (time).

We can find such a spatial correspondence during each stage of cosmic evolution. Whereas during ancient Saturn our Sun was a gigantic body of warmth that extended all the way out to the current orbit of the planet Saturn, a spatial contraction ensued that led to a reconfiguration of the Sun globe. This contraction took place between the ancient Saturn and ancient Sun stages of evolution. When the ancient Sun period commenced, the Sun globe—at that time a gigantic gaseous body raying out light—no longer filled space out to the orbit of Saturn; rather it had contracted to the current orbit of the planet Jupiter. When we observe Jupiter in the night sky, we can bring to consciousness that it is currently tracing out an orbit in the heavens, which marks what the extent of the Sun globe was during the ancient Sun evolution. Here there is a correspondence: orbit of Jupiter (space)—ancient Sun (time).

Then there was a further contraction of the solar nebula during the time that elapsed between ancient Sun and ancient Moon. At the beginning of the first stage of the ancient Moon evolution, our Sun globe—at that time a vast fluidic sphere filled with resounding tones—extended out to the current orbit of the planet Mars. The orbit that Mars is tracing out now marks what the extent of the solar nebula was during the first part of the ancient Moon evolution. However, during ancient Moon the cosmic body that was the ancient Moon divided into two parts. One part—the forerunner of our present Sun—contracted into the space where our Sun is currently located, and the other part remained like a great Moon orbiting around that Sun. This is why it is called the ancient Moon evolution. Here there is a correspondence: orbit of Mars (space)—ancient Moon (time).

Then there came a further contraction between ancient Moon and present Earth. This brings us to where we are right now, the present Earth evolution. In speaking of the Earth we can think of the Earth *plus* the Moon, because the Moon's orbit indicates the extent of the etheric body of the Earth. With the Earth plus the Moon we are considering both the physical and etheric bodies of the Earth. This is important to hold in consciousness. Initially, with the contraction of the solar nebula to the current orbit of the Earth, the Sun included Mercury, Venus, and the Earth plus Moon within itself. At a certain point during the present Earth evolution, the Sun (comprising Sun, Mercury

---

135 Robert Powell, *Hermetic Astrology,* vol. 2: *Astrological Biography* (San Rafael, CA: Sophia Foundation Press, 2006), pp. 292–298 discusses Uranus, Neptune, and Pluto in relation to the stages of cosmic evolution; see especially p. 292 for a diagram of the heliocentric system.

Chapter 5: The Macrocosmic Background to the Core Practice

and Venus) separated from the Earth (which still encompassed the Moon). When the Sun contracted still further, eventually to its present size, the planets Mercury and Venus separated out from the Sun, and the Moon separated out from the Earth.[136] The solar system arrived at its present structure—Saturn, Jupiter, and Mars having already separated out earlier from the solar nebula. Here there is a correspondence to space and time: orbit of Earth (space)—present Earth (time).[137]

Since the Mystery of Golgotha Christ is now united with this cosmic body we call the Earth. As indicated in the exercises "A Star Is above My Head" and "Christ in me" (described on page 63), one can consciously invite Christ into one's I. This is the first step. As referred to earlier, Christ came in order to overcome the consequences of the Fall which was brought about through Lucifer's intervention in the astral body. Let us recall that the seven chakras are the primary organs of the astral body. The intervention of Lucifer proceeded via the chakras, starting with the root chakra and working up, eventually to reach the crown chakra. Thus the seven chakras became permeated with Lucifer's influence. It was this that brought about the momentous event of the Fall, which was a "casting out" from Paradise, as described in the Book of Genesis—a truly devastating event in the history of humanity, which led in the course of time to the loss of the use of the chakras as organs of spiritual perception. It is Christ, the Lamb, who helps us to reverse and overcome this condition of the corruption of the chakras through Lucifer. By consciously taking Christ into the seven chakras, as outlined in the exercise of *Putting on the Resurrection Body*, Christ is able to work on the transformation of the luciferic influence permeating the chakras. Through Christ's activity, the chakras are not only restored to their pristine glory prior to the Fall, but are raised to a new level. Out of this a new clairvoyance is born—characterized by Rudolf Steiner with the word "Imagination" (as the first stage of three levels of higher knowledge, which he called Imagination, Inspiration, and Intuition)—leading humanity forward on the ascending path of evolution. Rudolf Steiner indicated that with the pouring out of the blood of Christ through the Mystery of Golgotha, the light, love, and life of Christ penetrated down into the heart of the Earth. This was the beginning of the process of Christ making our planet his body. Christ united with our planet to lead us through the "turning point of time" into the future, on the ascending path of evolution leading through the cosmic stages of future Jupiter, future Venus, and future Vulcan. The exercises presented in this book offer a way of aligning oneself with Christ as the guide (together with the Archangel Michael and with Sophia, the Bride of the Lamb) on the ascending path of evolution.

Let us now consider the future stages of evolution—Jupiter, Venus, and Vulcan—in relation to the heliocentric system. Do we find a space-time correspondence here? From the heliocentric image of our solar system it is apparent that the next contraction of the solar nebula (in terms of *humanity's proximity to the Sun*, not the actual physical dimension of the Sun) will result in a globe that extends out to the orbit of the planet Venus. Up until now I have used the expression "solar nebula," which is an astronomical expression. Now, though, I have chosen the expression "Sun globe" to express *humanity's relationship* (i.e., *proximity*) *to the Sun*. At present, here on the Earth, the Sun globe (in the sense that I am using it) extends from the Sun to the Earth, as the "sphere of influence" of the Sun (for human beings upon the Earth).

Each contraction of the solar nebula brings humanity to a new planet—in the heliocentric sequence Saturn, Jupiter, Mars, Earth, Venus, Mercury, Sun—drawing ever nearer to the Sun with each contraction. The future Sun globe delineating the next planetary orbit

---

136 Robert Powell, *Hermetic Astrology*, vol. 2: *Astrological Biography* (San Rafael, CA: Sophia Foundation Press, 2006), p. 145, figures 4 & 5.
137 The space-time correspondences described thus far in the four stages—ancient Saturn, ancient Sun, ancient Moon, present Earth—were indicated by Rudolf Steiner, *The Spiritual Hierarchies and the Physical World*, Complete Works vol. 110 (Great Barrington, MA: SteinerBooks, 2008), lecture of April 17, 1909.

as the future abode of humanity will correspond to future Jupiter. Through Christ (and Sophia) we are being led toward future Jupiter (time period), which will take place *spatially* in the sphere corresponding to the orbit of the planet Venus around the Sun. Then, at this next stage of planetary evolution, the Sun globe (meaning humanity's relationship to the Sun in terms of proximity to the Sun) will extend from the Sun to the orbit of Venus. Thus during future Jupiter humanity will be spatially closer to the Sun. This contraction to the Venus orbit at the future Jupiter (next) period of evolution was indicated by the words of Christ from the Apocalypse, paraphrased as, "I will give you the morning star" (Revelation 2:28). The morning star is the planet Venus, and the contraction from present Earth, delineated by the orbit of the Earth around the Sun, to future Jupiter, indicated by the orbit of Venus around the Sun, will place humanity in the Venus ("morning star") sphere. This is the promise of Christ. If we choose to follow him on the ascending path of evolution, he will give us the morning star, future Jupiter, delineated spatially by the planet Venus. Here again there is a correspondence: orbit of Venus (space)—future Jupiter (time). Christ, the Lamb, who holds the "seven stars" of the seven cosmic stages of evolution in his right hand, leads humankind step by step toward the goal to be attained during Vulcan evolution, the stage of Resurrection, of uniting with the Sun. Human beings of the future Jupiter evolution will be much closer to the Sun than at present on the Earth. It is important to prepare for this, as one needs to be prepared for this approach toward the Sun. The series of exercises presented in this book of entering into the stream of Christ's radiance are helpful by way of preparation. The cultivation of inner radiance, the practice of putting on the Resurrection body, is oriented toward the future, including passing over to future Jupiter. At the Jupiter stage of evolution we will no longer be in physical incarnation, but in an etheric/astral condition, which is a condition connected with Sophia—the woman clothed with the Sun, with the Moon under her feet, and a crown of twelve stars upon her head (Revelation 12:1).

After the Jupiter stage of evolution there will be a further contraction toward the Sun, when human existence will become united with the sphere of Mercury—the sphere traced out by the orbit of Mercury around the Sun. This contraction will occur between future Jupiter and future Venus. During future Venus humanity will be spatially even nearer to the Sun. Here again there is a correspondence: orbit of Mercury (space)—future Venus (time).

The final contraction will be from future Venus to future Vulcan, when the Earth will be reunited with the Sun. In other words, in this great panorama of the evolution of humanity we are moving steadily toward the Sun, eventually to become reunited with the Sun. It is Christ who is leading us toward the future Vulcan evolution, which will be when the Earth reunites with the Sun. Here again there is a correspondence: Sun (space)—future Vulcan (time).

The Book of Genesis points indirectly to a time during the first part of the present Earth evolution when the Sun was still connected with the Earth and the Moon. Then the Sun (still containing Mercury and Venus within it) separated out from the Earth plus Moon. That is what is referred to in the Book of Genesis with the words, "Let there be light." Then at a later stage of Earth evolution the planets Mercury and Venus separated out from the Sun, and then finally the Moon separated out from the Earth. The planets Mars, Jupiter, and Saturn had already separated out from the Sun globe which, prior to the event described with the words "Let there be light," filled the entire space extending up to the present-day orbit of the Earth around the Sun. So there was, near the beginning of the Present Earth evolution, a separation between the Earth and the Sun, with the planet Earth taking up its present orbit and the solar nebula contracting to the present physical location and dimension of the Sun. However, the Earth, through Christ, will become reunited with the Sun. This will be at the future Vulcan stage of evolution—the stage of Resurrection. It is only through the Resurrection body—the spiritualized physical body, transformed by the power of Christ's light, love, and life—that it will be possible to unite with the Sun. Recognizing the spatial aspect of the stages of evolution, we can see that the seven stages of evolution are embedded in the very structure of our solar system. If this were taught in astronomy classes in school, it would not only make sense of the structure of our solar system but would also bring meaning as to our existence—seen as part of the divine plan of evolution.

To summarize: Rudolf Steiner had perfect recall not only of his previous incarnations, but also of earlier stages of cosmic evolution. These seven stages of evolution through which the human being evolves are described by Rudolf Steiner in his book *An Outline of Esoteric Science*. Thus, by means of his spiritual faculties of perception, he was able to behold and describe not only the history of Earth evolution going back through various cultural epochs to Atlantis and even earlier, but also the history of each of the preceding stages of evolution, identified with the orbits of Saturn, Jupiter and Mars. He named these stages of evolution according to his clairvoyant perception, as already known by other initiates earlier in ancient Egypt. For example, he described the stage of evolution which took place within the orbit of the planet Jupiter as the *Sun* period; because the entire sphere bounded by the planet Jupiter was like a giant Sun. Similarly, the stage of evolution which took place within the orbit of the planet Mars he described as the *Moon* period of evolution, because of the moon-like globe that revolved around the orbit which is now occupied by Mars.

Together with the Earth the human being has passed through four stages of evolution: the *Saturn, Sun, Moon* and *Earth* stages of existence, in a series of contractions from Saturn's orbit around the Sun down to the present orbit of the Earth, during which the physical body, etheric body, astral body and the I became cosmically formed and bestowed upon the human being. These four stages of evolution—the three former evolutionary periods and the present Earth period—were named by Rudolf Steiner: Saturn, Sun, Moon, and Earth. These are to be followed by three future evolutionary periods, which Rudolf Steiner named: Jupiter, Venus, and Vulcan. Thus, according to Rudolf Steiner's cosmology, these seven stages of evolution relating to the development of the human being are:

Saturn   which took place within the orbit of the planet Saturn;

Sun   which took place within the orbit of the planet Jupiter;

Moon   which took place within the orbit of the planet Mars;

Earth   which is taking place in the orbit of the Earth around the Sun;

Jupiter   which will take place within the orbit of the planet Venus;

Venus   which will take place within the orbit of the planet Mercury;

Vulcan   which will take place in the sphere of the Sun.

Looking at the heliocentric planetary system, successive stages of evolution are indicated by the orbits of the planets around the Sun, each stage of cosmic evolution—by a process of contraction—drawing nearer toward the Sun. From the standpoint of the evolution of the human being, we are now at the fourth of seven stages of evolution. Outlined in general terms, in Rudolf Steiner's cosmology the mission of the first four stages of evolution—*Saturn, Sun, Moon*, and *Earth*—has been the establishment of the human being endowed with the I incarnated on the Earth in a physical, etheric, and astral body.

The stages of evolution are indicated by the names for the days of the week, where the present Earth evolution is divided into two halves: Mars (prior to the Mystery of Golgotha) and Mercury (post-Christian era). Saturday (Saturn), Sunday (Sun), Monday (Moon), Tuesday (Mars), Wednesday (Mercury), Thursday (Jupiter), Friday (Venus), and lastly we arrive at

Saturday (Vulcan)—this being the "higher octave" of the Saturn stage. The Anglo-Saxon names for the days of the week are partly derived from the names of the Germanic gods: Tiw = Mars, Wotan = Mercury, Thor = Jupiter, Freya = Venus. It should be noted that in the heliocentric system (as viewed from the Sun) the orbit of the Earth lies between that of Mars and Venus, where Mars represents a continuation from the past Moon stage and Venus leads into the future Jupiter stage of human evolution. However, according to Rudolf Steiner's esoteric cosmology, the names of the planets Venus and Mercury are interchanged. My research indicates that the names of the days of the week accorded to the stages of planetary evolution goes back to the Egyptians.[138] The planet the ancient Egyptians called Mercury is called Venus in modern astronomy, and the planet which they called Venus is called Mercury in today's astronomy. This interchange applies solely to the Egyptian naming of the planets, as in the tradition of Babylonian astronomy, Greek astronomy, Roman astronomy, and modern astronomy, the planets are named today in the same way as there were named by the Babylonians. Esoterically considered, in light of the Egyptian naming of the planets, the orbit of the Earth lies between that of Mars and Mercury. From this consideration, bearing in mind that it was the Egyptians who named the days of the week according to the esoteric cosmology, the validity of the designation of the two halves of Earth evolution as Mars and Mercury can be understood, and also why the future Venus stage of evolution is so called.[139]

---

138 Robert Powell, *History of the Planets* (Epping, NH: ACS Publications, 1989).

139 For further information concerning the naming of the weekdays by the Egyptians in relation to the stages of cosmic evolution, see Lacquanna Paul & Robert Powell, *Cosmic Dances of the Planets* (San Rafael, CA: Sophia Foundation Press, 2006), appendix 2.

Chapter 5: The Macrocosmic Background to the Core Practice

The "Staff of Mercury" and the Stages of Evolution

Here it is revealing to recall why earlier in this chapter the Staff of Mercury, also known as the *caduceus*, was referred to as an effective aid in hindering the invasion of ahrimanic forces into our consciousness. Against the background of the stages of cosmic evolution, the profound significance of the symbol of the Staff of Mercury can now be understood. It emerges from the following figure drawn by Rudolf Steiner[140]:

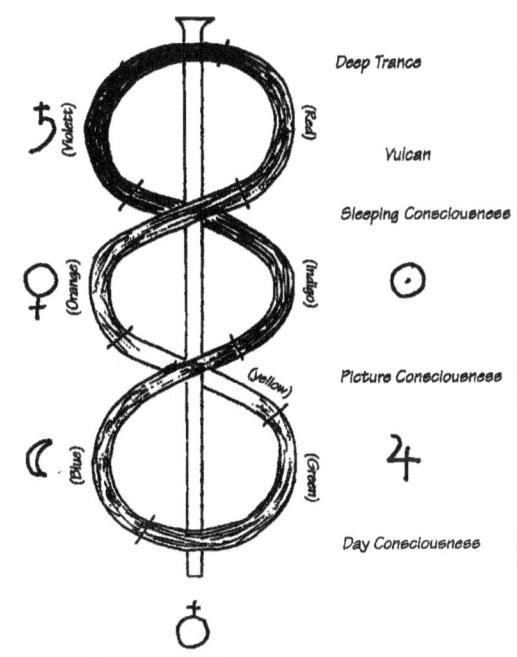

"Staff of Mercury" (depicting the stages of evolution)

Referring back to the Staff of Mercury figure on page 124, the above figure of the Staff of Mercury (*caduceus*) in relation to the stages of evolution depicts the cosmic archetype for the two snakes.

Archetypally the "black snake" is the descending stream of evolution depicted in the darker colors of the spectrum—Saturn (violet)

- Sun (indigo)
- Moon (blue)
- Earth evolution (first half) = Mars (green)
- and the "white snake" (archetypally) is the ascending stream of evolution depicted in the lighter colors of the spectrum as
- Earth evolution (second half) = Mercury (green)
- Jupiter (yellow)
- Venus (orange)
- Vulcan (red)

The vertical axis through the middle—"radiant yellow" (Rudolf Steiner)—is the axis that connects the Central Sun at the heart of our galaxy with the golden heart of our Earth, Shambhala. Christ and Sophia work along this axis—Christ from below, and Sophia from above.

In light of the hermetic axiom "As above, so below," the question arises as to how the Staff of Mercury is mirrored in the human being? In order to answer this question, it is helpful to consider the esoteric teaching concerning the *Sephiroth* Tree (known as the *Tree of Life*), which Rudolf Steiner spoke of on March 18, 1904, on September 8, 1910, and on May 10, 1924. In the sketch that Rudolf Steiner made of the human being in relation to the Sephiroth Tree in 1924, the three upper Sephiroth were drawn in relation to the human head, with *Kether* (Crown) above the head, *Chokmah* (Wisdom) in relation to the right side of the head, and *Binah* (Intelligence) in connection with the left side of the head. In this context he said:

> In the first place there are three forces at work upon the human head... The highest, the highest gift of the world, the highest spiritual gift, that could settle [from above] upon the human being, which could unite with one's head, if one knows much, was called *Kether* (Crown) in ancient Judaism. This was the highest. This was what spiritually formed the head from the universe. And then the head still needed two other forces. These two other forces approached him

---

140 Rudolf Steiner, *Esoteric Lessons* 1904–1909, Complete Works vol. 266/I (Great Barrington, MA: SteinerBooks, 2007), p.401.

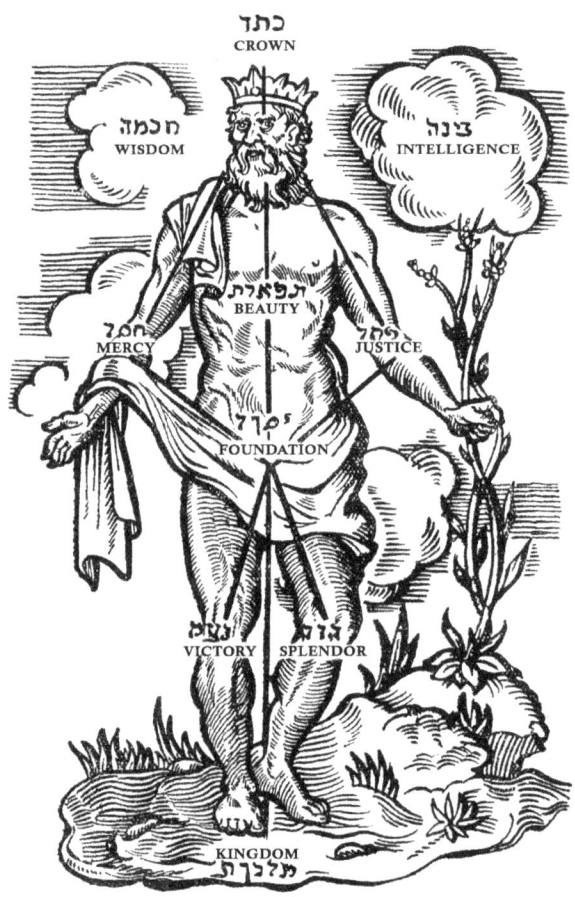

of Life[142] and Rudolf Steiner's figure, in turn, agrees with the arrangement of the Sephiroth in relation to the human being given by Henri Sérouya in his book on the Cabbala, which is reproduced here in English translation (see figure).[143]

The Cabbala denotes the Jewish tradition of esoteric knowledge, and the word Sephirah, which is the singular of the Hebrew word Sephiroth, means *sphere* in the sense of a "sphere of influence" or a cosmic sphere of existence. In the Cabbala the Sephiroth are understood to be ten emanations of God in the process of creation, the tenth emanation being the Earth. From another perspective (not that of Jewish esotericism) the other nine emanations correlate very precisely with the nine spiritual hierarchies of Christian tradition, who are regarded in Christianity as the forces of creation in creating humanity and the Earth—forces weaving between the Creator and humanity dwelling in the tenth sphere, that of the Sephirah Malkuth.

What is of particular interest for our consideration of the Staff of Mercury is the relation of the Sephiroth to the human being. Here it is important that these spheres (Sephiroth) are distinguished from the chakras. Whereas the chakras are organs in the astral body, the Sephiroth are spheres in the etheric (life) body—relating to the Tree of Life. As Rudolf Steiner noted in 1904, "The Tree of Life is the sum of the Sephiroth."[144] The Tree of Life is the archetype of the human etheric body, just as the Tree of Knowledge is the archetype of the human astral body. For example,

from the right and from the left. It was thought that the highest comes down from above [and] from right and left came the two other forces from the universe, which are spread out in the whole universe. The one that enters through the right ear was called Chokmah (Wisdom)...And from the other side came Binah. Today we would say Intelligence.[141]

This depiction of the first three Sephiroth in relation to the human head agrees with the figure that Rudolf Steiner drew of the human being in relation to the Tree

---

141 Rudolf Steiner, *Die Geschichte der Menschheit und die Weltanschauungen der Kulturvölker* ("The History of Humanity and the World Outlooks of Cultures"—Lectures to the Workers, vol. 7). Complete Works vol. 353 (Dornach, Switzerland: Rudolf Steiner Verlag, 1968), lecture of May 10, 1924.

142 Rudolf Steiner, *Über die Kabbala: Fragmentarische Notizen* ("Concerning the Kabbalah: Fragmentary Notes of a lecture held in Berlin on March 18, 1904") in: *Beiträge zu Rudolf Steiner Gesamtausgabe*, no. 29 (Dornach, Switzerland: Rudolf Steiner Verlag, Easter 1970), p.22.

143 Henri Sérouya, *La Kabbale* (Paris: Éditions Bernard Grasset, 1957), p.253.

144 Rudolf Steiner, *Über die Kabbala: Fragmentarische Notizen* ("Concerning the Kabbalah: Fragmentary Notes of a lecture held in Berlin on March 18, 1904") in: *Beiträge zu Rudolf Steiner Gesamtausgabe*, no. 29 (Dornach, Switzerland: Rudolf Steiner Verlag, Easter 1970), pp. 22–27.

in the human being, Kether (Crown) is a sphere in the etheric body in the region of the crown of the head, and has to be distinguished from the crown chakra, which is an organ in the astral body located in the region of the crown of the head. There is an inner connection between the crown chakra and Kether, but they are on different levels.

Kether is the highest Sephiroth on the Tree of Life, and the lowest is Malkuth (kingdom) which, as can be seen from the figure, relates to the feet—to the sphere beneath the soles of the feet—a sphere connected with the Earth. In the text below (see page 156) Malkuth is referred to as an "Earth sphere." As it is not in the astral body but in the etheric body, it is more appropriate to call it an "Earth sphere" in the human etheric body. This is a more accurate designation. However, usually no distinction is made between the chakras in the astral body and the spheres (Sephiroth) in the etheric body. And whereas most people are familiar with the chakras, they are not generally familiar with the spheres (Sephiroth) in the etheric body.

The Cabbala refers to ten Sephiroth, of which Kether is the first, and Malkuth the tenth. From the figure, following the vertical axis from Kether (Crown) to Malkuth (Kingdom), the axis passes through Tiphereth (Beauty) in the region of the heart and through Yesod (Foundation) in the region of the reproductive organs. It is interesting that there is an eleventh Sephirah called *Daath* (Gnosis), which is sometimes counted as part of the Tree of Life, but is more generally left out of consideration—and which is located between Kether and Tiphereth on the vertical axis.[145] Daath is a result of the uniting of the two Sephiroth Chokmah (Wisdom) and Binah (Intelligence). "Daath is the state of consciousness where intelligence and wisdom...become one."[146] On the microcosmic level, in the human being, Daath is mirrored in the place where the right brain (Chokmah) and the left brain (Binah) are united—called the *corpus callosum*—in the region of the cerebrum at the center of the brain.[147] In this place of connection between the right and left cerebral hemispheres is the microcosmic sphere of Daath. The right brain, mirroring Chokmah (Wisdom), could be said to be the wisdom side of the brain, having to do with intuitive, holistic skills, visual-spatial orientation, emotions, synthesis, creativity, the arts, and nonverbal, imaginative thinking. The left brain, mirroring Binah (Intelligence), could be said to be the intelligent side of the brain, having to do with logical, rational thinking, judgment and analysis, accuracy, facts and details, the sciences, and verbal, practical thinking. The uniting of the two cerebral hemispheres in the corpus callosum is where true knowing (Greek: gnosis) takes place, gnosis being the union (fusion) of wisdom and intelligence. As the corpus callosum is connected via the brain stem to the medulla oblongata in the region of the back of the neck, which functions primarily as the relay station between the brain and the spinal column, the location of Daath in the microcosm is usually depicted in this area of the human being's organism—in the neck/throat region.

The vertical axis from Kether (crown of the head) extends through Daath (neck/throat region), Tiphereth (heart region), Yesod (reproductive organs) to Malkuth (where the soles of the feet connect with the Earth). This is the vertical axis in the Staff of Mercury mirrored in the human being. As already mentioned, Rudolf Steiner indicates that one can visualize this vertical axis as radiant yellow. This color indication brings the vertical axis into relationship with the macrocosm, as emerges from the following description:

> The silver-sparkling blue below, arising from the depths of the Earth and connected with human weakness and error, is gathered into a picture of the Earth Mother. Whether we call her Demeter or Mary, the picture is of the Earth Mother. Thus it is that, as we gaze downward, we must bring together in imagination all the secrets of the depths that make up the

---

145 Http://en.wikipedia.org/wiki/da'at
146 *Meditations on the Tarot* (trans. Robert Powell; New York: Tarcher-Putnam, 2002), p. 506.

147 Http://en.wikipedia.org/wiki/Corpus_callosum.

material Mother of all existence. While in all that is concentrated in the flowing form above, we feel and experience the Spirit Father of everything around us. Now we witness the result of cooperation between the Spirit Father with the Earth Mother, bearing so beautifully within itself the harmony of the earthly silver and the gold of the heights. Between the Father and the Mother, we behold the Son.[148]

Imaginatively, we can extend the radiant yellow (gold) vertical axis of the Staff of Mercury up from Kether (crown of the head) to the *throne of the Father* at the galactic center (Central Sun)—to the "gold of the heights"—and we can extend this vertical axis down from Malkuth (soles of the feet) to the golden realm of Shambhala at the heart of the Earth. Whereas gold (radiant yellow) is the objective color of Shambhala, the subjective experience of the human being in clairvoyantly looking down to Shambhala is the color "silver-sparkling blue" as indicated by Steiner "arising from the depths of the Earth and connected with human weakness and error." The radiant yellow (gold) vertical axis from the Central Sun down to Kether (crown of the head) to Malkuth (soles of the feet) to Shambhala (golden heart of Mother Earth) is fundamental to all the exercises discussed in this book. It is the link between the microcosm and the macrocosm.

Returning to consider the two figures above, how are the "two snakes" entwining the central staff mirrored in the human being? Looking first at the figure of the stages of evolution on page 135, the "dark snake" of the descending phase of evolution—Saturn, Sun, Moon, Earth—is mirrored in the human being as also is the ascending phase of evolution—Earth, Jupiter, Venus, Vulcan. In relation to the figure on page 136, the individual stages of this path of descent are:

Saturn (violet)—from Kether via Chokmah to Tiphereth
Sun (indigo)—from Tiphereth via Geburah to Yesod

Moon (blue)—from Yesod via Netzach to Malkuth[149]

Having arrived at the feet (Malkuth), the "white snake" ascends from there on the ascending phase of evolution—Earth, Jupiter, Venus, Vulcan—and the individual stages of this path of ascent are:

Jupiter (yellow)—from Malkuth via Hod to Yesod
Venus (orange)—from Yesod via Chesed to Tiphereth
Vulcan (red)—from Tiphereth via Binah to Kether[150]

The following table indicates the individual stages of this path of descent in the classical Cabbalistic correspondence of the human being to the Tree of Life, where the Sephiroth Chesed and Geburah are identified with the right and left shoulders rather than the entire arms and hands, and the Sephiroth Netzach and Hod are identified with the right and left hips rather than the entire legs and feet.

I am aware that the color indications given in the above table differ slightly from Rudolf Steiner's figure (see

---

148 Rudolf Steiner, *The Four Seasons and the Archangels*, CW 223 & 229 (London: Rudolf Steiner Press, 1968), p.66.

149 The individual stages of this path of descent are expressed in Henri Sérouya's depiction of the human being in relation to the Tree of Life, which is the same as Rudolf Steiner's sketch from his lecture of March 18, 1904. There are other ways of depicting this, arising from the fact that normally Chesed and Geburah are shown in relation to the right and left shoulders and Netzach and Hod in relation to the right and left hips. Henri Sérouya's figure—and the same applies to Rudolf Steiner's 1904 figure—identifies Chesed and Geburah not just with the shoulders but with the entire arms and hands, and likewise identifies Netzach and Hod not just with the hips but with the entire legs and feet. This is only an apparent discrepancy. While it is correct to depict Chesed and Geburah in the location of the shoulders, the influences of these spheres stream through the entire arms and hands. Similarly, while it is accurate to depict Netzach and Hod in the location of the hips, the influences of these spheres stream through the entire legs and feet.

150 Ibid. It should be noted that in the 1924 sketch that Rudolf Steiner drew of the human being in relation to the Tree of life, while the Sephiroth Kether, Chokmah, Binah, Chesed, Netzach, and Malkuth are in the same positions as in the 1904 sketch, the Sephiroth Tiphereth and Geburah are interchanged, and also the Sephiroth Yesod and Hod are interchanged. The reasons for these interchanges are far too complex to go into here, and so neither of these interchanges is taken into consideration in this book.

Chapter 5: The Macrocosmic Background to the Core Practice

Cosmic stage of evolution	Rudolf Steiner's color indication	Path on the Tree of Life
Descending		
Saturn	Violet	Kether via Chokmah and Chesed to Tiphereth
Sun	Indigo	Tiphereth via Hod to Yesod
Moon	Blue	Yesod to Malkuth
Earth (first half)	Green	Malkuth
Ascending		
Earth (second half)	Green	Malkuth
Jupiter	Yellow	Malkuth to Yesod
Venus	Orange	Yesod via Netzach to Tiphereth
Vulcan	Red	Tiphereth via Geburah and Binah to Kether

page 135). However, it has to be remembered that this figure was produced from memory, and it could be that there was an error here with regard to the positioning of the colors on this Staff of Mercury. The reason for saying this is that in his lecture of December 28, 1907, Rudolf Steiner drew the same figure, but this figure from 1907 shows the color indications as I have given them in the table, except that it starts with black at the top, i.e., black is depicted at the top between violet and red.[151] In this 1907 figure, green is shown at the bottom, and yellow is indicated arising from the green at the bottom—as given in the above table. Regarding starting with black, Rudolf Steiner indicates:

> One gazes into the darkness (black) and gradually it begins to lighten up, turning to violet, then indigo, blue, green, yellow, orange, red, and then in reverse, until one has again risen to violet… If one gazes into the black in the endeavor to represent "darkness of soul" and then with the violet a mood of devotion, and so on with regard to the other colors—[indigo,] blue, green, yellow, orange—and then to call forth "joy of the soul" with the red, one's soul traverses a whole scale of feelings that are initially color impressions, but which become moral sensations. Thereby, that the form of the Staff of Mercury is mirrored in the soul in [such] feelings, something is inculcated in the soul which enables it to develop the higher organs [of spiritual perception]. Through this real symbol, we are transformed so that it [the soul] is able to take up the higher organs.[152]

The caduceus (Staff of Mercury) is a very real symbol which we can bring alive within ourselves in the way indicated here by Rudolf Steiner. After first establishing the vertical axis of the caduceus within, one can follow the curves of the "two snakes" entwining around this vertical axis in the way indicated in the above table or in the following figure.

---

151 Rudolf Steiner, *Mythen und Sagen. Okkulte Zeichen und Symbole* ("Myths and Folk Lore. Occult Signs and Symbols"), Complete Works vol. 101 (Dornach, Switzerland: Rudolf Steiner Verlag, 1992), p. 239.

152 Ibid., pp. 240–241.

Cultivating Inner Radiance and the Body of Immortality

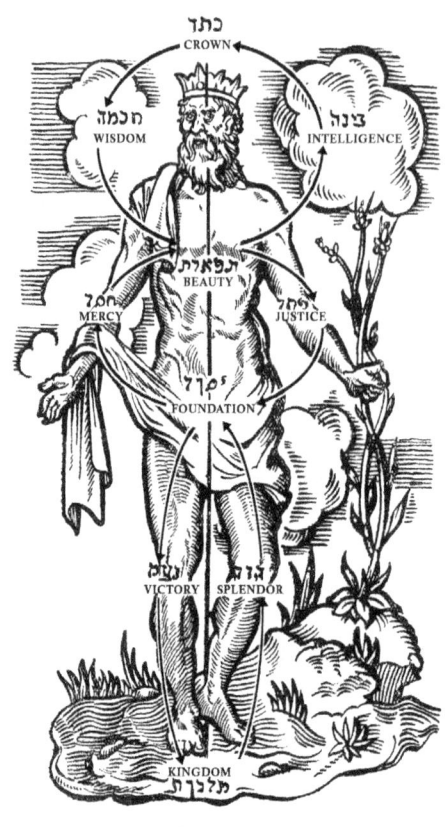

Although there are differences between the figure and the table, they are the same with respect to the vertical axis and the crossing points of the entwining curves across the vertical axis. That which the figure and the above table have in common is indicated in the following table, to which I have added the corresponding levels of consciousness associated with the stages of evolution:

Cosmic stage of evolution	Rudolf Steiner's color indication	Path on the Tree of Life	Corresponding level of consciousness
Descending			
Saturn	Violet	Kether to Tiphereth	Deep Trance
Sun	Indigo	Tiphereth to Yesod	Sleep
Moon	Blue	Yesod to Malkuth	Dream (Picture)
Earth (first half)	Green	Malkuth	Waking (Day)
Ascending			
Earth (second half)	Green	Malkuth	Waking (Day)
Jupiter	Yellow	Malkuth to Yesod	Imagination
Venus	Orange	Yesod to Tiphereth	Inspiration
Vulcan	Red	Tiphereth to Kether	Intuition

140

The table offers a key regarding activation of the "real symbol" of the Staff of Mercury within. The future stages of consciousness—Imagination, Inspiration, Intuition—are those associated with the future stages of evolution: Jupiter, Venus, and Vulcan. Imagination is a transformation of the Dream level of consciousness—having become conscious through the "I." Inspiration is a metamorphosis of the Sleep level of consciousness, which has become conscious through the activity of the "I." And Intuition is a Resurrection of the Deep Trance level of consciousness—having become conscious through the "I."

The goal of the next three stages of evolution—to be attained during the Jupiter, Venus and Vulcan stages of evolution—is the transformation by the human being, with Christ's help and guidance, of the three "vehicles" of the astral, etheric, and physical bodies, each with their corresponding level of consciousness, named Imagination, Inspiration, and Intuition.

These stages were all passed through by Jesus Christ in his life on Earth, whereby the last—and highest—stage of evolution was attained by Jesus Christ at the Resurrection. The appearance of Jesus Christ in his Resurrection body—the transformed physical body—signifies the accomplishment of the highest goal of humankind, the goal to be accomplished during Vulcan evolution. This stage of evolution will take place within the sphere of the Sun, and the presence of Christ's Resurrection body now on Earth—through his Second Coming in the etheric aura of the Earth—means that already a "ray of Sun" is present and active among humanity. From within his Resurrection body Jesus Christ continues to work in the guidance of humankind toward the attainment of the distant goal of Resurrection, that of the transubstantiation of the physical body. To align oneself with this goal of the creation of the Resurrection body, together with Christ, is the purpose and intention of the eurythmy sequence *Putting on the Resurrection Body*.

Let us recall Rudolf Steiner's words regarding the Staff of Mercury: "There is a remedy that will hinder ahrimanic beings from penetrating into our consciousness, a symbol that one must enliven within oneself. This is the Staff of Mercury, the luminous staff with a black snake and a brightly shining luminous snake."[153] He goes on to say: "Before every exercise the Staff of Mercury, after the exercise the Rose Cross... It is also very good to immerse ourselves in it [the Rose Cross] at the end of every exercise."[154] As with the Staff of Mercury, there is a way of bringing the Rose Cross alive within, which we shall now consider. One begins with establishing the Inner Cross, as indicated by Rudolf Steiner.

---

153 Rudolf Steiner, *Esoteric Lessons* 1904–1909, Complete Works vol. 266/I (Great Barrington, MA: SteinerBooks, 2007), p.393.
154 Ibid., p.394.

The Inner Cross—and—the Rose Cross—Meditations

The Inner Cross

One experiences the cross by allowing the forces of one's heart to stream out in full surrender and devotion:

1 into the arms and hands, imagining the horizontal axis of the cross—

meditative thought: [with] the firm will that the hands do only what is [right], good, beautiful, and beneficial for humanity;

> *[here one can stand with the arms and hands outstretched in the gesture of "Universal Love" and hold this gesture throughout the exercise of building up the Inner Cross +Rose Cross]*

2 into the [legs and] feet, adding the lower part of the vertical axis to the horizontal axis [of the cross]—

meditative thought: to stand firm and [with the firm will] that the feet go to do only what is right, good, beautiful [and beneficial];

3 into the larynx, completing the cross [by adding the upper part of the vertical axis]—

meditative thought: with the firm will to speak only what is right, good, beautiful, and beneficial;

4 into the brain—

[meditative thought]: with the innermost [firm] will to think only pure [and] good thoughts.

[Experience the cross through allowing the forces of the heart to stream with full surrender and devotion into the arms, legs, and head, creating an inner picture in relation to each of the four stages of the meditation.]

The above is my translation from the German conveying the essential meaning of this important meditation given by Rudolf Steiner in the first Esoteric School. As the meditation was only later written down from memory after it was spoken during an esoteric lecture by Rudolf Steiner, it may not be exact. For example, in the line concerning the feet, there is no mention in the "meditative thought" of the words "that the feet" in the German, but it is clear that they are meant to be included, which is the reason for including the words "that the feet" in the English translation.[155]

Having established the Inner Cross, the Rose Cross can be built up by placing seven roses around the Inner Cross, as indicated in the following meditation by Rudolf Steiner.

---

155 Rudolf Steiner, *Aus den Inhalten der esoterischen Stunden 1904–1909*, Complete Works vol. 266/I (Dornach, Switzerland: Rudolf Steiner Verlag, 1995), p.272. Words in [ ] added by RP. See also the English translation in: Rudolf Steiner, *Esoteric Lessons 1904–1909*, Complete Works vol. 266/I (Great Barrington, MA: SteinerBooks, 2007), p.222.

Chapter 5: The Macrocosmic Background to the Core Practice

Meditation on the Rose Cross

The cross, as if arising from burning wood.

Then on it [around it] seven roses—emerging reddish to gradually become radiantly brilliant.

The first rose radiates: left side of the head

May your warmth warm me through and through—

The second rose radiates: right side of the head

May your light irradiate me through and through—

The third rose radiates: left hand

May your activity stream through me—

The fourth rose radiates: right hand

May your peace pour through me—

The fifth rose radiates: left foot

May your ray empower me—

The sixth rose radiates: right foot

May your force permeate me—[156]

The seventh rose radiates: above
I am in your sphere.[157]

The above meditation on the Rose Cross given by Rudolf Steiner can be done together with the Inner Cross, while holding the eurythmy gesture of Universal Love. On closer examination, it is evident that the seven roses relate to seven of the Sephiroth on the Tree of Life. This becomes clearer still if the roses are placed in a slightly different sequence than that given above. The following version places the roses in a sequence that brings out the connection of each rose with a Sephirah on the Tree of Life, and this—preceded by the Inner Cross—is a most potent exercise. For the relationship of the Sephiroth to the human being, Kether in the region of the crown of the head, Chokmah at the right side of the head, Binah at the left side of the head, and so on, see the figure on page 136.

---

156   The German word "*Hub*" used in connection with the sixth rose, translated here as *force*, conveys the sense of a lifting impetus, whereby one can think of the *impulse or force in lifting the foot* when walking.

157   Rudolf Steiner, *Seelenübungen* (vol. II): *Mantrische Sprüche* ("Soul Exercises, vol. 2: Mantric Verses"), Complete Works vol. 268 (Dornach, Switzerland: Rudolf Steiner Verlag, 1999), p.186. Words in [ ] added by RP.

Meditation on the Rose Cross (with a different order of the roses)

The cross, as if arising from burning wood.

Then on it [around it] seven roses—emerging reddish to gradually become radiantly brilliant.

Kether	*The first rose radiates: above*
	I am in your sphere—
Chokmah	*The second rose radiates: right side of the head*
	May your light irradiate me through and through—
Binah	*The third rose radiates: left side of the head*
	May your warmth warm me through and through—
Chesed	*The fourth rose radiates: right hand*
	May your peace pour through me—
Geburah	*The fifth rose radiates: left hand*
	May your activity stream through me—
Netzach	*The sixth rose radiates: right foot*
	May your force permeate me—
Hod	*The seventh rose radiates: left foot*
	May your ray empower me.

In this meditation it is noticeable that of the ten Sephiroth comprising the Tree of Life, three Sephiroth are missing. These three Sephiroth belong to the vertical axis from Kether (crown) to Malkuth (feet). The missing Sephiroth from the central vertical axis are: Tiphereth (heart region), Yesod (region of the reproductive organs), and Malkuth (region of the feet). Precisely these three Sephiroth are addressed by Judith von Halle as relating to the closing words of the Lord's Prayer:[158]

For thine is the kingdom	*Malkuth* (Kingdom)
and the power	*Yesod* (Foundation)
and the glory	*Tiphereth* (Beauty)

---

158 Judith von Halle, *The Lord's Prayer* (London: Temple Lodge, 2007), pp. 62–64.

Based on this indication by Judith von Halle, the above exercise (Inner Cross/Rose Cross) can be closed with these words and gestures (see table):

Words from the Lord's Prayer	Corresponding Sephiroth	Accompanying gestures as indicated on pages 36 and 37 in relation to the gestures for these words of the Lord's Prayer
For thine is the kingdom	*Malkuth* (Kingdom)	the kingdom
and the power	*Yesod* (Foundation)	but deliver us from evil
and the glory	*Tiphereth* (Beauty)	give us this day our daily bread [AU-heart]
for ever and ever	*Kether* (Crown)	for ever and ever [fulfillment]
Amen/Aumeyn	*Tiphereth* (Beauty)	AMEN/AUMEYN

Let us recall Rudolf Steiner's words quoted above, "Before every exercise the Staff of Mercury, after the exercise the Rose Cross...It is also very good to immerse ourselves in it [the Rose Cross] at the end of every exercise." He says also:

> The symbol that helps us...is the Rose Cross: the black cross, the symbol of death; the seven red roses, the symbol of new, germinating life from the blood flowing forth from the Savior. A wonderful legend says that when the Savior died the bees came and sucked the pure, chaste blood as they otherwise sucked on the red rose blossoms. In the deepest sense the red roses are a symbol for the sacred blood of Christ. Evil powers must step back from those who place this black wooden cross with the seven blossoming dark red roses before their soul. For this reason we should let it live in us after every meditation. It is a symbol from which we can draw boundless power.[159]

---

159 Rudolf Steiner, *Esoteric Lessons* 1904–1909, Complete Works vol. 266/I (Great Barrington, MA: SteinerBooks, 2007), p.390.

Extension of the "Staff of Mercury" Exercise

"We can imagine the Mercury staff before every meditation, evenings and mornings, and also use it during meditation in order to ward off the evil influences."[160] The Staff of Mercury meditation can be done at the beginning of the entire sequence in practicing Right Standing—after finding the radiant yellow (gold) vertical axis from the Central Sun to the "star above the head" and then through the human being: Kether-Daath-Tiphereth-Yesod-Malkuth, and then from Malkuth to the golden realm of Shambhala, one can then in one's imagination add in the two "S" lines: one descending from Kether to Tiphereth to Yesod to Malkuth, and the other ascending from Malkuth to Yesod to Tiphereth to Kether (see figure on page 140).

After working with the Staff of Mercury in the way just described as an opening exercise for a time, a further refinement is possible in terms of the two "S" lines. Just as the vertical axis can be extended in the upward direction beyond Kether via the "star above the head" to the Central Sun and in the downward direction from Malkuth to Shambhala, so the two "S" lines can also be extended upward and downward. Looking at the figure on page 140, the upward "S" culminating with Vulcan meets (at Kether) the downward "S" beginning with Saturn. Imagine, however, that the downward "S" does not begin at Kether but commences at the Central Sun, and that likewise the upward "S" does not end at Kether but continues up to the Central Sun. The two "S" curves would then entwine the vertical axis all the way to the Central Sun.[161] Whereas the vertical axis extends up as a radiant yellow (gold), as it reaches up to the Central Sun it becomes more and more a supernal light. Similarly, the two "S" curves entwining the vertical axis from Kether to the Central Sun as they ascend are comprised increasingly of supernal light. This is the same light that streams from the Central Sun, which cannot be described in earthly terms. St. Paul speaks of the Father as "the King of kings and Lord of lords, who alone has immortality, and who dwells in the light which no human being can approach, that no human being has seen or can see" (I Timothy 6:15–16). The supernal nature of this light is such that in meditation it appears as black—here one can think of the vastness of the blackness of the night sky, against the background of which shine the stars. Rudolf Steiner's color indication for the top of the caduceus (region of Kether) is black (see description on page 139). This may seem paradoxical. The following words may be a help in grasping this paradox:

> Truth attained through synthesis is present at a deeper level of consciousness than that of the consciousness of self. It is found in darkness. It is from this darkness that the rays of light...of knowledge are emitted...as a result of...excursions into the region of this deeper level of consciousness...[where] contacts are established with the inner darkness, which is full of revelations of truth. The knowledge and power drawn from this dark and silent region of luminous certainty can well be described as the "gift of Perfect Night."[162]

In our discussion of the Staff of Mercury, it is interesting to note that in his lecture of September 25, 1907, Rudolf Steiner refers to the staff in connection with the Egyptian initiate Hermes Trismegistus.[163] And the "gift of Perfect Night" is also referred to in connection with Hermes, or rather it is mentioned in *Koré*

---

160 Ibid., p. 388.
161 Concerning the Central Sun (galactic center), see Robert Powell & Kevin Dann, *Christ & the Maya Calendar* (Great Barrington, MA: SteinerBooks, 2009), appendix 1 "The Central Sun," pp. 218–225.
162 Anonymous, *Meditations on the Tarot* (trans. R. Powell; New York: Tarcher/Putnam, 2002), pp. 221–222.
163 Rudolf Steiner, *Esoteric Lessons 1904–1909* (Great Barrington, MA: SteinerBooks, 2007), p. 204.

Kosmou, the sacred book of Hermes Trismegistus.[164] In imagining the continuation of the caduceus from Kether upward to the Central Sun, initially it is the blackness of night that arches above us. Then, in our endeavor to "sense behold" the *throne of God* at the Central Sun in the heights, out of the "perfect night" the supernal light flashes forth like lightning. "From the throne issue flashes of lightning" (Revelation 4:5). The two "S" curves of the caduceus reach up around the vertical axis like the "horns of Isis":

> There dawned upon her a remarkable clairvoyant vision: she [Isis] suddenly noticed that she still had the cow horns of ancient Egypt, in spite of having become a new Isis…Through the strength of her clairvoyance there one day arose in her the deep meaning…of that which is described in St. John's Gospel as the *Logos*…There arose…an actual golden crown of genuine substance…The power of the Word, the power of the Logos, must be laid hold of again. The cow horns of the ancient Isis must take on quite a different form.[165]

In this description of the Staff of Mercury, the "horns of Isis" take on a different form. They rise up from the crown (Kether) to one's Eternal Star, shining in the heights of Heaven, receiving the supernal light of the Central Sun from the *throne of God*. From the Eternal Star resounds the I AM. Then, in deepest humility, one can speak the words I AM in their true sense. The light-power of these words, resounding from the heights of Heaven, flashes down from above, all the way through the Staff of Mercury into the feet (Malkuth), and from there radiates into the depths of the Earth through the extension of the caduceus from Malkuth down to Shambhala—then returning back from Shambhala, passing through one in the form of the Staff of Mercury, back to the heights of Heaven, toward the Eternal Star, and from there to the Central Sun. This I AM experience is the experience of Christ, who is the divine I AM, within, who weaves "between the Spirit Father and the Earth Mother" (Rudolf Steiner).

The Staff of Mercury—by aligning us with the very foundations of existence—offers protection against the endeavor of the ahrimanic forces to penetrate into us. The I AM from one's Eternal Star shines into the "star above the head"—the eighth chakra, that of the higher I—and the exercise A Star Is above My Head (see page 62) takes the experience of the I AM presence (Christ) in the "star above one's head" as its point of departure. And it is not just this exercise that is transformed through the prior experience of the Staff of Mercury, but the entire sequence of exercises is lifted to a new level if the Staff of Mercury exercise is done at the beginning.

This can work within us throughout the day. We have the possibility of inwardly calling forth the caduceus at any time as a power of protection, realigning us with the spiritual foundations of existence in the heights and in the depths. The Staff of Mercury is called forth when we adopt the Right Standing posture with our legs and when, simultaneously, we bring our arms and hands up into the Fulfillment gesture—this is the gesture accompanying the words "for ever and ever" in the Lord's Prayer. The Fulfillment gesture evokes the "horns of Isis" and forms a Grail chalice in the region of the head, which is able to receive the grace streaming down from the heights of Heaven.

With Right Standing one first builds up the caduceus through the colors (see figure and table on page 140):

---

164 G.R.S. Mead, *Thrice Greatest Hermes* (York Beach, ME: Samuel Weiser, 1992), Book III, p.91: "the Black [Rite] that gives perfection" is the translation given here of the expression (from the Greek) translated as "the gift of Perfect Night" in the classic French translation of *Koré Kosmou* 32 by A.J. Festugière *Hermès Trismégiste Corpus Hermeticum* vol. III (Paris: Société D"Édition Les Belles Lettres, 1954), p.166. In *Koré Kosmou* 32 the "gift of Perfect Night" is said to have been bestowed on Hermes through his initiation by Kamephis.

165 Rudolf Steiner, *Ancient Myths: Their Meaning and Connection with Evolution*, Complete Works vol. 180 (Toronto: Steiner Book Center, 1971), pp. 39–40.

Saturn (violet)—from Kether to Tiphereth [right side]

Sun (indigo)—from Tiphereth to Yesod [left side]

Moon (blue)—from Yesod to Malkuth [right side]

Mars (silver-sparkling blue)—from Malkuth (green) to Shambhala (gold) [left side]

Mercury—(silver-sparkling blue) from Shambhala (gold) to Malkuth (green) [right side]

Jupiter (yellow)—from Malkuth to Yesod [left side]

Venus (orange)—from Yesod to Tiphereth [right side]

Vulcan (red)—from Tiphereth to Kether [left side]

Then, after Vulcan, one raises the arms into the Fulfillment gesture. Following the ascending stream (after Vulcan) further from Kether, it arches up through the raised left arm and hand into the realm of "for ever and ever" to one's Eternal Star, shining in the heights of Heaven which, in turn, is connected to—receiving from—the Central Sun, the *throne of God* at the heart of our galaxy. One then follows the stream back from the Central Sun to one's Eternal Star, streaming back down to pass through the right arm and hand, to take the path described above from Kether (crown) down to Malkuth (feet). In following the "Mars" stream (continuation of the "dark snake") down to Shambhala, this is inwardly connected with Christ's descent into the underworld after the end of the Crucifixion, in the wake of the earthquake that split the rock on Golgotha between his cross and the cross to the left of his cross. And in then following the "Mercury" stream (continuation of the "white snake") up from Shambhala, this traces the ascent of Christ back up from Shambhala on his path of "rising from the dead" to appear as the Risen One to the Blessed Virgin Mary on Golgotha and to Mary Magdalene in the garden of the holy sepulcher on Easter Sunday morning.

Right Standing (connecting with Shambhala in the depths) together with the Fulfillment gesture (connecting with the Central Sun via one's Eternal Star in the heights)—also visualizing the caduceus passing through the Sephiroth, enhanced by the colors—are appropriate gestures for calling forth the Staff of Mercury which, as described above, can be done at the start of the entire series, just as the Inner Cross/Rose Cross can be done at the end of the whole sequence of prayers and meditations.

The possibility for human beings to become conscious of the Father was opened by Christ, who came from the Central Sun—the *throne of God* referred to in Revelation, chapter 4, where Christ, the Lamb, is also described in connection with the throne. Christ came as the "light of the world" shining in the darkness (John 1:5). Christ spoke the words, "I and the Father are one" (John 10:30) and he also said, "No one comes to the Father except through me" (John 14:6). He taught the Lord's Prayer as a path to the Father. Thus, through Christ, the possibility is given of extending our consciousness to the Father, to the Central Sun, the throne of God. With the "S" ascending from Kether (region of the head), continuing the Vulcan section of the ascending "S", our prayers (for example, our praying of the Lord's Prayer) ascend to the Father. And with the "S" descending from the Central Sun down to Kether and continuing with the Saturn part of the "S" proceeding down from Kether, our prayers are answered by a stream of grace.

The path to the Father was opened by Christ some two thousand years ago. Now, in our time, the Etheric Christ is opening the path to Shambhala, to the Mother, to her realm at the heart of the Earth. Just as the two "S" curves can be extended upward from Kether to the Central Sun, so they can also be extended downward from Malkuth to Shambhala. Again referring to the figure and table on page 140, the descending "S" curve comes down from Yesod (blue) to Malkuth (green) and the ascending "S" curve passes up from Malkuth (green) to Yesod (yellow). The two "S" curves meet in Malkuth. Appropriately, the color of the caduceus in the region of Malkuth is green, which is the predominant color of the Earth.

In the practice of Right Standing the endeavor is to connect through Malkuth with Shambhala, to establish the vertical axis all the way down to Shambhala. The descending "S" curve can be imagined entwining the vertical axis, descending from Malkuth to Shambhala, representing the descending (Mars) half of Earth evolution. While Malkuth itself, in the region of the feet, can be imagined as a green sphere, the descending (Mars) "S" curve passing down from Malkuth to Shambhala is a silver-sparkling blue hue. We can send down our love and gratitude to the Mother along this descending (Mars) "S" curve. The response from the Mother ascends from Shambhala along the ascending (Mercury) "S" curve, which is also a silver-sparkling blue. The ascending "S" curve passes through Malkuth in the region of the feet and continues up to Yesod—Jupiter (yellow)—as indicated in the figure on page 140.

As a closing exercise to the entire sequence—in line with Rudolf Steiner's indications for protection—the Inner Cross/Rose Cross together with the closing words and gestures from the Lord's Prayer as indicated in the table on page 145 can be done. On this account these two "optional extra meditations"—the Staff of Mercury and the Inner Cross/Rose Cross—are included in the overview of the complete sequence on page 196.

The Relationship of the Chakras to the Seven Seals

Following this summary, let us now proceed to consider the correspondences between the seven seals and the seven chakras. There is a sketch by Rudolf Steiner that gives us a key to the relationship between the seals and the chakras. What it shows is the relationship of the chakras with the planets, and knowing this we can apply this relationship to the foregoing elaboration concerning the seven seals and discover the relationship between the chakras and the seals. In this sketch entitled "The Human Being in Relationship to the Planets," Rudolf Steiner depicts the Sun in the region of the heart chakra, Mercury in the region of the solar plexus chakra, Venus with the sacral chakra, and the Moon with the root chakra. For the upper chakras he depicts Mars in connection with the larynx, Jupiter with the third eye, and Saturn with the crown chakra.

The following figure is from the book *Cosmic Dances of the Planets*.[166] It is a tabulation of the correspondence between the planets and the lotus flowers (Sanscrit: *chakras*), also including Rudolf Steiner's color indications from his pastel sketch *Der Mensch in Beziehung zu den Planeten* (*The Human Being in Relation to the Planets*).

---

[166] Lacquanna Paul & Robert Powell, *Cosmic Dances of the Planets* (San Rafael, CA: Sophia Foundation Press, 2006), appendix 3.

Planet	Lotus Flower	Color
Saturn	8-petal	violet
Jupiter	2-petal	blue
Mars	16-petal	green
Sun	12-petal	yellow
Mercury	10-petal	orange
Venus	6-petal	red
Moon	4 petal	peach-blossom

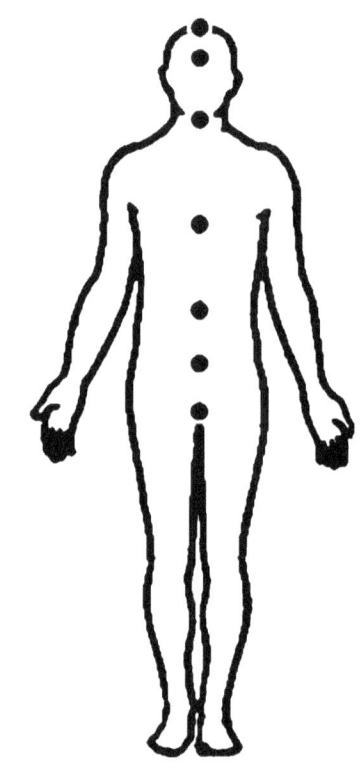

According to Rudolf Steiner's sketch, the crown chakra relates to the planet Saturn. The crown chakra is thus connected with the first seal, since the first seal relates to the ancient Saturn evolution. The words "I AM the Resurrection and the life" belong here, and the image of the Cosmic Christ on the first seal expresses exactly this ideal of the triumph of Resurrection. The crown chakra is the portal to the heavenly Father, and the Cosmic Christ is the one who opens up for humanity the path to the Father. As the Greater Guardian of the Threshold, Christ summons us across the threshold when we are ready. The crown chakra is thus implicitly represented in the first seal, and the words "I AM the Resurrection and the life" belong here.

Similarly, the sketch "The Human Being in Relationship to the Planets" indicates that the third eye chakra relates to the planet Jupiter, which has to do with the second seal and the ancient Sun evolution, during which the Sun globe extended out to the current orbit of the planet Jupiter. The image of the Lamb at the center of the second seal can be seen as a Sun-like power in connection with the "all-seeing eye" of the third eye chakra. The words of Christ, "I AM the light of the world" belong here. It is a matter of the light that illumines the world for spiritual vision.

Then we come to the larynx or throat chakra, that Steiner's depiction connects with the planet Mars, which has to do with the third seal and the ancient Moon evolutionary stage—during ancient Moon, the Sun globe extended out to the orbit of Mars. The larynx chakra corresponds to the third seal. The quality of Mars in the third seal comes to expression on the one hand with the sounding of the trumpets from above and on the other hand with the four apocalyptic riders below. The sounding from above and the expression of will below are indicative of Mars.

This Mars quality carries over from ancient Moon into the first half of the present Earth evolution and is depicted in the red pillar of the fourth seal, representing the present Earth stage of evolution. From the first to the second half of Earth evolution a transition from the Mars to the Mercury impulse is underway, whereby the second half has to do with the blue pillar, the Tree of Life, communion with which (after it had been cut off at the time of the Fall) was opened up to humanity by Christ through the institution of the Eucharist (Mass). War and combative impulses are connected with Mars—this is something that has to be overcome and transformed into something constructive and positive in order to make the transition from the Mars to the Mercury half of Earth evolution. The lower or egotistical I is what separates people from one another. However, the higher Christ-permeated I is what brings people together—"Where two or three are gathered in my name…" The activity of the I has to become uplifted in the impulse of community (Mercury)—instead of war (Mars)—if we are to follow the ascending path. The community impulse of Mercury is the opposite of the Mars impulse driven by self will.

From the image of the fourth seal it is evident that the red pillar represents the Tree of Knowledge and the blue pillar the Tree of Life. These two pillars are legs of the great cosmic being whose name is LOVE and who unites all humankind. The "mighty angel" coming down from Heaven (described in Revelation 10:1) is none other than Christ, who envelops the whole of the Earth evolution in the radiant Sun power of Divine Love. In the human being, the legs are the "wings" of the root chakra, just as the arms are the "wings" of the heart chakra. In most forms of dance the emphasis is on the movement of the legs, which connect from the root chakra to the Earth, whereby the lunar forces (visible to clairvoyant perception) stream from the Moon (root) chakra down through the legs and into the Earth and circulate back again. In eurythmy, however, the emphasis is on the movement of the arms, activating the "wings" of the Sun (heart) chakra.

Continuing with the correspondence between the chakras and the seven seals, Rudolf Steiner's sketch indicates the root chakra in relation to the Moon. In terms of the heliocentric astronomical perspective, the Moon denotes the extent of the Earth's etheric body, and the Moon sphere (the Earth's etheric aura) includes also the Earth as the physical body.

The fourth seal thus corresponds to present Earth evolution (Earth plus Moon), to which—of the seven chakras—the root chakra corresponds. The image of the fourth seal, with the two legs/pillars, clearly indicates the relationship of the Moon (root) chakra to the fourth seal.

From Rudolf Steiner's sketch it can be seen that he places Venus at the sacral chakra, which corresponds to the fifth seal—the Sophia Mystery—and the future Jupiter stage of evolution, during which the Sun globe will extend to the orbit of Venus. The sacral chakra has six petals, thus forming a six-pointed star,[167] which is a profound symbol relating to Sophia.[168] On this level, the fifth seal can be seen in relation to the Sophia Mystery. The six-pointed star (hexagram) is a symbol for the harmony between the heavenly and the earthly, between male and female, and between fire and water (the "marriage of opposites," thus creating harmony). Harmony is the signature of Venus and of the sacral chakra.[169] The hexagram is also known as the "seal of Solomon" and thus represents wisdom—the quality associated with King Solomon—which in turn relates to Jupiter as the planet of wisdom (Jupiter being the name for this future stage of evolution). However, there is a wonderful mystery here, which can only be mentioned briefly, and that is that the planet Venus traces out a five-pointed star (pentagram) in the course of eight years through its

---

167 Robert Powell, *Hermetic Astrology*, vol. 1 (San Rafael, CA: Sophia Foundation Press, 2006), p.247.
168 *Meditations on the Tarot* (New York: Tarcher/Putnam, 2002), chapter 19.
169 Rudolf Steiner, *Knowledge of the Higher Worlds and its Attainment*, Complete Works vol. 10 (Great Barrington, MA: SteinerBooks, 2006), chapter *Some Results of Initiation*: "The development of the six-petalled lotus flower situated in the center of the body…can only be achieved as the result of complete mastery and control of the whole personality through consciousness of self, so that body, soul and spirit form one harmonious whole." The I AM saying associated with this chakra—I AM the way, the truth, and the life—relates to these three levels of body, soul, and spirit.

conjunctions with the Sun.[170] And the pentagram is the symbol for the future Jupiter stage of evolution, which is the fifth stage, just as the cross (four-pointed star) is the symbol of the Earth stage (the fourth stage)—likewise the hexagram (six-pointed star) is the symbol for the future Venus stage of evolution (the sixth stage) and the heptagram (seven-pointed star) is the symbol for the future Vulcan stage of evolution (the seventh stage).

In terms of the hexagram as the symbol for the future Venus evolution, it is interesting that the planet Mercury traces out a six-pointed star in its conjunctions with the Sun in the space of a little more than one year.[171] Again, there is a mystery here, as the solar plexus chakra which, according to the sketch of the human being's chakras in relation to the planets, corresponds to Mercury, has the form of two pentagrams laid one over the other.[172] The solar plexus chakra relates to the sixth seal—the Michael Mystery—and the future Venus stage of evolution, when the Sun globe will extend to the orbit of Mercury. The symbolism expressed in the sixth seal relates to the solar plexus chakra, which is the door from the conscious self to our subconscious realms. The solar plexus is the point of transition from the conscious self to the realm of the subconscious, and Michael, as the Guardian of the Threshold on the macrocosmic level, also has the task of guarding this threshold within the microcosm of the human being. The words of Christ which are spoken in the first part of *Putting on the Resurrection Body* and which relate to the solar plexus chakra are "I AM the door." These words apply to the solar plexus chakra as the door from the conscious to the subconscious. It is noteworthy that Michael is depicted in this seal holding the eurythmic I gesture, which is the gesture for the Mercury sound I.

Finally, the heart chakra corresponds to the Sun and to the seventh seal. Here we find a relationship with the future Vulcan evolution, because at that stage the Sun globe will have contracted all the way into itself—the Earth will be reunited with the Sun. It is through the heart that we connect with our future home—the Sun—and this is depicted in the seventh seal as the mystery of the Holy Grail. Christ descended from the Sun at his incarnation upon the Earth, for the purpose of leading humanity and the Earth back to reunite with the Sun. This is the stage of Resurrection, i.e., humanity will complete the forming of the Resurrection body, the transformed physical body, by the end of the Vulcan stage of evolution. Jesus Christ attained this goal of evolution at the event of his Resurrection, when he became a "ray of Sun" upon the Earth in his life-radiant Resurrection body. Through a co-creative work together with him, the Risen One, the "first-born of the dead," we have the possibility of beginning the work of putting on the Resurrection body, as outlined in this book—a work that leads through the stages of transfiguration of the astral body into *manas* (future Jupiter—wisdom-filled spirit self) and the transformation of the etheric body into *buddhi* (future Venus—love-permeated life spirit) to the metamorphosis of the physical body into the Resurrection body, the stage of *atma* (future Vulcan—life-radiant spirit human) and reaching up even beyond this level to the Cosmic Christ, to his power of peace, to the source from which *manas, buddhi,* and *atma* originate.

The image of the seventh seal shows a transparent cube below—this is the "new Earth" (Revelation 21:1) that has been spiritualized through the power of Divine Love. In the words of Rudolf Steiner:

> With the event of Golgotha, when the blood flowed from the wounds of the great Redeemer, when the Cosmic Heart's blood penetrated the Earth and its forces poured down as far as its center, the Earth became illumined from within and light rayed outward into the surroundings... It is the mission of every single human being and of the whole of humanity to fill themselves with the Christ Spirit and to recognize themselves as a center living in this Spirit, through

---

170   Robert Powell, *Hermetic Astrology,* vol. 1 (San Rafael, CA: Sophia Foundation Press, 2006), p. 62.
171   Ibid., p. 135.
172   Ibid., p. 245.

which spiritual light, spiritual strength and spiritual warmth can flow into the Earth, thereby redeeming it and raising it aloft into spiritual realms.[173]

The new Earth is to arise through the activity of humankind, united with Christ, in spiritualizing the Earth—this is the significance of the transparent cube on the image of the seventh seal. At the same time, the "new Heaven" (Revelation 21:1) is depicted coming down from above, symbolized by the rainbow, the Grail chalice, and the dove.

> Then one of the seven angels...said to me, "Come, I will show you the Bride, the wife of the Lamb." And he carried me away in the spirit...and showed me the holy city, Jerusalem, coming down out of Heaven from God. It shone with the glory of God, and its brilliance was like that of a very precious jewel. (Revelation 21:9–11)

It is Sophia, the Bride of the Lamb, "coming down out of Heaven" shining with the brilliance of the Holy Grail like "a very precious jewel." For Sophia is the Heavenly bearer of the Holy Grail, just as in the Grail story Queen Herzeloyde is the bearer of the Grail in the earthly story of the quest of Parzival, the son of Herzeloyde. "As above, so below"—the Grail bearer Herzeloyde on Earth reflects the heavenly Grail bearer Sophia above. She is the Queen of Peace, and the rainbow is her sign, that of peace, as the harmonious collaboration and union of varying colors. And the dove as a symbol of peace is also associated with Sophia.[174] In chapter 8 of the Book of Genesis, after the Flood a dove returned to Noah with an olive branch in its beak, revealing the end of God's judgment and the beginning of a new covenant with humanity. The dove in the image of the seventh seal represents a new covenant with humanity, the covenant of the era of the heavenly Jerusalem, the holy city of the Lamb and his Bride, arising as the sacred marriage of Christ, bearing up the new spiritualized and transfigured Earth, with Sophia, the Bride, coming down from Heaven bearing the new Heaven. The new Jerusalem—comprising the new Heaven and the new Earth—is mirrored in human hearts as the sacred union of Christ and Sophia, the Lamb and his Bride. This is the mystery of the connection of the heart with the seventh seal, the mystery of the Holy Grail.

The progression outlined above of the correspondence between the chakras and the seven seals begins as a descent through the chakras, but then changes to an ascent. From the first seal to the third seal there is a descent from the crown chakra (ancient Saturn) to the third eye chakra (ancient Sun), to the larynx chakra (ancient Moon). Then with the fourth seal, to which the root chakra corresponds, there is a

---

173 Rudolf Steiner, *Concerning the History and Content of the Higher Degrees of the Esoteric School 1904–1914*, Complete Works vol. 265 (Tobermory, Isle of Mull, Scotland: Etheric Dimensions Press, 2005), pp. 453–455.

174 Bearing in mind that Sophia is the heavenly archetype for many of the goddesses of antiquity, the association of the dove with Sophia emerges in the following account by Anne Baring and Jules Cashford, *The Myth of the Goddess* (London: Penguin-Arkana, 1993), p.595: "The dove that—not in the Gospels but in the pictures of the Gospel stories—hangs above the head of Mary, whispers in her ear, or is poised midway between her and God across a stream of light in the moment of the Annunciation, is interpreted as having been sent by God to Mary as the epiphany of his presence: the image of the Holy Spirit. Yet the conjunction of dove and female in the earlier traditions would have been understood as the Mother Goddess with the dove that was her epiphany, and the two together as the Heavenly and earthly aspects of the goddess, which, in still earlier traditions, would have been unified in one being."

further descent—from the larynx chakra to the root chakra. Here there begins an ascent from the root chakra (present Earth) to the sacral chakra (future Jupiter) to the solar plexus chakra (future Venus); then this ascent culminates in the heart chakra (future Vulcan). This path of descent and ascent—relating to the descending path of evolution from ancient Saturn to the present Earth, followed by the ascending path from the present Earth to future Vulcan—indicates how one can work meditatively with the relationship between the seven seals and the chakras. The seven chakras are the "seven seals" in us, mirroring the macrocosmic seven seals, which in turn reflect the seven stages of evolution. And the evolutionary path of descent and ascent through our chakras is first a descending path from the crown chakra to the third eye chakra to the larynx chakra to the root chakra, and then an ascending path from the root chakra to the sacral chakra to the solar plexus chakra to the heart chakra.

Putting on the Resurrection Body—Part Four

This descending and ascending sequence represents a reality, which can be experienced. It is this that we seek to bring to realization—as an experience—in the fourth part of the core sequence *Putting on the Resurrection Body*. It is a matter of internalizing the reality of an influence that is continually streaming in from the world of the fixed stars, an evolutionary pulse pouring in through our solar system toward our Sun. I call this the *cosmic current*. Looking at our solar system heliocentrically, the cosmic current flows from outside our solar system, from the surrounding stars. Entering our solar system—again ignoring the outer planets and heavenly bodies such as Pluto, Neptune, and Uranus—the cosmic current flows through our solar system in the sequence: Saturn, Jupiter, Mars, Earth (plus Moon), Venus, Mercury, Sun.[175] This flow of the cosmic current is exactly that of the sequence outlined above in relation to the chakras: crown chakra (Saturn), third eye chakra (Jupiter), throat/larynx chakra (Mars), root chakra (Moon), sacral chakra (Venus), solar plexus chakra (Mercury), heart chakra (Sun).

In accordance with "As above, so below," the cosmic current continually flowing through our solar system also flows as a subtle stream of energy in the human being. In his lectures *Macrocosm and Microcosm*, Rudolf Steiner describes that during the 24-hour cycle of waking and sleeping we are in this current every night when we are outside the physical body, residing in the astral body and also every day when we are in the physical body. The cosmic current flows in the form of a figure 8, known in mathematics as a *lemniscate*. In order to grasp this, let us consider what Rudolf Steiner says concerning this in his lecture of March 22, 1910, which is lecture 2 of *Macrocosm and Microcosm*, entitled "Waking and Sleeping Life

---

175   There is also a *solar current* which flows out from our Sun, expressed in the flow of the *solar wind*, that streams in the opposite direction: Sun, Mercury, Venus, Earth (plus Moon), Mars, Jupiter, Saturn. This solar current is reflected in the microcosm of the human being. The reason for focusing upon the *cosmic current* is that it flows in the direction of the evolutionary sequence of the seven days of creation reflected in the structure of our solar system as described above in the space–time parallel between the planets and the evolutionary stages. In the words of Rudolf Steiner, *Macrocosm and Microcosm*, Complete Works vol. 119 (London: Rudolf Steiner Press, 1968), p. 57: "There is a living interplay between the planets and the Sun inasmuch as streams flow continually to and fro—from the planets to the Sun and from the Sun to the planets."

in Relation to the Planets." After describing that in the course of 24 hours the human being moves through a figure schematically represented as a figure 8—"During the night the human being moves around a kind of circle" and from his description the implication is that during the day the human being also moves around a kind of circle, whereby the two circles together form a figure 8, the crossing point being "the moment of going to sleep" and implicitly also the moment of awaking—Rudolf Steiner connects this figure 8 (lemniscate) with the ordering of the planets in the structure of our solar system:

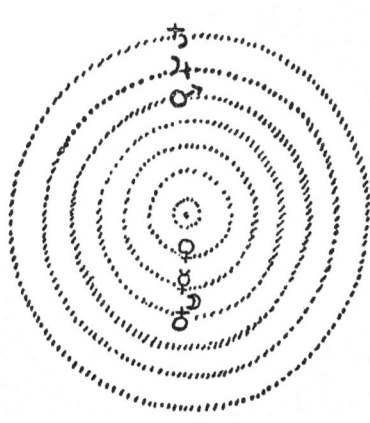

Think of the outer aspect of the solar system. The Earth revolves around the Sun at the center.... The Moon revolves around the Earth, and the planets usually called Mercury and Venus are nearer to the Sun and revolve around it. I emphasize here that in the course of time a change has taken place in the names of these two planets. The planet that is called Mercury today was formerly called *Venus*, and the planet called Venus today was formerly called *Mercury*. Therefore you should think of these designations reversed, so that they do not correspond with current astronomical designations. The planet lying nearer the Sun must be known as Venus and the planet lying further away from the Sun must be known as Mercury.

Here Rudolf Steiner draws attention to the Egyptian naming of the planets. The Egyptians named the planets in accordance with the stages of evolution and were the originators of the (now universal) custom of the naming of the days of the week after the planets— naming them in the order indicating the sequence of the evolutionary stages. For the Egyptians, the planet which we now call Mercury, which denotes the future Venus stage of evolution, was called by them Venus. They named this planet Venus knowing that it is the cosmic marker for the future Venus stage of evolution. Correspondingly, the planet which we now call Venus was called by the Egyptians Mercury. In this book, however, we have not followed the Egyptian names of the planets. Rather, we have adhered to the current astronomical names for Mercury and Venus, as Rudolf Steiner generally did in the earlier years of his lecturing activity (up to 1908) and as he did also in the latter period of his life (1913–1924)—although in 1924 he reverted in the karma lectures to the interchanged names, i.e., to the names as given in this lecture of March 1910 quoted from here. It was in the period 1908–1913, during which this lecture was held, that Rudolf Steiner referred (on numerous occasions) to the interchange of the names of the planets Venus and Mercury. In considering Rudolf Steiner's statements made in this lecture of March 1910 that we are quoting from here, and in looking at the two figures (reproduced here) associated with these statements that he drew during this lecture, this change of names must be kept closely in mind when he makes references to these two planets. Continuing further with his indications:

Further away than the Earth, the figure indicates Mars, Jupiter, and Saturn revolving around the Sun...In the space between the Earth and the Sun there will be the planets Mercury and Venus, and on the other side of the Sun, Mars, Jupiter, and Saturn. Leaving aside the Earth, the sequence will be: Sun, Venus, Mercury, Moon, on one side; Sun, Mars, Jupiter, Saturn, on the other. A looped line (see figure) drawn around the heavenly bodies is a lemniscate, with the Sun at the

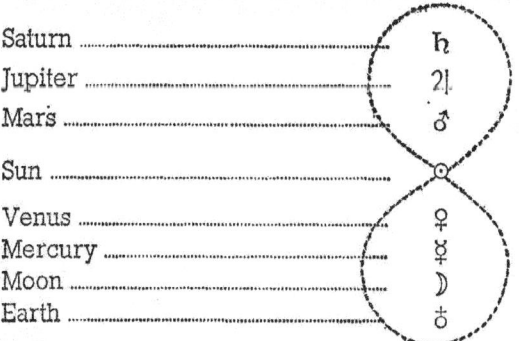

center of the loops—this is the same line as the one indicating the cycle of the human being's waking and sleeping life. Thus it is possible...for the planets to be arranged in the solar system in an order similar to that followed by the human being in completing the cycle of waking and sleeping. Taking the moment of going to sleep and that of waking as the center, the same spatial order can be indicated for the planetary system as for the daily life of the human being.[176]

This figure 8 of the cosmic current (see figure) is mirrored in the human being in a lemniscate as a flow of subtle energy running through the chakras. In the Core Practice *Putting on the Resurrection Body*, at the fourth stage of this meditation we focus our attention upon the flow of life energy running through us in a figure 8. Thus, if the gesture accompanying this stream were to start at the root chakra, relating to the present Earth stage of evolution, it then ascends up the front of the body through the sacral chakra and the solar plexus chakra to the heart chakra; passing through the heart chakra from the front to the back of the body, it then ascends up the spinal column and the back of the head to the crown chakra. Then it descends from the crown chakra frontally to the third eye chakra to the larynx chakra, passing down the front of the body, and goes again through the heart chakra from the front to the back of the body; it then continues to flow down the spinal column, returning to the root chakra to complete the figure 8. This is the "small figure 8" flowing around the chakras. However, there is also a "large figure 8" which includes the legs and feet.

Recalling that the fourth stage of evolution, that of the present Earth, corresponds to the Earth plus Moon, the "large figure 8" includes also the Earth, not just the Moon, as is the case with the "small figure 8." To understand this, it is helpful to contemplate again the schematic figure, reproduced earlier in this chapter, of *The Human Being in Relation to the Planets*. This figure shows the full human being, with the feet standing upon the Earth. In this figure a sphere representing the Earth can be imagined beneath the human being's feet. In the ancient Hebrew tradition this sphere is called Malkuth, meaning *kingdom*.[177] Prior to the separation of the Moon from the Earth, the Earth plus Moon was one body, and the corresponding circulation of life energy in the human being was as described above in relation to the small figure 8. When the Moon separated out from the Earth, the constitution of the human being also changed. One could then speak of an "Earth sphere" beneath the soles of the feet, where the feet rest upon the Earth. As referred to earlier in this book, the life energy flowing up from Shambhala, from the golden heart of Mother Earth, flows up into the feet and legs and then ascends to the region of the heart. The stream of life energy flowing up from Shambhala thus flows through the Earth sphere and is received by the soles of the feet. The large figure 8 extends down the legs to the feet, passing under the feet, and joins the stream ascending from Shambhala. How can one begin to experience this?

At the same time as the life energy of Mother Earth streams up from Shambhala—this being the yin (Earth) energy of Chinese tradition—the lunar forces stream down the legs from the Moon chakra (root chakra) to the Earth sphere beneath the feet.[178] Taking the preceding description of the small figure 8 as our point of departure, this description finishes with the downward flow down the spinal column to the root chakra. Here at the root chakra, the large figure 8 connects onto the downward flow to the root chakra and follows the flow further in connection with the downstreaming of the lunar forces from the root chakra,

---

176 Rudolf Steiner, *Macrocosm and Microcosm*, Complete Works vol. 119 (London: Rudolf Steiner Press, 1968), pp. 42–43.

177 Rudolf Steiner, *Lectures on the Gospel of St. Matthew*, Complete Works vol. 123 (London: Rudolf Steiner Press, 1965), p.134: "Everything, in fact, that the human being perceives in the physical environment was designated in the Hebrew secret doctrine as *Malkuth*, the kingdom."

178 Rudolf Steiner, *Karmic Relationships*, vol. 2, Complete Works vol. 236 (London: Rudolf Steiner Press, 1956), p.101: "Moon forces...are hidden from us only by the activity of...[the] legs. But now [to clairvoyant perception] all that has vanished. And in the background appears before us the creative Moon."

following this stream down the back of the legs under the feet to the earthly sphere beneath the feet. At the Earth sphere (Malkuth) the flow connects onto the ascending stream from Shambhala, which is followed in its flow streaming up the inside of the legs back to the Moon chakra and then continuing from there upward to the heart chakra via the sacral chakra and the solar plexus chakra—the flow then continuing as described above in relation to the small figure 8. In this way the small figure 8 becomes expanded—incorporated into—the large figure 8.

In part 4 of *Putting on the Resurrection Body*, the gesture accompanying the flow of energy through the large figure 8 is the eurythmy gesture for the sound M. The lemniscatory flow of life energy described here is a reality that one can come to experience through the practice of part 4 of *Putting on the Resurrection Body* in conjunction with the M gesture. In doing the gesture, tracing out the lemniscatory flow, it is important to accompany the flow of the M gesture through the figure 8 with one's awareness, as this awareness plays a significant role in bringing the flow of energy to consciousness—the same applies to all the other eurythmy gestures described in this book, especially to the streams that are enlivened through the practice of *Putting on the Resurrection Body*.

The figure 8 in part 4 is one of the four currents that are activated in practicing the four parts of *Putting on the Resurrection Body*. In the first part of this meditation, with the words "In purest out-poured light shimmers the Godhead of the world," we activate an ascending stream (flow) through the chakras in connection with the eurythmy gesture for the sound L to bring the light of Christ into the chakras. The current activated by the L is more than an ascending stream of life energy—it is a fountain of life energy—the focus here is upon the ascending stream through the chakras. In the second part of the meditation, with the words "In purest love toward all that lives radiates the Godhood of my soul," we activate a descending stream through the chakras in connection with the eurythmy gesture for the sound R to bring the love of Christ into the chakras. As with the L, the current activated by the R is more than the descending stream of life energy—it is a great circulatory stream—the focus here is upon the descending stream through the chakras. In the third part, with the words, "I rest within the Godhead of the world," we activate a spiral stream (larynx, solar plexus, third eye, sacral, crown, heart, then root) through the chakras in connection with the eurythmy sound AU to bring the life of Christ into the chakras. Then in the fourth part of the meditation *Putting on the Resurrection Body*, with the words, "I shall find myself within the Godhead of the world," we activate the current of life energy circulating through the figure 8 through the chakras (including the Earth sphere beneath the feet) to come into relationship with the transcendental level of the peace of Christ. In connection with each chakra we strongly visualize the image of the corresponding seal (of the seven seals) for that chakra.

Let us now consider the words that accompany the fourth stage of the Core Practice of *Putting on the Resurrection Body*. These are the seven "THOU ART sayings." Six of the "THOU ART sayings" belonging to this part 4 are not words spoken by Christ explicitly. However, they are implicit in various places in Revelation. In association with the crown chakra, contemplating the first seal, the words relating to this seal are "THOU ART the Alpha and Omega." As indicated in the first chapter of Revelation, the Cosmic Christ says, "I AM the Alpha and the Omega" (Revelation 1:8) and the form of the Cosmic Christ that is described in this chapter is the verbal description underlying what is portrayed in the first seal (Revelation 1:12–16). What is portrayed in the other six seals can be found—as verbal descriptions—in other chapters of Revelation. Although the six THOU ART sayings are not explicit as verbal descriptions in the chapters in Revelation relating to these seals, they are implicit in the spiritual reality (truth) underlying the image content of the remaining six seals.

Here, in connection with part 4 of *Putting on the Resurrection Body*, the form THOU ART is spoken instead of I AM, because this stage goes beyond the level of human evolution that is forseeable at the present point in time—a transcendental level as represented in the images of the seven seals. Although the seven seals correlate with the seven stages of evolution, the Cosmic Christ who oversees these seven stages is at a level transcending the seven stages themselves. He could say of himself "I AM the Alpha and the Omega," meaning the first stage (Alpha), that of ancient Saturn, and the last stage (Omega), that of future Vulcan. In order to be able to oversee these seven stages from ancient Saturn to future Vulcan, Christ is beyond them. And for human beings *within* these seven stages of evolution, it is only possible to look up to the Cosmic Christ transcending the seven stages of evolution and say THOU ART.

It is different with the "I AM" sayings. For Christ—he who is the divine I AM—came to the Earth to bestow the gift of the divine I AM on human beings, and meditating upon the seven "I AM sayings" in relation to the seven chakras is a way of connecting with Christ during present Earth evolution as the bestower of the I AM, to bring to realization the words "Not I, but Christ in me." Allowing the I AM sayings to reverberate within the chakras creates a resonance with the divine I AM, and thus the I AM form is appropriate here, especially as Christ gave the I AM sayings to us as mantras for the spiritualization of the chakras.

In our considerations so far, we have seen that the first seal corresponds to the ancient Saturn stage (Alpha) but also implicit within it is the future Vulcan stage (Omega). It is the Cosmic Christ on his path of Ascension that is represented in the image of this seal (see page 60), and correspondingly the focus is upon the crown chakra with the words, "THOU ART the Alpha and the Omega," since the path taken by the human soul at death is one of ascent through the crown chakra toward the Father. While on his path of Ascension to the Father, the Cosmic Christ appeared to John on the island of Patmos. John[179] was actually Lazarus-John, the name given to him after having been raised from the dead, on which occasion Christ spoke the words "I AM the Resurrection and the life" (Gospel of John, chapter 11), the I AM saying corresponding to the crown chakra. At this appearance the Cosmic Christ revealed to John (Lazarus) the content of Revelation containing the mysteries of the future. This appearance of the Cosmic Christ to John on Patmos was a prefiguring of Christ's appearance now to human beings around the globe, as the Etheric Christ. John experienced in advance what more and more human beings are now experiencing at this time of the Second Coming.[180] The image of the first seal—depicting the Risen Christ in his cosmic form[181]—thus relates to his current manifestation during the New Age (1899–4399), the age of the Second Coming of Christ, which extends from the last part of the Age of Pisces almost to the end of the Age of Aquarius (2375 to 4535). The Etheric Christ is now active in the Earth's etheric aura, preparing humanity and the Earth for the Age of Aquarius, which will start in some 360 years time, this being the time required for the vernal point to shift back from its present position at 5° Pisces into Aquarius, moving at a rate of one degree in 72 years.

Let us continue now with the second seal—in association with the third eye chakra, contemplating the second seal (see page 110), the Mystery of the Lamb, in relation to the words "THOU ART the Lamb of God." Through these words we form a relationship with divine peace—the transcendental level of Christ. The image of this seal depicts the Lamb in the midst of

---

179   Charles Tidball & Robert Powell, *Jesus, Lazarus, and the Messiah* (Great Barrington, MA: SteinerBooks, 2005), chapters 11 and 12.
180   See, for example, the descriptions by Estelle Isaacson of her experiences of the Etheric Christ in 2009 and 2011 that are published in *Prophecy-Phenomena-Hope: The Real Meaning of* 2012 (Great Barrington, MA: SteinerBooks, 2011), pp. 75–80, and pp. 89–92.
181   From the day of the Resurrection, for forty days the Risen One appeared in a more human form

Chapter 5: The Macrocosmic Background to the Core Practice

the four holy living creatures—the Bull, the Lion, the Eagle, and the holy living creature with a human face—as described in Revelation chapters 4 and 5. The Eagle is how the sign of Scorpio was seen in ancient times, and the holy living creature with a human face is the Waterbearer. The four holy living creatures—in Greek the word for holy living creature is *Zoa*—represent the circle of twelve *Zoa* comprising the zodiac. The word zodiac is usually translated as "animal circle." In fact, it is the circle of the holy living creatures around the throne of God and around the Lamb. As Rudolf Steiner described, "The etheric body of Christ embraces the zodiac."[182] The spiritual reality expressed in the image of the second seal is summarized in this sentence, "The etheric body of Christ embraces the zodiac." This is the Lamb (Christ) in the midst of the holy living creatures comprising the zodiac, of which there are twelve altogether, although only four of the twelve signs are depicted on this seal—the four fixed signs of the zodiac (Bull/Taurus, Lion/Leo, Eagle/Scorpio, Waterbearer/Aquarius). As described by Rudolf Steiner, each of these four signs has two "companion signs" accompanying on either side, making up the full circle of the twelve Zoa comprising the zodiac.[183] And this relates also to the etheric body of the human being, which was bestowed upon humanity during the ancient Sun stage of evolution, to which the second seal relates. Since the ancient Sun globe extended to the orbit of Jupiter, it is the planet Jupiter, and the chakra corresponding to Jupiter, the third eye chakra, that relates to the second seal. The Sun-like power of the Lamb at the center of the second seal is the cosmic power that can open the third eye—THOU ART the Lamb of God—the corresponding I AM saying being "I AM the light of the world," spoken at the healing of the man born blind. All who are not clairvoyant are like the man born blind, in need of healing, to have spiritual sight restored by the one who said of himself, "I AM the light of the world."

In association with the larynx chakra, contemplating the third seal, the relevant saying is, "THOU ART the Word." In this image there are three things which stand out. First, there are the seven trumpets sounding from above. They symbolize the resounding of the Word that brings all things into existence, indicating the tones of the *harmonies of the spheres* that resounded as creative forces into the shaping of the astral body during the ancient Moon stage of evolution. Second, in the center of the image of the third seal is the book with seven seals. This relates to the astral body, which was formed during the ancient Moon stage of existence, to which the third seal corresponds—the seven seals in the astral body being the seven chakras, which are the primary organs of the astral body. Third, below the book with seven seals are the four riders of the Apocalypse, followed by three sacred symbols: the pentagram (five-pointed star), hexagram (six-pointed star), and heptagram (seven-pointed star)—although this is not a regular heptagram, but a special version of it, called by Rudolf Steiner the star of the Lamb.[184]

As referred to earlier, the pentagram, hexagram, and heptagram are symbols for the three future stages of evolution: Jupiter, Venus, and Vulcan. The four Apocalyptic riders on their horses, represent the will forces at work within the astral body at different stages of evolution, which have to be "tamed" and directed by the I, and thus relate to levels of soul development, i.e., of the human I within the astral body. The first rider on the white horse represents an early stage of development of the human soul, when the soul was still pure, relatively speaking. The second rider on a fiery red horse symbolizes a war-like level of development of the soul. The third rider on a black horse indicates

---

182 Rudolf Steiner, *Esoterische Stunden 1910–1912* ("*Esoteric Lessons 1910–1912*"), Complete Works vol. 266/II (Dornach, Switzerland: Rudolf Steiner Verlag, 1996), p.459.

183 Robert Powell & Kevin Dann, *The Astrological Revolution* (Great Barrington, MA: SteinerBooks, 2009), pp. 14–17 discusses the spiritual reality of the Zoa underlying the constellations/signs of the zodiac, with many quotes from Rudolf Steiner identifying the circle of the twelve Zoa with twelve great colonies of sublime, exalted, majestic beings in direct proximity and in service of the Creator ("the one who sits upon the throne").

184 Rudolf Steiner, *Reading the Pictures of the Apocalypse*, Complete Works vol. 104a (London: Rudolf Steiner Press, 1993), lecture of April 22, 1907.

the level of soul development when the focus is upon the external, physical world—signifying a dying from the spiritual world, and symbolized as the realm of death (hence the black color). The fourth horse is a "pale horse, and its rider's name is *death*, and Hades followed him" (Revelation 6:8). This image relates to the present condition of the human soul, followed by Hades (Ahriman), the soul having become pale and death-like through being ensnared by ahrimanic forces. The fourth rider—representing the human soul at the present time—is at the low point of evolution. Ahead lies the ascending path, leading through the Jupiter, Venus, and Vulcan stages. As discussed earlier in this book, the ascending path has to be *willed* by the human being, who is inwardly called to turn to Christ and begin a work of co-creation together with him—the work of putting on the Resurrection body. Without this conscious decision to align oneself with Christ and take the ascending path, the human being by default falls prey to the encroachment/ensnaring of Ahriman. The time of decision is now!

In considering Earth evolution in association with the root chakra, we contemplate the fourth seal (see page 129), and the words: "THOU ART the Tree of Knowledge and the Tree of Life." To elaborate on the Tree of Knowledge of Good and Evil, let us consider that this tree is actually what is represented in Rudolf Steiner's great statue the *Representative of Humanity* (see the photo reproduction on page 2). It is carved in wood (elm). It is about thirty feet high—an enormous statue. Rudolf Steiner worked on this for seven years together with the English sculptress Edith Maryon. This sculpture is sometimes called *The Group*—the group being Christ in the center, Lucifer above and to the left of Christ, and Ahriman below and to the right of Christ. Then there is also the combination of Lucifer and Ahriman alongside to the right of Christ, an interlocking of Ahriman and Lucifer together. This statue has to do with the three temptations and three levels of activity of the double within the human being. Christ is obviously the central figure in this statue. Ultimately Christ is the true source of knowledge. In the Bible we read that it is Lucifer who tempts human beings to eat from the Tree of Knowledge of Good and Evil, and that is what happened. But it was not yet time for humanity to eat from this tree. Lucifer brought this about prematurely, and although Lucifer means the light bearer, Christ is the true light bearer—the true source of knowledge coming from the Tree of Knowledge of Good and Evil. In the Rosicrucian mysteries there was a saying, "Christus verus Luciferus." Translated from the Latin, this means: "Christ is the true Lucifer, i.e., *Christ is the true bringer of light* (Lucifer = "light bearer"). And in this statue we behold Christ as the source of good, and around him are the sources of evil. In this sense, this mighty statue mirrors something of the Tree of Knowledge of Good and Evil.

At the time of the Fall in the far-distant past of Earth evolution, during the age of Lemuria, the human being had hardly begun to develop the I and so was not in a position to cognize the mystery of good and evil, which can only be grasped by the I. In the twentieth century, however, Rudolf Steiner recognized that the time had arrived in human evolution when the mystery of good and evil needed to be unveiled. Without some knowledge of this mystery, it is not possible to understand the time in which we are living.[185]

The three temptations of Jesus Christ in the wilderness is the theme of the statue of *The Representative of Humanity* (see reproduction of this statue—also known as *The Group*—on page 2). It depicts the power of good in Jesus Christ, as the representative of humankind, overcoming the forces of evil that tempt human beings on three levels: on the level of the will (the first temptation, that of the will to power), the level of feeling (the second temptation, that of "casting oneself down from the pinnacle of the temple"), and the level of thinking (the third temptation, that of "turning stones into bread").

---

185 This theme is explored further in Robert Powell & Kevin Dann, *Christ & the Maya Calendar* (Great Barrington, MA: SteinerBooks, 2009) and in Robert Powell, *Prophecy–Phenomena–Hope: The Real Meaning of* 2012 (Great Barrington, MA: SteinerBooks, 2011).

Jesus Christ knew that every human being would be tempted in thought, word (feeling), and deed (will). What he lived through archetypally in the three temptations in the wilderness is an achievement that can be called upon by every human being, when being tempted. It is the I, ultimately, which is tempted—via the forces of thinking, feeling, and the will in the astral body, working down into the etheric body. Through succumbing to temptation, the double develops within the human being—actually not just one, but three doubles, relating to the three levels of temptation. These three doubles are called the luciferic double (force of the first temptation), the karmic double (force of the second temptation), and the ahrimanic double (force of the third temptation). We have to learn to free the luciferic double—I have discussed the redemption of Lucifer at length in *Christ & the Maya Calendar*.[186] Something of this mystery is connected with the figure of Lucifer above and to the left of Christ. The ahrimanic double has to be cast out beneath the feet—held in place, as depicted with Ahriman beneath the feet of Christ in the statue of *The Group*. This is accomplished through bringing to realization the moral strength of "Christ in me" and also with the help of the Archangel Michael as the Defender of Truth and Justice. Also, we have to transform within ourselves the karmic double (also called the human double). Through this transformation, there comes a time when the karmic/human double is no longer within us but *alongside* us. We are able to control it, and it becomes a servant of the good. The karmic double comprises both luciferic and ahrimanic forces, and it is this that is depicted as the figure alongside Christ in the statue of *The Group*. We accomplish this transformation through our moral development. The karmic double can only work within us if we keep falling prey to temptation. However, if we think good and noble thoughts, experience elevated feelings, and are doing good deeds through helping people, the karmic double is pushed out and goes through a metamorphosis to become a servant of the good.[187]

The fact that Rudolf Steiner was able to creatively manifest this great statue depicting the mystery of good and evil reveals that Rudolf Steiner is the guardian—on the human level—of the Tree of Knowledge of Good and Evil. As this guardian, he knew that through the advent of the Etheric Christ the time in evolution had arrived for the unveiling of the mystery of good and evil—that humanity had now reached a level of consciousness at which partaking of the Tree of Knowledge of Good and Evil could be in service of Christ. In the Garden of Eden it was not yet the right time for Adam and Eve to eat of this tree, i.e., to partake of knowledge of good and evil, for they (Adam = the human I; Eve = the human soul or astral body) did not have the strength to be able to choose good over evil. However, the time now is ripe, when the human I is able to cognize good and evil and to consciously choose between them. Thus, in the twentieth century, Rudolf Steiner was able to bring forth the knowledge of good and evil, which he spoke of in hundreds of lectures, and which he summarized in such a magnificent way in the statue of *The Group*. Prior to the twentieth century, before the onset of Christ's Second Coming, this unveiling of good and evil would have been premature, before its time, for humanity.

Continuing with the fourth seal, the image (see page 129) also depicts the Tree of Life, which is the other pillar we see in the fourth seal—the blue pillar. With Christ's institution of the Eucharist, in essence he communicated, "Through the substances of bread and wine you commune with me"—that is, you commune with the principle of divine life. Communion with Christ is communion with the Tree of Divine Life, access to which became opened up for humanity with the second half of evolution, starting with the institution of the Eucharist at the Mystery of Golgotha. In this sense—and bearing in mind what was

---

186 Robert Powell & Kevin Dann, *Christ & the Maya Calendar* (Great Barrington, MA: SteinerBooks, 2009), chapter 8: "The Redemption of Lucifer." For a discussion of the three doubles, see Valentin Tomberg, *Inner Development* (Great Barrington, MA: SteinerBooks, 1992).

187 Valentin Tomberg, *Inner Development* (Great Barrington, MA: SteinerBooks, 1992), chapter 2, discusses the three doubles.

said earlier about the (now) rightful eating from the Tree of Knowledge of Good and Evil—the "THOU ART words" in relation to the fourth seal in connection with the root chakra are, "THOU ART the Tree of Knowledge and the Tree of Life."

From the root chakra, now the ascent begins—corresponding to the ascending path of evolution—to the sacral chakra. In association with the sacral chakra (located about 3 inches below the navel), while contemplating the fifth seal in connection with the next stage of evolution, the Jupiter stage, the relevant words are: "Sophia is the Bride, THOU ART the Bridegroom." Whereas the other seals clearly relate to different aspects of the Cosmic Christ, how does the fifth seal express an aspect of the Cosmic Christ?

What we see in the image of the fifth seal (see page 112) is the figure of Sophia, who first appears midway through Revelation, in chapter 12, as the "woman clothed with the Sun, with the Moon under her feet, and on her head a crown of twelve stars" (Revelation 12:1). From chapter 21 of Revelation we learn that Sophia is the Bride of the Lamb. It is Christ, who is the Lamb, and thus Christ is the Bridegroom. This is the meaning of the words, "Sophia is the Bride, THOU ART the Bridegroom." And just as Christ is the overseer of the two halves of Earth evolution—connected with the Tree of Knowledge and the Tree of Life—the purpose of which is FREEDOM (through partaking, in the spirit of Christ, of the Tree of Knowledge, as shown to humanity by Rudolf Steiner) and LOVE (through communion with Christ, the Tree of Life, in the spirit of the words, "Christ in me"), so Sophia is the overseer of the Jupiter evolution, the mission of which is the transfiguration of the astral body into *manas* (spirit self), where the soul becomes "clothed with the Sun" (Christ within), "with the Moon under the feet" (the impure forces are cast out—trodden underfoot), and "on the head a crown of twelve stars" (united, i.e., reunited, with the cosmos, as prior to the Fall). The symbol of the Jupiter evolution is the pentagram traced out by Venus through its conjunctions with the Sun,[188] and tradition links Sophia with the rose, in the form of which the pentagram appears, in its five petals. It is more specifically the Virgin Mary who is connected with the rose—the prayer dedicated to her is the rosary, meaning "garland of roses"—and through Mary the connection is found with Sophia, who is the Rose of the World.[189]

From the sacral chakra, the ascent proceeds to the solar plexus chakra, related to the Venus stage of evolution, the mission of which is the development of *buddhi* (life spirit), which is the transformed etheric body, where the life body becomes permeated by the love of Christ and Sophia. The symbol for the Venus evolution is the six-pointed star (hexagram) traced out by Mercury in its conjunctions with the Sun.[190] In his lecture of January 2, 1906, Rudolf Steiner refers to the hexagram as the symbol for the Holy Grail.[191]

One aspect of the six-pointed star is that the two triangles can be seen in relation to Christ and Sophia—the upward pointing triangle representing the fire of the Logos, Christ, elevating and spiritualizing the Earth and humanity in the creation of the New Earth, and the downward pointing triangle

---

188 Robert Powell, *Hermetic Astrology*, vol. 1 (San Rafael, CA: Sophia Foundation Press, 2006), p. 62.
189 For the relationship of Mary to Sophia, see Valentin Tomberg, *Christ and Sophia* (Great Barrington, MA: SteinerBooks, 2006), chapter 12 of the section on the New Testament, the chapter on the Pentecost mystery of Sophia's union with the Virgin Mary. See also, Robert Powell, *The Sophia Teachings* (Great Barrington, MA: SteinerBooks, 2001, chapter 4: The Influence of Divine Sophia in the Western Mystical Tradition. And concerning the Rose of the World, see Daniel Andreev, *The Rose of the World* (Great Barrington, MA: SteinerBooks, 1997).
190 Robert Powell, *Hermetic Astrology*, vol. 1 (San Rafael, CA: Sophia Foundation Press, 2006), p. 135.
191 Rudolf Steiner, *Die Tempellegende und die Goldene Legende* ("The Tempel Legend and the Golden Legend"; CW 93; Dornach, Switzerland: Rudolf Steiner Verlag, 1982), p. 278. See also page 347, where Alexander Strakosch reports that Rudolf Steiner communicated to him, "The hexagram is the actual sign of Christ and the Venus evolution."

representing the water of Divine Wisdom (Sophia) streaming down from celestial heights, borne down by Sophia as the New Heaven. The hexagram thus represents the union, the *hieros gamos* ("sacred marriage"), of the Divine Masculine (Christ) and the Divine Feminine (Sophia) at the Venus stage of evolution, preceding the "reintegration of Heaven and Earth" at the Vulcan stage of evolution, which gives us a presentiment of the union of the Father and the Mother that will take place when the Earth reunites with the Sun—this being the higher octave of the mystery of the Holy Grail.

In association with the solar plexus chakra, contemplating the sixth seal (see page 110), the words relating to the image of this seal are, "Michael is the Guardian, THOU ART the Greater Guardian of the Threshold." What is the connection between Michael and the Cosmic Christ? Michael is at the "right hand of the place of sacrifice," which is to say Michael is at the right hand of Christ.[192] This is brought to expression in that Michael has the special task to guard the threshold to the spiritual world. He is called the Guardian of the Threshold, and Christ is called the Greater Guardian of the Threshold.[193] These words acknowledge that Michael is also in a certain respect an expression of the Being of Christ. Just as Sophia is inwardly united with Christ as the Bride (in relation to the Bridegroom) so Michael, as the Guardian of the Threshold, is united with Christ as the Greater Guardian of the Threshold. On the one hand the six-pointed star symbolizes the sacred union between Christ and Sophia, on the other hand it is also the Star of David, the symbol of the people of ancient Israel, whose Folk Spirit was the Archangel Michael.[194]

Just as the Archangel Michael was the Guardian of the people of ancient Israel, now, in our time, the Archangel Michael is the Guardian of the Threshold to the spiritual world. This is an "open secret" to those who know the content of the Michael School founded by Rudolf Steiner. Concerning the Michael School, he spoke out that "this school was founded by Michael" and that "the words of Michael are what should characterize the way which leads into the spiritual world."[195] By this, he means that the way—through nineteen lessons, each containing profound spiritual instructions, revealed in the content presented by Rudolf Steiner comprising the "lessons of the First Class" of the Michael School—is directly under Michael's guidance and that the words of the Michael School, although spoken by Rudolf Steiner, are actually the words of Michael. In each of the nineteen lessons of the First Class of the Michael School, the instructions for the spiritual path are given by the Guardian of the Threshold. Since, as Rudolf Steiner says, these instructions are "the words of Michael," it follows that (1) the (macrocosmic) Guardian of the Threshold and the Archangel Michael are one and the same, or

---

192 Rudolf Steiner, *Spirituelles Erkennen, Religiöses Empfinden, Kultisches Handeln* ("Spiritual Knowing, Religious Sensibility, Cultic Deeds"), Complete Works vol. 343 (Dornach, Switzerland: Rudolf Steiner Verlag, 1993), p.425: "Through the mediation of the Blessed Archangel Michael, who stands at the right hand of the place of sacrifice..."
193 Rudolf Steiner, *Knowledge of the Higher Worlds and its Attainment*, Complete Works vol. 10 (Great Barrington, MA: SteinerBooks, 2006), chapters *The Guardian of the Threshold* and *Life and Death: The Greater Guardian of the Threshold*. See also, Valentin Tomberg, *Inner Development* (Great Barrington, MA: SteinerBooks, 1992), chapter 5: *The Two Guardians of the Threshold*.
194 Rudolf Steiner, *Concerning the History and Content of the Higher Degree of the Esoteric School 1904–1914*, Complete Works vol. 265 (Tobermory, Isle of Mull, Scotland: Etheric Dimensions Press, 2005), p.443: "The Folk Spirit which united with Moses at his initiation and then dwelt in him was Michael." See also Dionysius the Areopagite, *Mystical Theology and the Celestial Hierarchies* (Fintry, England: Shrine of Wisdom, 1965), p.47: "Michael is called the Lord of the people of Judah."
195 Rudolf Steiner, *Esoterische Unterweisungen für die Erste Klasse* ("Esoteric Instructions for the First Class"), Complete Works vol. 270b (Dornach, Switzerland: Rudolf Steiner Verlag, 1999), p.174. See also vol. 270c, p.241: "The actual leadership of the [Michael] School lies with that spiritual power from whom the school was also founded and who has the leadership of the present age, working in the capacity of "Spirit of the Age" [*Zeitgeist*, Time Spirit]: the Archangel Michael" (from the afterword by Hella Wiesberger).

that (2) the (microcosmic) Guardian of the Threshold stands directly in the service of the Archangel Michael, who speaks through the Guardian of the Threshold.

In consideration of the two possibilities concerning the Archangel Michael in relation to the function of the Guardian of the Threshold, Thomas Meyer (in his recent publication of the content of the nineteen lessons of the First Class) draws the following conclusion.

> There is especially a being who needs to be taken into consideration...the Guardian of the Threshold. This real and actual spiritual being [is] of the rank of an Archangel[196]...He is to be met at all nineteen stages of the path of meditation [of the First Class of the Michael School] as a warning, protecting, advising companion. And he it is, also, who mediates access to the various beings of the [spiritual] hierarchies and to what they offer to teach along the course of this path of meditation. On September 11, 1924, Rudolf Steiner once indicated that the Guardian of the Threshold speaks "in Michael's commission" ["on the mandate of Michael"]. Thus it is made clear that this apparently nameless being is to some extent the most important helper on the *earthly* level of the School of Michael."[197]

Thomas Meyer comes to the conclusion that it is the Archangel Phanuel who is the Guardian of the Threshold: "We may see in Phanuel the real and actual Archangel individuality, who 'in Michael's commission' mediated the warnings, teachings, and mantras of the suprasensory–earthly Michael School."[198] This is an interesting idea, for which Thomas Meyer brings supporting evidence based on Rudolf Steiner's indication that in the initiation schools of antiquity the Archangel Phanuel "was the protector who was called upon by the one striving for initiation."[199] Thomas Meyer has found something of great significance here, with regard to the role of the Archangel Phanuel as a protector of initiation. On the other hand, it is possible to approach the question "Who is the Guardian of the Threshold?" from another perspective, as elucidated in the following. The approach followed here is to take into account the further question as to what actually takes place at the encounter with the Guardian of the Threshold. The result of successfully following this way of the Michael School is the meeting with the Guardian of the Threshold, who shows one the double, i.e., one's karmic double, which is the being comprising the sum total of all one's wrong thoughts, words, and deeds during the course of one's incarnations upon the Earth. This being, whom one has created oneself, is "a thoroughly horrid, ghostly being," who then speaks,

> I shall never leave your side once you have crossed my threshold. I shall always be there beside you in a form you can perceive. From then on, whenever you think or act wrongly, you will immediately see your fault as an ugly, demonic distortion in my appearance. My being will be changed and become radiantly beautiful only when you have made amends for all your wrongs and have so purified yourself that you become incapable of further evil. Then, too, I shall be able to unite with you as a single being in order to bless and benefit your further activity.[200]

In these words is revealed that the double performs a function of guarding the threshold and is capable along the path of moral development of being

---

196 Footnote by Robert Powell: here Thomas Meyer is citing Rudolf Steiner, *Von der Initiation* ("Concerning Initiation"), Complete Works vol. 138 (Dornach, Switzerland: Rudolf Steiner Verlag, 1986), p.63, where—in discussing the Guardian of the Threshold—Rudolf Steiner says, "This being belongs to the class of the Archangels."
197 *Der Meditationsweg der Michaelschule* ("The Path of Meditation of the Michael School"), (published by Thomas Meyer; Basel, Switzerland: Perseus Verlag, 2011), p.457.
198 Ibid., p.460.

199 Ibid., p.459—quoted from Rudolf Steiner, *Das Hereinwirken geistiger Wesenheiten in den Menschen* ("The Influence of Spiritual Beings upon Human Beings"), Complete Works vol. 102 (Dornach, Switzerland: Rudolf Steiner Verlag, 1984), lecture of April 20, 1908.
200 Rudolf Steiner, "The Guardian of the Threshold," in *How to Know Higher Worlds*: A Modern Path of Initiation (CW 10; Hudson, NY: Anthroposophic Press, 1994),

transformed into a servant of the good, "becoming radiantly beautiful." As Rudolf Steiner expresses it elsewhere: "One has to contemplate what appears to one as one's double—the guardian of the threshold—and interposes itself before one's higher self so that one is able to perceive the vast disparity between what one is now and what one is meant to become."[201] Thus, there is the Archangel, who is the Guardian of the Threshold for all humanity, and there is the individual's double, who is the personal guardian of the threshold for that individual. And there is also the Greater Guardian of the threshold, who is Christ.

The personal guardian of the threshold has two sides: one is the shadow side of the human being, the double that has to be transformed along the path of moral development into something "radiantly beautiful."[202] The other side of the personal guardian of the threshold is described as follows:

> Thus one stands at the boundary between the sense world and the world of spirit...in face of a reality which acts only as a suprasensory reality—however, as real and living as a human being. This is the guardian of the threshold...and one gets to know [the guardian]...as a being...which in a certain sense participated in the life of the Earth from the beginning, then however did not participate in what one experiences as a being of soul.... Here we come together with a being in relation to which one says to oneself: I have a being before me which learns and experiences much in the world, but it is not concerned with what one can experience on Earth as love, pain, and suffering, and also as mistakes and immoral behavior. It knows nothing and does not want to know anything of what took place until now in the depths of the human being.... The feeling arises: By passing through earthly cultures, you have of necessity acquired imperfections. However, you must return to the original condition. Upon the Earth you must find the way back again, and this being can show that to you, because it has not taken on your mistakes.[203]

From these words it is clear that the personal guardian of the threshold has a higher side as well as a shadow side. The higher side, as described above, has to do with the higher self, preserving the true image of the human being from before the Fall; and the shadow side, the double, is the sum total of all the errors and moral failings of the human being throughout all earthly incarnations. The human being is between these two and has to work upon transforming the shadow nature of the double in order to be able to cross the threshold, and is helped in this by the higher self. Thus the encounter with the guardian of the threshold has these two sides.

In Rudolf Steiner's use of the expression "Guardian of the Threshold," whereas he specifies "Greater Guardian of the Threshold," when he is speaking of Christ, he does not always distinguish between the Archangel who is the macrocosmic Guardian of the Threshold and the personal guardian of the threshold for that individual. (Capitals are used here to distinguish between the two.) Through the encounter with the Archangelic Guardian of the Threshold, the individual's personal guardian of the threshold becomes a "mouthpiece" of the Archangelic Guardian of the Threshold. In other words, the microcosmic guardian of the threshold then serves the macrocosmic Guardian of the Threshold, as can be seen from consideration of the above words "I shall never leave your side..." spoken by the microcosmic guardian of the threshold. It is this "mouthpiece" relationship that is implied by Rudolf Steiner in the following words: "Then comes the moment in which the words of the guardian of the

---

201 Rudolf Steiner, *An Outline of Esoteric Science*, Complete Works vol. 13 (Great Barrington, MA: SteinerBooks, 1997), chapter 5: *Knowledge of Higher Worlds—Initiation*. Translation revised by RP after comparison with the original German text.

202 See the discussion on page 164 concerning the karmic double that functions as the personal guardian of the threshold.

---

203 Rudolf Steiner, *Von der Initiation* ("Concerning Initiation"; CW 138; Dornach, Switzerland: Rudolf Steiner Verlag, 1986), lecture of August 27, 1912.

threshold resound decisively, the words of the guardian of the threshold as if coming from Michael himself, as if coming from worlds afar."[204] These words make it clear that the microcosmic guardian of the threshold is the "mouthpiece" of the Archangel Michael, who is the macrocosmic Guardian of the Threshold. In the German original, no distinction is made between the macrocosmic Guardian of the Threshold and the microcosmic guardian of the threshold, and since this relationship was evidently kept veiled by Rudolf Steiner, this has led to confusion with regard to the identity of the Archangelic being who is the macrocosmic Guardian of the Threshold.

However, once one beholds the Archangel Michael as the macrocosmic Guardian of the Threshold, who shows one one's personal guardian of the threshold, and one then experiences the latter speaking "in Michael's commission," the macrocosmic–microcosmic relationship is clear, as expressed in the following words: "After the guardian has told us how we have to prepare ourselves [to cross the threshold]—and we feel: such preparations have to be—then as from Michael, as from worlds afar, his word resounds."[205] Here again the "mouthpiece" relationship—that the words of Michael from afar are spoken to the individual via his or her personal (microcosmic) guardian of the threshold—is evident. In this context it has to be remembered that the entire content of the Michael School was given to Rudolf Steiner by the Archangel Michael, the macrocosmic Guardian of the Threshold, speaking through Rudolf Steiner's personal (microcosmic) guardian of the threshold—a purified and elevated being in service of Michael. Rudolf Steiner's personal guardian of the threshold is thus—within the Michael School founded by Rudolf Steiner—the archetypal representative for each and every individual's personal guardian of the threshold (at least, for each individual within the School of Michael founded by Rudolf Steiner). And, moreover, it is important in this matter to bear in mind that Michael—as the macrocosmic Guardian of the Threshold—is the "right hand" of Christ, who is the Greater Guardian of the Threshold.

The mystery of the Guardian of the Threshold remains veiled until one crosses the threshold. The macrocosmic Guardian of the Threshold for humanity is the Archangel Michael—"This being belongs to the class of the Archangels" (in the words of Rudolf Steiner quoted earlier). Once this veil is lifted, an extraordinary light is shed upon much of Rudolf Steiner's life work, which culminated with the founding of the School of Michael. The Archangel Michael, as the macrocosmic Guardian of the Threshold, founded the Michael School on Earth through Rudolf Steiner, through Rudolf Steiner's "radiantly beautiful" personal (microcosmic) guardian of the threshold. Thanks on the one hand to the impeccable nature of this macrocosmic–microcosmic relationship between the Archangel Michael and Rudolf Steiner's personal guardian of the threshold, and on the other hand to Rudolf Steiner's extraordinary ability to transmit exactly what he received, it is *Michael's words* that are to be found as the instructions of the Guardian of the Threshold in every one of the nineteen lessons of the First Class of the Michael School. This excursus concerning the Guardian of the Threshold is given here in order to clarify the background to the expression, "Michael is the Guardian, THOU ART the Greater Guardian of the Threshold" spoken in relation to the sixth seal, whose image expresses the mystery of Michael as the macrocosmic Guardian of the Threshold at the "right hand" of Christ (see page 110).

Finally, in connection with the heart chakra, contemplating the image of the seventh seal, the words relating to the Cosmic Christ as expressed here are, "THOU ART the Holy Grail." The seventh seal reveals the mystery of the Holy Grail. We see in this image the uniting of the "new Heaven," coming down from above, with the "new Earth," spiritualized and raised up from below. The new Earth, completely spiritual-

---

204 Rudolf Steiner, *Esoterische Unterweisungen für die Erste Klasse* ("Esoteric Instructions for the First Class"; CW 170c; Dornach, Switzerland: Rudolf Steiner Verlag, 1999), p.119.
205 Ibid.

ized through Christ's sacrifice, his out-pouring of Divine Love, appears below in this form of a transparent cube. The rainbow and the dove together with the Grail chalice at the top represent the new Heaven that is brought down from celestial heights by Sophia. "I saw a new Heaven and a new Earth...the holy city, new Jerusalem, coming down from Heaven, from God, prepared as a bride adorned for her husband" (Revelation 21:1–2). On the level of the microcosm, the sacred wedding of Christ, the Lamb, and his bride, Sophia, takes place in the heart chakra—it is here that the "holy city" is born within the human being. This is one aspect of the mystery of the Holy Grail.

With the help of an understanding of the Staff of Mercury, it is possible to grasp the deeper significance of the spiral form emerging from the two snakes encircling the new Earth—the whole connecting the new Heaven and the new Earth. The spiral form is exactly that shown in the figure on page 153. The symbols for the new Heaven—the Grail chalice, the rainbow, and the dove—when seen in relation to the figure on page 140, are in the region of the head.

> The spiral has its significance in the bodies of the world; and these bodies of the world represent a form with which human beings will identify themselves one day. By then the reproductive force of the human being will be cleansed and purified. Then the larynx will be the organ of reproduction.... The transformed larynx in us will be the chalice, which one calls the Holy Grail. And just as the one, so also the other will be purified that connects itself with this organ of reproduction. This will be an essence of the world force, of the great force of the world. And this world spirit in its essence is represented by the image of the dove beneath the Grail chalice. Here the dove is the symbol of the spiritualized fructification which will proceed from the cosmos, when the human being will have become identified with the cosmos. The entire creative aspect of this process is represented by the rainbow. This is the all-embracing seal of the Holy Grail.[206]

Now contemplating the two snakes beneath the spiral:

> The physical body...is the lowest. The spiritual, the highest, is the opposite. It is represented through "counter dimensions" [belonging to "counter space"]. Here, in the course of evolution, these counter dimensions form themselves into a being, which one can best represent as flowing together into the world of passions, desires, instincts. This is the case initially. Later, they become something else. They are more and more purified.... However, they proceeded from the lower drives, which are symbolized by the snakes. This process is symbolized by the flowing together of the counter dimensions in two snakes in relation to one another. In that humanity is purified, humankind ascends upon what is called the "world spiral." The purified body of the snake, this world spiral, has a deep significance.[207]

There is yet another aspect to the lower part of this image of the seventh seal. The two snakes, connect onto the world spiral. The world spiral is in exactly the form represented by the Staff of Mercury in the figure on page 135. As discussed earlier (see page 148), the Staff of Mercury can be pictured continuing further from the figure down to Shambhala—representing the two halves of Earth evolution (Mars and Mercury)—and the two snakes can be brought into connection with this downward continuation of the Staff of Mercury. At the Vulcan stage of evolution, when the Earth, right down into physical substance, will be completely spiritualized and permeated with Divine Love, the Earth will turn inside out. The inner layers of the Earth will become the outer aspect of the Vulcan-Earth. This means that Shambhala in the heart of the Earth will rise up to the Earth's surface. This is an important aspect of the "new Earth" represented by the transparent cube—then surrounded by the two snakes representing the forces of the two halves of Earth evolution.

---

206 Rudolf Steiner, *Bilder okkulter Siegel und Säulen* ("Images of the Esoteric Seals and Pillars"; CW 284; Dornach, Switzerland: Rudolf Steiner Verlag, 1993), pp. 77–78.
207 Ibid., p.77. The end of this quotation connects onto the beginning of the proceeding one.

Ultimately the union of the "new Earth" with the "new Heaven" will signify the union—or rather the reunion—of the Earth and humanity with the Sun. This is a profound aspect of the mystery of the Holy Grail. The seventh seal expresses how the interior of the Earth becomes transformed—as an important aspect of the Grail Mystery.

Relatively few people are able and willing to delve deeply into the Grail Mystery, which is only now being unveiled at this time of the Second Coming of Christ.

It takes courage and great inner effort. However, this is the calling of Michael to us in our time. Michael is the great protector of truth and justice. As long as that is our first and foremost striving—truth and justice—we can be in alignment with the Archangel Michael. Rudolf Steiner made a great sacrifice to descend from higher realms to bring Michael's extraordinary spiritual teachings. He made this sacrifice because he saw that Michael was battling on behalf of humanity and the Earth and resolved to help him. This is a very important sacrifice for us to hold in consciousness.

Concerning the Interval of Silence — Significant to the Practice

Now let us look once again at the four main events of the Christ Mystery in relation to the four levels we focus upon in the Core Practice of the sequence *Putting on the Resurrection Body*: the Transfiguration; the Crucifixion; the Resurrection; and the Ascension. We receive the light of Christ through the seven I AM sayings. This light was revealed to the disciples Peter, James, and John on Mount Tabor at the Transfiguration. Thus, the stage of spirit self (*manas*) was manifested by Christ at his Transfiguration, when he was radiant with light. This is the goal, through working with the seven I AM sayings of Christ, of bringing the light of Christ into each chakra so that the lotus flowers become transfigured. The Transfiguration is the great archetype for the level of *manas*.

In the description of this level of Transfiguration in connection with the first stage of *Putting on the Resurrection Body*, it is indicated that "during the resting contemplation holding the AU-heart gesture after completing the exercise, one focuses one's inner gaze upon the scene of the Transfiguration, inwardly invoking the divine light of the Transfiguration that was streaming through all seven of Christ's chakras."

A period of "resting contemplation" is recommended not only at this first stage but also at the end of each of the four stages of *Putting on the Resurrection Body*. The significance of inner contemplation after a meditation is expressed by Rudolf Steiner in these words:

> It has already often been said during esoteric lessons how the person meditating has to allow complete peace and quiet to enter into the soul after the meditation. At first the meditation still plays into the soul like a tone that slowly fades away. The soul has to become empty, completely empty, in order to receive from spiritual realms. One has to patiently and persistently practice this. One must remain quiet and peaceful, even if for a long time one does not experience anything. One can rejoice if this peace and quiet is attained at all.[208]

Focusing on the Transfiguration in connection with the words, "In purest out-poured light shimmers

---

208 Rudolf Steiner, *Aus den Inhalten der esoterischen Stunden 1910–1912* (*Esoteric Lessons 1910–1912*; CW 266/II; Dornach, Switzerland: Rudolf Steiner Verlag, 1996), p.456.

the Godhead of the world" together with the seven I AM sayings and the seven healing miracles corresponding to the seven chakras is a powerful experience. During the resting contemplation thereafter, as the "tone slowly fades away," the following (and similar) thoughts can fill one's consciousness—and it may be that one wishes to sit during this time, rather than stand.

Through "Christ in me / Sophia in me" I unite myself with the ascending phase of evolution under the guidance of Christ and Sophia. This ascent leads from the Earth to Jupiter evolution, from the objective state of consciousness here on Earth to the imaginative state of consciousness belonging to Jupiter—the evolutionary stage marked by the orbit of Venus in the heavens. The ancient Egyptians, from whom the naming of the days of the week comes, called Venus "Mercury." Since Venus ("Mercury") calls us toward the Jupiter stage of evolution, this second half of Earth evolution—that began with the coming of Christ—is called the Mercury phase of the Earth. I unite myself with this ascending phase by connecting with Christ's words and deeds.

Now I immerse myself into the scene of Christ's Transfiguration, the archetype for the spirit self (*manas*) that is the next level of the human being (beyond the I) to be developed during the Jupiter stage of evolution. By uniting with Christ and Sophia—Christ through whose sacrifice the "new Earth" is being created, and Sophia who is bearing the "new Heaven" down from celestial heights—already now I consciously begin the work of transforming my astral body into *manas* (spirit self). Just as all seven chakras of Jesus Christ were permeated by the light of the divine I AM (Christ) at the Transfiguration, so now I allow the light of Christ to stream into all seven lotus flowers, that my astral body may be transfigured into *manas*—each chakra radiant with the light of Christ. This is a work that I choose *consciously* together with Christ, in the light of the Transfiguration, and in the spirit of the words, "In purest out-poured light shimmers the Godhead of the world."

One of the consequences of the Fall that ensued through Lucifer's penetration into the seven chakras of the astral body was that the lotus flowers became disfigured (in comparison with their original pristine condition prior to the Fall). When Christ came to the Earth, his mission was to overcome the consequences of the Fall. In order to heal the seven chakras, he performed seven healing miracles—each healing miracle being related to one of the seven divine I AM sayings. For example, at the healing of the man born blind Christ spoke the words "I AM the light of the world." Each one of us, insofar as we do not have clairvoyance through the opening of the "third eye," is "blind" to the world of spirit. Each one of us is in need of the healing light of "I AM the light of the world" in the third eye chakra—the 2 petal lotus flower. Each one of us can turn to Christ, to the archetype of the miracle of the healing of the man born blind, and invoke the power of this healing miracle for the opening of the 2 petal lotus flower, that our blindness be healed, that we may spiritually see again through a new, conscious, Christ-filled clairvoyance (Imagination).[209]

Such thoughts as these in relation to the miracle of the healing of the man born blind for the healing of the 2 petal lotus flower (third eye) can be formed inwardly in connection with each of the seven healing miracles corresponding to the seven I AM sayings corresponding to the seven chakras. In this way—through the archetypes of the Transfiguration and the seven healing miracles—my astral body is purified and illumined by the divine I AM, to become transfigured into *manas* (spirit self). "In purest out-poured light shimmers the Godhead of the world."

In connection with the next stage of *Putting on the Resurrection Body*, where the Crucifixion, the seven sayings from the Cross, and the seven stages of the Passion, are the focus—here it is a matter of the next

---

209 Valentin Tomberg, *Christ and Sophia* (Great Barrington, MA: SteinerBooks, 2006), pp. 242–267 offers an abundance of profound insights not only into the miracle of the healing of the man born blind but also into the other six healing miracles as well.

level beyond *manas*, that of *buddhi* (life spirit). *Buddhi* is attained by way of receiving Christ's love-permeated etheric substance streaming into the etheric body and transforming it. The activity of Christ's healing was one of raying out *buddhi*. Everywhere he went, he not only taught but was also engaged in healing activity, streaming out *buddhi*. The people at the places he visited needed only to be in his presence and they could be healed of their illnesses and infirmities. This, ultimately, is also our goal—the goal of eurythmy—that all the way down to the level of the etheric body we become permeated with the love of Christ so that the love-permeated etheric substance of our transformed etheric body becomes a healing force streaming out from us. Every eurythmy gesture done lovingly, if it is permeated by love streaming from the heart into the arms and hands and legs and feet, can stream out as a healing force into the etheric realm.

During the Crucifixion Christ was pouring out Divine Love for humanity and for the whole planet. It was at the Crucifixion that Christ spoke the seven words (sayings) from the Cross. For example, the saying "Today you shall be with me in paradise" is what he spoke to the repentant criminal to his right (viewer's left), who said to him, "Lord remember me when you come into your kingdom." Then Christ spoke from his heart lovingly to this criminal. Imagine the agony of death through Crucifixion, which is one of the most painful experiences anyone could possibly undergo, and in the midst of his suffering he said from his heart filled with love, "Today you shall be with me in paradise." With these words, he offered the criminal redemption. This is an example of the degree and extent of Christ's compassion, reaching out with his heart full of love, even as he was in the agony of death through Crucifixion. These words of Christ, "Today you shall be with me in paradise," relate to the heart chakra. And the other six sayings from the Cross (in relation to the other six chakras) each bring to expression the power of Divine Love that was streaming through each of Christ's chakras during the Crucifixion—each one of the seven sayings of the Cross corresponding to a particular chakra.

Whereas the Transfiguration was the pouring out of the light of Christ, the Crucifixion was the pouring out of the love of Christ. Focusing upon the Crucifixion in connection with the words, "In purest love toward all that lives radiates the Godhood of my soul" together with the seven sayings from the Cross and the seven stages of the Passion corresponding to the seven chakras is very potent. Throughout the entire second stage of the core exercise of *Putting on the Resurrection Body*, and also during the resting contemplation holding the AU-heart gesture after completing the exercise, one focuses one's inner gaze upon the scene of the Crucifixion, inwardly invoking the Divine Love that was pouring out at the Crucifixion, while contemplating the seven sayings from the Cross and the seven stages of the Passion. During the resting contemplation thereafter, the following (or similar) thoughts can fill one's consciousness—and it may be that one wishes to sit during this time, rather than stand.

Through "Christ in me / Sophia in me" I unite myself with the ascending phase of evolution under the guidance of Christ and Sophia. This ascent leads from the Earth to Jupiter evolution and then to Venus evolution, from the objective state of consciousness here on Earth to the imaginative state of consciousness belonging to Jupiter, then to the inspirational state of consciousness belonging to Venus—the evolutionary stage marked by the orbit of Mercury in the heavens. The ancient Egyptians, from whom the naming of the days of the week comes, called Mercury "Venus." And since Mercury ("Venus") calls us toward the Venus stage of evolution, the Egyptians called that planet "Venus," which traces out a six-pointed star in its conjunctions with the Sun—the hexagram being the symbol of Venus evolution. I unite myself with this ascending phase by connecting with Christ's words and deeds—with the stages of the Passion.

Now I immerse myself into the scene of Christ's Crucifixion, the archetype for the life spirit (*buddhi*) that is the next level of the human being (beyond the spirit self) to be developed during the Venus stage of

Chapter 5: The Macrocosmic Background to the Core Practice

evolution. By uniting with Christ and Sophia, already now I consciously begin the work of transforming my etheric body into *buddhi* (life spirit). Just as all seven chakras of Jesus Christ's astral body were permeated by the love of the divine I AM (Christ) at the Crucifixion, and this love streamed from the level of his astral body into his etheric body, and streamed out around the world and into the Earth, so now I allow the love of Christ to stream into all seven lotus flowers, that my astral body may radiate love into my etheric body to become transformed into *buddhi*—each chakra pouring out the love of Christ. This is a work that I choose *consciously* together with Christ, immersing myself in the Divine Love pouring out from the Cross at the Crucifixion, and in the spirit of the words, "In purest love toward all that lives radiates the Godhood of my soul."

One of the consequences of the second Fall that is currently underway through Ahriman's penetration into the etheric body is that humanity and the Earth are coming more and more under the sway of forces of death—the subterranean forces of electricity, electromagnetism, and atomic power, for example. There are also other death forces at work on different levels here, including more subtle, non-physical levels. The expression "death forces" is used here in the wider sense of that which is antithetical to divine life. When Christ came to the Earth, he came to bestow the gift of divine life on humanity and the Earth. The path that he took through the stages of the Passion was for this purpose, to open up the gift of divine life—that blossomed forth at the Resurrection. It is to this gift that we open ourselves in taking up the path of putting on the Resurrection body.

Christ's path entailed sacrifice (the first five stages of the Passion, culminating with the Crucifixion), Entombment (the sixth stage), and Resurrection (the seventh stage). The death forces proceed from the "Lord of Death" as Ahriman is known.[210] To overcome death, i.e., to overcome Ahriman, Christ went through the death on the Cross and the subsequent Entombment in the grave of the Earth.[211] Christ "took on" the death forces and the forces of evil in the Earth's interior with a view to overcoming and transforming them. The descent down to Shambhala was at the same time an encounter with the forces of evil in the interior of the Earth. Through receiving the Mother forces of Shambhala—in conjunction with the Father forces from the Central Sun that shone into him during the Crucifixion—he resurrected from the dead and thereby overcame Ahriman, the Lord of Death, who no longer had any power over him, and he also overcame evil by way of his path of descent and ascent through the subterranean spheres of the Earth in which the forces of evil reside. His Resurrection was the triumph over death, and also over evil—the latter simply by virtue of his presence in an "unassailable form" (the Resurrection body) in each of the subterranean realms where the most varied forms of evil are to be found.

As well as allowing Christ's love to flow in a descending stream into the seven chakras through the seven sayings from the Cross, we can connect with the karmic stream of the Mystery of Golgotha through immersing ourselves meditatively in the seven stages of the Passion. These seven stages can also be followed as a descending path through the chakras. The descending path of the stages of the Passion begins with the highest activity, that of the "washing of the feet," which is exemplified by the Creator, who serves *all*, and ends with the Resurrection, which started with Christ receiving the Mother forces from Shambhala—the forces that were needed for the completion of the Resurrection body. Let us now review the path of the stages of the Passion descending through the seven chakras: the washing of the feet, which is the resolve of the highest in the human being to serve humanity and the Earth, working from the heights (crown chakra, corresponding to Saturn) to the depths (Malkuth, the Earth sphere in the region of the feet); the scourging (third eye chakra, corresponding to Jupiter)—this be-

---

210 Valentin Tomberg, *Christ and Sophia* (Great Barrington, MA: SteinerBooks, 2006), p.288.

211 Ibid., pp. 297-300—"The Defeat of Ahriman"

ing the attack of the hostile forces of Lucifer (from the left) and Ahriman (from the right) assaulting the human I (center of consciousness in the Jupiter chakra) in order to knock it out of alignment from the stream of foot-washing/service flowing down from above to below; the crowning with thorns (larynx chakra, corresponding to Mars)—this being the "reward" at this stage of the path, requiring mastery of the will, speech, and thought, at which the meeting with the Guardian of the Threshold takes place; the carrying of the cross (heart chakra, corresponding to the Sun)—this being the resolve to bear not only one's karmic cross but also the cross of Christ, the mission which Christ bestows upon one, relating to the deepest level of one's heart; the Crucifixion (solar plexus chakra, corresponding to Mercury) is the voluntary immobilization of one's freedom of movement in order to stand in the vertical axis between the Central Sun and Shambhala as a servant of Christ in the temple of the world—this being the stage of meeting him as the Greater Guardian of the Threshold; Entombment (sacral chakra, corresponding to Venus) constitutes the voluntary immersion of oneself and one's spiritual impulse (given to one by Christ) as a sacrifice borne by love into the grave of the Earth in trust, in hope, and in faith that it will one day resurrect; and Resurrection (root chakra, corresponding to the Moon and, by extension, to the Earth) is the birth of the miracle of divine life arising as a consequence of the path of sacrifice leading through the voluntary "giving oneself over" to death. Resurrection is a miracle which, although it cannot be "made" to happen, will happen if the path of the stages of the Passion is truly followed in imitation of Christ.[212]

In contemplating the Resurrection in connection with the root chakra, following the Entombment (sacral chakra), it is important to bear in mind that just as the crown chakra is the "portal to the Father," so the root chakra is the "portal to the Mother." In passing from the Entombment to the Resurrection, the descent to Shambhala, to the Mother, is also to be taken into consideration, and in fact is the real focus when

---

[212] Ibid., pp. 268–290; "The Way of the Passion" offers a wealth of inspiration concerning the stages of the Passion.

meditating upon the Resurrection in relation to the root chakra—in the sense, as described already, that Christ descended to Shambhala in order to receive from there the forces of the Mother needed for the completion of his Resurrection body. The descent through the root chakra to the Mother is the focus here, whereas the actual Resurrection leads us to the third stage of *Putting on the Resurrection Body*. The reason for saying "Resurrection" here rather than "descent to Shambhala" is out of respect for the tradition that the Resurrection is the seventh stage (of the seven stages of the Passion). As is evident from part 3 of the Core Practice, the Resurrection embraces all seven chakras and the whole human organism on all levels, so it is not specifically a matter of the root chakra in connection with the Resurrection—but as the "portal to the Mother" the root chakra is key with regard to Christ's descent down to Shambhala following the Entombment (the sixth stage of the Passion).

Such thoughts as these can be formed inwardly in connection with each of the seven sayings from the Cross bringing the love of Christ into the seven chakras and in relation to the seven stages of the Passion, including the archetype of the Crucifixion central to this second stage of *Putting on the Resurrection Body*, and which also extends to the Resurrection—central to the following stage of this Core Practice. At the second stage the seven chakras of my astral body are filled with love by the divine I AM, and through Divine Love streaming from my astral into my etheric body, the latter becomes transformed into *buddhi* (life spirit). Bringing alive the seven stages of the Passion within is a bulwark against the penetration of Ahriman into my etheric body. "In purest love toward all that lives radiates the Godhood of my soul."

Then at the third stage of *Putting on the Resurrection Body*, where the central focus is the Resurrection and the stage of *atma* (spirit human, or the Resurrection body), the goal of this part of the meditation is to immerse oneself in the streaming of the *life* of Christ, just as it is the *light* of Christ at the first stage in connection with the Transfiguration and the *love* of

Christ at the second stage in relation to the Crucifixion. After the Resurrection, during the forty days leading up to the Ascension, there were times when the Risen One breathed upon the disciples, and in so doing he was transmitting *atma*.[213] The breath of life streamed from the Risen One to the disciples.

Whereas the Transfiguration was the raying out of the light of Christ and the Crucifixion was the pouring out of the love of Christ, the Resurrection was the streaming out of the life of Christ. Focusing upon the Resurrection in connection with the words, "I rest within the Godhead of the world" together with the seven sayings of the Risen One and his seven gifts corresponding to the seven chakras is very strengthening. Throughout the entire third stage of the core exercise of *Putting on the Resurrection Body*, and also during the resting contemplation holding the AU-heart gesture after completing the exercise, one focuses one's inner gaze upon the scene of the Resurrection, inwardly receiving the divine life streaming out from the Risen One, as did Mary Magdalene at her encounter with him in the garden of the holy sepulcher on Easter Sunday morning (described on page 27). During the resting contemplation thereafter, the following (or similar) thoughts can fill one's consciousness—and it may be that one wishes to sit during this time, rather than stand.

Through "Christ in me / Sophia in me" I unite myself with the ascending phase of evolution under the guidance of Christ and Sophia. This ascent leads from the Earth to the Jupiter evolution to the Venus evolution and then to the Vulcan evolution, from the objective state of consciousness here on Earth to the imaginative state of consciousness belonging to Jupiter, to the inspirational state of consciousness belonging to Venus, to the intuitive level of consciousness belonging to Vulcan—the evolutionary stage marked by the Sun in the heavens. In the naming of the days of the week there is no day named for the Vulcan stage

---

213   In this connection it is interesting that the German word for breathing, *atmen*, comes from the same root as the Sanscrit word *atma*.

of evolution, since it is the octave of the Saturn stage, i.e., it is the octave of "Saturday." Inwardly looking up toward the Sun, to the future Vulcan stage, I unite myself with the ascending phase—leading to Vulcan—by connecting with Christ's words and deeds—uniting myself with the impulse of Resurrection.

Now I immerse myself into the scene of Christ's Resurrection, the archetype for the spirit human (*atma*) that is the next level of the human being (beyond the life spirit) to be developed during the Vulcan stage of evolution. By uniting with Christ and Sophia, already now I consciously begin the work—in seed form—of transforming my physical body into *atma* (spirit human). Just as all seven chakras of Jesus Christ's astral body were permeated by divine life at the Resurrection, and this divine life cascaded down from the level of his astral body into his etheric body, and from there into his physical body that became his Resurrection body, so now I allow the divine life of the Resurrection to stream into all seven lotus flowers—each chakra streaming out the life of Christ—that my astral body may stream divine life into my etheric and physical bodies. This is a work that I choose *consciously* together with Christ, immersing myself in the divine life streaming out from the Risen One, in the spirit of the words, "I rest within the Godhead of the world."

At the Vulcan stage, I am to become a Sun being—with the Sun as my abode—indwelling the Resurrection body that I am beginning to develop in seed form already now, during the Earth evolution, through starting to work consciously toward this distant goal together with Christ. The path that Christ took through the stages of the Passion, culminating with the Resurrection, was for the purpose of opening up for humanity and the Earth the gift of divine life, and it is to this gift that we open ourselves in taking up the path of putting on the Resurrection body. In his Resurrection body Christ achieved the perfect union of spirit and matter. His Resurrection body comprised spirit-permeated matter. For this, the highest spirit—that of the Father raying out from the Central Sun—and the spiritual core of matter belonging to the realm of the Mother, Shambhala, had to unite in Christ. This union of Heaven and Earth signifies complete peace and at-oneness with existence. It is this that comes to expression in the words, "I rest within the Godhead of the world."

As well as allowing the divine life of the Risen One to flow in a spiraling stream clockwise through the seven chakras in connection with the seven sayings of the Risen One, we can open ourselves to the seven gifts of the Risen One also by way of following the spiral stream through the seven chakras in the reverse direction (counterclockwise), contemplating each gift in relation to the corresponding chakra. The significance of the spiral is referred to on page 167, and in this connection Rudolf Steiner refers to the "world spiral" which is an expression of the movement of our Sun through cosmic space. Thus, as our Sun moves around the Central Sun—once every 227 million years—it makes a spiral movement through cosmic space. Resurrection is a Sun mystery, and in focusing upon the Resurrection it is appropriate to adopt the spiral movement reflecting the "world spiral." Resurrection is a miracle which can only happen through grace, yet nevertheless we have to do all we can to align ourselves with the impulse of Resurrection by contemplating this miracle again and again with the help of the seven sayings of the Risen One.

Such thoughts as these can be formed inwardly in connection with each of the seven sayings of the Risen One bringing divine life into the seven chakras and in relation to the seven gifts of the Risen One, central to this third stage of putting on the Resurrection body. At the third stage the seven chakras of my astral body are filled with divine life, and through divine life streaming from my astral into my etheric and physical bodies, with the help of the gestures of eurythmy, the seed is sown for the transformation of my physical body into *atma* (spirit human). Opening myself to the seven gifts of the Risen One, I have the possibility of participating in his work of sacred magic for the redemption of the Earth and humanity. "I rest within the Godhead of the world."

Summarizing, the path of putting on the Resurrection body leads through Transfiguration, Crucifixion, Resurrection, and Ascension:

1. transfiguration of the astral body into *manas*, corresponding to the Jupiter stage of evolution and the level of consciousness known as Imagination;

2. transformation of the etheric body into *buddhi*, corresponding to the Venus stage of evolution and the level of consciousness known as Inspiration;

3. resurrection of the physical body (*atma*), corresponding to the Vulcan stage of evolution and the level of consciousness known as Intuition; and

4. ascension reaches up toward—in honor of—the Cosmic Christ in the realm of eternity, whose essence is *eternal peace*, the source of *manas, buddhi,* and *atma,* and who from beyond the seven stages of planetary evolution guides humanity and the Earth through all seven stages: Saturn, Sun, Moon, Earth, Jupiter, Venus, Vulcan.

With the path of putting on the Resurrection body, it is a matter—already now, during Earth evolution—of developing the seeds of *manas, buddhi,* and *atma,* and of orienting oneself toward the transcendental peace of the Cosmic Christ.

The transcendental peace of Christ—"the peace that surpasses understanding" (Philippians 4:7)—is what we strive toward in the fourth stage of putting on the Resurrection body. The Ascended One revealed the content of Revelation—summarized in the seven seals of the Apocalypse—to John on the Island of Patmos for a reason, and now is the time for the unveiling—the *Apocalypse*. The Ascended One went to the transcendental level of existence, prior to returning to the Earth through his Second Coming. Here, at the fourth stage of the Core Practice, it is a matter of going beyond the foreseeable stages of evolution to a higher level, inwardly reaching up toward the transcendental level of the Ascended One, the Cosmic Christ, in order to fortify ourselves with the *truth* that lives both macrocosmically and microcosmically in the great mystery of the evolution of humanity. This is ultimately what we are drawing upon when we are occupied with the seven seals from Revelation.

As already indicated, at the fourth level of putting on the Resurrection body, understanding how the seven seals relate to the seven chakras, it is evident why this is such an important practice for these times. The seven seals communicate something very profound to us on a very high level. The seven seals go beyond the Risen One to the Ascended One. The Risen One appeared to the disciples over a period of forty days. Then there began his Ascension. It was on his path of Ascension, some 62 years after Ascension Day, from another level of existence, that the sublime and majestic being of the Ascended One, the Cosmic Christ, appeared to John on Patmos. And now is the time for this revelation to John to be unveiled, as our fortifying source of truth at this time of the Second Coming.

Per Spiritum Sanctum Reviviscimus
—Through the Holy Spirit the soul awakens!

Such thoughts as these can be formed inwardly in the period of inner contemplation at the conclusion of the fourth part of *Putting on the Resurrection Body*—in connection with each of the seven THOU ART sayings relating to the Cosmic Christ bringing "the peace that surpasses understanding" into the seven chakras and in relation to the seven aspects of the Cosmic Christ, central to this fourth stage of the Core Practice. At the fourth stage the seven chakras of my astral body are filled with divine peace, and through divine peace streaming from my astral into my etheric and physical bodies, with the help of the gestures of eurythmy, the seed is sown for the possibility of participating in the Cosmic Christ's work of sacred magic for the redemption of the Earth and humanity, uniting Heaven and Earth. "I shall find myself within the Godhead of the world."

Putting on the Resurrection Body and Overcoming the Ahrimanic Double

Lastly, a word about the title *Inner Radiance* for the entire sequence, of which the Core Practice is *Putting on the Resurrection Body*:

> There are schools—occult or other—which teach and practice *crystallization*, and there are other schools which teach and practice *radiation*, i.e., the complete de-crystallization of the human being and transformation into a "sun," into a center of radiation. "Then the righteous will shine like the sun in the kingdom of the Father" (Matthew 13:43)—this is the practical aim of "schools of radiation," to which that of Christian hermeticism belongs.[214]

The Choreocosmos School, which owes much to the founder of the stream of Christian hermeticism, is also a "school of radiation." The sequence of exercises presented in this book under the title *Cultivating Inner Radiance and the Body of Immortality* is intended as a contribution through which inner radiance may triumph over the crystallizing death forces now rampant in the modern world. And it is a response to St. Paul's words expressing Christ's call to us to clothe ourselves with the body of immortality, the Resurrection body.

However, it is important to emphasize that *Cultivating Inner Radiance and the Body of Immortality* is not in any way proposing that this book is the *sole* answer to the ahrimanic encroachment taking place in the modern world—it is a spiritual response. In addition, there are many practical aspects—for example, shielding devices for one's home, such as a grounded copper mesh, which would suffice to stop virtually all electromagnetic radiation. These practical aspects are very important and are too numerous and complex

---

214 *Meditations on the Tarot* (trans. Robert Powell; New York: Tarcher-Putnam, 2002), p.354.

to go into here.²¹⁵ *Putting on the Resurrection Body* is a spiritual response as may be understood from the following considerations.

Earlier in this chapter, reference was made to the three doubles. It is above all the ahrimanic double that is of central importance for our considerations here, as is evident from these words of Rudolf Steiner:

> In the coming centuries it will be increasingly important that human beings come to know that they bear within a double, an ahrimanic-Mephistophelian double.... There are various forces coming up from the Earth—magnetic, electric, but also forces that work much more into the realm of life forces—which influence human beings in different ways at various points on the Earth, differentiated according to geographical location.... However, it is the double...which primarily relates to these forces streaming up from the Earth. Human beings in body, soul, and spirit, have an *indirect* relationship with the Earth and with that which streams up from the Earth at various locations—indirect, because the double has the most intimate relationship with that which streams up. These beings, who as ahrimanic-mephistophelian beings take hold of human beings a short time before they are born, have their quite special tastes.... Now, all this [knowledge concerning the ahrimanic double] has only become so extremely important in the fifth post-Atlantean period and will be especially important for human beings already in the immediate future.²¹⁶

Underlying this indication was the clear perception on the part of Rudolf Steiner that in the immediate future human beings would be engaged in a protracted struggle with the ahrimanic forces encroaching upon the human being by way of technology.

Here it is clear that it is above all the ahrimanic double which is strengthened through the encroachment of the invisible forces of technology (electromagnetism and so on). And when Rudolf Steiner speaks also of "forces that work much more into the realm of life forces," are we to think in this respect—among other implications known to Rudolf Steiner at that time—of the peculiarly lifeless "life forces" that human beings take into themselves when eating genetically manipulated food? How are human beings going to be able to cope with the encroachment of such influences that are so prevalent in our time?

It is the power of the Mystery of Golgotha—especially Christ's Resurrection—that overcame and overcomes Ahriman.²¹⁷ It is this power that lives in the Resurrection body and which has the potential to equip human beings with the spiritual forces needed in order to overcome the pernicious effects of GM food, electromagnetic radiation, etc., all of which belong to the influences of *crystallization* at work upon the human being. *Putting on the Resurrection Body* opens up the possibility for one—through grace—to enter into the stream of radiation—inner radiance—which is needed in order to overcome the ahrimanic double. This book provides a healing antidote and a path—together with Christ—toward meeting the great struggle of our time, a struggle in which every human being is increasingly involved, and which can be won only with the help of Christ. However, in speaking of Christ, we are not talking of the "simple man of Nazareth." Rather, it is a matter of a great cosmic being—as outlined in the next chapter.

---

215 Robert Powell, *Prophecy-Phenomena-Hope: The Real Meaning of 2012* (Great Barrington, MA: SteinerBooks, 2011) for details.

216 Rudolf Steiner, *Individuelle Geistwesen und ihr Wirken in der Seele des Menschen* ("Individual Spiritual Beings and Their Working in the Human Soul"; CW 178; Dornach, Switzerland: Rudolf Steiner Verlag, 1992), pp. 61–64. In reading this quote, it has to be remembered that Rudolf Steiner made these statements prior to the onset of Christ's Second Coming in 1933. Since that time, it is now possible for human beings to have a *direct* relationship with the Earth, with Shambhala, through Christ.

217 Robert Powell & Kevin Dann, *Christ & the Maya Calendar* (Great Barrington, MA: SteinerBooks, 2009), pp. 213–214: *The Defeat of Ahriman*.

Chapter 6

THE COSMIC NATURE OF CHRIST IN LIGHT OF THE HERMETIC TRADITION

In chapter 7 there is a discussion of Rudolf Steiner's indication concerning focusing on an image in order to allow spiritual truth to dawn in one's consciousness. Among his various suggestions for an image or thought content to focus on was "As above, so below"—the fundamental axiom of hermeticism. He indicated that one could hold this phrase steadily in one's consciousness, focusing upon it in the region of the brow—the location of the third eye chakra. "As above, so below" is evidently a creative mantra on the path toward the future Jupiter evolution for humanity.

Along the lines of the hermetic principle—"As above, so below"—let us now contemplate some further hermetic considerations concerning the Resurrection body:

> The theme of Resurrection being of the order of "last things," but all the same [it is] accessible to intuitive cognition.... The idea, ideal, and work of Resurrection, therefore, make appeal to that which is most creative, most generous, and most courageous in the human soul. For the soul is invited to become a conscious and active instrument of accomplishment—neither more nor less—of a miracle on a cosmic scale.[218]

This is a wonderful point of departure in order to come to an understanding of the cosmic dimension of Christ out of the tradition of Christian hermeticism, which is explored in its profound depths and breadths in the book *Meditations on the Tarot*. This book contains an impulse for the future. It is the foundational work for the new spiritual stream of Christian hermeticism, written by a spiritual teacher who has a covenant with the students of this work. The experience of many people, including myself, in working with this book deeply and intensely is that it conveys a profound spiritual teaching that leads one into direct connection with the Etheric Christ.

In this sense it is a magical work, for there is more between the lines than is expressed on the printed page. The central theme of the author, as its title says, is *Meditations on the Tarot*. It comprises a series of spiritual meditations on the Major Arcana of the Tarot in light of the hermetic tradition to which the Tarot belongs.

These images—the Major Arcana of the Tarot—represent spiritual archetypes. In contemplating them one begins to enter into a living experience of these archetypes, each of which is teaching us something profound. This book containing meditations on the twenty-two Major Arcana comprises a series of twenty-two images. Originally the Tarot was a game of cards that originated in Italy in the fifteenth century. Then, in 1781, the French Egyptologist and esotericist, Court de Gébelin, found that these images comprise the *Lost Book of Thoth* or Hermes, who was the great teacher of the Egyptians.[219] Exactly the same idea

---

218 *Meditations on the Tarot* (trans. R. Powell; New York: Tarcher-Putnam, 2002), pp. 555–558. Words in brackets [ ] added by RP.

219 Court de Gébelin included an essay on the Tarot in his *Le Monde primitif, analysé et comparé avec le monde moderne* ("The Primitive World, Analyzed and Compared

was later put forward by Rudolf Steiner, who refers to the Tarot as the *Lost Book of Hermes* (*Lost Book of Thoth*).[220] Here it is necessary to distinguish between the Greek god called Hermes from mythology and the human being Hermes, who was an Egyptian. He is usually called Hermes Trismegistus to distinguish him from the Greek god. The Greek god Hermes is the god of the planet Mercury. Similarly, Aphrodite is the goddess of the planet Venus, Chronos is the god of the planet Saturn, and so on. The Greeks worshipped the planets as gods.

For the Egyptians Hermes Trismegistus was a human being. His birth is not exactly dated. Through my research I have been able to hone in more or less to the historical period when Hermes lived—around the time of the building of the great pyramid at Giza, approximately 2500 BC. In order to understand the Egyptian Hermes, we can use an analogy with Moses.

Moses was the great teacher of the people of Israel. However, he was not the founder of this people. The patriarchs Abraham, Isaac, and Jacob were the founders of the tradition of ancient Israel. Moses incarnated into the Hebrew tradition inaugurated by the patriarchs. In the same way, the Egyptian culture or civilization was founded by an individual known as King Menes, the legendary first Pharaoh Menes (Hebrew: Misraim). He was said to have lived about 3000 BC.

---

to the Modern World"), (Paris, 1781), vol. viii. It was his immediate perception, the first time he saw the Tarot deck, that it held the secrets of the Egyptians. Writing without the benefit of Champollion's deciphering of the Egyptian language, Court de Gébelin developed a reconstruction of Tarot history, without producing any historical evidence, which was that Egyptian priests had distilled the ancient *Book of Thoth* into the images of the Tarot. In this way he initiated the interpretation of the Tarot as an arcane repository of timeless esoteric wisdom.

220 Rudolf Steiner, *Concerning the History and Content of the Higher Degrees of the Esoteric School 1904-1914*, CW 265 (Tobermory, Isle of Mull, Scotland: Etheric Dimensions Press, 2005), p.396.

In the Hebrew language Menes is known as Misraim. In Hebrew that is also a name for the land of Egypt. The beginning of this first Egyptian dynasty, when Menes (Misraim) is said to have lived, is dated to be about 3000 years before the beginning of the Christian era. Hermes lived about 2,500 years before Christ, approximately five hundred years after King Menes, the first Pharaoh and the founder of the first dynasty of Egypt. This places Hermes in the time of the fourth dynasty of Egypt, known as the *pyramid age*. There is a mysterious connection here. Hermes came to the people of Egypt as a great teacher of wisdom. He imparted knowledge of hieroglyphs, rituals, and all kinds of esoteric wisdom to the Egyptians.

What Hermes imparted was zealously guarded by the Egyptian priesthood. This constituted the founding of what is called the *Hermetic tradition*, embracing the ancient mystery wisdom. When we look at the culture of Egypt, we see also two other great ancient cultures—those of India and China—which embodied mystery wisdom in a very profound way. The ancient mystery wisdom was carried primarily by three great traditions in antiquity: those being Egypt, India, and China.

The Egyptian tradition is closer to us than that of India or China. Significantly, there was a fructification of the tradition of ancient Israel that took place from Egypt, which occurred through Moses, who was born about 1200 years before the Christian era.

Moses led the people of Israel from the Egyptian captivity through the desert and onward toward the Promised Land, where the Israelites later settled. Prior to the exodus from Egypt, Moses had been initiated into the Egyptian mystery wisdom stemming from Hermes. The most significant aspect of the mystery wisdom that—through Moses—became transmitted from Egypt to Israel is the *Cabbala*, which has its origins in the mystery tradition of ancient Egypt. The Cabbalistic tradition of Israel was carried from Egypt by Moses. We find, therefore, that the mystery tradition of Egypt was extraordinarily significant for ancient Israel.

Chapter 6: The Cosmic Nature of Christ in Light of the Hermetic Tradition

The endeavor of the author of the book *Meditations on the Tarot* is to bring about in our time a renaissance of the Egyptian mystery wisdom in a new form, fused with the stream of Christianity. It is perhaps the first time that anyone has undertaken this on such a scale.

It is a very far-reaching attempt to introduce into mainstream Christianity these profound esoteric teachings belonging to the hermetic tradition extending back to Hermes. Through these esoteric teachings there is the potential to bring about a transformation of traditional Christianity from within. Such was the calling of the author of this work who, however, chose to remain anonymous.

In the Foreword he refers to the Hermetic tradition that goes back to the founder of this tradition, Hermes. It is appropriate, therefore, to contemplate this great teacher of the Egyptian people. In so doing, we can begin to appreciate the teaching and the mission of this individuality who had such a great impact on the people of ancient Egypt and whose earthly mission coincided with the time of the building of the Great Pyramid.

What we know of the teachings of Hermes is summarized in the words "As above, so below"—as in the heavens above, so also on the Earth below. I would like to give just one example of this hermetic axiom so that we have an idea of what Hermes was bringing to humanity.

When we look at the starry heavens we see a myriad of stars. Some 4,500 years ago, Hermes was able to see the correspondences between stars in the heavens and places on the Earth below. This correspondence signifies that any particular place on the Earth can be seen as linked to a particular star in the heavens. By way of the inspiration coming through Hermes at the time of the building of the Great Pyramid at Giza, it was understood that the particular location of Giza is linked to one of the three stars in the belt of Orion.

In both the northern and southern hemispheres we can see these three stars in Orion's belt pointing to Sirius, which is the brightest star in the heavens. In the teaching of Hermes the star Sirius was seen to be the abode of the Egyptian goddess Isis. Hermes taught that the *whole* of the starry heavens is an expression of the goddess Isis, but that the star Sirius is a particularly powerful representative of the nature of Isis. He also taught that the whole constellation of Orion is connected with the god Osiris, who is both the husband and the brother of Isis. In particular, as seen from the northern hemisphere, the lower left-hand star, Alnitak, of the three marking the belt of Orion is the star "above" in the heavens that corresponds with the place below on the Earth, which is the location of Giza. This extraordinary revelation underlay the building of the Great Pyramid. Those who have been in the King's Chamber and the Queen's Chamber of the Great Pyramid will know that this pyramid has shafts—so-called "air shafts," but which are actually "star shafts"—that lead from these inner chambers to the outer walls of the pyramid. The shaft in the south leading from the King's Chamber pointed toward the star Alnitak, the lower left-hand star in the belt of Orion, at the time when the Great Pyramid was built.

Correspondence between the Great Pyramid and Alnitak[221]

This is the only pyramid that has shafts leading from the inner chambers to the outer walls of the pyramids. At the time of the building of the Great Pyramid the

---

221 Robert Bauval–Adrian Gilbert, *The Orion Mystery* (London: Arrow Books, 1994), p.256.

shaft leading from the King's Chamber pointed toward the star Alnitak, which is the lower left hand star of the three stars forming the belt of Orion (as viewed in the northern hemisphere).

I have worked out exactly when this alignment took place. It was in the year 2495 BC. Its position at the time of its daily culmination aligned exactly with the extension of the southern star shaft leading from the King's Chamber of the Great Pyramid then being built. Evidently the Great Pyramid at the time of its construction was purposefully built to align with the star Alnitak.[222] This is an example of the hermetic axiom "As above, so below" summarizing the essence of the mystery wisdom of Hermes that was infused into Egyptian culture and took effect right down into the details of the building of the Great Pyramid. The alignment with the star Alnitak was intrinsic to the structure of the pyramid.

First a serious misconception concerning the Great Pyramid has to be clarified. This was not a burial place for the pharaoh Cheops. It was an initiation chamber. The sarcophagus in the King's Chamber was a place for the one to be initiated. Whether the pharaoh or an Egyptian priest, the one undergoing initiation would lie in the sarcophagus and would go through a ritual simulating death. In the case of a successful initiation he returned from the experience having united with Osiris. This can be read in the ancient Egyptian pyramid texts.[223] For the Egyptians the soul of Osiris was connected with the constellation of Orion.

This is evident not only in the pyramid texts but also through the alignment of the Great Pyramid

with Alnitak taken in conjunction with the text of the initiation rituals. The initiate experienced a connection with Osiris-Orion, in particular with the three stars of the belt of Orion, which was symbolically mirrored on Earth by the three pyramids at Giza, with the Great Pyramid corresponding to Alnitak, the central pyramid to Alnilam, and the third (smaller) pyramid to Mintaka. Alnitak, Alnilam, and Mintaka are the names of the three stars comprising the belt of Orion. I say "symbolically," because this is the right word when viewing the three pyramids together here on Earth "below" corresponding to the three stars in Orion's belt "above." With regard to the correspondence between the Great Pyramid and Alnitak, however, this correspondence is not merely symbolic. It is real.[224]

---

222 Ibid., p 209 for the artistic representation of the Great Pyramid–Alnitak alignment shown in the figure. See also Robert Powell & David Bowden, *Astrogeographia* (forthcoming) for details—www.astrogeographia.org. Some writers have suggested that the Great Pyramid is a more recent construct erected upon the foundation of a more ancient monument.

223 *The Ancient Egyptian Pyramid Texts* edited and translated by R.O. Faulkner (Oxford: Clarendon Press, 1914).

224 See Robert Powell & David Bowden, *Astrogeographia* (forthcoming). See also www.astrogeographia.org.

Only in our time now is it possible to know what this correspondence between the three pyramids at Giza and the three stars in the belt of Orion was all about. The reason for mentioning this symbolic correspondence of the three pyramids at Giza with the three stars in the belt of Orion is to illustrate the fundamental axiom of Hermes—"As above, so below."

Hermes transmitted his teachings orally to the Egyptian priesthood. An essential aspect was the teaching about Isis and Osiris and their offspring Horus. To understand these teachings, which have a cosmological significance, we can explore their background. The essence to be grasped here is that Hermes had a specific mission for the Egyptian people and this mission was to add something to the great mystery tradition of humanity.

His teachings were about initiation and the connection with Isis and Osiris. These teachings were transmitted orally. They were first written down about 150 years later in the period of the fifth and the sixth dynasties BC. We are talking about some of the oldest texts of humanity, the pyramid texts, that were not discovered until the year 1890 and that were first published in English translation in 1914.

It was the age of the fourth dynasty which was that of the building of the three pyramids at Giza, the construction of the Great Pyramid dating to around 2500 BC. These three pyramids—according to the hermetic axiom "As above, so below"—mirror the three stars in the belt of Orion: Alnitak, Alnilam, and Mintaka.[225] Later, there were smaller pyramids built in Sakkara during the fifth and sixth dynasties. In five of those pyramids were found inscriptions which were discovered in the year 1890.

The first English translation of these pyramid texts was published in 1914 by Raymond O. Faulkner. The pyramid texts are all about Isis and Osiris, and their son Horus, as well as depicting their struggle with Seth, the evil brother of Osiris. Osiris represents the light and Seth the darkness.

In addition, as described in the pyramid texts, they speak of the Egyptian initiation rituals, which were introduced to the Egyptians by Hermes and which focus upon Osiris, Isis, and Horus.

If we try to understand the larger background and the context for the incarnation of Hermes on the Earth at that specific time and the teachings he was bringing, we have to look back even further historically to the ancient tradition associated with Noah.

We know of the ancient story of the Flood. Noah saved his people by building an ark prior to the onset of the deluge. What is not generally known is that Noah is the same individual who is referred to in the Hindu tradition as the Manu. Manu was the great teacher in the Hindu tradition, and the seven Holy Rishis, who inaugurated the Hindu tradition in ancient India, were disciples of Manu.

Let us consider the deeper significance of the ancient tradition associated with Noah (Manu). He was the one who was holding—preserving within himself—the whole of the ancient wisdom. Noah's ark is the symbol of the preservation of the ancient wisdom from the time prior to the Flood. The Flood was the great water catastrophe that destroyed the ancient continent of Atlantis, which was located in the region of the Atlantic Ocean.

Noah transmitted the ancient Atlantean wisdom—albeit in a new form—to India, and the seven Holy Rishis were the disciples of Noah (Manu), who transmitted this ancient Atlantean wisdom at the start of the culture of ancient India, which was the first culture to flourish at the start of the historical period following the destruction of Atlantis.

However, the task was much greater than the transmission of wisdom to ancient India. The task of

---

225 The Greek letters of these three stars marking the belt of Orion are *Mintaka (delta)*, *Alnilam (epsilon)*, and *Alnitak (zeta)*.

Manu (Noah) was to oversee the development of the whole unfolding of humanity's evolution following the Atlantean catastrophe, to shepherd this unfolding through a series of seven civilizations: India, Persia, Egypt and Mesopotamia, Greece and Rome, Europe, Russia (Slavic), and America.

This covers the time period from the age of Cancer through the age of Capricorn, a period of seven zodiacal ages (Cancer, Gemini, Taurus, Aries, Pisces, Aquarius, Capricorn), each lasting for 2,160 years—the period of time for the vernal point to retrogress through one star sign of thirty degrees at a rate of one degree every 72 years. This sequence of seven zodiacal ages began with the ancient Indian cultural epoch that flourished during the age of Cancer (8426–6266 BC).[226] The period immediately preceding this was the time of Noah (Manu), who lived when the Great Flood took place at the end of the age of Leo. Since the time of Atlantis that ended with the Flood, Manu guides the tradition of mystery wisdom, shepherding its unfolding from culture to culture. Noah (Manu) administered the primal wisdom in India through the seven Holy Rishis, and he continues to work through all the great teachers of humanity.

Thus the Manu coordinates the activities of the great teachers of humanity, those referred to in the Hindu tradition as the *Rishis* and in the Buddhist tradition as *Bodhisattvas*. They are the great teachers of humanity. From the perspective of Noah (Manu), the Flood came as a result of humankind's ignorance and resulted in a fall from the blessedness of communion with the spiritual world. Since the Deluge, humanity has become increasingly cut off from the realm of spirit. From incarnation to incarnation human beings are seeking to find the way back to the world of spirit. In the Bible the Fall is referred to as the "expulsion from paradise," when humanity's gradual severance from the realm of spirit began. The Flood came much later, at the close of the age of Leo, the end of the seventh Atlantean cultural period, as a result of humanity's erroneous path—a path based on ignorance. Since these long past times, from incarnation to incarnation, human beings have searched for ways back to spirit realms.

This search has many names in different traditions. In the West, one of the names used to designate this search is the *quest for the Holy Grail*. This designation, expressing the essence of rediscovery of the realm of spirit, signifies the coming back into living relationship with the spiritual world which we have lost through the course of time. The quest for the Holy Grail symbolically expresses this journey. It is a matter of penetrating the veil of ignorance, to then find the Holy Grail as the great pearl of priceless treasure, which is a profound symbol for the blessedness of communion with the world of eternal spirit.

As we know, the story of the Grail is linked with the coming of Christ. It is associated with the event of Christ's Last Supper at which the holy chalice containing the sacred blood and the consecrated bread was used by Christ.

In a deeper sense this mystery of the Holy Grail has to do with the Earth, and this is expressed by the sacrifice of Christ whose pure blood flowed upon the ground for the redemption of the Earth. Then the body of Christ was laid to rest in a sepulcher within the Earth. The words that he spoke at the Last Supper, "This is my body, this is my blood," were literally fulfilled by way of his sacrifice for the whole Earth, which received his body and blood as a sacrament through the Mystery of Golgotha on Good Friday in the year AD 33.

The Grail story is concerned with this great mystery which has to do, on the one hand, with the restoration of humankind to the level of the spirit through communion with Christ (Last Supper) and on the other hand with the redemption of the whole Earth (Mystery of Golgotha). In the book *Meditations on the*

---

226   See Robert Powell, *Hermetic Astrology,* vol. 1 (San Rafael, CA: Sophia Foundation Press, 2007), p.56, 63, for a tabulation of the dates of the zodiacal ages and the corresponding cultural epochs.

Tarot it is indicated that the great mystics bear witness to this mystery of the Holy Grail, who exemplify that it is possible to attain an ongoing relationship with the living spirit.

Now I would like to give an example of such a mystic, who is alive at the present time. I am referring to Judith von Halle, a young woman who was born in 1972. On Good Friday in 2004 she received the stigmata at the age of 32 and since that time has been living in communion with the Risen Christ and has been blessed with profound visions of the life of Christ. Since the time she received the stigmata she has not eaten—not because she does not want to but because she is unable to, as it is only water that her body is able to take without having an adverse reaction, becoming sick.

She bears the stigmata, five wounds located as follows: one in each hand, and one in each foot, and one to the right of her heart, a little lower down than the heart, just to the right of the central vertical axis running through the body, in the same place where Longinus plunged the spear into Christ's body all the way through to his heart, thus piercing his heart, so that blood and water flowed forth from this wound. Generally she experiences Christ's Crucifixion every Friday, and sometimes on Saturday and Sunday she also experiences his descent into the underworld and his subsequent Resurrection. At each of my meetings with her, she has been in good health—and this despite not having eaten for many years. She does occasionally drink some water. Her existence without food is a miracle. She indicated that she is nourished by the Resurrection body of Christ which gives her all she needs. By not eating, she is manifesting to the world the truth of the words, "Man does not live by bread alone but by every word that proceeds from the mouth of God" (Matthew 4:4).

That these words are literally true is demonstrated by the example of those stigmatists—human beings who have received the wounds of Christ—who live without any intake of food, a contemporary example being Judith von Halle. I have written about her in my recent book *Christ and the Maya Calendar*.[227] This book places this miracle of the stigmata within the context of our time and offers an explanation as to why it has happened now. I am mentioning this because Judith von Halle is an example of someone who has attained the power of the Grail.

In the Grail legends the Grail is depicted as something that is not visible to the physical senses but is a suprasensory reality that nourishes those who come into connection with it. In this sense Judith von Halle has found the Grail: she is nourished by the Resurrection body of Christ, and she takes no food or drink—except occasionally small quantities of water—and yet she has everything that she needs to live. She has not eaten any food since Easter 2004, when she received the stigmata, and is a living example of the mystery of putting on the Resurrection body through communion with Christ's Resurrection body. (This is one outstanding contemporary example which, however, does not mean that it is necessary to receive the stigmata in order to begin putting on the Resurrection body.)

What Judith von Halle is living is a fulfillment of the Grail Mystery, which has to do with "suprasensory communion" or "nourishment of the spirit."[228] She is able to live solely through communion with Christ's Resurrection body. As she writes in her first book, *And if He had Not Been Raised*, "The life force emanating from the Resurrection strengthens me inwardly so much that I can be outwardly nourished by it."[229] The first part of her book discusses the stigmata in the context of putting on the Resurrection body, whereby Judith von Halle also uses the expression "phantom" (Rudolf Steiner) and thus she speaks of "putting on

---

227 Robert Powell & Kevin Dann, *Christ & the Maya Calendar* (Great Barrington, MA: SteinerBooks, 2009), appendix 2.
228 Judith von Halle, *And if He had Not Been Raised: The Stations of Christ's Path to Spirit Man* (London: Temple Lodge, 2007), p.43.
229 Ibid., p.23.

the phantom."²³⁰ In the context of the hermetic tradition represented by the book *Meditations on the Tarot*, the stigmata are "the future organs of the will."²³¹

What does this have to do with Hermes, the founder of the hermetic tradition? Returning to the Egyptian initiate Hermes, who lived around the time of the building of the Great Pyramid, as will emerge in the following, he proclaimed Christ in cosmic realms already in pre-Christian times; and it is this level of understanding that we need again now, as it provides an important background to the Inner Radiance sequence—including the Core Practice *Putting on the Resurrection Body*—presented in this book. We are led to understand that Hermes was spiritually a disciple of the great wisdom teacher of humanity, the Manu, known in the Old Testament as Noah. The Manu's teaching indicated that humanity went through the great catastrophe of the Fall and in the course of time lost contact with the realm of spirit. Consequently there had to be some kind of divine intervention for humanity to rediscover the living spirit. In referring to this future divine intervention, the Manu did not use the word *Christ*. However, already in ancient times he was aware that a divine being—whom we now call Christ—would later incarnate on the Earth to bring that impulse which human beings need to be able to return to a connection with the living spirit.

The Manu was aware that this divine incarnation would take place because he spiritually beheld the divine being of Christ, whom he called *Vishvakarma,* in starry heights and saw him approaching our Sun. A teaching—that evidently originated with the Manu or with one of his disciples (one of the seven Holy Rishis)—concerning the great being *Vishvakarma* is to be found in the Rig Veda, one of the most ancient and sacred texts of Hindu tradition.²³²

The seven Holy Rishis who lived in India in the age of Cancer were disciples of the great wisdom teacher of humanity; they were direct students of the Manu. The Hindu tradition expressed in the Vedas goes back to the seven Holy Rishis and to their teacher, the Manu. One of the disciples of the Manu who spiritually beheld the approach of *Vishvakarma* toward the Sun subsequently reincarnated around 6000 BC in Persia during the age of Gemini (6266–4106 BC) and bore the name Zarathustra. It was around this time—early in the age of Gemini—that the descent of *Vishvakarma* from starry heights to unite with our Sun was complete.

Zarathustra came to humanity with the mission to proclaim the great being that the Manu and the seven Holy Rishis called *Vishvakarma*. He came as a witness as to how this great being, *Vishvakarma*, had descended from the world of fixed stars and had now united with our Sun.

Here it is a matter of grasping a picture of great cosmic events. The descent of Christ from the starry heavens to unite with our Sun was proclaimed by Zarathustra, who founded the religion of Zoroastrianism, known as *the religion of the Good*. In the teaching of Zarathustra, this being whom we call Christ and whom the seven Holy Rishis called *Vishvakarma*, he called *Ahura Mazda*, meaning "the aura of the Sun."²³³

Zarathustra said that he received his teaching directly from Ahura Mazda. Interestingly, in the teaching of Zarathustra an opposing power, whom he refers to as *Ahriman*, the dark opponent of Ahura Mazda, is also spoken of.

Here we find the theme of an opposing force in that teaching which preceded the Egyptian teachings of

---

230 Ibid., p. 44.
231 *Meditations on the Tarot*, p. 110.
232 *Vishvakarma* ("all-accomplishing, all-creator") is believed by Hindus to be the *"principal universal architect,"* the architect who fabricated and designed the divine architecture of the universe, the Lord of Creation. In the Rig Veda he is visualized as the *ultimate reality*, from whose navel all visible things emanate—http://en.wikipedia.org/wiki/Vishvakarman.

233 Rudolf Steiner, *Die Beantwortung von Welt- und Lebensfragen durch Anthroposophie* ("Answering Questions Concerning Life and the World through Anthroposophy"; CW 108;1 Dornach, Switzerland: Rudolf Steiner Verlag, 1979), p. 131; "To his initiates Zarathustra could speak of the great 'aura of the Sun,' Ahura Mazdao, the god of the Good."

Seth as the evil brother of Osiris. In other words, the opposition between Ahura Mazda (Christ) and Ahriman (Satan) taught by Zarathustra recurs in the teaching of Hermes in the depiction of Seth (Satan-Ahriman) as the opponent of Osiris (Christ-Ahura Mazda). At this juncture it may seem as though we have departed considerably from the theme of this chapter. However, there is a reason for going into this background. The reason is that Zarathustra, who was a disciple of the Manu himself, had initiated two of his most outstanding students and thus prepared them for the task of further contributing to the unfolding of humanity's spiritual wisdom. One of these students of Zarathustra later incarnated in Egypt as Hermes Trismegistus. The other student of Zarathustra later incarnated in the people of Israel as Moses.[234] On this account there is a link between Moses and Hermes, because in an earlier life they were both disciples of Zarathustra having been prepared by Zarathustra, who was acting on behalf of the Manu; and they both were clothed in his wisdom-filled sheaths.[235]

In referring to the Manu, the seven Holy Rishis, Zarathustra, Hermes, and Moses we are speaking of great individuals—teachers of humanity—with special missions. Each of them had a mission to help prepare the way for the incarnation of the divine being we now call Christ. Christ came to the Earth to bring—through his sacrifice—the divine intervention, the power of the spirit, to enable humanity to return to the spirit. This divine intervention is not just for the benefit of Christians and Christianity. It applies to the whole of humankind. Christ's sacrifice on Golgotha was not just for a limited group of people. The sacrifice of this great divine being was for the whole of humanity and served as the fulfillment of the mission and purpose of Earth evolution itself.

We can follow the incarnation of this divine being through the various stages as borne witness to by the great teachers of humankind. This early stage of Christ's activity, working down from the level of the fixed stars, was beheld by the Manu and the seven Holy Rishis, and at this stage Christ was designated by the name *Vishvakarma*. The next level, after Christ's descent from the starry heavens to work directly from the Sun was borne witness to by Zarathustra some eight thousand years ago, where for Zarathustra Christ was known as *Ahura Mazda*. About 3,500 years later, around 2500 BC, during the Egyptian epoch, in the age of Taurus, Hermes then proclaimed yet a new level of activity of this divine being whom he called Osiris.

We have to understand that the Osiris of the Egyptians is the same as the being we call Christ. In other words, Osiris was a pre-Christian, pre-incarnatory form of Christ, who prior to his incarnation was still in a cosmic form. What stage had the incarnation of Christ–Osiris reached in Egyptian times, when Hermes made this proclamation concerning the mystery underlying the worship of Isis and Osiris in the Egyptian religion? At that time Christ–Osiris–Ahura Mazda was still united with the Sun but was working from the Sun through the Moon. Thus the main festival of Osiris was celebrated at the time of the Full Moon. It was because Osiris was working through the phases of the Moon that Hermes taught that the festival of Osiris was to be celebrated at the Full Moon, when the Moon was at full strength. Then for a period of fourteen days, which is the time from the Full Moon to the subsequent New Moon, it is the Moon's waning period. The Moon diminishes in size and intensity night by night as it is waning.

This diminishing was brought to expression in the teaching of Hermes concerning the dismemberment of Osiris by his evil brother Seth—who was called Ahriman by Zarathustra. According to the Egyptian legend, Seth dismembers Osiris stage by stage into fourteen parts or members. The cosmic background to this myth is that the waning Moon diminishes in size night by night through the fourteen nights from Full Moon to New Moon as a cosmic image of the dismembering of Osiris into fourteen parts.

---

234 Rudolf Steiner, *According to Matthew: The Gospel of Christ's Humanity*, CW 123 (Great Barrington, MA: SteinerBooks, 2003), lecture of September 2, 1910.
235 Ibid.

According to this myth, then Isis, the wife of Osiris, at the time of the New Moon begins to search for the parts of Osiris and starts to "re-member" Osiris. She puts Osiris back together again in fourteen stages from the New Moon to the Full Moon, which is the time of the waxing Moon when it is seen to grow in size from night to night—again for a period of fourteen days. Thus we see that the Egyptian legend of the dismembering of Osiris by Seth into fourteen parts and the subsequent re-membering of Osiris by Isis through fourteen stages was the content of the cosmic myth taught by Hermes to bring to expression that the being of Osiris was working from the Sun through the phases of the Moon.

At the same time, however, Hermes brought another level of the being of Osiris to expression in the teaching that Osiris was associated with the world of the fixed stars—in particular with the constellation of Orion. Now, in our time, against the background of current knowledge of the structure of the Milky Way galaxy, it is possible to understand the teaching about Orion being the abode of Osiris. As a starting point in coming to an understanding of this teaching, let us look at a map of the galaxy. We see from a map of the Milky Way galaxy that the galactic center is surrounded by myriads of stars. What can be said about this?

Briefly, our Sun is one of about 100 billion stars orbiting around a great center referred to in astronomy as the *galactic center*.

Our Sun is located on the Orion arm of the galaxy, which is called the Orion arm because when we look up at the constellation of Orion we are looking toward the center of our local arm of the galaxy).[236]

Now let us consider this in relation to Hermes' teaching described earlier. The being now called Christ has been proclaimed in different cultures under different names. In pre-Christian times it was a matter of a series of proclamations in various cultures—ancient India (the seven Holy Rishis), ancient Persia (Zarathustra), ancient Egypt (Hermes)—in preparation for his incarnation upon the Earth. It was Hermes who taught the Egyptians about Christ already in pre-Christian times. St. Augustine refers to the fact that there were "Christians before Christ."[237]

Hermes referred to Christ—at that time working from the Sun through the phases of the Moon—as Osiris. He spoke of the constellation of Orion as the "abode of Osiris." Let us think of this in the context of modern astronomy, which has determined that our Sun belongs to the Orion arm of the Milky Way galaxy—this arm being thus named because, when we look in the direction of Orion, we are looking toward the center of the local arm of our galaxy. Later I shall elucidate further upon the deeper significance of this aspect of Hermes' teaching.

---

236 A team of astronomers has taken an important step toward mapping the Milky Way by accurately measuring the distance to the star-forming region W3OH in the Perseus spiral arm, the nearest arm to us. This long strand of stars streaks out of the Milky Way's disk in the same manner as others seen in galaxies across the universe. This diagram shows the position of the Sun in relation to the various spiral arms of our Milky Way galaxy, as seen from above the galactic north pole—source: www.Science.com.

237 St. Augustine: "That which is known as the Christian religion existed among the ancients" (*Retractiones* I, xiii).

Chapter 6: The Cosmic Nature of Christ in Light of the Hermetic Tradition

The final stage of incarnation of the divine being we call Christ was the birth on Earth of the God-Man, Jesus Christ. Christ is not merely a human being. This is a fundamental misconception. We are speaking of a divine being.

In my research, and particularly in my book *Chronicle of the Living Christ*, I have shown that the numerous miracles and acts of Christ were linked with the starry heavens, thus proving that he was a cosmic being. I have shown that Christ was working with cosmic forces when he performed miracles. He was working with different stars of the heavens. For example, the feeding of the 5000 took place when the Sun was aligned with the star *Deneb* marking the head of the Northern Cross. (The constellation of the Northern Cross was referred to by the Greeks as the Swan, and *Deneb*, meaning *tail* in Arabic, refers to the tail of the Swan.)

The healing activity of Christ has a cosmic dimension. I have given the example of the feeding of the 5000 and the alignment of the Sun with the powerful star Deneb at that miracle—Deneb being one of the most luminous first magnitude stars, a white supergiant, that we can see with the naked eye. Deneb's luminosity is currently reckoned to be about 60,000 times that of our Sun, with a diameter more than 100 times that of the Sun, making it one of the largest white stars known.[238]

A second example is the healing of the paralysed man at the pool of Bethesda. At this miracle, which took place ten days prior to the feeding of the 5000, the Sun was aligned with the star Sadr marking the heart of the Northern Cross (for the Greeks Sadr marked the breast of the Swan—*Sadr* means *breast* in Arabic). Like Deneb, Sadr is a very luminous star, about 65,000 times more luminous than our Sun. It is a second magnitude star, more than 1,500 light years away. These two—the solar alignment with Deneb and Sadr at the miracles of the feeding of the 5,000 and the healing of the paralyzed man—are just two of a number of such examples indicating that Christ was mysteriously aligned with, and perhaps even calling upon, the forces of powerful stars at his healing miracles.[239]

Contemporary Christianity, by and large, has lost sight of the cosmic dimension of Christ. What my research points to is that Christ originated from the galactic center, which is not a supermassive black hole as described by modern astronomy. It is a suprasensory spiritual reality, and it is simply an inadequacy on the part of modern astronomy not to be able to describe a suprasensory reality, such as the cosmic heart of our galaxy.

There are mystics who have seen this suprasensory reality and have given it different names—for example: the *throne of God* (Dante) or the *Star Fire / Astro Fire* (Daniel Andreev), which rays out from the heart of the galaxy, pouring out as the power sustaining every single star in the galaxy, including our Sun. One mystic of the twentieth century who beheld the galactic center in mystic vision was Daniel Andreev, who wrote:

> I remember seeing a glowing mist of stunning majesty, as though the creative heart of our universe had revealed itself to me in visible form for the first time. It was *Astrofire*, the great center of our galaxy.[240]

Just consider our Sun and its enormous power and strength. It holds eight or nine planets and a myriad

---

238 According to the May 12, 2011, Wikipedia list of stars in Cygnus, the Swan, Deneb's luminosity is about 270,000 corresponding to an absolute magnitude of −8.73 at a distance of about 3,200 light years (http://en.wikipedia.org/wiki/List_of_stars_in_Cygnus). However, these values of Deneb's *luminosity* and *distance*, derived from the Hipparchos catalog, have recently been revised downward to *approximately* 60,000 at a distance of 1,550 *light years*. Even at half the distance indicated by the Hipparchos catalog, this still makes Deneb the most distant first magnitude star; http://en.wikipedia.org/wiki/Deneb (Nov. 1, 2011).

239 Robert Powell & Kevin Dann, *The Astrological Revolution* (Great Barrington, MA: Steiner Books, 2010), chapter 5 describes the research into the cosmic dimension of Christ in detail.

240 Daniel Andreev, *The Rose of the World* (Great Barrington, MA: Lindisfarne Books, 1997), p.198.

of other celestial bodies (asteroids, etc.) in their orbits. After contemplating the power of our Sun, let us try to imagine the power of the galactic center, known in esoteric teaching as the Central Sun, which has at least 100 billion stars orbiting around it that are held in their orbits by the power of the Central Sun.[241] This gives us some sense of the enormous power and majesty of the galactic center.

Among the ancient texts, the Central Sun is referred to as the *Divine Sun* in the *Gayatri mantra* from the Rig Veda, considered to be the most ancient of the sacred Sanscrit texts known as the Vedas:

Gayatri Mantra

Om bhur bhuvas svah

tatsavitur varenyam bhargo devasya dhimahi,

dhiyo yo nah prachodayat.

Om shantih shantih shantih. (Rig Veda)

We invoke the three worlds of mortal, immortal, and divine planes.

We choose the Supreme Light of the Divine Sun.

We aspire that it may impel our minds.

Om peace peace peace. (trans. Sri Aurobindo)[242]

Whereas the Central Sun was known of in ancient times through mystical experience, the difference is that now—through the diligence of modern astronomy—its location at the center of the galaxy is known.

Above I referred to the connection between two events in the life of Christ and two very luminous stars—Deneb and Sadr—in the constellation of the Swan. What this research points to—and only a fragment of the research is discussed here—is that Christ is connected to every single star in the heavens. At first this sounds like an extraordinary claim. Nevertheless, my research findings indicate that Christ originated from the galactic center and thus has a relationship with all the stars in the galaxy. (At least this can be held in consciousness as a hypothesis.)

The incarnation of Christ on the Earth has to do with the mystery of a divine being who descended from the Central Sun (galactic center) to the Earth and united with the human being Jesus of Nazareth in order to restore the Earth and humanity and reestablish spiritual contact to the supreme reality of the Creator, whom he called the *Father*—a spiritual reality having to do with the galactic center and with the myriads of stars in the heavens. Christ said, "In my Father's house are many mansions" (John 14:2). The many mansions are the many stars in the heavens, all in evolution. We are all in evolution. At that time Christ could not say to his disciples, "I have come from the galactic center." Nobody would have had any idea what he was talking about. It was hardly possible at that time to grasp the cosmic dimension of Christ, who originated from the Central Sun at the heart of our galaxy and descended in stages to incarnate upon the Earth. Now, however, we are in a position to gain an overview of the Cosmic Christ and his path of incarnation.

The first stage was his descent from the heart center—also known as the Central Sun—of our Milky Way galaxy to unite with the Orion arm, which is our local part of the galaxy.[243] Here we can begin to understand why Hermes taught that Osiris came from Orion and that Orion was the abode of Osiris. One can only comprehend this against the cosmic background that I have described above. Long ago, in the far-distant

---

241 Robert Powell & Kevin Dann, *Christ & the Maya Calendar* (Great Barrington, MA: SteinerBooks, 2009), appendix 1: *The Central Sun*.

242 Http://www.aurovilleradio.org/spirituality/the-path/915-learning-about-mantras.

243 The Orion Arm, to which our Sun belongs, comprises almost all of the stars that we can see with the naked eye. When we look up to the constellation of Orion, we are looking toward the center of our local arm, and on this account it is called the Orion Arm.

past, Christ descended from the heart of our galaxy, the Central Sun, to unite with the Orion arm of the galaxy. Hermes, one of the great teachers of humanity, was aware that, upon looking up to Orion, here the cosmic presence of Osiris was strongest. Since the constellation of Orion lies at the heart of our local arm of the galaxy, it follows that when Christ united with the Orion Arm, his presence—while embracing all (almost all) of the stars visible in the heavens—was focalized in the constellation of Orion. Even though, at the time of Hermes, Osiris was no longer indwelling the starry heavens (Orion Arm), having descended to unite with the Sun during the age of Gemini, somehow the mystical faculty of this great teacher of the Egyptians intuited the connection of Osiris with the constellation of Orion—perhaps as a residue of that past epoch when Osiris-Christ's presence was focused most strongly through the constellation of Orion at the heart of our local arm of the galaxy.

Now I would like to mention a different aspect, one that connects the constellation of Orion with the land of Egypt. My research shows that certain of the great mystery centers on the Earth are connected with different stars. For example, certain stars in the constellation of Orion are connected with specific mystery centers. Perhaps the most well known of these is the mystery center of Giza where the Great Pyramid is located, connected with the star Alnitak belonging to the belt of Orion. As already referred to, there is a correspondence between the Great Pyramid and Alnitak in Orion's belt. Another correspondence is that between the star Bellatrix, marking the left shoulder of Orion, and the temple of Artemis at Ephesus where the mysteries of the Divine Feminine were celebrated.

Astrogeographia is the name of the science of correspondences between stars in the heavens and earthly locations. *Astrogeographia* exemplifies the teaching of Hermes: "As above, so below."[244] Through *Astrogeographia* it emerges that the lower part of Orion is projected onto the land of Egypt, whereas the upper part (head and shoulders) is mirrored on Earth in Turkey.[245]

From the foregoing, it emerges that Hermes is best understood when seen in the line of great teachers whose mission it was to prepare for the incarnation of Christ on the Earth.

We can begin to grasp the full significance of Hermes and his mission by way of comparison with Moses who lived about 1,200 years after Hermes. Moses beheld Christ in the burning bush. What was this experience? It was the experience of a new stage of the incarnation of Christ, still coming from the Sun, through the Moon (as proclaimed by Hermes), and—at the time of Moses—descending into the realm of the elements, particularly the element of fire.

When Moses asked, "Who are you?" The response of Christ from the burning bush was—in Hebrew—*Ehyeh asher Ehyeh*, which means "I AM THE I AM." It was Christ, the divine I AM, announcing himself to Moses. Just as Hermes proclaimed Christ—under the name Osiris—to the Egyptians, so Moses proclaimed Christ as *Ehyeh asher Ehyeh* ("I AM THE I AM") to the people of Israel.

The esoteric name of Christ is I AM. The advent of Christ on Earth signified the commencement of his mission to bestow the divine I AM upon human beings. The search for the Holy Grail is the search for Christ as the bearer of our individual divine I AM.

Moses was a great teacher in the line of teachers bearing witness to the revelation of Christ at different stages of incarnation descending from the galactic center to finally incarnate upon the Earth. The witnessing began with the Manu, followed by the seven Holy Rishis, Zarathustra, Hermes, and then Moses—each proclaiming a different phase of the incarnation of the great cosmic being whom we call Christ.

---

244 Robert Powell & David Bowden, *Astrogeographia* (forthcoming). See also the web site www.astrogeographia.org.

245 See www.astrogeographia.org.

Moses can be viewed as a link in the sequence of the great teachers of humanity whose mission it was to proclaim the revelations of Christ in his stages of descent from the world of stars to the world of the elements. The whole life of Moses was dedicated to the coming of the Messiah into a physical body, which was attained at the baptism of Jesus in the River Jordan. In this line we have been considering, the last of the great teachers/proclaimers in this series was John the Baptist, who was present on Earth to bear witness to the descent of Christ into the physical body of Jesus and also to proclaim this event. When he baptized Jesus, he had a majestic clairvoyant vision, on account of which he proclaimed: "Behold the Lamb of God, who bears the sins of the world," having clairvoyantly beheld the divine being of Christ in the form of a dove of light descending down from Heaven upon Jesus.

It is against this background of the great teachers proclaiming the stages of Christ's incarnation that we can begin to understand Hermes—who he was and what his mission was about and, indeed, what the Egyptian mystery wisdom was all about. It is evident that in the Egyptian religion there was a multitude of gods. However, the central god of the Egyptians was Osiris. The mystery rites that were celebrated—for example at the Great Pyramid—were focused on the mystery of death and Resurrection. It was this which was implanted into the Egyptian soul, the ritual of death and rebirth in Osiris, to become a reborn soul.

This was a presentiment on the soul level of what was subsequently enacted on Earth on a physical level through the death and Resurrection of Jesus Christ. With the death and Resurrection of Christ came the fulfillment of the goal of human evolution, which is the Resurrection. What Jesus Christ attained in one single incarnation will take the rest of humanity many, many incarnations. Reincarnation is the path that leads gradually toward Resurrection, if we seek it— since it is intrinsic to the mystery of Christ that we are left completely free. Nobody is forced to take the path of Christ leading to Resurrection.

It is possible, as expressed in the words of St. Paul, for the mortal body—on the path toward Resurrection— to put on the immortal, imperishable Resurrection body: "When this perishable [body] will have put on the imperishable, and this mortal will have put on immortality" (I Corinthians 50:53). These words of Paul indicate precisely what is meant in taking the path of putting on the Resurrection body described as the Core Practice of the Inner Radiance sequence presented in this book. From incarnation to incarnation one can again and again take up the great work of "putting on the immortal, imperishable Resurrection body," which signifies engaging in a co-creative activity together with Christ in the creation of one's own Resurrection body.

Judith von Halle, referred to earlier, is an example of a contemporary human being who is consciously engaged in the great work to such a high degree that she no longer requires food but is able to live directly from the Resurrection body of Christ. By putting on the Resurrection body she has achieved "foodlessness," which is a stage on the path of development of the Resurrection body. For Judith von Halle it was an act of grace to begin putting on the Resurrection body, which, however—at least potentially—is there, held by Christ, for every single human being. It is Christ's gift to everyone, to each and every individual, and this is central to the mystery of the Holy Grail.

Against this background we can see that Hermes was preparing for the mystery of the death and Resurrection of Christ in teaching the Egyptian people of the death and Resurrection of Osiris. Moreover, when we contemplate Isis with her child Horus, we have a presentiment at that time of ancient Egypt of what came into consciousness later with the image of the Madonna and child. When we contemplate Isis and Horus it is a prefiguring of the image of the Madonna holding the child. Horus for the Egyptians was a presentiment of the child Jesus.

There are many different aspects to this mystery. What we are considering is one aspect which can help us to see the book *Meditations on the Tarot* in a new light. We see that what is brought forth in the book is a Resurrection of the Egyptian mysteries through a Resurrection of that which came into the world through Hermes. This was carried over to Israel through Moses, and later was borne witness to by John the Baptist, then Christianized through Christ, and now is arising in a metamorphosed way in our time as the book of Thoth: *Meditations on the Tarot*.

Why did this occur in our time of the twentieth/twenty-first century (recalling that the book *Meditations on the Tarot* was completed in 1967)? This has to do with the greatest mystery of our time, which is encapsulated in the words "Second Coming." Reference was made to Christ's Second Coming when Jesus was asked by his disciples, "What will be the sign of your [second] coming?" (Matthew 24:3).

The signs of the Second Coming encapsulate a mystery connected with our time. It is referred to in detail in several of my works, including the recent book, *Christ and the Maya Calendar*, where I have gone into the mystery of Christ's Second Coming.[246] It is not a physical incarnation but a radiant manifestation of Christ in the etheric world as a new presence for humanity all around the globe (the Greek word for the Second Coming is *parousia*, meaning *presence*). If we choose to do so, we can receive Christ into our hearts and minds as a living presence, a living and guiding power in our lives. And the mystery of the book *Meditations on the Tarot* is that it was written in direct response to the event of Christ's Second Coming.[247] It was written to open up a path to humanity to experience the *parousia*, the Divine Presence of Christ in our time. And this, also, is the central purpose of the Inner Radiance sequence described in this book.

---

246 Robert Powell & Kevin Dann, *Christ & the Maya Calendar*, chapter 8: *The Rose of the World*, and appendix 2, "The Good News."
247 *The Wandering Fool: Love & its Symbols—Early Studies on the Tarot with Three Lectures on Hermeticism* by Robert Powell (San Rafael, CA: LogoSophia, 2009), pp. 6–7.

The work *Meditations on the Tarot* has come as a gift to humanity in our time—as a Resurrection of what Hermes brought in ancient Egypt. Just as there was the descent of the Cosmic Christ from the Central Sun at the heart of our galaxy through various stages: (1) the fixed stars, (2) the Sun, (3) from the Sun working through the phases of the Moon, (4) from the Sun working through the Four Elements, and (5) incarnating into a human being—Jesus of Nazareth—for a period of three and a half years, so now are we able to participate in his Second Coming.

The Second Coming is a mirror image in our time of that which was proclaimed in ancient Egypt by Hermes concerning the coming of Osiris (Christ in his pre-incarnatory form), who is now coming again in our time on a cosmic level in a way that bears similarity to the time of Hermes. This new level of activity of Christ in our time is coming to expression in various ways, one of them being what is expressed in *Meditations on the Tarot* as a profound teaching that signifies a metamorphosis of the teaching of Hermes, on which account this teaching is called *Christian hermeticism*. We are able through this book, when we enter into its content deeply and intensely, to find a relationship with Christ in his Second Coming. This book is an expression of a new form of Christianity. It is a fusion of the Christian and the Egyptian traditions. It leads us into a new dimension and to new spiritual experiences.

How may we understand the Second Coming as a mirror image of the activity of Osiris–Christ during the third cultural epoch at the time of Hermes? The term *cultural epoch* signifies a period of time during which the vernal point, on account of its precession through a zodiacal sign, gives rise to a particular kind of culture on the Earth. Ancient Egypt was the time of the age of Taurus, and the corresponding culture that flourished in Egypt during that time is called the *third cultural epoch*, because it flourished in the third age since the great flood that destroyed ancient Atlantis. According to esoteric teaching, there were seven zodiacal ages and seven corresponding cultures on Atlantis, and these are followed by a further seven ages and corresponding cultures comprising the historical period in which our present civilization is unfolding.

At the present time, we are now in the fifth cultural epoch, corresponding to the age of Pisces. And the Second Coming of Christ during the present age of Pisces (fifth culture) mirrors the time of Hermes, which was during the age of Taurus (third culture). The fourth cultural epoch during the age of Aries, this being the central age during the unfolding seven zodiacal ages, stands alone and thus does not mirror another age (note the sequence: Taurus–third age, Aries–fourth age, Pisces–fifth age). Whereas the fifth culture (Pisces) mirrors the third (Taurus), the sixth culture (Aquarius) will mirror the second (Gemini), and the seventh culture (Capricorn) will mirror the first (Cancer).

From the time of the coming of Christ during the age of Aries (fourth cultural epoch), the onward flow of evolution requires from humanity the fulfillment of the task of Christianizing[248] the religions of old, through bringing the power of Divine Love into the wisdom of antiquity as a force of renewal. Otherwise humanity faces the possibility of a second fall, a fall into the subearthly realms.[249] We can see it as a work of divine providence that the book *Meditations on the Tarot* has been written as a guide for us all. This book is an expression of a new form of Christianity. It is a fusion of the Christian and the Egyptian mystery wisdom, and it leads us into a new dimension, a new realm of experience, which has to do with the mystery of Christ's Second Coming.

The author of this book is one who can be called a *friend of Christ*. He was one who received from Christ himself the task of writing this book and of working as a guide for all human beings who are seeking the guidance of the living being and the living presence of Christ. That is what underlies this work.

Against the background of what I have presented above, it is evident that the author of *Meditations on the Tarot* can also be viewed in the line of the great teachers of humanity. He is one such teacher in our time in the post-Christian era, who is bringing the teaching for the ascending phase of this great movement of Christ on his path of return to the heavenly Father, leading humanity stage by stage on the ascending path leading to the Resurrection. He connected onto the great teacher Rudolf Steiner—this connection shows in their horoscopes, where the Sun's location (14½° Aquarius) at his birth aligned exactly with the position of the Sun (14½° Aquarius) at Rudolf Steiner's birth (see dedication on page 241). Whereas Rudolf Steiner's task was to prepare for the onset of Christ's Second Coming in the etheric aura of the Earth in 1933, the task of the author of *Meditations on the Tarot* was to help humanity align with the Etheric Christ in the period after 1933.[250]

As through antiquity Christ descended from the heights of our galaxy down to the Earth, so now he is uniting with the etheric aura of the Earth all the way down to the golden heart of the Earth (Shambhala), from there to begin his ascending movement from the depths in the spiritualization of the Earth, creating the "new Earth."

And the time we are in now, during the present age of Pisces,[251] approximately mirrors the time of Hermes

---

248 The word *Christianize* does not refer simply to the religion of Christianity but rather refers to the process that has ensued since Christ's incarnation into the world as a majestic divine being on Earth through the gift he bestowed upon the Earth and all humanity through his sacrifice on Golgotha.
249 See Robert Powell, "Subnature and the Second Coming," in *The Inner Life of the Earth* (ed. Paul V. O'Leary).

250 The author of *Meditations on the Tarot* is the second of the three spiritual teachers referred to in: Robert Powell, *The Most Holy Trinosophia and the New Revelation of the Divine Feminine*, pp. 100ff, "The Three Spiritual Teachers" (incarnating one after the other, successively in the course of the nineteenth and twentieth centuries, with the task of helping humanity to align with Christ in the etheric realm).
251 Rudolf Steiner, *The Christ Impulse and the Development of Ego Consciousness*, CW 116 (Hudson, NY: Anthroposophic Press, 1976), p.111—"As a result of the Sun reaching a certain point in the constellation of Pisces at

during the age of Taurus—*Meditations on the Tarot* bearing the impulse of resurrecting the Egyptian mysteries inaugurated by Hermes, the founder of the hermetic tradition.

On a personal level, having translated the book *Meditations on the Tarot* from French into English, and having studied the new art of movement, eurythmy, inaugurated by Rudolf Steiner, I have been blessed from two sides with impulses leading to Christ in the etheric realm. One approach to the path through eurythmy is described in this book. The path through *Meditations on the Tarot* entails the inner way of mysticism, gnosis, and sacred magic (see table on page 217).

Returning to the content of this book *Cultivating Inner Radiance and the Body of Immortality*, arising from the impulse of eurythmy, in honor of Rudolf Steiner as the one through whom the gift of this new etheric form of movement came into the world—now at this time of the 100-year anniversary of the birth of eurythmy—I would like to close with two very special verses given by Rudolf Steiner during the foundational course *Eurythmy as Visible Speech*:

The first verse is given in the context of the interweaving of the eurythmic *Peace Dance* with the "*I-and-You*" exercise. [252]

> *The wishes of the soul are quickened,*
>
> *The deeds of the will are growing,*
>
> *The fruits of life are ripening.*
>
> *I feel my destiny,*
>
> *My destiny finds me.*
>
> *I feel my star,*
>
> *My star finds me.*
>
> *I feel my aims,*
>
> *My aims find me.*
>
> *My soul and the world are one.*
>
> *Life grows more radiant around me.*
>
> *Life grows more arduous for me.*
>
> *Life grows more abundant within me.*

---

the vernal equinox, a certain etheric clairvoyance may be acquired." This new etheric clairvoyance is arising, as Rudolf Steiner indicated, as a result of Christ's return in the etheric realm—from 1933 onward.

252 Rudolf Steiner, *Eurythmy as Visible Speech*, Complete Works vol. 279 (Weobley, England: Anastasi, 2005), p.142—translation amended by RP after comparison with the German original.

The second verse—*the eurythmy verse*—is a meditative verse given by Rudolf Steiner to eurythmists.

> *I seek within myself*
> *The working of creative forces,*
> *The life of creative powers.*
> *The powerful pull of the Earth*
> *Speaks to me*
> *Through the word of my feet.*
> *The forming might of the air*
> *Speaks to me*
> *Through the singing of my hands.*
> *The force of the light of Heaven*
> *Speaks to me*
> *Through the thinking of my head.*
> *How the world—in the human being—*
> *Speaks, sings, thinks.*

When you have meditated upon such words as these, you will discover that you can say to yourselves:

"It is as though I have awakened out of a cosmic sleep into the heavenly realm of eurythmy."[253]

---

253   Ibid., pp. 152–153—translation amended by RP after comparison with the German original.

Chapter 7

FROM THE EUCHARIST TO THE SECOND COMING OF CHRIST

Sources

Sources of the songs, prayers, and meditations

- PD Peter Deunov
- SF Sister (Saint) Faustina
- RP Robert Powell
- RS Rudolf Steiner
- VT Valentin Tomberg
- T   traditional

Rudolf Steiner is the founder and originator of eurythmy; Robert Powell is responsible for the eurythmy gestures and forms associated with each prayer and meditation, and also for correspondences with the chakras of the Seven Stages of the Passion, the Seven Gifts of the Risen One, the Seven THOU ART Sayings, and the seven seals of the Apocalypse.

Valentin Tomberg is the source of the correspondences with the chakras of the Seven Petitions of the Lord's Prayer, the Seven I AM Sayings, the Seven Healing Miracles, the Seven Words from the Cross, and the Seven Sayings of the Risen One. These correspondences are indicated in his *Lord's Prayer Course* available as a course of study from the Sophia Foundation; and for those who read German, published in four volumes—*Der Vaterunser-Kurs* (Taisersdorf, Germany: Achamoth Verlag, 2008–2010). Deepening into the correspondences indicated by Valentin Tomberg is possible—to ever-deeper and more profound levels—through study of what he says about them in the *Lord's Prayer Course* and in his biblical studies, published in the book *Christ and Sophia* (Great Barrington, MA: SteinerBooks, 2006).

Overview of the Inner Radiance sequence

The sequence of songs, prayers, and meditations is presented here in the way it is ideally practiced. Of course, each individual may choose otherwise—to arrange the sequence appropriately for themselves. The following is optimal in terms of the unfolding of the sequence from one practice to the next. Once one has learned it, if practiced peacefully (unhurriedly), the entire sequence takes approximately half an hour—if the pauses between each practice are brief, whereby it should be noted that in the case of the four parts of the Core Practice *Putting on the Resurrection Body*, it is recommended to pause for a period of up to two minutes between each part in order to allow the content to resonate within, as described in chapter 5 in consideration of the various levels of the Core Practice in relation to the future stages of evolution: Jupiter, Venus, and Vulcan.

Index

The page numbers indicate the starting page where reference is made to the relevant song, prayer, or meditation in this book. The page numbers emphasized in bold face indicate the starting page where the practice is described, and the additional page numbers indicate where in this book supplementary reading material relating to the practice of the relevant song, prayer, or meditation is to be found.

		Pages
Introduction: Right Standing	RP	**41**
The Staff of Mercury	RS—developed by RP	123, 135, **146**
Sung version of AUM	PD	**81**
Singing the Concordances	RS—developed by RP	**81**
The Lord's Prayer (T) as Chakra Prayer	VT	**35**
AMEN / AUMEYN meditation	VT—developed by RP	33, **38**
"A Star Is above My Head"	RS	**62**
"Christ in me"	RS	**63**
"Sophia in me"	RP	**63**
"Michael-Sophia in Nomine Christi "	VT	**63**
Prayer for the Protection of Mother Earth	RP—latter part: SF	**64**
Salutation to the Sun	RP	**66**
"Prayer for Putting on the Resurrection Body"	RP—latter part: SF	**67**
The *Morning Meditation*	RS—see page 2—	
	is the starting point for the Core Practice	
Putting on the Resurrection Body:		
First stage: The Transfiguration	VT	**45**, 168, 214
Second stage: The Crucifixion	VT—stages of the Passion: RP	**48**, 170, 215
Third stage: The Resurrection	VT—seven gifts of the Risen One: RP	**52**, 173, 215
Fourth stage: The Ascension	RP	**56**, 174, 215
"Christ in me"	RS gave this as "Christ in us"—see page 197	**68**
"Sophia in me"	RP—adapted from "Christ in me"	**68**
"Michael-Sophia in Nomine Christi"	VT	**68**
The Star of the Lamb	RS	**69**
Meditation on the Etheric Christ	VT—developed by RP	**71**
AUM meditation	T [Sanskrit]—introduced to the West by RS	**78**
Sung version of AUM	PD	**81**
IAO meditation	RS—developed by RP	**85**
Sung version of IAOUE	(music PD—developed by RP)	**103**
Inner Cross / Rose Cross meditation	RS—developed by RP	**142**

The above tabulation, while giving the name of the originator of each song, prayer, and meditation, does not provide source references. However, by referring to the pages indicated, most of the source references relating to contributions by Rudolf Steiner and Peter Deunov can be found—usually given in the footnotes. In the case of Valentin Tomberg's indications, the reader is referred to his *Lord's Prayer Course* available from the Sophia Foundation and to the biblical studies published in *Christ and Sophia*; and for Sister (Saint) Faustina to the official website www.faustina.ch/index_en.htm.

Chapter 7: From the Eucharist to the Second Coming of Christ

Further Considerations

While most of the source references can be found in the way described above, there are some that still need to be addressed.

A Star Is above My Head by Rudolf Steiner[254]—this is one of many meditations given by Rudolf Steiner relating to the "star of the higher self" above the head (see page 62).

In the exercise "Christ in me" the opening gestures are for the sounds IAO which, as described in chapter 5, express Christ as: I AM ("I") the Alpha ("A") and the Omega ("O"). "Christ in me" was given by Rudolf Steiner as "Christ in us,"[255] which has been adapted here from the group sacramental form to the individual meditative prayer form. "Christ in us" comes as the culmination of the Offering Service given by Rudolf Steiner for celebration by religion teachers for young people attending the Waldorf Schools. The structure of the Offering Service is in four parts, corresponding to the structure of the *Eucharist* (known as the *Mass* in the Church and as the *Act of Consecration* in the Christian Community founded by Rudolf Steiner). Traditionally, the four parts of the Mass are: Gospel Reading, Holy Offering/Sacrifice, Transubstantiation, and Communion. In the Offering Service the communion is on a spiritual level, without partaking of the consecrated substances of bread and wine. The essence of this spiritual communion is expressed in the words:

> Christ in us.
> His radiant, light-filled spirit in our spirit.
> His pure, loving thought in our soul.
> His undefiled, sin-free heart in our heart.
> Christ, we receive thee:
> For the healing of our body,
> For the healing of our soul,
> For the healing of our spirit.

For the individual prayer form—"Christ in me"—I have adapted the words of "Christ in us" by changing "we" to "I," "us" to "me," and "our" to "my." Also, in terms of suitability in the English language, in translating this I have substituted in the fourth line "his grace-filled sacred heart" in place of "his undefiled, sin-free heart." The latter ("sein lautres, sündenreines Herz") sounds wonderful in German, but has an unfamiliar quality to it in the English language, whereas "his grace-filled sacred heart" is familiar to some from the tradition of *devotion to the sacred heart*.[256] Adapted to "Christ in me," this meditative prayer corresponds with the words of St. Paul "not I, but Christ in me," which are the central words for the second half ("Mercury half") of Earth evolution. On this account, "Christ in me" is a highly significant meditative prayer for our time, relating to the core meaning of life on Earth.

It is important, though, to bear in mind the context in which Rudolf Steiner originally gave this—as the culmination of a most sacred and holy sacrament to help young people find their true I. The teachers celebrating the Offering Service generally devote much time to aesthetically and spiritually preparing the space according to Rudolf Steiner's indications and to intensive inner preparation in order to speak the sacred words, culminating with "Christ in us," spiritually corresponding to receiving the holy sacrament through communion at the culmination of the Eucharist. Instead of communion through consecrated bread and wine, it is a matter of directly receiving Christ's spirit and his thoughts and his heart in spirit, soul, and

---

254 Rudolf Steiner, *Seelenübungen mit Wort- und Sinnbild-Meditationen* ("*Soul Exercises with Word and Image Meditation*"), Complete Works vol. 267 (Dornach, Switzerland: Rudolf Steiner Verlag, 1997), p. 412.
255 *Freie Sakramente: Die allgemein-priesterlichen Sakramente Rudolf Steiners* ("*The Free Spirit of the Sacraments: The Universal-Priestly Sacraments given by Rudolf Steiner*") (ed. Volker David Lambertz; Markdorf, Germany: Pro-Drei-Verlag, 1997), p. 384.

256 Robert Powell, *Consecration to the Immaculate Heart of Mary Sophia and Consecration to the Sacred Heart of Jesus Christ* (San Francisco: Sophia Foundation, 2007) discusses the significance of the devotion to the sacred heart of Jesus Christ. In the "Christ in me" exercise some readers may prefer the line "his undefiled, sin-free heart in my heart" (Rudolf Steiner) instead of "his grace-filled sacred heart in my heart."

body. Here—and this holds also for the future—Christ enters into a direct and immediate inner relationship with the human being. Rudolf Steiner said of this service, that it could be celebrated everywhere where there would be a need for it.[257]

"Sophia in me" is adapted from "Christ in me" and has—in terms of "order of magnitude"—a significance similar to "Christ in me," except that it is a matter of communion with Sophia, the Bride of the Lamb, rather than with Christ, the Lamb. One point of difference is that the words "her grace-filled immaculate heart" are substituted in place of the words "his grace-filled sacred heart."[258]

"*Michael–Sophia in Nomine Christi*" ("Michael and Sophia in the name of Christ") is given by Valentin Tomberg as the *spiritual motto* of the community dedicated to AnthropoSophia.[259]

"Prayer for the Protection of Mother Earth"—the opening eurythmy gestures for this prayer (A, U, M, I, Universal Love) follow the same sequence as for the AUM meditation and thus call upon the four primal powers of good: A—Father / U—Son / M—Holy Spirit / I—Jesus Christ as the incarnated God–Man, the ideal toward whom we strive. The four primal powers of good are discussed later in this chapter in connection with Rudolf Steiner's Foundation Stone meditation.

"I See the Sun"—the closing words of this meditation are adapted from "Christ is already here."

"Prayer for Putting on the Resurrection Body"—the same comments regarding the opening eurythmy gestures (A, U, M, I, "Universal Love") as made above in relation to the four primal powers of good apply also to this prayer.

The Meditation on the Etheric Christ was communicated by Valentin Tomberg during an esoteric lecture he held in Amsterdam at Easter 1941.[260] This was in the midst of the apocalyptic struggle with the anti-Christian forces that arose in 1933 and began their assault upon humankind exactly at the time of the onset of Christ's return in the etheric realm.[261] This apocalyptic struggle is continuing now on a global level, and the Meditation on the Etheric Christ is perhaps even more relevant now than when it was given in 1941. The words of this meditation were spoken during the course of a lecture—of which only fragmentary notes were made. The significance of these words—as a meditation on the Etheric Christ—is not indicated at all in the notes of the lecture. Herewith a literal translation (see facing page), from the lecture notes, in the left column—alongside Robert Powell's adaptation in the right column.

Comparing the differences between the left and right columns for the words of the meditation "Christ is already here," there are several points to be noted. First, at the time when Valentin Tomberg beheld the Etheric Christ "standing in the south of the Earth"—Easter 1941—this was shortly (eight years) after the onset of the Second Coming in 1933. At that time it was appropriate to state that "Christ is not yet moving; he is still standing." Since that time, Christ is opening the path to Shambhala.[262] Second, as the lecture notes are fragmentary, it is possible that some of the words spoken

---

257 Volker David Lambertz, ed., *Freie Sakramente: Die allgemein-priesterlichen Sakramente Rudolf Steiners* ("The Free Spirit of the Sacraments: The Universal-Priestly Sacraments given by Rudolf Steiner"; Markdorf, Germany: Pro-Drei-Verlag, 1997), p. 257.
258 Robert Powell, *Consecration to the Immaculate Heart of Mary Sophia and Consecration to the Sacred Heart of Jesus Christ* (San Francisco: Sophia Foundation, 2007) discusses the significance of the devotion to the sacred heart of Jesus Christ and to the immaculate heart of Mary Sophia.
259 Valentin Tomberg, *Inner Development* (Great Barrington, MA: SteinerBooks, 1992), p. 32.

260 Valentin Tomberg, *Mitteilungen aus der Arkandisziplin* ("Communications from the Arcane Discipline") (Taisersdorf, Germany: Achamoth Verlag, 2003), p. 13.
261 Robert Powell, *Prophecy—Phenomena—Hope: The Real Meaning of 2012*, discusses Rudolf Steiner's prophecy relating to 1933—see page 32: "Before the Etheric Christ can be comprehended by human beings in the right way, humanity must first cope with encountering the beast who will rise up in 1933."
262 Robert Powell, "Subnature and the Second Coming," *The Interior of the Earth* (ed. Paul V. O'Leary), pp. 69–141.

Chapter 7: From the Eucharist to the Second Coming of Christ

by Valentin Tomberg were not written down. In translating from the German, I have endeavored to sense where words might have been left out—for example, the words "out of free will." On this account I added in these words when translating, "The human being has to do this," so that this becomes "The human being has to do this out of free will." Third, the expression "standing up for Christ" ("eintreten für Christus") is better expressed as "aligning oneself with Christ" in English. Fourth, in translating from German into English, holding in consciousness that the English-speaking world is very different from the German-speaking, I made allowance for what is acceptable in the English language. Fifth, the "horror" referred to by Valentin Tomberg toward the end of this meditation was that of the Second World War, which was raging in Europe at that time. Lastly, the addition of AUM at the end rounds out this meditation in an appropriate way.

Literal translation from the lecture notes	Adaptation by Robert Powell
Christ is already here	Christ is already here
He is standing in the south of the Earth	From the south of the Earth
And waves are proceeding from him	Waves are proceeding from him across the world
Every human being is now able to create the connection with him	Every human being is now able to create a connection with him
The human being has to do this	The human being has to do this out of free will
Christ is not yet moving; he is still standing	Christ is opening the path to Shambhala
However, human beings are able to go to him, to create a connection with him	And human beings are able to approach him, to create a connection with him
For this, only two things are necessary	For this, two things are necessary
Knowledge of Christ and Antichrist	Knowledge of Christ and Antichrist
And standing up for Christ	And aligning oneself with Christ
If one chooses one of the two streams streaming through the world	If one chooses one of the two streams now streaming through the world
Christ or Antichrist	Christ or Antichrist
A radiant blue stream and a black stream	A radiant blue stream and an ahrimanic stream
When one chooses, thereby one is already taken into one of the two streams	When one chooses one is already taken into one of the two streams
Through the power of Christ one is immeasurably strengthened	The power of Christ is immeasurably strengthening
With him one can peacefully pass through all this horror	With him one can pass through all trials and remain peaceful
Through his power one can endure to an unbelievable degree	Through his power one can endure to an extraordinary degree
He bestows such great power	He bestows great power
	AUM

The Spiritual Awakening of Humanity—What is at Stake

Those readers who regularly practice the Inner Radiance sequence will discover that it is a practical realization—not in full, but in seed form—of the evolutionary path into the future through the stages of planetary evolution under the guidance of Christ and Sophia. The whole Inner Radiance sequence is important in this respect. However, certain exercises are direct "signposts" with respect to stages of the evolutionary path into the future, as indicated in the table.

Planetary Stage of Evolution	Corresponding Stage of Development of the Human Being	Corresponding Exercise(s) from the Inner Radiance Sequence
Mercury (second half of Earth evolution)	Bringing to realization "Not I, but Christ in me"	A Star Is above My Head "Christ in me"
Jupiter	Transfiguration of the astral body into spirit self (*manas*)	First part of *Putting on the Resurrection Body*
Venus	Transformation of the etheric body into life spirit (*buddhi*)	Second part of *Putting on the Resurrection Body*
Vulcan	Metamorphosis of the physical body into spirit human (*atma*)	Third part of *Putting on the Resurrection Body*
Eternity	Attunement to the Cosmic Christ in the realm of *eternal peace* beyond the stages of planetary evolution	Fourth part of *Putting on the Resurrection Body*

To embark on the path of putting on the Resurrection body entails turning to Christ prayerfully to humbly ask to participate with him in a co-creative work leading into the future, toward the goal of Resurrection. As Judith von Halle expresses it:

> This gaze into the etheric world—into that sphere in which the Christ being is [now] revealing himself in his etheric appearance—is essentially possible to human beings at the present time. And if one comes to the experience of the reality of Christ through gazing upon his etheric form, one beholds surrounding him a vast, seemingly infinite number of etheric seedlings, which through the Mystery of Golgotha the Representative of Humanity [Christ] has prepared for every human soul, for every one of us. They are preserved there until the moment when one—out of the freedom bestowed upon us—develops the impulse, taking the well deliberated decision in recognition of one's true spiritual being, to develop it further and thus also to shape and form one's own seedling of the new body from the etheric seedling preserved for one there.[263]

Also, there is what is expressed in the words of Christ, "Ask, and you will receive; seek, and you will find; knock, and it will be opened to you"—this is the right attitude to hold in embarking upon the path of putting on the Resurrection body.

---

263 Judith von Halle, *Joseph von Arimathia und der Weg des Heiligen Gral* ("Joseph of Arimathea and the Path of the Holy Grail," Dornach, Switzerland: Verlag für Anthroposophie, 2011), pp. 34–35.

Chapter 7: From the Eucharist to the Second Coming of Christ

Some readers may be familiar with the lecture *Cosmic "I" and Human "I"* that Rudolf Steiner held on January 9, 1912, in which he depicts that the task of Christ now, during Earth evolution, is the bestowal of the I AM upon human beings—in the spirit of St. Paul's words, "Not I, but Christ in me" (Christ understood as the I AM or the cosmic I).[264] This is undoubtedly true, and this is acknowledged as the point of departure for the whole Inner Radiance sequence—see also the table on page 200. However, it also emerges in this lecture that there are counter-forces adversarial to Christ that seek to lead human beings into temptation by teaching them "that they could become superhuman even during earthly evolution."[265] Against this background, some readers might think that the path outlined in this book—in particular the Core Practice *Putting on the Resurrection Body*—might constitute a temptation of this kind. Nothing could be further from the truth, since the entire path proceeds *together with Christ*—bearing in mind the above-mentioned point of departure. As indicated above, "To embark on the path of putting on the Resurrection body entails turning to Christ prayerfully to humbly ask to participate with him in a co-creative work leading into the future, toward the goal of Resurrection."

What is at stake here? It is the whole future of humanity and the Earth that is at stake. In becoming aware of the cosmic stages of evolution, gradually the realization dawns that countless spiritual beings have sacrificed themselves for the sake of humanity's coming into being through the Saturn, Sun, Moon, and Earth stages of evolution. The greatest sacrifice of all was the descent of Christ into the human being Jesus of Nazareth and, subsequently, his passing through the Crucifixion on Golgotha and his descent down to the heart of the Earth, Shambhala. This sacrifice was made in order to turn around the course of evolution from a descending path to an ascending one—hence the expression "the turning point of time" for the Mystery of Golgotha.[266] Yet most human beings of the present time give hardly a thought to Christ's sacrifice, let alone to the drama of the unfolding of the cosmic stages of evolution which form the backdrop to his sacrifice. What is at stake is that through becoming buried in materialism modern human beings could forget their true mission, which is, through Christ, to evolve into the future through receiving from Christ the I AM (cosmic I), and consequently to evolve through the future stages of planetary evolution—Jupiter, Venus, and Vulcan—ultimately toward the development of the Resurrection body. The path outlined in this book is intended to serve the spiritual awakening of humanity toward becoming aware of this glorious future that awaits us—the Resurrection body!

Fortunately, Rudolf Steiner described the relationship of Christ to the higher members of his own being—spirit human (*atma*), life spirit (*buddhi*), and spirit self (*manas*)—and it is helpful to hold this in consciousness when contemplating the path into the future, toward the Resurrection body/spirit human/*atma*.

> Christ left behind him in the Sun that which...is called *spirit human*, the seventh member of the human being....Christ left his *spirit human* on

---

264 Rudolf Steiner, *Cosmic "I" and Human "I"* available as a PDF from the SteinerBooks website "Spiritual Research Center" (edition © 2008 by SteinerBooks): http://steinerbooks.org/research/archive.php.
265 Ibid., p. 19.

266 The Mystery of Golgotha embraces three mysteries: the Good Friday mystery of the Crucifixion; the Holy Saturday mystery of the descent to Shambhala; and the Easter Sunday mystery of the Resurrection. Up until fairly recently in the history of Christianity, the Easter Saturday mystery has—by and large—remained veiled. Now, with the Second Coming of Christ, the path to Shambhala is opening up for humanity. In the words of Rudolf Steiner, "Human beings will be guided to it [Shambhala] by him whom they will see when, through a vision like that of the event [of Christ's appearance to Saul, who became Paul] in Damascus, they reach the land of Shambhala....The Christ event [the Second Coming], however, which will be granted to human beings in this century [the twentieth, and into the future, from 1933 to 4433—the age of Christ's presence—*parousia*—in the etheric realm] through their newly awakened [spiritual] faculties, will bring back the fairyland of Shambhala" (*Christ Impulse and the Development of I Consciousness* [CW 116; Spring Valley, NY: Anthroposophic Press, 1976], pp. 112–113).

the Sun and around the Earth his *life spirit*...the Earth was swathed, as it were, by the *life spirit* of Christ....Christ came down to Earth leaving his *spirit human* on the Sun and his *life spirit* in the atmosphere around the Earth, bringing down his "*I*" and his *spirit self* to the Earth.[267]

The Foundation Stone Meditation

In relation to the cosmic being of Christ, obviously for the human being the path toward the development of the Resurrection body is to be distinguished from that of Christ as the cosmic bearer of the human being's higher members: spirit human, life spirit, spirit self, and the I AM. With regard to the path of putting on the Resurrection body outlined in this book, the old adage applies, "The proof of the pudding is in the eating"—meaning: to fully test something you need to experience it yourself. Everyone who honestly and sincerely persists with the Inner Radiance sequence for a time in the right spirit will sooner or later come to experience—through the words of Christ in conjunction with the eurythmy gestures—the grace of Christ streaming into the chakras, as an experience of inner radiance ("Christ in me"). This is the "proof" that this path is authentic; a path taken by the human being together with Christ.

It is thanks to Rudolf Steiner that knowledge of the divine plan (Sophia)—expressed in the "seven days of creation" (Saturn, Sun, Moon, Earth, Jupiter, Venus, Vulcan)—has been communicated to humanity. This teaching is the heart of AnthropoSophia, which is "a path of knowledge to guide the spiritual in the human being to the spiritual in the universe."[268] What Rudolf Steiner communicated is the "road map" of spiritual evolution. What is described in this book is a path of taking up a practice signifying embarking upon the way into the future according to this "road map." The content of this book, therefore, is a practical realization of the path of AnthropoSophia—a path that connects onto the Resurrection as the guiding impulse into the future. This content is in the spirit of Rudolf Steiner's AnthropoSophia and is intended to raise to new life the precious seeds of knowledge—concerning the divine plan—sown by Rudolf Steiner, so that AnthropoSophia arises within as a powerful inner source of strength from which one can meet the challenges of our time adequately equipped to do so.

Rudolf Steiner placed himself in service of the Etheric Christ, with whom he was in a living relationship. AnthropoSophia, including eurythmy, was born out of this relationship. By entering into the stream of the Etheric Christ through eurythmy, it is possible to experience the arising of AnthropoSophia within oneself as a living power. We need this living power—imbued with the strength of Christ's Resurrection—to overcome the flood of evil now coming up in the world: a flood that is also arising within each human being and which has to be overcome first of all *within* before one is in a position to stand up to evil in the world.

The living relationship between Rudolf Steiner and the Etheric Christ unfolded in such a way that the ascending path of Rudolf Steiner met with the descending path of the Etheric Christ at a certain point in time.[269] This was in the year 1923, after Rudolf Steiner had suffered the devastating blow of losing the temple he had built for the Etheric Christ. This temple, the sublime building known as the "First Goetheanum," was destroyed by fire in the night of New Year's Eve 1922/1923. Out of the loss experienced by Rudolf Steiner came the gift of receiving from the

---

267 Rudolf Steiner, *Karmic Relationships*, vol. 8, Complete Works vol. 240 (London: Rudolf Steiner Press, 1975), lecture of August 27, 1924—translation amended by RP after comparing with the German original.
268 http://steinerbooks.net/aboutrudolf.html.

269 The term *Etheric Christ* applies in particular to Christ in his Second Coming, to his manifestation in the Earth's etheric aura since 1933. In addition, here the term is used in an extended sense, applied to Christ from 1899 to 1933, at that time on his path of "incarnation" on his way into the Earth's etheric aura. In this extended sense, the term *Etheric Christ* is applied to Christ in his relationship to Rudolf Steiner in the period of preparation for his Second Coming.

Etheric Christ the plan for a spiritual temple to be built in human hearts. The impulse for the realization of the plan of this spiritual temple was given by Christ through Rudolf Steiner on December 25, 1923, with the speaking of the Foundation Stone meditation for about eight hundred people assembled on that morning.[270]

The next morning Rudolf Steiner indicated that the verses of this meditation were "heard from the World Word," i.e., from the Logos/Christ.[271] This is particularly evident for the first three verses of this meditation, each of which begins with the words "human soul" addressed by Christ to the human being. However, it is clear that the fourth verse was born in Rudolf Steiner as an answer on behalf of humanity—in the form of a meditative prayer—to the Etheric Christ in his Second Coming, that he may "warm our hearts" and "enlighten our heads." The words of this great meditation are given on the following pages.

---

270 Rudolf Steiner, *The Christmas Conference for the Foundation of the General Anthroposophical Society 1923–1924*, cw 260 (Great Barrington, MA: SteinerBooks, 1990)

271   Ibid., lecture of December 26, 1923.

Human Soul!
Thou livest in the limbs
Which bear thee through the World of Space
Into the Spirit's Ocean Being.
Practice *Spirit Recollection*
In depths of soul,
Where in the Wielding Will
 of World Creating
Thine own I
Comes to being in God's I.
And thou wilt truly *live*
In Human World Being.

For the Father Spirit
 of the Heights holds sway
In Depths of Worlds
Begetting Being:
Seraphim, Cherubim, Thrones!
Let there ring out from the Heights
What in the Depths is echoed.
This speaks:
Ex Deo nascimur.
The Spirits of the Elements hear it:
In East, West, North, South—
May human beings hear it!

Human Soul!
Thou livest in the beat of heart and lung
Which leads thee through the Rhythm of Time
Into the realm of thine own soul's feeling.
Practice *Spirit Awareness*
In balance of the soul,
Where the Surging Deeds
 of the World's Becoming
Thine own I
Unite with the World I.
And thou wilt truly *feel*
In Human Soul Weaving.

For the Christ Will
 in the encircling Round holds sway
In Rhythms of Worlds
Bestowing Grace on the soul:
Kyriotetes, Dynamis, Exusiai!
Let there be fired from the East
What in the West is formed.
This speaks:
In Christo morimur.
The Spirits of the Elements hear it:
In East, West, North, South—
May human beings hear it!

Chapter 7: From the Eucharist to the Second Coming of Christ

Human Soul!
Thou livest in the resting head
Which from the Grounds of Eternity
Opens to thee the World Thoughts.
Practice *Spirit Beholding*
In stillness of thought,
Where the Eternal Aims of Gods
World Being's Light
On thine own I bestow
For thy free willing.
And thou wilt truly *think*
In Human Spirit Foundations.

For the World Thoughts
 of the Spirit hold sway
In Beings of Worlds
Beseeching Light:
Archai, Archangeloi, Angeloi!
Let there be prayed from the Depths
What in the Heights will be granted.
This speaks:
Per Spiritum Sanctum reviviscimus.
The Spirits of the Elements hear it:
In East, West, North, South—
May human beings hear it!

At the turning point of time
The Spirit Light of the World
Entered the Stream of Earthly Being.
Darkness of Night had held its sway.
Day-radiant Light streamed into human souls:
Light that gives warmth
To simple Shepherds' Hearts.
Light that enlightens
The wise Heads of Kings.

O Light Divine,
O Sun of Christ,
Warm Thou our hearts,
Enlighten Thou our heads,
That Good may become—
What from our hearts we found
And from our heads direct

With single purpose. (Rudolf Steiner)[272]

---

[272] Rudolf Steiner, *The Christmas Conference for the Foundation of the General Anthroposophical Society 1923–1924*. See also Lacquanna Paul & Robert Powell, *The Foundation Stone Meditation in the Sacred Dance of Eurythmy* (San Francisco: Sophia Foundation, 2007); and Valentin Tomberg, *Studies on the Foundation Stone Meditation* (San Rafael, CA: LogoSophia, 2010)..

Note that the words "O Sun of Christ" in the fourth verse relate to the Etheric Christ, in the same way that the expression "Christ Sun" in the Salutation to the Sun ("I see the (Christ) Sun..." on page 66). "Christ Sun" is the literal translation from the German *"Christus Sonne"* in the fourth verse of the "Foundation Stone Meditation."

The Foundation Stone Meditation and the Second Coming

Foundation Stone meditation	Stages of Planetary Evolution	Level in the Human Being	Corresponding Level of Consciousness	Relationship to the Holy Trinity
Fourth verse relates to the present stage	Mercury (second half of Earth evolution)	"Christ in me"	Spiritualized "objective consciousness" (see facing page*)	Jesus Christ (as the incarnated God–Man) (see facing page**)
Third verse prefigures Jupiter in seed form	Jupiter	Transfiguration of the astral body into spirit self (*manas*)	Imagination "practice spirit beholding"	Holy Spirit *Per Spiritum sanctum reviviscimus*
Second verse prefigures Venus in seed form	Venus	Transformation of the etheric body into life spirit (*buddhi*)	Inspiration "practice spirit awareness"	Son *In Christo morimur*
First verse prefigures Vulcan in seed form	Vulcan	Metamorphosis of the physical body into spirit human (*atma*)	Intuition "practice spirit recollection"	Father *Ex Deo nascimur*

The communication of the Foundation Stone meditation by Christ on his descending path can be understood as the "baptismal event" in the Second Coming of Christ, comparable to the baptism of Jesus in the River Jordan, when Christ incarnated into Jesus.[273] Normally baptism follows birth. This is true on the physical level. On the etheric level of Christ's Second Coming, the baptism (Christmas 1923) preceded the birth (January 1933).[274] In relation to Christ's Second Coming, Rudolf Steiner played the role that John the Baptist had played at the baptism in the River Jordan two thousand years previously. At that event of the physical baptism, John the Baptist announced the baptism by speaking the words, "Behold the Lamb of God, who bears the sins of the world" (John 1:29). With the Second Coming of Christ, Rudolf Steiner announced the baptism—heralding Christ's Second Coming as an etheric event—by speaking the words of the Foundation Stone meditation.

These words are of spiritual significance as a "portal" to the *parousia*, the presence of Christ in the Earth's etheric aura. Moreover, these words also contain the seed impulse into the future—through the future stages of planetary evolution—as indicated in the table above.

---

273 Robert Powell, *Chronicle of the Living Christ* (Hudson, NY: Anthroposophic Press, 1996), pp. 35–38.

274 Robert Powell, *The Christ Mystery: Reflections on the Second Coming* (Fair Oaks, CA: Rudolf Steiner College Press, 1999), pp. 69–74 describes that whereas the period of Christ's activity while physically incarnated upon the Earth lasted for only 3½ years from the baptism to the Resurrection, the *parousia* (the presence of Christ in the etheric realm) extends for some 2,500 years (1933–4433), near the end of the age of Aquarius in 4535. In other words, Christ's Second Coming extends for 442 years (1933–2375) within the last part of the age of Pisces, and 2,058 years (2375–4433) throughout most of the age of Aquarius, noting that the 2,160-year period of the age of Aquarius lasts from 2375 to 4535.

*Objective consciousness is the consciousness developed by virtue of incarnation into a physical body. It is this quality of objectivity that is striven for in science, whereby the realization has come in modern science that there is an *observer effect*, meaning that the *act of observing* influences the phenomenon being observed. *Spiritualized objective consciousness* is objective consciousness permeated by the warmth, light, and goodness of "Christ in me"—through Christ's warmth in one's heart, his light in one's mind, and his goodness in one's will, as it is expressed in the fourth verse of the Foundation Stone meditation: "Warm thou our hearts, enlighten thou our heads, that good may become, what from our hearts we found and from our heads direct with single purpose."

**Jesus Christ as the incarnated God-Man, also known as the *Divine Person (Persona)*, is the *fourth power of good* in world existence—the three other *powers of good* being the Father, the Son, and the Holy Spirit: see Valentin Tomberg, *Christ and Sophia* (Great Barrington, MA: SteinerBooks, 2006), appendix: *The Four Sacrifices of Christ and the Reappearance of Christ in the Etheric*, pp. 359–360.

The three Latin expressions given in the previous table were referred to by Rudolf Steiner as the "Rosicrucian mantras." The literal translation from the Latin into English is, "From God we are born. In Christ we die. Through the Holy Spirit we are revived." According to Rudolf Steiner, these Latin mantras mean: "In God the Father we are born. In Christ we die…. Through the Holy Spirit we will resurrect."[275] The Resurrection, of course, is directly connected with Christ, and so the question arises as to what exactly is meant by, "Through the Holy Spirit we will resurrect?" If we understand that the Holy Spirit leads us toward the future, toward the realization of the divine plan, which culminates with Resurrection, we can grasp that the sense of these words is that under the guidance of the Holy Spirit we are led toward the future goal of evolution, which is Resurrection. Elsewhere, Rudolf Steiner translated *Per Spiritum Sanctum reviviscimus* as, "Through the Holy Spirit we are reborn, reawakened,"[276] which is in line with the understanding that the Holy Spirit is the spiritual awakener through whom we are enlightened, i.e., spiritually reborn. In addition, when Rudolf Steiner gave the Foundation Stone meditation, he gave his own unique translation—or, rather, two different renditions—of the three Rosicrucian mantras, the second (in brackets) being a more personal version of these mantras, rendered in the "I" form rather than in the "we" form:[277]

> *Ex Deo nascimur*—From the Divine humanity is born [I—Father (reverence for the Father)]
>
> *In Christo morimur*—In Christ death becomes life [I—Son (love for the Son)]
>
> *Per Spiritum Sanctum reviviscimus*—In the world thoughts of the [Holy] Spirit the soul awakens [I—Spirit (union with the Holy Spirit)]

The three Rosicrucian mantras, which were central to the First Esoteric School founded by Rudolf Steiner, form the culmination of the first three verses of the Foundation Stone meditation. The quintessence of the first three verses is expressed by the three Rosicrucian mantras, just as the quintessence of the fourth verse can be expressed as "Christ in me."

---

275 Rudolf Steiner, *Aus den Inhalten der esoterischen Stunden II, 1910–1912* ("Esoteric Lessons, 1910–1912," cw 266/2; Dornach, Switzerland: Rudolf Steiner Verlag, 1996), p.466.

276 Rudolf Steiner, *Aus den Inhalten der esoterischen Stunden II, 1910–1912*, p.151.

277 See Lacquanna Paul & Robert Powell, *The Foundation Stone Meditation in the Sacred Dance of Eurythmy* (San Francisco: Sophia Foundation, 2007) for this particular translation into English by RP of Rudolf Steiner's rendition of the three Rosicrucian mantra into German in the context of the Foundation Stone meditation. For the "I" form of the Rosicrucian mantras, see Rudolf Steiner, *Esoterische Unterweisungen für die Erste Klasse*, vol. 3 ("Esoteric Instructions for the First Class," cw 241c; Dornach, Switzerland: Rudolf Steiner Verlag, 1977), p. 237.

The Foundation Stone Meditation and the Morning Meditation

Morning Meditation opening verse	Morning Meditation mantras	Foundation Stone meditation	Four stages of Putting on the Resurrection Body
In purest out-poured light shimmers the Godhead of the world	HE WILLS spirit human *atma*	For the Father–Spirit in the heights holds sway	First part
In purest love toward all that lives radiates the Godhood of my soul	SHE FEELS life spirit *buddhi*	For the Christ Will in the encircling round holds sway	Second part
I rest within the Godhead of the world	IT THINKS spirit self *manas*	Human soul, thou livest in the resting head	Third part
I shall find myself within the Godhead of the world	I AM "I"	"Christ in me"	Fourth part

In working with the Foundation Stone meditation—and eurythmy is a help in deepening into it[278]—it becomes apparent that the seed for this meditation was living already in the *Morning Meditation* taught by Rudolf Steiner in the First Esoteric School, which existed from 1904 to 1914.[279] The four sentences of the opening verse comprising part 1 of the *Morning Meditation* are reproduced on page 2 of this book alongside Rudolf Steiner's sculpture of Jesus Christ as the *Representative of Humanity*. In connection with this juxtaposition, we can think of Rudolf Steiner's words concerning the *Morning Meditation*: "Here in this meditation we find Christ as our highest leader, our highest guru, who guides us in a direct and immediate sense, if we turn to him."[280] How do the words of this meditation relate to the Foundation Stone meditation? There is a direct correspondence between these two meditations, as can be seen from the table.

The first column of the table above shows the four sentences comprising the opening verse that is the first part of the *Morning Meditation*. The second column contains the four mantras belonging to the second part of the *Morning Meditation*, for which Rudolf Steiner gave the following juxtaposition:

I AM	"I"
IT THINKS	spirit self
SHE FEELS	life spirit
HE WILLS	spirit human[281]

---

278 Ibid.
279 Rudolf Steiner, *From the History & Contents of the First Section of the Esoteric School 1904–1914*.
280 Rudolf Steiner, *Aus den Inhalten der esoterischen Stunden II, 1910–1912* (*Esoteric Lessons II, 1910–1912*), p.90.

281 Rudolf Steiner, *Seelenübungen mit Wort- und Sinnbild-Meditationen* ("Soul Exercises with Word and Image Meditations"), CW 267 (Dornach, Switzerland: Rudolf Steiner Verlag, 1997), p.111.

The four mantras were originally described by Rudolf Steiner in connection with a breathing exercise.[282] The mantras can be worked with in connection with the chakras—I AM (third eye chakra); IT THINKS (larynx chakra); SHE FEELS (heart chakra); HE WILLS (solar plexus chakra)—as described by Rudolf Steiner,[283] without doing the breathing exercise.[284] For he also gave the four mantras as a meditation without the breathing exercise—for example:

> With the sense that *"from the spiritual world my self flows to me,"* concentrate upon the center of the forehead and thereby guide to this place the words:
> I AM.
>
> Then with the sense that *"the spiritual world lives on the soul level in the silent word,"* concentrate upon the larynx and thereby guide to this place the words:
> IT THINKS.
>
> Then with the sense that *"the spiritual world creates its knowledge itself,"* concentrate upon the heart, arms, and hands and guide into this region the words:
> SHE FEELS.
>
> Then with the sense that *"the spiritual world creates knowledge of itself within me,"* concentrate upon the aura, which is thought of as surrounding the body in an egg shape; thereby guide into this region the words:
> HE WILLS.[285]

The relationship of these four mantras to the four verses of the Foundation Stone meditation is evident from the content of the four verses of the Foundation Stone meditation. The first verse, for example, is directed to the human being's will; HE WILLS refers to the will of the Father. "In HE WILLS, the HE signifies God, within whose will we instate our whole being...HE is the word of power for the cosmic will, the cosmic spirit whose will acts from out of itself, whereas the human will is brought into action through the outer world. This HE is the creative primal power of the world."[286] It is in "purest out-poured light" that the Godhead, the creative primal power of the world is revealed. In the words of St. Paul:

> God, the blessed and only Ruler, the King of kings and Lord of lords—he who is the blessed and only Sovereign—who alone is immortal and *who lives in unapproachable light*, whom no one has seen or can see: To him be honor and might forever. Amen. (1 Timothy 6:15–16)

It was this "unapproachable light"—the "purest out-poured light" of the Godhead—that radiated through and shimmered around Jesus Christ at the Transfiguration on Mt. Tabor. In connection with the opening verse of the *Morning Meditation*, beginning with the words, "In purest out-poured light shimmers the Godhead of the world," Rudolf Steiner drew a figure. Alongside this figure, he wrote: "Eye—Godhead / Triangle—spirit human-life spirit-spirit self / Rays—'I' / Illumined clouds—astral body / Dark clouds—etheric body / Unillumined surrounding—physical body." From this figure, it is evident that the Godhead is the source of "purest out-poured light."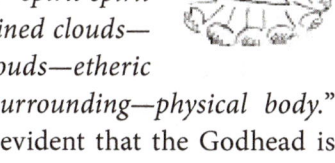

The second verse of the Foundation Stone meditation is directed to the realm of feeling in the human being, connected with the "beat of heart and lung"; SHE FEELS relates to the world soul, Sophia,

---

282 Rudolf Steiner, *Guidance in Esoteric Training*, CW 245 (London: Rudolf Steiner Press, 1972), pp. 25–26. To deepen the *Morning Meditation*, it helps to read the whole relevant section in *Guidance in Esoteric Training*, pp. 24–33. For German-speaking readers, a wealth of material on the *Morning Meditation* is in the German edition: *Anweisungen für eine esoterische Schulung* (Dornach, Switzerland: Rudolf Steiner Verlag, 1979), pp. 35–47; and in Rudolf Steiner, *Seelenübungen mit Wort- und Sinnbild-Meditationen*, CW 267 (Dornach, Switzerland: Rudolf Steiner Verlag, 1997), pp. 101–115 and 134–215.

283 Rudolf Steiner, *Anweisungen für eine esoterische Schulung* ("*Guidance in Esoteric Training*"), Complete Works vol. 245 (Dornach, Switzerland: Rudolf Steiner Verlag, 1979), pp. 39–41.

284 Valentin Tomberg, *Lazarus, Come Forth!* (Great Barrington, MA: SteinerBooks, 2006), p. 248. Tomberg offers helpful indications for breathing exercises in general.

285 Rudolf Steiner, *Seelenübungen mit Wort- und Sinnbild-Meditationen*, p. 114.

286 Rudolf Steiner, *Guidance in Esoteric Training*, pp. 26, 33 (translation amended by RP after comparing with the original German).

who—since her entrance onto the stage of world evolution around 1775—is working ever more intensely together with Christ, whose will, which "holds sway in the encircling round," is united with the world soul, Sophia.[287] "In SHE FEELS, the SHE signifies the cosmic soul—meaning that we should practice feeling not personally, but impersonally, as is the case with the cosmic soul...SHE is the word of power for the cosmic soul, who streams out feeling from herself, whereas human feeling streams in through the stimulus from outside. This feeling of the world soul is the creative cosmic love which brings all things into existence."[288] This last sentence is clearly also a reference to Christ, the Logos, "through whom all things were made" (John 1:3). And in the context of the foregoing words concerning the world soul, Sophia, the whole quotation by Rudolf Steiner can only be understood against the background of the union of Christ and Sophia. It is in "purest love toward all that lives" that Christ and Sophia, the Lamb and his Bride, are revealed in their spiritual unity as the creative cosmic love of the world, and it was this love that poured through Jesus Christ at the Crucifixion on Golgotha.

The third verse of the Foundation Stone meditation relates to the faculty of thinking in the human being, that arises in the "resting head"; IT THINKS relates to the Holy Spirit. "In IT THINKS, the IT signifies the universal cosmic thinking which should live impersonally in our words...IT is the word of power for the cosmic thinking: that is, for those beings in the higher world to whom creative thinking belongs in just the same measure as sense perception belongs to human beings below them."[289] It is in "resting in the Godhead of the world" that the Holy Spirit, as the creative cosmic thinking of the world, is revealed in "spirit beholding," and it is this that is referred to by Rudolf Steiner in his unique translation—or, rather, rendition—of the "Holy Spirit" words: *Per Spiritum Sanctum reviviscimus* ("In the world thoughts of the [Holy] Spirit the soul awakens"—"And then we are illumined with the certainty that we ascend to the Spirit, resurrect in the Spirit. *Per Spiritum Sanctum Reviviscimus.*"[290] Hence the connection of IT THINKS—and, correspondingly, also the third verse of the Foundation Stone meditation (as well as the words "I rest within the Godhead of the world")—with the event of Christ's Resurrection.

The fourth verse of the Foundation Stone meditation, where the human being turns in prayer to receive the warmth of Christ in the heart, the light of Christ in the head, and the goodness of Christ in the will, is directed to the human I and—through the I—to the I AM, and thus refers to the I united with the cosmic I AM (Christ) in the spirit of the words "Christ in me." "One will gradually realize that intellectual, soul, and moral power of the highest order comes to birth within by immersing oneself in the right way in the I AM, and that one thereby brings oneself into a more and more conscious relationship to a higher world."[291] Through meditating upon the I AM—and in the *Morning Meditation* the mantra I AM is brought into relation to the third eye chakra—"One comes to experience something like...I resolve to place myself within the whole context of the world."[292] What is expressed here is

---

287 Http://www.sophiafoundation.org, articles, "Sophia and the Rose of the World" (article); it discusses the descent of Sophia from cosmic heights into our local part of the galaxy, beginning around the year 1775.
288 Rudolf Steiner, *Guidance in Esoteric Training*, pp.26, 33 (translation amended by RP after comparing with the original German).
289 Ibid.

290 Rudolf Steiner, *Aus den Inhalten der esoterischen Stunden 1910–1912* (*Esoteric Lessons 1910–1912*), Dornach, Switzerland: Rudolf Steiner Verlag, 1996), p.201. It is interesting that in the first vol. of the Esoteric Lessons, Rudolf Steiner used the expression "resurrect in the Holy Grail" as a rendering of *Per Spiritum Sanctum reviviscimus* (*Esoteric Lessons 1904–1909*, CW 266/I (Great Barrington, MA: SteinerBooks, 2007), p.440.
291 Rudolf Steiner, *Guidance in Esoteric Training* (translation amended by RP after comparing with the original German).
292 Ibid.

another way of saying: "I shall find myself within the Godhead of the world." The discovery of oneself in the I AM is the goal of the fourth verse of the Foundation Stone meditation and it is also the goal of meditating upon the words "I shall find myself within the Godhead of the world." The strength of the I AM is revealed as the power to unite Heaven and Earth, this being "the whole context of the world," and it was this power of the I AM indwelling Jesus Christ that shone forth at his Ascension to heaven from the Mount of Olives at the start of his journey to the Father. "I am ascending to my Father and your Father, to my God and your God" (John 20:17). In other words, Christ's path of Ascension to the Father was a bringing to realization (as a divine archetype) of "I shall find myself within the Godhead of the world"—this being the fourth line of the opening verse of the *Morning Meditation*.

The *Morning Meditation* begins with the opening verse (see page 2) as the first part of the meditation. The four mantras—I AM, IT THINKS, SHE FEELS, HE WILLS—comprise the second part. As already mentioned, Rudolf Steiner originally indicated breathing instructions in connection with the four mantras, but these mantras can also be meditated upon in relation to the chakras without applying the breathing instructions.

Concentration on an Image/ Thought Content

The third part of the *Morning Meditation* entails concentration upon an image/thought content. "For a while one fills one's consciousness completely with one single image in which one is entirely absorbed, so that during this time nothing else whatever is present in the soul."[293] As an example of this, Rudolf Steiner describes, "In the soul—completely at peace—one has to call up one single image: *Above, everything as below; below, everything as above*. One has to live for ten minutes (according to one's inner sense, not according to the clock) in such images [as those] that one can attain through applying this [one single] image to the [various] manifestations of the world."[294] Elsewhere, Rudolf Steiner simplified this one single image to "As above, so below, which is imprinted into the frontal brain directly for approximately 2½ minutes."[295] In connection with "As above, so below"— the fundamental axiom of hermeticism—he drew a figure indicating:

> *above*—*atma, buddhi, manas,* "I"
> *below* [corresponding to the above, the following:]
> I [above] / [below] the blood [the I lives in the blood]
> *manas* [above] / [below] the nerve-sense system [the astral body lives in the nerve-sense system, and *manas* is the transfigured astral body]
> *buddhi* [above] / [below] digestion-procreation [the etheric body lives strongly into the digestive and procreative processes, and *buddhi* is the transformed etheric body].[296]

Although Rudolf Steiner does not indicate an above-below correspondence for *atma*, he does draw the figure of a circle for *atma*, which in another (related) figure becomes an oval form surrounding the lower human being (the metabolic-limb system, including the legs and feet) upon which he wrote the mantra HE WILLS.[297] As already described, he connects HE WILLS with *atma*, and thus the following above-below correspondence for *atma* emerges:

> *atma* [above] / [below] the lower human being (the metabolic-limb system, including the legs and feet). However, since *atma* is the metamorphosis of the physical body, in an extended sense the Resurrection body (spirit human/*atma*) has to do with the original form of the whole physical body, as comes to expression in these words:

---

293   Ibid., p.26.

294   Rudolf Steiner, *Anweisungen für eine esoterische Schulung* (*Guidance in Esoteric Training*), p.39—words in brackets [ ] added by RP.

295   Rudolf Steiner, *Seelenübungen mit Wort- und Sinnbild-Meditationen* (Dornach, Switzerland: Rudolf Steiner Verlag, 1997), p.127.

296   Ibid.—words in brackets [ ] added by RP.

297   Ibid., p.138.

Concentrate upon the entire surface of the body and thereby meditate on
> HE WILLS.

One "pours out" one's whole body with this
> HE WILLS.

Thereby one pays attention to the living warmth which permeates the whole body, and one remains peaceful for a time, quietly living into this sensation.[298]

So much for the "As above, so below" correspondence indicated by Rudolf Steiner for part 3 of the *Morning Meditation*. This was not the only "one single image" that he gave for the concentration exercise of part 3. Different people in the First Esoteric School received different images, although it is known that some people received the same image/thought content. Herewith some further examples: "*My strength—I in me—I will—I am steadfast—Repose in strength—Strength in repose—Soul warmth permeates me.*"[299] Now, without being given an image by Rudolf Steiner, it is a matter of choosing one for oneself and practicing concentration upon this image/thought content.

> Completely at rest, one concentrates upon a short thought content, which should be *totally clear and comprehensible* so that one does not allow the unconscious or subconscious reminiscences to play in. Rather, one remains in spiritual activity with fully attentive consciousness. Then one allows the thought content to fall away from consciousness and seeks to retain the energy to remain for a short time consciously without thought content. Thereby one connects one's faculty for knowledge to that quiet energy which is necessary in order to grasp the spiritual and which otherwise usually falls through the mesh of normal thinking and thus does not come to consciousness.... The significance of this exercise lies partly in calling forth a stronger soul activity than is usual. As in the case of physical events, where at critical points the quantitative is transposed into the qualitative, so also the intensification of the normal faculty of knowledge can become that which has the spiritual world as its object.[300]

A slightly different nuance regarding this concentration exercise (part 3 of the *Morning Meditation*) is brought out in the following characterization:

> A word or sentence is given to us for contemplation. This concentration on a sentence or a word—for example, *strength*—is very important. This is a kind of watchword, a word of power that is adapted exactly to the soul constitution of every individual. One should let this word resonate in one's soul as one would strike a tuning fork. And as one listens to the sounds of a tuning fork fading away, so one should, after meditating on the word, let the sound of it fade away in the soul: one should devote oneself to what has been brought about in the soul by the word.[301]

In the fourth part of the *Morning Meditation*, "Then we pass on to complete absorption, for five minutes, in our own divine ideal. This exercise must be enacted with the utmost devotion and reverence."[302]

> In conclusion, one meditates five minutes or more on his or her divine ideal. What kind of ideal it may be does not come into consideration; what is of concern is only the creation of the proper mood in the soul. It does not matter whether one thinks of the master or of the celestial sphere. Atheists have even come who thought they did not have a divine ideal. But their attention was drawn to the celestial sphere, which nevertheless draws forth a feeling of devotion and reverence from everyone.[303]

---

298   Ibid., p.108.
299   Rudolf Steiner, *Anweisungen für eine esoterische Schulung*, p.37.
300   Rudolf Steiner, *Seelenübungen mit Wort- und Sinnbild-Meditationen*, pp.79–80.
301   Rudolf Steiner, *Esoteric Lessons 1904–1909*, p.193.
302   Rudolf Steiner, *Guidance in Esoteric Training*, p.26.
303   Rudolf Steiner, *Esoteric Lessons 1904–1909*, p.193.

Deepening into the Core Practice "Putting on the Resurrection Body"

Once having understood the correspondences between the *Morning Meditation* and the Foundation Stone meditation, one can also hold these correspondences in consciousness when practicing the Core Practice *Putting on the Resurrection Body*. For example, as one speaks/thinks the words "In purest out-poured light shimmers the Godhead of the world" in the first part of the Core Practice, where then the words are spoken "*Putting on the Resurrection Body*—the first stage: the Transfiguration," one can inwardly contemplate the correspondences associated with these guiding thoughts/images. One way of doing this is to expand the number of L's at the start of this first part from three to ten, where with each L one adds a further correspondence, as described below in detail.

However, before coming to this description, it is necessary to clarify that there are two different—seemingly contradictory—perspectives with regard to the correspondences under consideration. This is because there are two ways in which the four sentences comprising the opening verse of the *Morning Meditation* can be considered: the macrocosmic and the microcosmic. Beginning with the microcosmic perspective: in the table on page 200 these four sentences are looked at from the perspective of the human being on the ascending path of evolution, looking to the Jupiter evolution in connection with the Transfiguration ("In purest out-poured light shimmers the Godhead of the world"), to the Venus evolution in connection with the Crucifixion ("In purest love toward all that lives radiates the Godhood of my soul"), to the Vulcan evolution in connection with the Resurrection ("I rest within the Godhead of the world"), and to the realm of eternity, that of eternal peace, in connection with the Cosmic Christ at the Ascension ("I shall find myself in the Godhead of the world"). This microcosmic perspective is the one that we have been working with hitherto and which underlies the speaking of the three L's at the start of the first part of *Putting on the Resurrection Body*—similarly with the speaking of the three R's at the start of the second part, the speaking of the three AU's at the start of the third part, and the speaking of the three M's at the start of the fourth part.

Now, looking at the table on page 206, with the introduction of the correspondence with the four verses of the Foundation Stone meditation, a macrocosmic perspective comes in, revealed in the fact that the sequence of the four verses of the Foundation Stone meditation is reversed in this table. For the Foundation Stone meditation was communicated from the macrocosmic level by Christ on his descending path toward his Second Coming. And if we look at the table on page 208, where the verses of the Foundation Stone meditation are properly arranged in descending sequence and are simultaneously placed in correspondence with the four mantras and the four sentences of the opening verse of the *Morning Meditation*, we see that then the macrocosmic perspective with regard to these four sentences is revealed. The "purest out-poured light" is then no longer understood solely as the result of the transfiguration of the astral body into *manas* (Jupiter evolution), but as the "clothing" of the Father. Similarly, the "purest love toward all that lives" is then no longer specifically the consequence of the transformation of the etheric body into *buddhi* (Venus evolution), but is the out-pouring of the Son as the power of Divine Love streaming throughout all existence. Likewise, "resting in the Godhead" is then no longer comprehended solely as the result of the metamorphosis of the physical body into *atma* (Vulcan evolution), but as the point of departure of the Holy Spirit, in the sense that "the fruit of the spirit is...peace"—Galatians 5:22—and peace is an expression of resting in the Godhead of the world." Lastly, the "finding of oneself in the Godhead of the world" is then no longer specifically an attunement to the Cosmic Christ in the realm of eternity, but is the state of "Christ in me"—the immersion of the I in the I AM.

It is this macrocosmic perspective that comes to expression in the correspondences associated with speaking the seven L's (after the first three L's) at the start of the first part of *Putting on the Resurrection Body*—similarly with the speaking of the seven R's (after the first three R's) at the start of the second part, the speaking of the seven AU's (after the first three AU's) at the start of the third part, and the speaking of the seven M's (after the first three M's) at the start of the fourth part, as indicated below. (Instead of "speaking," the word "thinking" could also be used here, depending upon whether in practicing this exercise one prefers to speak the words out loud or to think them inwardly.)

Having indicated these two perspectives—the microcosmic and the macrocosmic—the following description outlines this deepening into the Core Practice *Putting on the Resurrection Body*, whereby the apparent contradiction between the macrocosmic and microcosmic perspectives brings with it a profound deepening of this practice:

Part One of the Core Practice

Microcosmic perspective (three L's with right foot forward)
- L   "In purest out-poured light shimmers the Godhead of the world"
- L   *Putting on the Resurrection Body*
- L   the first stage: the Transfiguration

Macrocosmic perspective (seven L's with left foot forward)
- L   *Ex Deo nascimur* (first Rosicrucian mantra in Latin)
- L   "From the Divine humanity is born" (Foundation Stone meditation)
- L   "I—Father" (reverence for the Father)
- L   "Practice spirit recollection" (first verse of the Foundation Stone meditation)
- L   Intuition (highest level of consciousness, prefiguring Vulcan evolution)
- L   Gnosis (corresponding to Intuition in Christian hermeticism)
- L   HE WILLS (mantra from the *Morning Meditation*)

Part Two of the Core Practice

Microcosmic perspective (three R's with right foot forward)
- R   "In purest love toward all that lives radiates the Godhood of my soul"
- R   *Putting on the Resurrection Body*
- R   the second stage: the Crucifixion

Macrocosmic perspective (seven R's with left foot forward)
- R   *In Christo morimur* (second Rosicrucian mantra in Latin)
- R   "In Christ death becomes life" (Foundation Stone meditation)
- R   "I—Son" (love for the Son)
- R   "Practice spirit awareness" (second verse of the Foundation Stone meditation)
- R   Inspiration (level of consciousness prefiguring Venus evolution)
- R   Mysticism (corresponding to Inspiration in Christian hermeticism)
- R   SHE FEELS (mantra from the *Morning Meditation*)

Chapter 7: From the Eucharist to the Second Coming of Christ

Part Three of the Core Practice

    Microcosmic perspective (three heart-AU's / or three AU's, arms extended, circling clockwise)
        AU   "I rest within the Godhead of the world"
        AU   *Putting on the Resurrection Body*
        AU   the third stage: the Resurrection
    Macrocosmic perspective (seven AU's, arms extended, circling counterclockwise)
        AU   *Per Spiritum Sanctum reviviscimus* (third Rosicrucian mantra in Latin)
        AU   "In the world thoughts of the [Holy] Spirit the soul awakens" (Foundation Stone meditation)
        AU   "I—Spirit" (union with the Holy Spirit)
        AU   "Practice spirit beholding" (third verse of the Foundation Stone meditation)
        AU   Imagination (level of consciousness prefiguring Jupiter evolution)
        AU   Sacred magic (corresponding to Imagination in Christian hermeticism)
        AU   IT THINKS (mantra from the *Morning Meditation*)

Part Four of the Core Practice

    Microcosmic perspective (three M's with right foot forward)
        M   "I shall find myself within the Godhead of the world"
        M   *Putting on the Resurrection Body*
        M   the fourth stage: the Ascension
    Macrocosmic perspective (seven M's with left foot forward)
        M   *Iesous Christos Theou Yios Soter* (Greek)
        M   "Jesus Christ, Son of God, Savior" (translation from the Greek)
        M   "Christ in me" (personalized version of Rudolf Steiner's "Christ in us")
        M   "That good may become" (fourth verse of the Foundation Stone meditation)
        M   "O Sun of Christ" (Christ-permeated consciousness) [304]
        M   "As above, so below" (formula of initiation in Christian hermeticism)
        M   I AM (mantra from the *Morning Meditation*)

In the fourth part of the Core Practice it is a matter of honoring Jesus Christ as the incarnated God–Man, and one traditional Christian saying that brings this to expression is, in Greek, *Iesous Christos Theou Yios Soter*,[305] translated into English as "Jesus Christ, Son of God, Savior." Jesus Christ is the fourth power of good, after the Father, the Son, and the Holy Spirit. While the three Rosicrucian mantra apply to the Father, the Son, and the Holy Spirit, there is no Rosicrucian mantra for Jesus Christ as the fourth power of good. However, on the sarcophagus in the crypt of Christian Rosenkreuz, the original founder of the Rosicrucian movement, these words, among various inscriptions, were written in Latin: *Jesus mihi omnia*. This saying—meaning "Jesus is everything to me"—honors Jesus but it does not honor Jesus Christ, whereas "Jesus Christ, Son of God, Savior" does. It is also an acrostic for the Greek word *I Ch Th Y S* (ichthys), meaning fish—reminding us of the words of Jesus Christ, "Follow me, and I will make you fishers of men" (Mark 1:17), as one of his many sayings relating to fish. "Jesus Christ, Son of God,

---

304 "O Sun of Christ" is an expression of the human being's striving for Christ-permeated consciousness—an abbreviation from the fourth verse of the Foundation Stone meditation for "O Sun of Christ, warm thou our hearts, enlighten thou our heads."

305 Approximate pronunciation: Yay-*sous* Krees-*tohs* Thay-*oo* We-*ohs* So-*tair* (with emphasis always on the second syllable—italicized).

Savior" was for early Christians a brief profession of faith in the divinity of Jesus Christ as the redeemer of humankind. "Christ in me" brings to expression the central content and meaning of the fourth verse of the Foundation Stone meditation, which culminates with the words, "That good may become, what from our hearts we found and from our heads direct with single purpose." "As above, so below," as discussed earlier in this chapter, was indicated by Rudolf Steiner as a key to initiation (see page 211) and is referred to in the book *Meditations on the Tarot* as the formula for initiation.[306]

The following table provides an overview with respect to deepening into the Core Practice *Putting on the Resurrection Body*. The table is intended to be read (primarily) column by column.

---

306   Anonymous, *Meditations on the Tarot*, p.88.

Eternity: Stages of planetary evolution	Cosmic Christ; Realm of Eternal Peace	I shall find myself within the Godhead of the world (Ascension)	Macrocosmic Perspective (Descending)	Rosicrucian mantras for the Father, Son, and Holy Spirit	Translation of mantras	Expression of mantras in the "I" form	Foundation Stone Meditation Spiritual Practice	Corresponding states of consciousness	Morning Meditation Mantras
Vulcan metamorphosis of Ancient Saturn	Physical body becomes spirit human (*atma*)	I rest within the Godhead of the world (Resurrection)	In purest out-poured light shimmers the Godhead of the world	Father: *Ex Deo nascimur*	From the Divine humanity is born	"I"–Father (reverence for the Father)	First verse: "Practice spirit recollection"	Intuition (gnosis)	HE WILLS
Venus metamorphosis of Ancient Sun	Etheric body becomes life spirit (*buddhi*)	In purest love toward all that lives radiates the Godhead of my soul (Crucifixion)	In purest love toward all that lives radiates the Godhead of my soul	Son: *In Christo morimur*	In Christ death becomes life	"I"–Son (love for the Son)	Second verse: "Practice spirit awareness"	Inspiration (mysticism)	SHE FEELS
Jupiter metamorphosis of Ancient Moon	Astral body becomes spirit self (*manas*)	In purest out-poured light shimmers the Godhead (Transfiguration)	I rest within the Godhead of the world	Holy Spirit: *Per Spiritum sanctum reviviscimus*	In the world thoughts of the Spirit the soul awakens	"I"–Spirit (union with the Holy Spirit)	Third verse: "Practice spirit beholding"	Imagination (sacred magic)	IT THINKS
Mercury metamorphosis of the first half of Earth evolution	"Christ in me"—from the "I" to the I AM	Microcosmic Perspective (Ascending)	I shall find myself within the Godhead of the world	God–Human: *Iesous Christos Theou Yios Soter*	Jesus Christ, Son of God, Savior	Christ in me	Fourth verse: "That good may become"	"O Sun of Christ" (as above, so below)	I AM

The Significance of Valentin Tomberg's "Lord's Prayer Course"

For readers unfamiliar with Valentin Tomberg's Lord's Prayer Course, it is important to know that the *Morning Meditation* was foundational for this course—a course embodying the most profound Christian esotericism, which is a source of inspiration for much of the content of the Inner Radiance sequence, especially for the Core Practice *Putting on the Resurrection Body*. In discussing the four sentences of the opening verse of the *Morning Meditation*, Valentin Tomberg indicated in his notes for the Lord's Prayer Course:

First sentence concerning light = gnosis
Second sentence concerning pure love
    = true mysticism
Third sentence concerning resting in the Divine
    = [sacred] magic (this resting is very active)
Fourth sentence concerning finding oneself
    = true Mystery Being

True Mystery Being represents the perfectly free human being, united in body, soul, and spirit, in the unity of mysticism, gnosis, and sacred magic. Gnosis, mysticism, and [sacred] magic, united in the fourth = Mystery Being. Only thus can one find oneself. Life and death in Resurrection, only then can one begin to speak of a self in the deeper sense.

From these words of Valentin Tomberg, it is possible to understand why—in connection with deepening into the *Morning Meditation* underlying the sequence *Putting on the Resurrection Body*—the terms "gnosis," "mysticism," and "sacred magic," terms that are foundational for the spiritual stream of Christian hermeticism discussed in chapter 6, are included here together with the ancient Egyptian saying "As above, so below" expressing the essence of "true Mystery Being." With "true Mystery Being"—i.e., true initiation— it is a matter of "life and death in Resurrection," which, ultimately, is what the path of putting on the Resurrection body is about. Hence the significance for "true Mystery Being" of "As above, so below" as a significant formula of initiation in our time, just as it was an initiation formula in ancient Egypt.

As indicated in the index at the start of this chapter, many of the correspondences of the sayings of Christ with the chakras stem from Valentin Tomberg, from his Lord's Prayer Course—for example, the correspondence of the seven sayings of the Risen One to the seven chakras. In this instance, however, for the sake of completeness, it needs to be pointed out that whereas it holds true that Valentin Tomberg is the source for the correspondences with the upper five chakras, the correspondences in part 3 of *Putting on the Resurrection Body* for the two sayings of the Risen One corresponding to the two lower chakras stem from Robert Powell:

> Sacral chakra (6-petal lotus flower)
> —Peace be with you
>
> Root chakra (4-petal lotus flower)
> —Receive the Holy Spirit

For the sacral chakra Valentin Tomberg does not give a saying of the Risen One. Instead, he refers to the encounter of the two disciples Luke and Cleophas with the Risen One on their way to Emmaus on Easter Monday and indicates three significant aspects of this encounter pertaining to the sacral chakra: that the Risen One gave the two disciples instruction concerning the meaning of the Holy Scripture; that in the company of the Risen One the two disciples experienced that their hearts were burning; and that they finally recognized him in the breaking of the bread. This is described in the last chapter of the Gospel of St. Luke. Immediately after experiencing this, Luke and Cleophas hurried to Jerusalem to join the disciples, who were all, except for Thomas, gathered together with Nicodemus and Joseph of Arimathea in the hall of the Last Supper, the Coenaculum. There, as described in the Gospel of

Luke—and this is also found in the Gospel of John—the Risen One appeared to the disciples. According to John, he blessed them and spoke the words "Peace be with you" (John 20:19). These words, therefore, belong together with the Emmaus experience (in continuation from that experience) and thus are appropriate for the sacral chakra.

Regarding the root chakra, Valentin Tomberg also does not indicate a saying of the Risen One for this chakra but instead draws attention—in relation to this chakra—to three stages of manifestation of the Risen One as described in chapter 20 of the Gospel of John:

1 when Mary Magdalene sees him and thinks that he is the gardener. "Do not touch me, for I have not yet ascended to the Father" (John 20:17)
2 when he appears to the ten disciples without Thomas
3 when he appears to the eleven disciples including Thomas

With respect to the second one of these three manifestations, Jesus "breathed on them and said to them 'Receive the Holy Spirit'" (John 20:22), on which account this saying of the Risen One—by way of extension, since it was spoken in this connection—can be related to the root chakra. As Valentin Tomberg states, "At the first appearance his Resurrection body was not completed—Christ had not yet ascended to the Father. At the second appearance Christ breathed on the disciples. At the third appearance his Resurrection body was complete."

In connection with the correspondences of the sayings of the Risen One indicated by Valentin Tomberg for the five upper chakras, it also needs to be borne in consciousness that the saying he gave for the heart chakra—"I saw a new heaven and a new Earth" (Revelation 21:1)—is not to be found in the four gospels but in Revelation, whereas the other sayings of the Risen One all stem from the four gospels. However, since Revelation was communicated to John by the Cosmic Christ on his path of Ascension following the period of forty days' manifestation as the Risen One, by way of extension the words "I saw a new heaven and a new Earth" can be thought of implicitly in connection with the Risen One. Further, it should be noted that the words "I saw a new heaven and a new Earth" are the words of John, perhaps inspired by words of the Cosmic Christ such as "Behold a new heaven and a new Earth." Through the revelation to him of the Cosmic Christ, John beheld "the holy city, New Jerusalem"—to which the words "I saw a new Heaven and a new Earth" refer. He saw "the holy city, New Jerusalem, coming down out of heaven from God." As discussed in chapter 5 in connection with the seventh seal, these words relate to the descent of the new heaven from above, borne down from celestial heights by Sophia, the Bride of the Lamb. And he saw the "new Earth" arising through the sacrifice of the Lamb. Again, as indicated in the discussion on the seventh seal, these words refer to the spiritualization of the Earth through the sacrifice of Christ. The interpenetration of the new heaven and the new Earth gives rise macrocosmically to the "holy city, New Jerusalem" and microcosmically this union of the new heaven and the new Earth takes place in the heart chakra, the 12-petal lotus flower—hence the connection of the saying "Behold a new heaven and a new Earth" with the heart chakra.

Eucharist—Morning Meditation—Foundation Stone Meditation

In the *Lord's Prayer Course* Valentin Tomberg draws a parallel between the four parts of the *Morning Meditation* and the four stages of the Eucharist. According to him, the opening verse of the *Morning Meditation* corresponds to the gospel reading; the four mantras relate to the holy offering/sacrifice; the concentration upon one single image of part 3 of the *Morning Meditation* is inwardly connected with transubstantiation; and the absorption in one's own divine ideal (part 4 of the *Morning Meditation*) corresponds to communion.

The Eucharist was instituted by Jesus Christ as the path of uniting with him, through four stages, culminating with communion. This was two thousand years ago, whereby the final stage of this union is by way of communion with Christ through the sacred substances of consecrated bread and wine. Against the background of its correspondence with the Eucharist, to which Valentin Tomberg draws attention, the *Morning Meditation* appears as a new path to Christ—at this time of his Second Coming—in which the Eucharist is celebrated *within* as an act of consciousness. Like the four stages of the Eucharist, which correspond to the four levels of the human being, the *Morning Meditation* and also the Foundation Stone meditation relate to these four levels. Herewith my translation of some of Valentin Tomberg's notes on the *Morning Meditation* from the Lord's Prayer Course:

In purest out-poured light shimmers the Godhead of the world	To gain a glimpse into the world of the revelation of God	(gnosis)
In purest love toward all that lives radiates the Godhood of my soul	The harmony of Divine Love and my love	(mysticism)
I rest within the Godhead of the world	Offering oneself up, one finds the [true] self	(sacred magic)
I shall find myself within the Godhead of the world	If one gives oneself up to God, one finds the true self	(true Mystery Being)

> Looking into the world to find God, the human being can know God because the human being has love and divinity in the soul.
>
> The union of God in the world and within the soul = resting within the Godhead of the world (resting within the spiritual world).

Chapter 7: From the Eucharist to the Second Coming of Christ

I AM	One learns to say I AM in eternal gratitude toward God, whom one has to thank for this bestowal [of existence]. (Thankfulness)
IT THINKS	All wisdom must be in service of love.... All logic which is activated in the world is there to support and care for the I AM. (Concern for the I AM)
SHE FEELS	To speak SHE FEELS in the sense of Christ's Resurrection means speaking it in the same way as I AM and IT THINKS are spoken—in the light of world conscience.
HE WILLS	"Not my will, but thy will be done." To think God's will and to say HE WILLS in accordance with the SHE FEELS of world conscience... This is faithfulness to the Resurrection.... The Resurrection is the key to speaking HE WILLS.

- Concentration on a point: It is possible to focus one's gaze ever more sharply, to become more and more concentrated: an ever brighter but also narrower ray—heightened attentiveness... The Christian way is to go ever further until one passes over to moral content... to come to the moral aspect.

- Spiritual ideal: An attitude of "beholding in wonder" the miracle of existence. What does this signify? A Christian liturgy... it becomes resurrected if it is undertaken in the spirit of truth and is pursued in its moral depth.

- Divine ideal = Communion

- Concentration = Consecration [Transubstantiation]

- I AM, IT THINKS, SHE FEELS, HE WILLS = Offering [Holy Sacrifice]

- Opening verse "In purest out-poured light..." = Gospel

- These are the four stages of the Mass (Eucharist).

- Thus, the *Morning Meditation* is of importance not only for those who practice it, but also for the world. It is like a Mass (Eucharist). It is a preparation for the future if one practices this meditation; it prepares for future times.

Following on from Valentin Tomberg's words, in addition, the *Morning Meditation*, as shown above, is the seed from which the Foundation Stone meditation—communicated by Christ at the "baptismal event" announcing his Second Coming—developed. The *Morning Meditation* is like the root of a tree—the tree itself is the Foundation Stone meditation. A line of development emerges from the time of Christ's life on Earth two thousand years ago to his Second Coming by way of descent from cosmic heights to indwell the Earth's etheric aura as the *parousia* (Divine Presence) in our time:

Eucharist (Mass)—*Morning Meditation*—Foundation Stone meditation.

In this line of development, the *Morning Meditation* can be seen as an *annunciation* of the approaching Foundation Stone borne down from cosmic heights by Christ on his path of "incarnation" toward his Second Coming as the *parousia* (Divine Presence) in the etheric aura of the Earth.[307]

As indicated in the table on page 217, the four stages of the Core Practice of the Inner Radiance sequence can be seen in relation to the four sentences of the opening verse and the four mantras of the *Morning Meditation*, and also in correspondence with the four verses of the Foundation Stone meditation. Thus the Core Practice *Putting on the Resurrection Body* can also be seen in this line of development—moreover, as a path to realization of that toward which this line of development is unfolding, the ultimate goal of which is Resurrection, i.e., the transformation of the physical body into the Resurrection body. The traditional path of the Eucharist is one of receiving the consecrated bread as a "seed" for the transformation of the physical body into the Resurrection body, just as receiving the consecrated wine is a stimulus for the union of the I with the I AM in the spirit of the words "Christ in me." Now, in our time of the Second Coming, the traditional path of the Eucharist toward transformation of the physical body into the Resurrection body is supplemented—and the content of this book, in particular the Core Practice *Putting on the Resurrection Body*, is intended as a contribution that each person can take up individually, a contribution to the line of development outlined above.

---

[307] The words of the Foundation Stone meditation are the "clothing" for the Foundation Stone itself, which is a suprasensory reality perceptible to spiritual vision in the form of a dodecahedron. Known by various names—the Holy Grail, the Stone of the Wise, and so on—this suprasensory reality is the NEW that Christ through his Second Coming has brought down from cosmic heights as that which can be spiritually received into human hearts as a reality in our time. See Valentin Tomberg, *Studies on the Foundation Stone Meditation* (San Rafael, CA: LogoSophia, 2010).

Inner Radiance Sequence: Further Refinements: (1) General

With the movement exercises, it is helpful to allow the breath to "just be," and likewise with the gestures, to follow the flow of the gestures. This might require some adjustments in relation to the way they are described in this book. Our angels like to participate with us, and one can come into the experience of their presence through the gestures; for example, one can be open for angelic inspiration in shaping the gestures.

It is possible that during the exercises one may feel some discomfort or even pain. This can come about because, in activating the flow of life energy, one might experience some blockages within one's organism, and this can bring pain or discomfort. Just as water works away steadily as it flows over a rock, gradually wearing it down, likewise activating the flow of life energy will in time clear away all blockages. Thus, if one experiences pain or discomfort due to blockages or toxicity, it is important not to give up but to continue the Inner Radiance sequence—not forcing anything, but "bathing" in the flow of life energy, which cleanses and lifts us to a higher level of experience.

At the other end of the spectrum, instead of experiencing pain, it is possible that one experiences such a tremendous influx of light and life energy that it can feel almost overwhelming. Rather than making oneself continue with the Inner Radiance sequence beyond one's level of comfort, one can do some other activity of a grounding nature—gardening or some other practical activity, going for a walk, cooking, eating, and so on. It may be helpful to build up the practice slowly over time. One should never overdo it, but rather build up step by step, knowing that the practice of the Inner Radiance sequence, if carried through in the right spirit, is reorganizing the various "bodies" (physical, etheric, and astral bodies) as well as engaging the "I" consciously on the path of "dying into Christ," the divine I AM—in short, knowing that this is a profound undertaking. As it is expressed in the Foundation Stone meditation: "In Christ, death becomes life."

In this connection, it is important to bear in mind that the spiritual world never gives us more than we can bear. At the same time, in the case of a co-creative work together with the spiritual world, one has to be prudent—always listening for guidance and taking care to follow one's intuitive sense. It is a matter of the noble "middle way" as Gautama Buddha expressed it, without excess in one direction or another, always seeking balance and harmony.

The theme of symmetry is addressed in the following specific indications, and—for the sake of symmetry—with the Inner Radiance sequence it is possible to repeat the meditation A Star Is above My Head after the second *"Michael-Sophia—in nomine Christi."* Then, just as the three meditations "Christ in me," "Sophia in me," and *"Michael-Sophia—in nomine Christi"* are practiced both before and after the Core Practice *Putting on the Resurrection Body*, so in this case—in the spirit of symmetry—A Star Is above My Head would also be practiced both before and after. Then these four meditations would together comprise not only part of the introduction to the core of the Inner Radiance sequence but would also be part of the conclusion following *Putting on the Resurrection Body*.

Inner Radiance sequence— further refinements: (2) Specific

In relation to deepening into the Core Practice described on pages 214 to 215, there the indication is given for three L's, three R's, three AU's, and three M's followed by seven L's, seven R's, seven AU's, and seven M's. For the sake of symmetry, the initial three L's, three R's, three AU's, and three M's can be expanded to seven of each by including at the beginning:

L (or R or AU or M)—Glory to the Father in the heights
L (or R or AU or M)—and to the Mother in the depths
L (or R or AU or M)—and peace on Earth
L (or R or AU or M)—to all beings of good will

followed by the three L's, three R's, three AU's, or three M's as described on pages 214 to 215.

Closing section of the Core Practice:	Practicing the gesture:	In connection with these words— spoken (or thought)	Addition: closing with
First section	L	In purest out-poured light shimmers the Godhead of the world	AUMEYN (as described on page 40)
Second section	R	In purest love toward all that lives radiates the Godhood of my soul	AUMEYN
Third section	AU	I rest within the Godhead of the world	AUMEYN
Fourth section	M	I shall find myself within the Godhead of the world	AUMEYN

And at the end of each of the four sections of the core exercise, after speaking (or thinking) the closing words in conjunction with the closing gesture, one can—as indicated in the preceding table—add in the final closing word "AUMEYN," together with the gestures for "AUMEYN" described on page 40. At the end of each of the four sections this would mean—instead of proceeding directly to the heart-AU gesture—in conjunction with speaking the word "AUMEYN" one would finish with the sequence of gestures described on page 40; Universal Love, A horizontal, U horizontal, M horizontal, and then, finally, the heart-AU gesture (see table on the previous page).

One last point, which has already been discussed on page 168, but on account of its importance it is mentioned here again: quiet time (inner silence) at the end of each of the four sections of the Core Practice is very important as also a brief moment of reflection at the end of each individual prayer or meditation, and especially important is a period of quiet rest after the conclusion of the entire Inner Radiance sequence—in order to allow the grace of the spiritual world to flow in as a resonance in response to one's endeavor through the eurythmic movement.

Preparation for the Inner Radiance Sequence: An Experience

There is much more that could be said about the line of development from the Eucharist to the Second Coming of Christ and about the mysteries of the Resurrection body. This, however, will have to wait for a follow-up book, in which level two of the Core Practice *Putting on the Resurrection Body* will be presented.

On a closing note, as preparation for the Inner Radiance sequence, practicing the consecrations is helpful,[308] as described in the following letter I received from a participant in the Choreocosmos School:

> The prayers you have taught us have true sacred power.... I was saying the consecration to the Sacred Heart, along with the consecration to the Immaculate Heart, as I have done every day since you first communicated these consecrations to us. When I prayed the words with all my heart, "Fulfill my prayer that the powers of evil withdraw from me and the Life of Shambhala flow into me," I realized that this lives as an answered prayer—as this has been my experience of the golden-white light coming up from Shambhala, streaming like a fountain through me. This prayer has become a living experience.... As I walk about I experience the golden light of Shambhala coming up through my feet, arising through my chakras to the crown of my head, and then beyond to my Eternal Star. Like a fountain it then recirculates back to Shambhala. This is the *Circle of Life* and, much like the Tree of Life, the human roots, our feet, receive the Mother from below, on the one hand, and on the other hand we reach up to the heavens, to the Father, through our chakras, and thereby Earth and Heaven—the Mother and the Father—are united in us through the Deed of the Son, the God–Man, Jesus Christ. May we grow strong roots and may the fountain of the Circle of Life rise through us all.

---

308 Robert Powell, *Consecration to the Immaculate Heart of Mary Sophia and Consecration to the Sacred Heart of Jesus Christ* (San Francisco: Sophia Foundation, 2007).

Chapter 8

ASTROSOPHY AND SCIENTIFIC RESEARCH

Readers of this book *Cultivating Inner Radiance and the Body of Immortality*, especially those who take up the practice of the Inner Radiance sequence, will sooner or later discover that working with the flow of life forces through the gestures of eurythmy in conjunction with the words of Christ leads one into connection with the cosmos. As Rudolf Steiner expressed it already in 1921, "In our age it never occurs to someone that their being belongs not to the Earth alone but to the cosmos beyond the Earth. Knowledge of our connection with the cosmos beyond the Earth—that is what we need above all to make our own."[309] *Knowledge of our connection with the cosmos* is the goal of astrosophy ("star wisdom"), which is a vast field of research and endeavor, as readers of the yearly *Journal for Star Wisdom* will know. Eurythmy, as described in this book and as practiced in the Choreocosmos School of Cosmic and Sacred Dance, is *a path toward experience of cosmic realms of existence*. Astrosophy and eurythmy thus belong together in terms of knowledge and experience.

The central focus of this book is upon the path of experience—a path through eurythmy to the Etheric Christ, who is united with the whole galaxy, as comes to expression in the AMEN/AUMEYN meditation on pages 38 to 40. In various publications, as can be seen from those listed below, it is my goal through scientific research to help fulfill the words of Rudolf Steiner quoted above by researching into the connections between the cosmos, the Earth, and the human being. This began long ago with a quest to learn what the true nature of the "star of the magi" was. Following this line of pursuit led not only to one hundred percent certainty with regard to penetrating the mystery of the "star of the magi" but also to a whole series of further discoveries that are outlined below.

As Isaac Newton remarked in a letter of February 5, 1676, "If I have seen further, it is by standing on the shoulders of giants."[310] In quoting Newton I certainly do not intend to say that I have seen further than other researchers in the field of astrosophy, but rather I wish to acknowledge that it is thanks to "standing on the shoulders of giants" that I have been able to carry out research that has led to some scientific discoveries. And this, of course, is the whole basis of the scientific tradition, that the fruits of the work of our predecessors are gratefully acknowledged and taken up and, according to circumstances, led further.

The most outstanding "giant" upon whom most of the work in the field of astrosophy and in the realm of eurythmy is based is Rudolf Steiner (1861–1925), through whom eurythmy came into the world some one hundred years ago. To him an enormous debt of gratitude is owed. Then there are all the other "giants"—too numerous to mention—whom I would also like to thank, especially mathematician and astronomer Elisabeth Vreede (1879–1943), who took up the work of pioneering astrosophy, based on Rudolf Steiner's numerous indications in this field; Willi Sucher (1902–1985), who—continuing on from Elisabeth Vreede—was a great pioneer of astrosophy, who also encouraged me to do further astrosophical

---

309 Rudolf Steiner, "Offspring of the World of Stars," lecture of May 5, 1921, in: *Materialism and the Task of Anthroposophy*, CW 204 (Hudson, NY: Anthroposophic Press, 1987).

310 I. B. Cohen, "Isaac Newton"; Charles Coulston, ed. *Dictionary of Scientific Biography*, vol. 10 (New York: Scribner's, 1974), p. 55.

research into the mysteries of the life of Christ and to study eurythmy as a path to a living connection with the cosmos; and all my eurythmy and choreocosmos colleagues (see acknowledgments on page 236) and fellow astrosophy researchers, many of whom are contributors to the yearly *Journal for Star Wisdom*.

It came as a surprise upon nearing completion of this book when Professor Bernt Rossiwall engaged me in conversation about my scientific discoveries—the result being the following list of fourteen discoveries—which are offered here as foundational guidelines for astrosophical research and for those who take up the path outlined in this book. May this list serve as an underpinning of *knowledge of our connection with the cosmos* (Rudolf Steiner).

The following is only a list, underlying which are many profound things that are impossible to express in such an abbreviated outline, and so these short descriptions need to be understood simply as "signposts" to much larger considerations that are indicated in the reference works included with the entries in this list. It will be noted that the common thread between the cosmologically oriented research indicated in the list and the content of this book is the focus upon Christ and the mystery of human evolution. Having begun my quest many years ago for the One who is the focus of the mystery of the "star of the magi," with the content of this book we find the same focus again—now, however, elaborated as a path through eurythmy to Christ.

Robert Powell's Scientific Achievements
A contribution by Bernt Rossiwall

With interest I have been following Dr. Robert Powell's work now for some twenty-one years, and it is a privilege to point out—from an academic standpoint—some of his scientific achievements, spread over a wide area of research:

In his scientific work, Robert Powell's main achievements are:

1 reconstructing the ancient Babylonian zodiac—now known as the *sidereal zodiac* ("zodiac of the stars")—defined by the two primary marking stars: Aldebaran ("the Bull's eye") at 15° Taurus in the middle of the constellation of the Bull, and Antares ("the heart of the Scorpion") at 15° Scorpio in the middle of the constellation of the Scorpion (see *History of the Zodiac*, appendix 1, for the reconstruction of the original zodiac—preceding all other definitions of the zodiac);

2 deciphering the "star of the magi" in relation to a series of astronomical events beginning with the threefold conjunction of Jupiter and Saturn in the year 7 BC and culminating with the full Moon in Virgo on the evening of March 5, 6 BC (see *Chronicle of the Living Christ* and *Christian Hermetic Astrology: The Star of the Magi and the Life of Christ*);

3 discovering the birth and death dates of Jesus, Mary, and John the Baptist (see *Chronicle of the Living Christ* and *Christian Hermetic Astrology: The Star of the Magi and the Life of Christ*);

4 determining the dates of most of the events in the life of Jesus Christ described in the four gospels with an accuracy of 99.999999999997%, thus finding for the first time in history the exact chronology of events in the life of Christ (see *Chronicle of the Living Christ, Christian Hermetic Astrology: The Star of the Magi and the Life of Christ* and Anne Catherine Emmerich, *Visions of the Life of Jesus Christ*, 2012—see footnote 38 on page 33);

5 discovering the importance of "mega stars"—very luminous stars like Betelgeuse and Antares (both red supergiants), and Deneb and Rigel (both blue-white supergiants)—in Christ's healing miracles; this discovery indicates that, in terms of stellar influences, the *starry heavens in their entirety* are potentially significant, i.e., that it is not simply a matter of observing the movements of the Sun, Moon, and planets just against the background of the zodiacal constellations but also that *stars (and their corresponding constellations)* above and below the zodiacal constellations can play a role; the key concept in connection with this discovery is that of *stellar meridians* ascending or descending from each star and intersecting the sidereal zodiac as "lines of energy" which are crossed by the Sun, Moon, and planets in their orbits around the zodiac, thereby—by way of crossing these "energy lines" (stellar meridians)—conjoining with stars which can be far above or below the zodiac in latitude; here again, the sidereal zodiac is of key importance as the frame of reference for describing and understanding this discovery of the potential significance (in terms of stellar influences) of the entire starry heavens (see *The Astrological Revolution*);

6 the discovery of two astrological rules of reincarnation, thus raising astrology to the level of a science—the science as to how destiny is carried over by the stars from one incarnation to the next; this finding proves scientifically (a) the reality of reincarnation, (b) that the ancient Babylonian zodiac—the original zodiac, now known as the *sidereal zodiac*—is the authentic astrological zodiac, and (c) that not only geocentric planetary positions in the sidereal zodiac but also the heliocentric positions of the planets in the sidereal zodiac are important.[311]

7 the discovery of the importance in astrology of the astronomical system of Tycho Brahe as the basis for the "Tychonic horoscope" (also known as the *hermetic horoscope*); the hermetic (Tychonic) horoscope, which is essentially the heliocentric horoscope showing the heliocentric sidereal positions of the planets but including also the Sun, Moon, ascendant, and other elements from the geocentric sidereal framework, is just as important as the traditional geocentric horoscope; whereas the latter is referred to as a "map of the soul," the hermetic horoscope can be seen as a "map of the spirit," indicating the individual's spiritual talents and faculties (see footnote 311);

8 the discovery of the importance of the conception horoscope as determined by the hermetic rule (rule of Hermes) from the birth horoscope in so far as the conception horoscope relates to the *birth horoscope* of the preceding incarnation, just as according to Rudolf Steiner the birth horoscope carries over from the *death horoscope* of the preceding incarnation—this relationship being one of the fundamental laws underlying astrological biography... another fundamental law being Willi Sucher's discovery that the seven-year rhythm in the human biography is determined by the lunar sidereal cycles between conception and birth (see *Chronicle of the Living Christ* and titles listed in footnote 311);

---

311 See *The Astrological Revolution: Unveiling the Science of the Stars as a Science of Reincarnation and Karma*; *Elijah Come Again: A Scientific Approach to Reincarnation*; *Hermetic Astrology*, vol. 1: *Astrology and Reincarnation*; and *Hermetic Astrology*, vol. 2: *Astrological Biography*.

9 the discovery that for each individual *four* horoscopes apply—the heliocentric/hermetic conception horoscope relating to the physical body ("map of the spirit seed of the human form"); the geocentric conception horoscope relating to the etheric body ("map of the life forces"); the geocentric birth horoscope relating to the astral body ("map of the soul"); and the heliocentric/hermetic horoscope relating to the "I" ("map of the spirit") (see *Elijah Come Again: A Scientific Approach to Reincarnation*);

10 the discovery of a constant rhythm of 1,199 years, which is the rhythm of the *Venus pentagram* (the time taken for the Venus pentagram to make one complete rotation of the sidereal zodiac), as the time-lag between the start of a new zodiacal age and the beginning of the corresponding cultural epoch; this discovery confirms the importance of what Rudolf Steiner described as the 600-year rhythm of a "cultural wave"—this being half of the 1,199-year rhythm (see *The Astrological Revolution: Unveiling the Science of the Stars as a Science of Reincarnation and Karma* and *Hermetic Astrology*, vol. 1: *Astrology and Reincarnation*);

11 the discovery of the rhythm of a period of exactly 33⅓ years—having determined this to be the precise length of the life of Jesus Christ—thereby confirming the 33⅓-year rhythm as fundamental not only for individual biographies but also for history, as indicated by Rudolf Steiner in 1917 (see *Chronicle of the Living Christ, Christian Hermetic Astrology: The Star of the Magi and the Life of Christ*, and *The Christ Mystery: Reflections on the Second Coming*);

12 the discovery of the astronomical basis of *astrogeographia* as a new science, in which a one-to-one correspondence between the celestial sphere, that of the starry heavens, and the terrestrial sphere, that of the earthly globe, is *astronomically* and also—as determined by mathematician David Bowden—*mathematically* specified; in other words, according to astrogeographia each location on the earth corresponds to a star in the heavens: for example, Jerusalem aligned closely with the red supergiant star Betelgeuse at the time of the building of the temple of Solomon (see *Astrogeographia* by Robert Powell & David Bowden, 2012);

13 the discovery, outlined in chapter 5 of this book, that the heliocentric structure of our solar system indicates the "plan of creation" through seven stages of planetary evolution (the "seven days of creation")—Saturn, Sun, Moon, Earth, Jupiter, Venus, and Vulcan; this discovery helps to "redeem" the materialistic conception of the cosmos that was inaugurated in the world through the introduction of the heliocentric system by Copernicus and Kepler, in that the meaning and purpose of the existence of humanity and the Earth is revealed within the context of the stages of planetary evolution marked by the heliocentric structure of the solar system; at some future time this deeper meaning of the heliocentric solar system will no doubt be taught by science alongside the purely astronomical facts, so that the very meaning of existence will be conveyed to human beings through being taught this deeper significance of the structure of our solar system;

14 the discovery that Kepler's three laws of planetary motion underlying the heliocentric system provides confirmation of Rudolf Steiner's indication concerning the existence of three ranks of spiritual beings indwelling the Sun:

"spirits of form," who maintain the elliptical form of the planets in their orbits (first law);

"spirits of movement," who regulate the dynamics of the movements of the planets in their orbits (second law);

"spirits of wisdom," who uphold the wisdom-filled ordering—in terms of the mutual relationships of the distances/time periods specific to each planet—to one another (third law);

this discovery, by highlighting that there is a spiritual dimension to the laws of planetary motion, also helps to "redeem" the materialistic conception that came into our culture at the time of Copernicus and Kepler (sixteenth/seventeenth centuries).

In addition to initiating the discussion that led to the above compilation of his scientific discoveries, I would like to add that I was present at a lecture in Pforzheim, Germany, on October 22, 2006, when Robert Powell presented his discovery of the deeper meaning of the three laws of planetary motion as outlined in (14) above; after the lecture we visited the Kepler museum in nearby Weil-der-Stadt, where Johannes Kepler was born on December 27, 1571 (corresponding to January 6, 1572 in our modern calendar).

In conclusion, particularly with regard to the discovery of two rules of astrological reincarnation—number 6 in the list, however, this also applies to other discoveries in the list—I would like to add these little-known words written by Rudolf Steiner in 1903:

At the present time there may be many who would very much like to quickly learn about the teachings of spiritual science. They will no doubt find it inconvenient if one first presents scientific facts in a comprehensible way and in such a light as to serve as a foundation for the development of spiritual-scientific content. They say: we want to hear something about spiritual science and you tell us about scientific things which every educated person knows.... [They] believe that it is unnecessary to prove convictions about karma and reincarnation with the results of science. They do not know that *this is the task of*...*the inhabitants of Europe and America and that without this foundation* [they]...*are not truly able to come to the insights of spiritual science*.[312]

Prof. Bernt Rossiwall, DDr., Founding member of Institut für Astrosophie (IFA) in 2003, a non-profit research institute for the support of Astrosophy

---

312 Rudolf Steiner, *Luzifer-Gnosis* (CW 34; Dornach, Switzerland: Rudolf Steiner Verlag, 1960), p. 90, footnote 3.

AFTERWORD

It is impossible to do justice to the theme underlying this book—eurythmy as a path to Christ in the etheric realm—since words, while offering a "first level approximation," cannot truly capture the essence of what eurythmy really is nor can they adequately convey an experience of the Etheric Christ in its depth and profundity. Moreover, everyone who comes to an experience of Christ will describe it differently, because Christ has an individual and personal relationship with each person.

Given the impossibility of putting the indescribable into words, rather than attempting to do so, instead I shall outline a description below of the activity of choreocosmos, comprising cosmic and sacred dance—arising from eurythmy and focusing upon eurythmy as a spiritual path centered upon Christ and Sophia—as practiced in the Choreocosmos School. However, before coming to this, there is an important point to be emphasized.

This book, written in honor of the one hundredth anniversary of the birth of eurythmy, is a small contribution offered as a path to Christ in the etheric realm—a path one can explore—the practice of which can lead one to a living experience of a deeper level of existence. For readers who are already familiar with the works of Rudolf Steiner, the inclusion in this path of a variety of other sources—such as Peter Deunov (1864–1944), Valentin Tomberg (1900–1973), and St. Faustina (1905–1938)—may seem unusual. However, the inclusion of a broader selection of sources, after starting with Rudolf Steiner as the primary source, is in the spirit of Sophia, who is seeking to lead humanity toward becoming one spiritual family: the Rose of the World. For Sophia, it is a matter of bridging between various spiritual streams—for example between the experience of the Etheric Christ as undergone by a traditional Catholic nun, St. Faustina, during the 1930s, and the experience of Rudolf Steiner who, as mentioned already, was the "John the Baptist" for the return of Christ in the etheric realm, who experienced the Etheric Christ on a more cosmic level in the period prior to his death in 1925. In this example, it is a matter of bridging traditional Christianity and the new Christianity arising through Christ's Second Coming—the bridge being the Etheric Christ. With Peter Deunov and Rudolf Steiner, it is a matter of bridging between the Slavic "heart approach" to spirituality and the Western "mind approach"—both approaches, in the case of these two great spiritual teachers of eastern and western Europe, leading to Christ in the etheric realm. And in the case of Valentin Tomberg and Rudolf Steiner it is a matter of bridging between a "mystical-magical" and a "gnostic-philosophical" approach to spirituality, both of which led in the lives of these two highly developed individuals to encounters with the Etheric Christ.

What all of these individuals have in common is *experience of the Etheric Christ,* on which account they are included as contributors to a spiritual path leading to Christ in the etheric realm, each contributing a different tone to the "symphony of the whole" orchestrated by Sophia from spiritual heights and focusing upon Christ's Presence (*parousia*) in the etheric aura of the Earth—a presence that has been with us since the early twentieth century and which will be with us for another 2,400 years as the guiding impulse, together with Sophia's inspiration from the heights, for the unfolding of the entire future evolution of humanity and the Earth.

Afterword

Those who have experienced the activities of the Choreocosmos School of Cosmic and Sacred Dance in Europe, Australia, or North America know something of the profound depth of experience offered by coming together in community to celebrate Christ through this sacred form of movement—for example, through the Choreocosmos celebration of the nine Beatitudes. Participants also know that Choreocosmos is a service to the ranks of the nine spiritual hierarchies—Angels, Archangels, Archai, Exusiai, Dynamis, Kyriotetes, Thrones, Cherubim, and Seraphim. Each cosmic dance belonging to the cycle of 84 cosmic dances expressing the seven planets in the twelve signs of the zodiac is an expression of the weaving of the spiritual hierarchies, who weave in cosmic realms between the Creator and humanity.

For example, the Moon in Aries—where the Moon was located (in the middle of the constellation of Aries) at Christ's Ascension—is an expression of the Angels, active in the Moon sphere, against the background of the collective activity of the entire colony of beings of the first hierarchy (Seraphim, Cherubim, Thrones) weaving through the starry region of the heavens that manifests outwardly as the constellation (sidereal sign) of Aries.

To learn this cycle of 84 cosmic dances is to learn the cosmic alphabet that expresses the essence of the Cosmic Christ now weaving in the etheric realm in conjunction with the nine spiritual hierarchies. Choreocosmos is thus a metamorphosis of the ancient temple dances held at the mystery centers of antiquity to honor the spiritual hierarchies known at that time as the "gods." Choreocosmos is a unique new expression of the ancient service of human beings in honor of the spiritual hierarchies whose activity underlay the creation of the world—an activity that lives on in the shaping and unfolding of human destiny, this being the real meaning and significance of astrology.

The Choreocosmos School of Cosmic and Sacred Dance, founded in the year 2000, exists to support the development of two aspects of eurythmy: cosmic and sacred dance. The Choreocosmos School comprises a community dedicated to Christ in the etheric realm and to the service of the nine spiritual hierarchies working in conjunction with Christ. Something of this is also alluded to in the transcript of two of my lectures included as chapter 5 in this book. Moreover, it is important to bear in mind that the activity of choreocosmos is focused not only on Christ, known as the Lamb, but also upon the Bride of the Lamb, known as Sophia. In the words of Rudolf Steiner: "Christ will appear in spiritual form in the twentieth [and twenty-first] century not simply because something happens outwardly, but to the extent that we find the power represented by Holy Sophia."[313] These words indicate the significance of Sophia for attuning to Christ in the etheric realm—for beholding the Etheric Christ. This is central to the founding of the Sophia Foundation[314] and to other Sophia communities around the world.[315] The Sophia Foundation is the main sponsor of the Choreocosmos School of Cosmic and Sacred Dance.

It is appropriate here to indicate briefly how the relationship between Christ and Sophia, the Lamb and his Bride, comes to expression in choreocosmos. As described in the last two chapters of Revelation, the future of the Earth is known as the heavenly Jerusalem—"Behold a new heaven and a new Earth" (Revelation 21:1). The new Earth is arising through the sacrifices of Christ, the Lamb, in spiritualizing the Earth to become the new Earth. At the same time the new heaven is descending from above, from celestial heights, borne down by the Bride of the Lamb, known as Sophia. In the future the great event of the sacred wedding (*hieros gamos*) of the Lamb and his Bride will

---

313 Rudolf Steiner, *Isis Mary Sophia: Her Mission and Ours* (Great Barrington, MA: SteinerBooks, 2003), p.213. Comment in brackets [ ] inserted by RP.
314 The Sophia Foundation is a non-profit foundation dedicated to help serve the creation of a new culture based on love and wisdom. The Sophia Foundation was founded by Robert Powell, Karen Rivers, and others in Nicasio/San Rafael, California, during the Holy Nights at the end of the year 1994: www.sophiafoundation.org.
315 For example, the Sophia community in Australia: http://sophia-australis.com.

take place. This union of Christ ascending, raising the new (transfigured) Earth, with Sophia, bearing on her path of descent the new heaven (she is "clothed with the Sun, with the Moon under her feet, and on her head a crown of twelve stars"—Revelation 12:1), will give rise to the heavenly Jerusalem as the new heaven and the new Earth—united. This glorious future, a vista of which is opened up to us through attuning to Christ and Sophia, the Lamb and his Bride, by way of choreocosmos (as a spiritual practice), is the great vision that inspires the activity of the Choreocosmos School.

Engaged in the cosmic and sacred dances, we may become aware of the in-streaming of the Etheric Christ and find that we are able to receive his stream of Divine Love into our hearts (meaning the threefold physical, etheric, and astral heart), which we are then able to direct downward from the region of the heart through our legs and feet toward the golden realm of Shambhala, the realm at the heart of Mother Earth, thereby participating in the work of the Etheric Christ in transforming the Earth spiritually into the new Earth. Our participation in Christ's work of transformation is facilitated by way of expressing our love and gratitude to Mother Earth through our gestures and movements, allowing this to flow all the way down to Shambhala. From there we may be graced with receiving something of the "breath of life" that streams up from the Mother in response to the expression of our love and gratitude toward her.

Correspondingly, when participating in cosmic and sacred dance we can direct our attention upward to Sophia in celestial heights, who is now streaming in her grace from the starry heavens, in particular focused through the "heart meridian" running through the celestial sphere formed by the twelve constellations of the zodiac ("with a crown of twelve stars on her head"). Feeling our love and gratitude toward Sophia as the bearer of the divine plan—she who is divine wisdom—we allow our love and gratitude during the cosmic and sacred dances to stream from the heart region through our arms and hands, each gesture streaming out love and gratitude. It is also possible to allow the stream of love and gratitude from our hearts to flow directly upward through the crown chakra—this chakra opening toward Sophia's crown of twelve stars, the twelve sidereal signs of the zodiac. In this way through choreocosmos we connect with the new heaven now being brought down by the Bride of the Lamb, on the one hand, and with the new Earth being raised up as Shambhala by the Lamb on the other hand.

There is much more that could be described of the worldwide activity of the Choreocosmos School of Cosmic and Sacred Dance. An important aspect explored in this book is that the activity of choreocosmos opens a path to Christ in the etheric realm—to the Etheric Christ—whose mission is to lead humanity to the experience of Shambhala in the creation of the new Earth.

The Inner Radiance Sequence and the Core Practice of Putting on the Resurrection Body—Experiences

I have testimony, a positive experience to report regarding the practice of putting on the Resurrection body and cultivating inner radiance, which I did religiously during my travels.

When I returned home, I consulted with my health care practitioner for detox baths and such to help with the inevitable accumulated toxicities from travel: primarily jet fuel fumes, radiation from flying, and all the fragrances I encountered. These always come up. But this time she didn't get anything for jet fuel or radiation and commented that the face mask I use must be helping a lot. (Although it did not prevent the need for detoxing measures with my previous travel and I had even forgotten to use it at a critical time during that last 11-hour flight home from Europe.)

I mentioned to her that I had made a point of bathing in the Mediterranean sea—soaking in salt water is generally beneficial—when I had a chance, and she said that had helped a lot. But I was only able to do that a few times in five weeks of travel, and there was still that last 11-hour flight back to the U.S. to explain.

So what was different? Reflecting later, I realized the difference was the daily practice of *Putting on the Resurrection Body* and the resulting protection, some kind of inner radiance, which I did not necessarily feel—meaning I did not feel like a radiant being or even have a conscious feeling of Christ's presence. But after five weeks of travel with two 11-hour flights and other short flights in between, she was unable to pick up any problems with radiation from air travel or jet fuel toxicity in my system!

So that's my testimony. I believe it really works—what has been said about the protection offered by this practice is true! In addition, whenever I do it, it leaves me with a feeling of peace, calm, and centeredness.

—M.R. (Palo Alto, California)

This morning, after I had completed the Inner Radiance Core Practice of *Putting on the Resurrection Body* I thanked Christ for healing my chakras through his grace and then I prayed to the angels of the various planets that they may radiate their light, love, and life through my chakras in order that I might bless Mother Earth and her creatures in love and gratitude. Then I bowed down lovingly and thankfully toward Mother Earth. Suddenly I felt how I was lifted out of my body, expanding to an enormous size, although I was still connected with my body. I beheld the radiant Earth below me. I bowed down toward the Earth and was able to lovingly embrace the whole, radiant Earth.

—F. S. (Germany)

THE SCHOOL OF COSMIC AND SACRED DANCE

Developed by Robert Powell, Ph.D.—a eurythmist, movement therapist, and cofounder of the Sophia Foundation—the School of Cosmic and Sacred Dance was founded to serve those seeking spiritual awakening, a living experience of the cosmos, and a sense of wholeness and healing.

Education in cosmic and sacred dance aims to develop movement skills, foster healing, enhance each individual's spiritual growth, and to open a gateway to a new wisdom of the stars. The cosmic dances initiate a learning process that leads to an inner knowing or "gnosis" relating to the wisdom inherent in the movements, gestures, and choreographies of the cosmic archetypal forms.

Through learning to move together harmoniously in a group, community is fostered as the movement itself helps to expand each person's awareness.

In dancing according to the principles of cosmic harmony, one feels part of an organic whole, while remaining an individual. Consciousness is expanded beyond this planet, so that one feels part of a greater whole on a cosmic level. One begins to experience universal/cosmic citizenship.

Through the experience of cosmic and sacred dance in one's heart, one's gestures, and in one's limbs—and by way of the knowledge and understanding connected with this experience—the cosmos begins to come alive in one's whole being as a "living organism."

Choreocosmos Schooling

The schooling offered by Choreocosmos aims not only at developing movement skills and healing abilities, but also at enhancing the individual's spiritual growth and opening the door to star mysteries leading to a new wisdom of the stars. In response to requests for a training in cosmic dance, Choreocosmos is offering a schooling intended to train participants to teach and give courses on cosmic dance. Proceeding course by course, those who successfully complete the training will then be in a position to teach. It is envisaged that completion of the training will take several years, depending upon the number of courses each participant attends each year.

Upon completing the training of the School of Cosmic and Sacred Dance, it will be possible to take these dances back to one's own community—or to take them to other communities—to help awaken the dawning consciousness of the new star wisdom and the star mysteries of Divine Sophia, and thus to be able to offer to one's fellow human beings the possibility of experiencing universal or cosmic citizenship.

Intrinsic to this schooling in cosmic and sacred dance is an experience of music and prayer being moved in forms of sacred geometry, which engage the consciousness, the heart and the limbs. Thereby the holy waters of the flowing life forces that move within each human being are set in motion in sacred patterns—leading to healing and spiritual awakening.

Study and Ideal

In addition to cosmic and sacred dance, there is the study aspect of the schooling: entering into an understanding of the new star wisdom as belonging to the Mysteries of Sophia, the Divine Wisdom of the cosmos. The study activity entails learning about the planets, the signs of the zodiac, and the four elements (Fire, Air, Water and Earth). It also involves becoming acquainted with spiritual exercises—complementary to the cosmic and sacred dances—that can help open the way to knowledge and experience of the star mysteries of Divine Sophia.

Entering into these star mysteries, one comes to experience that there is a continual exchange of divine energy between the cosmos, the Sun and the Earth. This cosmic energy is Divine Love which weaves throughout the entire universe. The cultivation of love is the spiritual ideal of the School of Cosmic and Sacred Dance. In doing the cosmic and sacred dances, we seek to connect our hearts and minds with Divine Love and with the Supreme Consciousness that pervades all existence.

The Choreocosmos School of Cosmic and Sacred Dance, while based in America (under the auspices of the Sophia Foundation), offers the training also in other countries. As a "moving school," with an underlying cosmic language as its basis, it seeks to be universal in scope. The stars belong to everyone and they are united with us all. Our image of the heavens is of a world working in beauty and divine harmony, and the more we enter into communion with the world of stars, the more our gestures and our whole lives begin to correspond to the harmony of the heavens. The cosmic dances, when moved in harmony, serve to create a vessel receiving higher spiritual impulses flowing down from the heavens into earthly life. At the same time, we learn through cosmic dance to "speak to the stars." This work can be seen as a spiritual training and discipline to take into one's daily life and practice. In due course of time it is anticipated that there will be an increasing number of qualified teachers of cosmic and sacred dance. For further information, please contact the Sophia Foundation or visit the Sophia Foundation website.

ACKNOWLEDGMENTS

An immense debt of gratitude is owed to Rudolf Steiner for pioneering the new art form of eurythmy, and to Marie Steiner for her dedication in shepherding the unfolding of this new art form—and to all the dedicated eurythmists who have contributed to the unfolding of the impulse of eurythmy in the world. I am especially grateful to my eurythmy teacher in Dornach, Lea van der Pals (1909–2002), of whom Rudolf Steiner said when she was still a young girl taking a children's eurythmy course: "She is an artist!"

My heartfelt gratitude also goes to my my wife Lacquanna Paul (also a choreocosmos graduate) for her editorial help, her unfailing encouragement, and her sketches of some of the eurythmy gestures. Many thanks also to Lesley King and to choreocosmos graduate Josie Scott for some of the sketches and to Malcolm Glover for his cover design. Heartfelt thanks also to pianist and composer Marcia Burchard, who has been and continues to be such a support for the Choreocosmos School and who contributed the two scores for singing *Shantih Shantih Shantih Aum* at the end of the Sanskrit version of the AUM meditation. And my heartfelt gratitude is extended also to Estelle Isaacson for the contribution of her visions to the foreword.

I am most grateful to Fort Schlesinger, Monique Camp, and choreocosmos graduate Linda Delman, who have helped cosmic and sacred dance to flourish by offering space on their respective properties in Northern California; to anthroposophical medical doctor Heinrich Sandkühler and his wife Ingrid—both choreocosmos graduates—for creating a center for choreocosmos at their home in Pforzheim, Germany; to all the graduates of the Choreocosmos School, each of whom have supported and contributed to the choreocosmos impulse—of whom I would especially like to thank eurythmist Gudrun Gundersen for her inspiring thoughts and helpful comments regarding the prayers and meditations included in this book, and Kelly Calegar, who made the inclusion of chapter 5 possible, for which I am deeply grateful. Special thanks to eurythmist and choreocosmos graduate Uberta Sebregondi for her shepherding of the activities of the Choreocosmos School in Italy, and to Lynne Klugman for initiating the choreocosmos workshops in Australia.

In gratitude also to the board of the Sophia Foundation for the continuing support of the Choreocosmos School of Cosmic and Sacred Dance, especially to cofounder Karen Rivers, also a choreocosmos graduate, for her collaboration and helpful suggestions, and board member and choreocosmos graduate Cheryl Mulholland for facilitating the production of a Choreocosmos School brochure and choreocosmos videos (www.sophiafoundation.org).

I would also like to thank publishers Chris Bamford and Gene Gollogly of SteinerBooks for taking on the manuscript and William Jens Jensen for his work in enabling this book to become available.

There are also many others who have helped in one way or another, to whom my gratitude and appreciation are extended without naming everyone explicitly.

Robert Powell

December 4, 2011—conjunction (inferior) of Mercury with the Sun at 17° Scorpio
There was an inferior conjunction of Mercury with the Sun at the Transfiguration on
Mt. Tabor; and the Sun was at 17° Scorpio at the first conversion of Mary Magdalene (see
Journal of Star Wisdom 2011, page 145).

ABOUT THE AUTHOR

ROBERT POWELL was born in 1947 in Reading, England, and studied mathematics at the University of Sussex, graduating with a Master's degree. At the same time, he developed an interest in astronomy and this, in turn, led him to explore the roots of astrology, the ancient science of the connections between the stars and human beings.

In the early 1970s, while researching these fields at the British Museum Library in London, Robert discovered the Rudolf Steiner Bookshop and Library on Museum Street. From that moment on, Steiner's Anthroposophy or spiritual science became the esoteric or spiritual context in which he was to work: a path and a guide. Steiner's many works provided the epistemological, cosmological and Christological foundations he sought to continue his work. Through Steiner, he was led to the work of both the astrosophist Willi Sucher (1902–1985) and the Russian sophiologist Valentin Tomberg (1900–1973).

From 1978 to 1982, Robert, while continuing his research, was in Dornach, Switzerland, at the Goetheanum, where he completed a training in eurythmy, a new art of movement developed by Steiner. Since graduating from eurythmy school, still continuing to study, research and lecture on themes arising from the practice of esoteric Christianity and astrology, Robert has lived and worked as a eurythmist and movement therapist in Kinsau, near Munich, Germany.

The writing of his Ph.D. thesis on the original scientific definition of the zodiac—a thirty year odyssey—started in 1974 when he began doing the initial research on the history of the zodiac at the libraries of the British Museum and the Warburg Institute in London. Completion of the doctoral procedure took place in December 2004 at the Polish Academy of Science (Institute for the History of Science) in Warsaw.

Robert has an enduring passion for the stars and was awarded a Ph.D. for his contribution to the History of the Zodiac. He is an internationally renowned lecturer. Through the content of his talks given during conferences and workshops, his living knowledge of the stars is woven into his presentations. As well as being a scholar of the history of astronomy, Robert is also a movement therapist trained in the art of eurythmy (from the Greek, meaning beautiful, harmonious movement).

Focusing upon the cosmic aspects of eurythmy, he founded the Choreocosmos School of Cosmic and Sacred Dance and teaches a gentle form of healing movement—the sacred dance of eurythmy—as well as the cosmic dances of the planets and signs of the zodiac. He leads these sacred and cosmic dances—dancing with the stars—in the endeavor to create harmony between the heavens, the earth, humanity, and nature. He presents Choreocosmos workshops in Australia, Europe, and North America.

Robert is also cofounder with Karen Rivers of the Sophia Foundation of North America, through which Robert and Karen lead pilgrimages to sacred sites around the world: 1996, Turkey; 1997, the Holy Land; 1998, France; 2000, Britain; 2002, Italy; 2004, Greece; 2006, Egypt; 2008, India; 2010, Grand Canyon, Arizona; 2012, South Africa. Through the Sophia Grail Circle, Robert and Karen facilitate sacred celebrations dedicated to the Divine Feminine.

Robert is the author of many books, including most recently *The Astrological Revolution* and *Christ and the Maya Calendar* (both coauthored by Kevin Dann), and *The Mystery, Biography & Destiny of Mary Magdalene*. His latest books are *Prophecy-Phenomena-Hope: The Real Meaning of 2012* and *Cultivating Inner Radiance and the Body of Immortality*, and he has a new book in preparation: *Astrogeographia* (coauthored with David Bowden). For further information on his books and courses, visit www.sophiafoundation.org; www.astrogeographia.org; and http://steinerbooks.org/author.html?au=492.

Administrative Office:
525 Gough St. 103
San Francisco, CA 94102

Telephone / Fax · (415) 522-1150
Email · sophia@sophiafoundation.org
www.sophiafoundation.org

PUBLICATIONS BY ROBERT POWELL

Divine Sophia, Holy Wisdom. Booklet describes the Sophia impulse and the work of the Sophia Foundation. Outlines the significance of Sophia for America and for our time.

The Astrological Revolution: Unveiling the Science of the Stars as a Science of Reincarnation and Karma by Robert Powell and Kevin Dann. Humanity has for many centuries employed astrology to penetrate the mystery of the stars' relationship to human destiny. Through the newly discovered rules of astrological reincarnation, it has been discovered that the sidereal zodiac presents an authentic astrological zodiac, enabling a new practice of astrology—one that offers tools to reestablish a wisdom-filled astrology in the modern world.

Christ and the Maya Calendar, 2012 & the Coming of the Antichrist by Robert Powell and Kevin Dann. Explores the significance of the year 2012 and the Mexican mysteries, drawing on Revelation as well as Rudolf Steiner's work. New research is presented to help the reader navigate the Apocalyptic scenario currently unfolding. The Second Coming of Christ is the true event of our time; the incarnation of Satan/Ahriman is its shadow, and Divine Sophia is the antidote to the negative consequences of Ahriman's incarnation. Also discusses the significance of young anthroposophist Judith von Halle, who since Easter 2004 has borne the stigmata—the visible signs of the wounds of Christ.

The Christ Mystery: Reflections on the Second Coming by Robert Powell. The fruit of many years reflection on the Second Coming, its cosmological aspects, the approaching trial of humanity, and the challenges of living in apocalyptic times, against the background of "great signs from heaven."

Christian Hermetic Astrology: the Star of the Magi and the Life of Christ by Robert Powell. Consists of discourses set in the "Temple of the Sun," where Hermes and his pupils gather to meditate on the cosmic aspects of the birth, miracles, and passion of Jesus Christ. Outlines a modern path of the magi leading to a Christian star wisdom.

Introduction to the Christian Star Calendar by Robert Powell. A guide to working with the *Journal for Star Wisdom* (formerly the *Christian Star Calendar*) on a daily basis, including information on mega stars, the 36 decans, and many other topics.

Chronicle of the Living Christ, the Life and Ministry of Jesus Christ: Foundations of Cosmic Christianity by Robert Powell. Based on the visions of Anne Catherine Emmerich, includes a day by day chronicle of the three and a half year ministry of Jesus Christ with horoscopes of the birth and death of Jesus, Mary, and John the Baptist and events in the life of Christ.

Cosmic Dances of the Planets by Lacquanna Paul & Robert Powell. Study material describing the seven classical planets and their forms and gestures in cosmic dance, with diagrams, including a wealth of information on the planets.

Cosmic Dances of the Zodiac by Lacquanna Paul & Robert Powell. Describes the twelve signs in relation to the stars. Provides meditation material and outlines the zodiacal forms and gestures in cosmic dance, with diagrams, and new research on the 36 decans and 12 zodiacal signs.

Elijah Come Again, A Prophet for Our Time, A Scientific Approach to Reincarnation by Robert Powell. Presents a scientific approach toward the foundation of a new "science of the stars" as the "science of karma," unveiling the mystery of human destiny and the fulfillment of Elijah's mission at this time, for earth and humanity, in the next step underlying our spiritual evolution. Explores the various incarnations of the Elijah—John the Baptist–Raphael–Novalis individuality, whom Rudolf Steiner described as "a radiant and splendid forerunner…with whom you are to prepare the work that…will lead humankind past the great crisis in which it is involved."

Hermetic Astrology I, Astrology and Reincarnation by Robert Powell. Includes a comprehensive basis for a new science of karmic astrology, specific reincarnation examples, the astrology of the ancient Babylonians and Egyptians, the New Age, the Second Coming of Christ, and more.

Hermetic Astrology II, Astrological Biography by Robert Powell. A detailed look at embryonic life—conception to birth—in relation to the unfolding of destiny in human biography through seven-year periods. Also includes historical examples of karmic relationships, the esoteric significance of the outer planets, working with the lunar rhythms in meditation, and much more. Astrological biographies of Richard Wagner and Rudolf Steiner.

History of the Zodiac by Robert Powell. Penetrating study of the history of the zodiac; restores the sidereal zodiac to its rightful place as the original zodiac, and traces it back to the Babylonians in the 5th century BC. First submitted in 2004 as Robert Powell's Ph.D. Thesis.

Journal for Star Wisdom edited by Robert Powell. A guide to the correspondences of Christ in the stellar and etheric world. Includes articles of interest by various authors and a complete sidereal ephemeris and aspectarian, geocentric and heliocentric. Published yearly in October/November of the preceding year. In addition to the ephemeris and aspectarian, every issue contains an article by Robert Powell and there are many interesting articles by other authors as well, for example by Daniel Andreev, William Bento, Kevin Dann, Wain Farrants, Brian Gray, Robert Schiappacasse, Richard Tarnas, and David Tresemer.

Lazarus, Come Forth! by Valentin Tomberg (formerly titled *Covenant of the Heart*). Profound meditations of a Christian esotericist on the mysteries of the raising of Lazarus, the Ten Commandments, the Three Kingdoms (God, Man, and Nature), and the Breath of Life. Translated from German into English by Robert Powell & James Morgante.

Meditations on the Tarot: A Journey into Christian Hermeticism by an anonymous author. The twenty-first century classic of Western spirituality. "Hermeticism is an athanor erected in the individual human consciousness, where the mercury of intellectuality undergoes transmutation into the gold of spirituality." Translated from French into English by Robert Powell.

The Most Holy Trinosophia and the New Revelation of the Divine Feminine by Robert Powell. Discusses Sophia as a Trinity—Mother, Daughter, and Holy Soul—and as the feminine aspect of the Divine Godhead. Also, an introduction to the Divine Feminine by Daniel Andreev, author of *The Rose of the World*, and a foreword by Carol Parrish, founder of the Sancta Sophia Seminary.

The Mystery, Biography, and Destiny of Mary Magdalene, Sister of Lazarus John & Spiritual Sister of Jesus by Robert Powell. Sifts through the misunderstandings and distortions to reveal the true Mary Magdalene, her mission and her relationship to Jesus as the Beloved Disciple.

Prophecy–Phenomena–Hope: The Real Meaning of 2012 by Robert Powell. This new book focuses on two important and significant prophecies by Rudolf Steiner. The first (from 1909) concerns the Second Coming of Christ, his appearance to humanity as the Etheric Christ. The second prophecy (from 1919) represents the shadow side of Christ's Second Coming.

The Sign of the Son of Man in Heaven: Sophia and the New Star Wisdom by Robert Powell. An excellent introduction to Sophia's star wisdom. Addresses Christ and the Zodiac, the End of the Century, the Sophianic Millennium, the Sign of the Son of Man in Heaven, and other themes.

The Sophia Teachings by Robert Powell. In this text the author uncovers a secret stream of wisdom flowing through the heart of Christianity: the feminine principle known in Greek as "Sophia," or Divine Wisdom. Robert Powell surveys teachings from Christianity's mystical past concerning Sophia, spanning the Greek philosophers, King Solomon, the visions of Hildegard of Bingen, the Russian Sophiologists, Mary as the Mother of Christ, Our Lady of Guadalupe, and Sophia as "Mother of all Humanity."

Inner Life of the Earth, Exploring the Mysteries of Nature, Subnature & Supranature edited by Paul V. O'Leary. Discusses how forces from the interior of the Earth affect human and earthly evolution. Robert Powell's chapter, *Subnature and the Second Coming*, discusses the significance of Christ's incarnation, by which he united with the Earth.

If you would like to order any of the above-mentioned publications, please go to the Sophia Foundation website www.sophiafoundation.org and click on "Book Store."

A new book—*Astrogeographia*, by Robert Powell & David Bowden—is to be published in September 2012.

The following works published as study material for the Sophia Grail Circle are available from the Sophia Foundation administrative office:

    Prayer Sequence in Sacred Dance by Lacquanna Paul & Robert Powell

    Morning Meditation in Eurythmy by Robert Powell

    Morning Meditation to Sophia in Eurythmy by Karen Rivers

    The Foundation Stone Meditation in the Sacred Dance of Eurythmy by Lacquanna Paul & Robert Powell

    Consecration to the Immaculate Heart of Mary Sophia & Consecration to the Sacred Heart of Jesus by Robert Powell

For further information regarding the above Sophia Grail Circle Study Material
- visit www.sophiafoundation.org and click on Meditational Study Materials
- or use the following direct link: https://sophiafoundation.org/activities/meditation_study/.

DEDICATION

To the Future, to the Spiritual Development of Humanity and the Earth

In the context of humanity's spiritual evolution, this book is dedicated to the Etheric Christ and his messengers, above all to Rudolf Steiner and Valentin Tomberg, both of whom (as referred to at the end of chapter 6) were born when the Sun was at 14½° Aquarius (♒) in the constellation of the Waterbearer, both of whom came to prepare humankind for the coming Age of Aquarius (2375–4535) by opening paths to the new mysteries of the Etheric Christ, who in his second coming is the *new Waterbearer* pouring out *buddhic* life force in radiant blue light for humanity and the Earth—this being the fulfillment of the "sign of the Son of Man in heaven" (Matthew 24:30).

Rudolf Steiner was born on February 25, 1861, at 11:25 p.m., and Valentin Tomberg was born on February 14, 1900, at 9:50 p.m. (date in the old Russian calendar, corresponding to February 26 in the

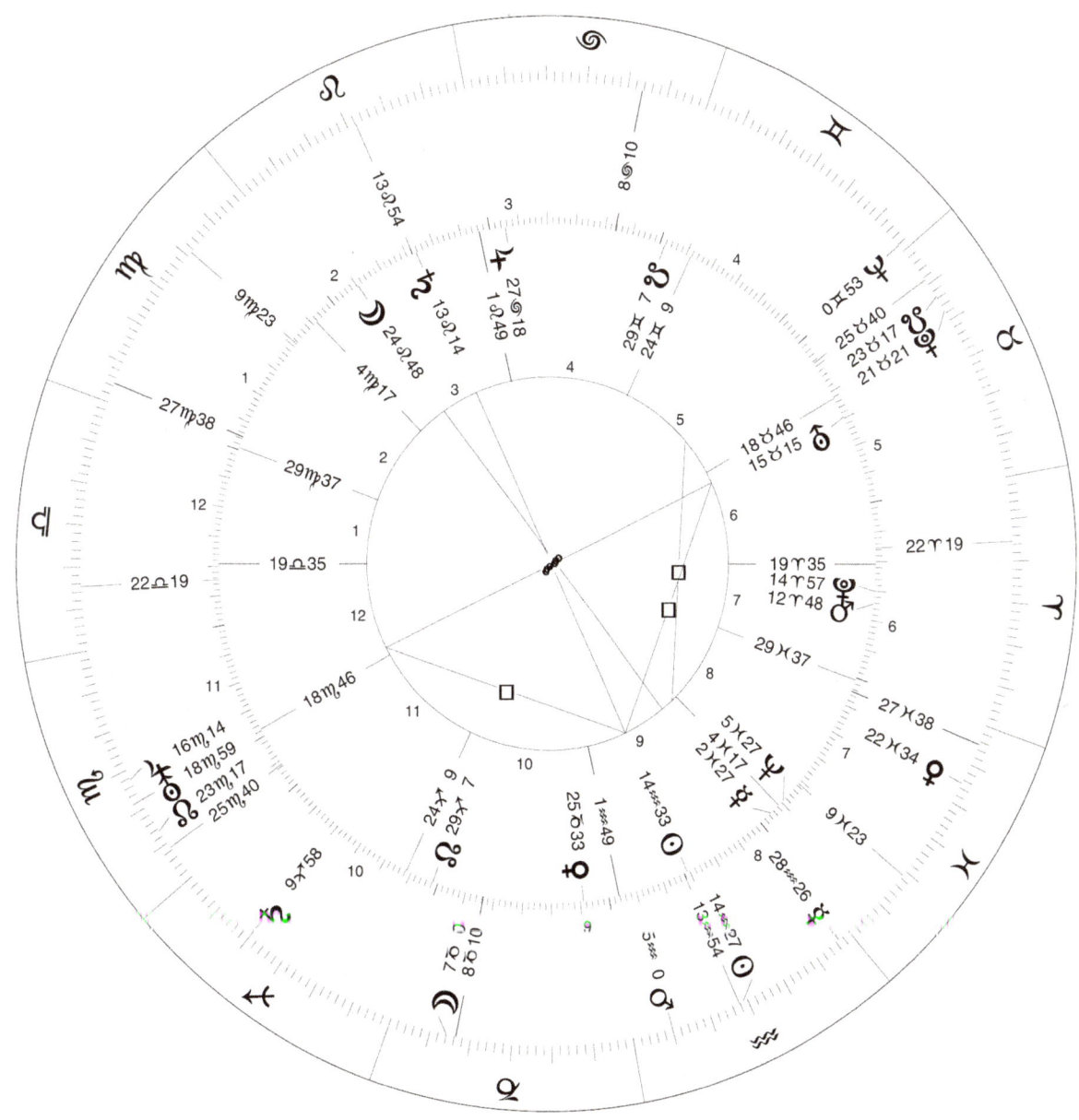

modern Western calendar); see comparison horoscope on page 241. In the comparison horoscope look for ♒ in the outer circle and 9 in the inner circle, to see that the Sun at Rudolf Steiner's birth was at 14°33' Aquarius (14♒33) and the Sun at Valentin Tomberg's birth at 14°27' Aquarius (14♒27). In other words, the position of the Sun at the birth of these two individuals differed by only 0°06'. Since the position of the Sun at someone's birth indicates the essence of the spiritual impulse of that individual, the comparison horoscope reveals that, in terms of his true spiritual impulse, Valentin Tomberg chose to incarnate at that precise moment in time, in 1900, at the start of the New Age, in order to connect onto the essence of Rudolf Steiner's impulse, which was the proclamation of the coming of Christ in the etheric realm, this being the "greatest mystery" of the New Age that, according to Rudolf Steiner, began at that very time.

A key to understanding the relationship between Rudolf Steiner and Valentin Tomberg is found by considering the year 1933, the year in which Valentin Tomberg's esoteric work began. As Elisabeth Vreede wrote in her foreword: "Valentin Tomberg's *Studies of the Old Testament*...represent the beginning of an extended work.... The twelve studies on the Old Testament, begun in Autumn 1933, were followed by another series of twelve on the New Testament."[1] As indicated on page 192: Whereas Rudolf Steiner's mission was to prepare for the onset of Christ's Second Coming in the etheric aura of the Earth in 1933, Valentin Tomberg's task was to help humanity align with the Etheric Christ in the period from 1933 onward. His profound works on the esoteric mysteries of the Old Testament, the New Testament, and the Apocalypse of John, as well as his *Studies on the Foundation Stone Meditation* and other works, were preparatory in this task, which began to unfold from 1932/1933. And then, during the war years, came the Lord's Prayer Course, in which Valentin Tomberg, through his inner connection with the Etheric Christ, gave to humanity a means of coming into relationship with Christ in his Second Coming.

On account of the circumstances in Europe at that time (Hitler's coming to power in 1933 and the resulting conflict, culminating with World War II, from 1939 to 1945), Valentin Tomberg's work, as an ambassador from 1933 onward of the Etheric Christ, was buried from sight for most human beings. Now, in this book, especially in the sequence *Putting on the Resurrection Body*, a distillation of the content of the Lord's Prayer Course is given in conjunction with the etheric form of movement known as eurythmy, whose birth in 1912 we are celebrating now, one hundred years later. Here the work of these two great teachers, both of whose lives were in service of the Etheric Christ (in Rudolf Steiner's case, leading up to 1933, and with Valentin Tomberg from 1933 on) are brought together. May each reader of this book find a path to the Etheric Christ through the content presented here—a way leading to the one who said of himself: "I AM the way, the truth, and the life."

---

1   Valentin Tomberg, *Christ and Sophia*, p. xxxi.

www.ingramcontent.com/pod-product-compliance
Lightning Source LLC
Chambersburg PA
CBHW081208170426
43198CB00018B/2888